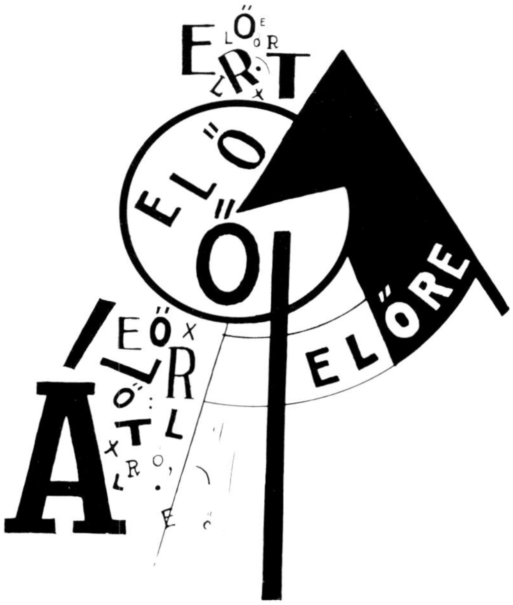
ELŐRE

STANDING IN THE TEMPEST | painters of the HUNGARIAN AVANT-GARDE 1908-1930

S. A. MANSBACH

With contributions by Richard V. West,
István Deák, Júlia Szabó, John E. Bowlt,
Krisztina Passuth, and Oliver A.I. Botar

Santa Barbara Museum of Art
Santa Barbara, California

The MIT Press
Cambridge, Massachusetts
London, England

Cover: Composition with Six Figures
by Sándor Bortnyik (Detail), 1918.
Half title: Forward by Lajos Kassák, 1923.
Frontispiece: View of Tabán
by Sándor Galimberti, c1910.

Published by the Santa Barbara Museum of Art
1130 STATE STREET
SANTA BARBARA, CALIFORNIA 93101

This publication and the exhibition which accompanies it are funded in part by the National Endowment for the Humanities and the National Endowment for the Arts, both federal agencies, and by Northern Trust of California.

Exhibition Itinerary:

SANTA BARBARA MUSEUM OF ART, SANTA BARBARA, CALIFORNIA
MARCH 16–MAY 11, 1991

NELSON ATKINS MUSEUM, KANSAS CITY, MISSOURI
JULY 14–SEPTEMBER 8, 1991

KRANNERT ART MUSEUM, CHAMPAIGN, ILLINOIS
JANUARY 18–MARCH 1, 1992

Design: Lorraine Wild, with Lisa Nugent and Susan Parr
Editor: Bonnie Simrell
Senior Editor: Steven Mansbach
Cartographer: Kirsten Zecher
Typography: Continental Typographics, Chatsworth, California
Printed in Singapore.

LIBRARY OF CONGRESS CATALOGING-IN-PUBLICATION DATA
Mansbach, Steven A., 1950-
Standing in the tempest: painters of the Hungarian Avant-garde, 1908–1930 / S.A. Mansbach; with contributions by Richard V. West...[et al.].
p. cm.
Includes bibliographical references and index.
ISBN 0-262-13274-5 (MIT hbk.)
ISBN 0-89951-079-5 (SBMA pbk.)
1. Nyolcak (Group of artists) 2. Aktivisták (Group of artists) 3. Avant-garde (Aesthetics) — Hungary — History — 20th century. 4. Art, Modern — 20th century — Hungary. I. West, Richard V. II. Santa Barbara Museum of Art. III. Title.
N6820.5.N93M36 1991
709′.439′1207473 — dc20 90-49893
CIP

Contents

Editor's Note

Transliteration of Russian in this book follows the system used by the Slavic Review, except for the names of well-known individuals, which appear in the form that is most often encountered in works on Russian art written in English. Hungarian names have been rendered in Hungarian style, with the exception of the Hungarian custom of reversing the order of given and surnames. Those appear here in the Western style of given name first, followed by surname.

6

Board of Trustees

Museum Staff

ADMINISTRATION

Richard V. West, *Director*
Thomas R. Mathews, Jr., *Assistant Director for Administration*
Petty Stevens, *Personnel and Office Manager*
Julie Senn, *Administration Department Secretary*
Elizabeth Bradley, *Executive Secretary to the Director*
°Karen McGinnis and Chelsea Brown, *Receptionists*

CURATORIAL

Robert Henning, Jr., *Assistant Director for Curatorial Services*
Nancy Doll, *Curator of 20th Century Art*
Susan Tai, *Curator of Asian Art*
Terry Atkinson, *Designer*
Sharen O'Riordan, *Curatorial Administrative Assistant*
°Silvia Tyndall, *Preparator*

COLLECTIONS MANAGEMENT

Cherie Summers, *Registrar*
Elaine Cobos, *Assistant Registrar*

EDUCATION

Deborah Tufts, *Curator of Education*
Ron Crozier, *Librarian*
Beverly Decker, *Museum Educator*
Frances Thorpe, *Assistant to the Curator of Education*

DEVELOPMENT

Barbara B. Luton, *Director of Development*
Shelley S. Ruston, *Director of Special Programs*
Virginia Cochran, *Grants and Public Relations Director*
Kathy O'Leary, *Events and Volunteer Coordinator*
Cathy Pollock, *Publications Manager*
Kelly L. Cretti, *Membership Manager*
°Lisa Higgins, *Programs Assistant*
Joan Enasko, *Development Assistant*
Adis Morales, *Development Secretary*
°Vicki Allen, *Grants and Public Relations Assistant*

ACCOUNTING

Gale Poyorena, *Controller*
Sharon Beckett, *Accounting Supervisor*
Marilyn Skiöld, *Accounting Clerk*
Kurt Angersbach, *Admissions and Information Clerk*

MUSEUM STORE

Penny Mast, Museum Store Manager
°Lauren Baldwin and Libby McCollum, *Museum Store Assistants*

MAINTENANCE AND INSTALLATION

John A. Coplin, *Facilities Manager*
Jerry Travis, *Museum Technician*
Dane Goodman, *Museum Technician*
Alfonso Bravo, *Building Technician I*
Gene Brundin, *Building Technician II*
Raul Matamoros, *Building Custodian*
John Morales, *Building Custodian*

SECURITY

Walter Hildbrand, *Chief of Security*
Noel Assayech, *Deputy Chief of Security*
Alexander Grabner, *Senior Security Guard*

SECURITY GUARDS

Kurt Angersbach
Steven Bissell
Bert Espinoza
Phillip Liddicoat
Michael Woxell
°Michael Caulfield
°Mansour Matin
°Mario Munarolo
°Joan Nikola-Lisa
°Ann Skiöld
°Peter Stettinivus

°*part-time employee*

A project as complex and pioneering as this could not have been accomplished without the efforts of many individuals, agencies, and museums in the United States and Hungary. The inspiration and scholarly guidance of Dr. Steven A. Mansbach were key to every step of development. With the greatest perseverance, he nurtured the evolution of this publication and the related exhibition over a period of six years, years of great change in Eastern Europe and in the state of research in the field. In turn, Dr. Mansbach and I wish to thank the international roster of scholars who contributed the essays that illuminate so many aspects of the Hungarian avant-garde phenomenon: Oliver A.I. Botar, Dr. John E. Bowlt, Dr. István Deák, Krisztina Passuth, and Júlia Szabó.

The interest of our Hungarian colleagues and the outstanding generosity of Hungarian museums in sharing their collections with us were crucial. At the Hungarian National Gallery, our thanks go to General Director Dr. Lóránd Bereczky and Deputy Directors Géza Csorba and György Horváth for their kind assistance. The unparalleled cooperation and support of Dr. László Beke, Chief Curator, and his staff made it possible for us to bring the key masterpieces of Hungarian avant-garde artists to the American public for the first time. It was a personal pleasure to work with Dr. Beke in selecting the works that are included here. We also wish to thank Dr. Éva Bajkay, Curator of the Gallery's graphics collections, for her kind suggestions. Gallery Curators Gábor Bellák and András Zwickl not only assisted in verifying loan data, but provided the artists' biographies for this publication. We thank also Károly Petheő, Chief Conservator, for preparing the works for the exhibition. We are indebted to former Deputy Director Gyöngyi Éri, who was instrumental in securing the early interest of the Hungarian authorities in the idea of making the Hungarian avant-garde better known to to a wider audience outside Hungary and who, with her husband Dr. István Éri, provided unfailing hospitality and advice on our frequent visits to Budapest.

Others in Hungary we wish to acknowledge for their assistance are: Miklós Mojzer, Director, and Brigitta Czifka, Curator, Museum of Fine Arts, Budapest; György Várkonyi, Deputy Director, and Dr. Ferenc Romváry, Chief Curator, Janus Pannonius Museum, Pécs; Dr. János F. Várga, Hungarian Film Archives, and Dr. József Marx, Hungarian Film Institute, Budapest; Ferenc Sárkány, International Exhibitions section of the Hungarian Ministry of Education and Culture, Budapest; and members of our honorary International Advisory Council, Levente Nagy and György Iványi. In Washington, D.C., we received assistance and valuable advice from the cultural attachés of the Hungarian Embassy, Victor Polgár and his successor, Béla Szombati.

During the course of our work, we were fortunate to have the help of the United States Embassy in Budapest. Former U.S. ambassadors Nicholas M. Salgo and Mark Palmer both took personal interest in the development of this project and supported its inclusion in United States-Hungarian cultural exchange agreements. American cultural attachés Csabo Csikas and João Escödi were always willing to assist when needed.

In the United States, we have many people to thank. Paul Kövesdy, a long-time staunch champion of Hungarian modernism, initially suggested the idea and transmitted his enthusiasm to our former Curator of Modern Art, Diane Shamash. In the course of developing the idea, we had the interest and support of many people, including the members of our honorary International Advisory Council: George Soros, Tibor de Nagy, György Kepes, the late Andor Weininger, and Pierre-Frantz Chapou. Dr. Scott Simmon, then of the Library of Congress, worked with us to locate important Hungarian documentary and feature films to enhance our understanding of the cultural and social forces at work during this period. Special appreciation is due to Eva Haller for her generous support of Dr. Simmon's research trip to Budapest. Dr. Tibor Frank, visiting Fulbright Professor at the University of California, Santa Barbara, deserves our thanks for his advice and many helpful suggestions.

The complex task of seeing this publication through from inception to finish was skillfully handled by the Museum's Publication Manager, Cathy Pollock. No problem was too great for her to tackle and to resolve. The equally demanding challenge of text editing was capably met by Bonnie Simrell, whose editing skills and sense of form shaped the numerous parts of the book into a consistent whole. We owe a word of thanks to our text reviewers, Éva Forgács and András Fűrész, for helping clarify references, names, and orthographic questions. The original translation of certain essays and citations written in Hungarian were done by Adam I. Topolansky and Judith Hollosy. The entire manuscript and its numerous revisions were impeccably word-processed by Ethel Geary. The map was researched and created by Kirsten Zecher. The interest and support of Roger Conover of MIT Press from the very start of this publication is greatly appreciated. The handsome appearance of this publication is due to the design skills of Lorraine Wild, who like everyone else involved on this project, spent far more time on it than anticipated in order to create an important and lasting contribution to our knowledge of a significant aspect of twentieth-century art.

Finally, I wish to thank the staff of the Santa Barbara Museum of Art for their help and assistance. Special appreciation is due Elizabeth Bradley, Executive Secretary; Cherie Summers, Registrar; Virginia Cochran, Grants and Public Relations Director; Anne Farrell, former Associate Director of Development; Cynthia Adams, former Grants Assistant; Nancy Doll, Curator of 20th Century Art; and Terry Atkinson, Museum Designer, for their efforts on behalf of the realization of this publication and related exhibition. I am grateful to Marc Wilson, Director of the Nelson-Atkins Museum, and Stephen S. Prokopoff, Director of the Krannert Art Museum, University of Illinois, for their vision in sharing the exhibition with a broad audience. Particular thanks are also due to Steven Mansbach's wife, Julia E. Frane, and mine, Ennan, for their forbearance and support during the years this project dictated so much of our activities.

And now a word about our sponsors: without the positive and significant support of the National Endowment for the Humanities and the National Endowment for the Arts, both federal agencies, this project would have been difficult to contemplate and impossible to implement. Our thanks to the great staffs of the museum programs in both agencies who are so rarely acknowledged but who were vital to the realization of this project. We also thank Northern Trust of California for sponsoring the Santa Barbara showing of our exhibition, and Dr. István Schlégl for helping support the publication of this book.

Richard V. West
Director (1983–1991)
Santa Barbara Museum of Art

ANONYMOUS LENDERS
BERLINISCHE GALERIE, BERLIN
BÉLA CZÓBEL MUSEUM, SZENTENDRE
DR. NICHOLAS ÉBER, UNTERENGSTRINGEN, SWITZERLAND
KÁROLY FERENCZY MUSEUM, SZENTENDRE
MR. AND MRS. THOMAS O. HECHT, MONTREAL
HUNGARIAN ADVERTISING AGENCY ARCHIVES, BUDAPEST
HUNGARIAN NATIONAL GALLERY, BUDAPEST
PAUL KÖVESDY COLLECTION, NEW YORK
KUNSTHALLE NÜRNBERG
MUSÉE D'ART MODERNE, CENTRE POMPIDOU, PARIS
MUSEUM OF FINE ARTS, BUDAPEST
MUSEUM OF MODERN ART, NEW YORK
MUSEUM OF THE MODERN AGE, BUDAPEST
LEVENTE NAGY COLLECTION, BUDAPEST
NATIONALGALERIE, BERLIN
HERMAN OTTO MUSEUM, MISKOLC
JANUS PANNONIUS MUSEUM, PÉCS
RIPPL-RÓNAI MUSEUM, KAPOSVÁR
SAN FRANCISCO MUSEUM OF MODERN ART
GALERIE DR. I. SCHLÉGL, ZÜRICH
STAATSGALERIE, STUTTGART
YALE UNIVERSITY ART GALLERY, NEW HAVEN

RICHARD V. WEST

THE AVANT-GARDE: MARCHING IN THE VAN OF PROGRESS

It is we artists who will serve you as avant-garde...what a magnificent destiny for the arts is that of exercising a positive power over society, a true priestly function, and of marching forcefully in the van of all the intellectual faculties....[1]

This passionate declaration by the Utopian Socialist Henri de Saint-Simon in the early years of the nineteenth century appears to be the first use of the term *avant-garde* to describe a new militant role for the artist. No other expression could have more vividly described the transformation of the artist's role in society during the tumultuous closing decade of the eighteenth century and early years of the nineteenth. Nor would the military analogy have been lost on Saint-Simon's contemporaries: in truth, the leading artists of the day were perceived by many (not in the least the artists themselves) as engaged in a battle with the forces of repression, both political and artistic. Saint-Simon exhorts the artist to become both priest and warrior, spearheading human progress. And the artists of France fulfilled that plea in the revolutions that followed, in 1830, in 1848, and in the Paris Commune of 1870.[2]

As the political tides receded in the late nineteenth century, however, the term lost its original potency. In *fin-de-siècle* Europe, the energies of the avant-garde were directed inward toward aesthetic skirmishes, not major social battles. A "radical" artist could be a conservative citizen, or completely apolitical, alienated, aloof. *L'art pour l'art* became the battle cry, and avant-garde artists laid siege to the public's eyes, not minds. Or did they? Alienation was not limited to the artist; it was a malaise that could be found at all levels of society. Could it be that the artist's intense scrutiny of society and self was a form of suppressed political comment?[3]

However one interprets the conflicting developments of the late nineteenth century, it is clear that artists emerging into the twentieth were imbued with a new sense of militancy. In Hungary, particularly, all the elements that would galvanize artists into more

Richard V. West, Director of the Santa Barbara Museum of Art from 1983 to 1991, has organized a number of exhibitions devoted to early modernism and central European art, including Painters of the Section d'Or and Munich and American Realism in the Nineteenth Century. Born in Czechoslovakia, he studied at the Academy of Fine Arts, Vienna and continued his graduate studies in art history at the University of California, Berkeley.

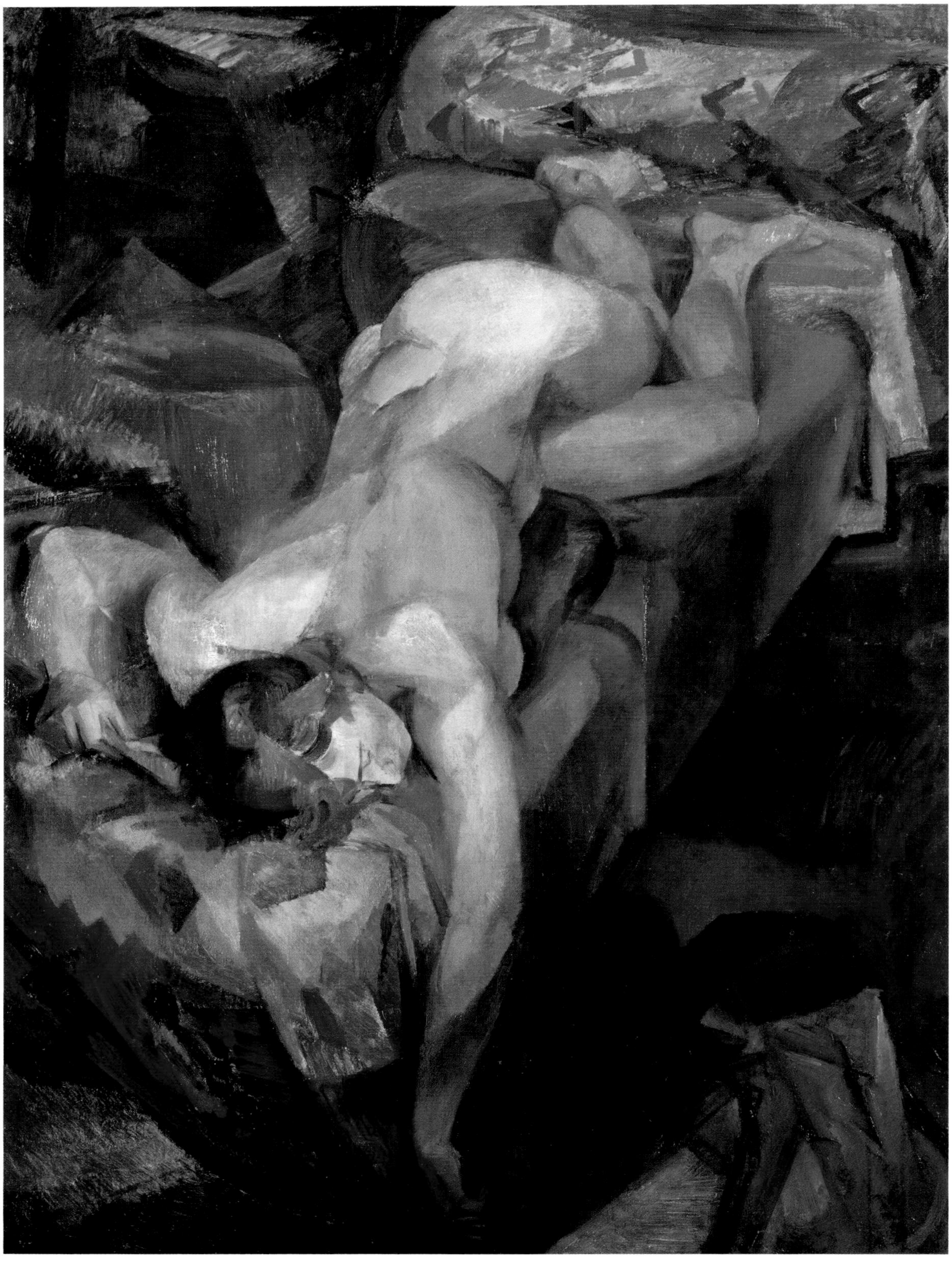

142. IMRE SZOBOTKA, Reclining Nude, 1921

active roles were in place by the early 1900s: a sophisticated society able to provide a forum for new ideas; a growing realization that the Austro-Hungarian monarchy had fossilized, imposing a dead hand on all aspects of life and culture; and an emerging group of charismatic thinkers and theoreticians able to state social dilemmas in new terms and propose fresh answers.

Does this sound familiar? As this is written, artists all over Central Europe have acted as priests and warriors, most recently spearheading the evolution of renewed democratic ideals in their homelands. Press commentators express concern that the new civic forums guiding the destiny of these countries are made up of "untried" artists and intellectuals, not seasoned politicians. Is this concern well founded? I think not. Once again artists have taken up the standard of liberty and assumed the role that Saint-Simon predicted would be theirs. Historically, such periods are brief. What is important, however, is that at critical junctures of human history, artists focus and give shape to the deepest aspirations of their epoch and thus articulate and encourage movements toward fundamental change.

At one such juncture, between 1908 and 1930, Hungarian artists experienced the exhilaration of marching in the van of progress, just as now a new generation of Hungarian artists are participating in the restructuring of their homeland. *Standing in the Tempest* documents the emergence of these dynamic artists and thinkers in Hungary in the early decades of the twentieth century, and follows the changing fortunes of avant-garde art in the face of monarchical repression, political dissent, engagement with the proletariat, and ultimate diffusion under the tremendous pressures of political and cultural transformation. Because of the nature of these national and international shifts from the 1930s almost until now, the great significance of the Hungarian role in the revolution we now call "early modernism" has been obscured. In 1908, the Hungarian theoretician and philosopher György Lukacs likened an exhibition of Hungarian avant-garde artists to a "declaration of war," so it is not surprising that many of the key documents and works were lost or suppressed as movements and governments rose and fell. Although certain Hungarian artists (such as László Moholy-Nagy) are recognized for their later achievements outside Hungary, little has been done to show the source of their artistic philosophy and development. Nor has much attention been given the important role of Hungarian avant-garde thought and aesthetics on the development of other avant-garde movements in Russia, Poland, Czechoslovakia, Yugoslavia, Romania, and elsewhere.

This study provides both the visual evidence and the scholarly documentation to substantiate the Hungarian role as a leading one in the evolution and crystallization of modernist aesthetics in the early twentieth century. It also reveals the pivotal activities of many Hungarian artists in later developments elsewhere in Europe and in the United States, developments that still resonate in the visual arts of the last decade of the twentieth century. We hope that our efforts will serve to renew public recognition of the incredibly complex and diverse history of early modernism.

1. Henri de Saint-Simon, Opinions Littéraires, philosophiques et industrielles (Paris, 1825), first cited in Donald D. Egbert, "The Idea of 'Avant-Garde' in Art and Politics," *The American Historical Review* 73 no. 2 (December 1967) p. 343, and subsequently quoted in Linda Nochlin, "The Invention of the Avant-Garde: France, 1830-80," *Art News Annual*, no. 34 (1968), p. 5. I am grateful to Dr. Henri Dorra for pointing out this passage to me.

2. This history is discussed at length in Nochlin, op. cit.

3. The idea that an artist's interest in intense psychological states, even madness, could be a covert political statement is discussed in Jane Kromm, "Marianne and the Mad Women," *Art Journal* 46, no. 4 (Winter 1987), pp. 299-304. This entire issue of *Art Journal*, edited by Linda Nochlin, is devoted to the theme "The Political Unconscious in Nineteenth-Century Art."

13. SÁNDOR BORTNYIK, Red Sun, 1918-19

INTRODUCTION

S. A. MANSBACH

The Hungarian avant-garde of the early twentieth century may appear to be an esoteric subject, particularly to Western audiences. Indeed, its manifold achievements and contributions to the history of modern art and aesthetics have been largely unheralded in Western scholarship, even if many of its artists and theorists are now accepted as principal figures in the genesis and reception of modernism. Many American collections are enriched by works of Moholy-Nagy, Breuer, Molnár, and any number of other Hungarian modernists. Nevertheless, of all the European (and American) protagonists in the drama of modern art, the Hungarian avant-garde played a distinctive role that today is among the least known and most undervalued.

This relative obscurity contrasts oddly with conditions three-quarters of a century ago when the Hungarians were creatively shaping the character, defining the meanings, and determining the implications of modernist artistic expression. Contemporary journals of the 1910s and 1920s from London to Leningrad were filled with articles by and about these Hungarian pioneers of modern aesthetics and art. Names of artists such as Kassák, Bortnyik, and Uitz, and of critics such as Kállai and Kemény, were common copy in the advanced periodicals of their time. Moreover, contemporaneous art history and philosophical debate themselves were influenced richly by the contributions of other Hungarians — Károly (Charles) Tolnay, Arnold Hauser, Frederick Antal, Leo Popper, and György Lukács, to name a few — who advocated in their writings and lectures the progressive aesthetics (and often politics) of their countrymen.

In large measure, the momentous shift from ready recognition early in the century to relative obscurity is the consequence of tumultuous political and cultural events during the last seventy-five years, a turbulence that not only submerged the thriving cultures of "Mitteleuropa," but moved their historical presence from the center of European consciousness to the periphery of Western awareness. In this violent dislocation, Hungary — like so much of East-Central Europe — was assigned to a Soviet-dominated Eastern Europe, where until relatively recently its free contacts with the West were severed and its essential connections to its own avant-garde past degraded. Thus, the Hungarian artists (and their apologists) best known in the West are those such as László Moholy-Nagy who elected emigration or whose work entered early the international modernist mainstream. Unfortunately, the signal achievements of those important artists who chose in the mid-1920s to return to or remain in Hungary (or to emigrate to the Soviet Union) have been largely erased from popular recognization.

Some responsibility for the eclipse of the Hungarian avant-garde rests with the nature, attitudes, and actions of the artists themselves. Always standing in the political opposition — to the Habsburg monarchy, to successive revolutionary regimes, to the ultramontane government of conservative reaction, to the German occupiers, and to the post-World War II communist system — progressive Hungarian artists rarely saw their work broadly endorsed or their accomplishments seriously studied or fairly assessed. In fact, it has only been in the last decade or so that the rich heritage of the avant-garde has been fully acknowledged by Hungarian scholars and its art widely exhibited to the public.

Unlike almost every other contemporaneous art movement, the Hungarian avant-garde tolerated, at times even appeared to encourage, diversity in style and breadth in outlook. While the Dutch De Stijl group or the Russian suprematists insisted on a purity of formal expression, the Hungarians adopted a much more heterogeneous perspective, not infrequently promoting concurrently expressionism, futurism, cubism, and constructivism. One finds represented among the Hungarian Activist painters, for example, a panoply of early twentieth century styles, yet adherence to a relatively uniform, if somewhat vague, socialist world view.

With such diversity, it was always difficult for the Hungarian avant-garde to speak with a single voice, despite the authoritative claims of Lajos Kassák, Béla Uitz, Sándor Bortnyik, and others. Thus, historians and critics found the movement difficult to characterize easily or succinctly, despite the numerous texts authored by the artists themselves. Furthermore, many of the important documents written by and about the avant-garde appeared in Hungarian, which posed a language barrier between the artists and the vast majority of Western scholars and audiences. Most Hungarian avant-gardists spoke additional languages, primarily German. However, during their formative years in Hungary and, later, their early years in exile in Vienna and Berlin, all sought to maintain contact with one another and with their homeland. To do this, they frequently employed the Hungarian language.

Finally, the Hungarians often served as the link or bridge between the dynamic developments in Eastern Europe and the West. For the Hungarian artists themselves, this was both a singular advantage and a definite drawback. On the one hand, they benefited directly and early from the aesthetic innovations taking place in Russia and throughout much of Eastern Europe. On the other hand, their unmediated (though selective) embrace of these new trends too often was misunderstood in the West, and distinctive and significant Hungarian accomplishments frequently were attributed to those other artists and movements whose work, ideas, and achievements the Hungarians promoted and adapted to their own needs.

In the light of the dynamic and world-shaping developments of 1989 in Hungary and its Eastern European neighbors, it seems particularly fitting that the 1990s should bring a new appreciation and assessment of the remarkable character of the aesthetics and intentions, successes and limitations of the Hungarian avant-garde through which to reclaim from historical obscurity the movement's essential influence on the development of international modernism. This assessment is undertaken, then, not as a celebration of cultural or national chauvinism but as a responsible step in integrating into the rich and complex history of modern art and aesthetics one of its most important elements: the Hungarian contribution.

The scope of this assessment is an ambitious one: It requires study not only of the avant-garde movement and its principal protagonists, but also of the social, political, and historical backdrop for their unfoldment and activity. Integration of the movement into the international arena then demands an appreciation of the interplay among the other avant-garde movements, artists, and literary figures with whom the Hungarians came in contact.

In view of the profound scope of this undertaking, it was necessary for reasons of clarity and impact to select from a vast profusion of artistic works, interpretations, writings, and other documentation those examples that best serve to enhance our understanding of the development of Hungarian avant-garde aesthetics, intentions, and applications. By focusing on painting, for example, with ancillary attention paid to graphics and selected documentary material, this book acknowledges the primacy of two-dimensional work within the Hungarian movement as compared with the relatively restricted role of Hungarian achievements, however noteworthy, in the three-dimensional media.

Unlike the (largely paper) architecture and sculpture of the Russian and Soviet avant-garde movements, these media constituted largely a secondary mode of expression for Hungary's progressive artists and commentators. With some exceptions, particularly among Hungarian artists in German exile who were affiliated with the Bauhaus, there was relatively little opportunity for architectural work owing to the harsh circumstances of voluntary exile and domestic conditions that discouraged commissions for political radicals. Furthermore, such versatile artists as János Máttis Teutsch, Lajos Kassák, and (especially) László Moholy-Nagy, for whom architecture and sculpture had particular importance, often expressed their aesthetic constructs equally well in two-dimensional works.

Another carefully considered decision was the exclusion of photography from our undertaking. Of all the visual arts of the mature period of Hungarian avant-garde activity (and after), photography is the most widely known and often exhibited in the United States. In recent years there have been several important studies and exhibitions devoted to the photography of André Kertész, Brassaï, Kepes, and Moholy-Nagy. In fact, the widespread appreciation of modern Hungarian photography receives important, if indirect, support in this study, which investigates the artistic and cultural environment from which Hungarian photography emerged and to which it so creatively responded.

This study focuses primarily on Hungarian artists who were instrumental in articulating the avant-garde's varied objectives and expressing them pictorially. Not included are those significant artists of Hungarian nationality or extraction whose art or activities had little direct bearing on the course of Hungarian modernism and its contribution to the international avant-garde. Thus, Vilmos Huszár, for example, who played an instrumental role within the Dutch De Stijl group but who had little association with, or direct influence on, the Hungarian avant-garde, is not represented.

This interpretive assessment of the Hungarian avant-garde focuses principally on the years between 1908—when a group of eight Hungarian painters with emphatically progressive aesthetic, social, and stylistic tendencies coalesced—and the year 1930, by which time the heroic period of experimentation, accomplishment, and dissemination had essentially run its course. These two decades embrace the period of greatest accomplishment for the avant-garde, for it was roughly in these 20 years that the artists and their apologists developed a progressive means of expression and concomitant political and social world view that achieved a stunning degree of clarity and forcefulness. Moreover, it was exactly in this period that Hungarian avant-garde aesthetics had its decisive impact on the evolution of modern art.

Almost no historical phase, modern or otherwise, can be said to emerge or conclude decisively at a single moment. Indeed, the following essays acknowledge the rich artistic and cultural background out of which the first truly avant-garde artistic group emerged. Nor did progressive Hungarian art cease abruptly in 1930. By this date, however, conditions in Hungary compelled artists who had been its leading figures to reappraise their assertive role in avant-garde activity. Many withdrew from engaged aesthetics, thereby paving the way for a new generation of artists who would soon distinguish themselves by their formal experimentation. For members of the Hungarian avant-garde who had elected to remain abroad, 1930 marked the approximate end of their close association with their fellow countrymen as joint participants in a collective movement. By 1930, many who had moved to the West had begun to distance themselves from a strong identification as Hungarian émigré artists, and a significant number had established close ties with other modernist movements.

Like most pioneers and impresarios within the international avant-garde, many Hungarians by 1930 experienced a profound disappointment with their inability to restructure reality through art. As a consequence, one readily detects among a great number of Hungarian avant-gardists a tendency to jettison (or at least to moderate) long-held ideological commitments and idealistic world views. This was especially true among those who had elected to return to their homeland during the 1920s to find contemporary political and social conditions increasingly hostile toward the propagation of the tenets and forms of modern art. Thus, by the end of the decade, the most innovative phase of Hungarian avant-garde expression was over.

For those Hungarians whose radical social commitment remained undiminished and who sought asylum and opportunity primarily in the Soviet Union, the 1930s turned out to be a period of comparatively restricted activity, limited artistic experimentation, and frequent disappointment. The freedom and responsibility they sought to exercise in the service of socialist aesthetics ultimately proved anathema to Stalin's conception of radical art.

The Hungarian avant-garde left a profound legacy despite its brief quarter-century span of mature creativity. The innovative formal solutions avant-garde artists brought to the fine and applied arts have fundamentally shaped the morphology of modern art as well as helped to determine the very image of the contemporary world. Furthermore, the passion and intelligence with which these artists participated in the international discourse on art have affected the very way in which we think, write, and speak about modernist aesthetics. These are laudable accomplishments; how Hungarian painters endeavored to achieve them is the essential subject of the present volume.

It is both timely and fitting that a large-scale study on the Hungarian avant-garde be undertaken in America, drawing on the scholarship of both American and European art and cultural historians. During the period 1908-30, the Hungarians themselves sought direct contacts with American artists, collectors, museums, and scholars, and they valued their connections with American journals and writers. Moreover, an idealized image of America as a country of limitless energy, innovation, and progress occupied a privileged position in their own world view, as is evidenced in several of their publications. This conviction, though shared broadly by almost all participants in the international avant-garde of the early twentieth century, was to play a consequential role a decade or so later. In the 1930s when affiliates of the Hungarian avant-garde felt compelled to emigrate once again, it was primarily to the United States that László Moholy-Nagy, Marcel Breuer, György Kepes, Andor Weininger, and dozens of other Hungarian artists brought the passion, commitment, and experience that they had acquired during the preceding two decades. In America, they found conditions favorable to their ideas and art, and there they created what might be recognized as the final phase of their progressive "new vision" of a modern art for modern man, an ideal image first articulated in an earlier time and place by the Hungarian avant-garde.

TO ACQUAINT THE READER with the historical, political, and cultural background from which the Hungarian avant-garde emerged, this volume opens with an overview of Hungarian social history by István Deák of Columbia University. Professor Deák attends closely to the dynamic events in nineteenth and twentieth Hungarian history that shaped profoundly the aesthetic and social perspectives of the avant-garde artists.

The character, objectives, and achievements of the Hungarian avant-gardists are next assessed in my own essay, in which the history of Hungarian modern art is substantially reinterpreted in light of recent scholarly studies and from the perspective of an American art historian.

Júlia Szabó, a senior researcher at the Hungarian Academy of Sciences, next examines trends and techniques in Hungarian painting at the turn of the century and their influences on the visual experiments of the avant-garde.

John Bowlt, professor at the University of Southern California, investigates the remarkable role and contributions, as well as connections and interactions between the Hungarian avant-garde and Russian art, both progressive and conservative, during the first third of the century.

In a complementary essay, Krisztina Passuth of the Museum of Modern Art of the City of Paris surveys the connection between Hungary's avant-garde painters and apologists and those of other progressive movements in East-Central Europe.

The volume concludes with two particularly useful sections compiled by Oliver A.I. Botar: a substantial comparative chronology of significant events within the Hungarian avant-garde, international avant-garde, and political spheres; and an extensive selected bibliography embracing primary and secondary sources.

This map has been simplified for the purposes of the book. Political boundaries of the entire former Austro-Hungarian monarchy are not included. For ease in identification, countries and major European cities are given in English, regardless of the name current in 1920. Traditional Hungarian place names are rendered in Hungarian; the present names of former Hungarian centers now part of other countries are shown in parentheses.

ISTVÁN DEÁK

HUNGARY: a brief political & cultural history

Hungary is a small country, a mere speck on the map of the world or even on that of Europe. But before 1918, it was three times as large, and unlike today's chastised Hungarians, its inhabitants tended to think of themselves as uniquely dynamic and successful. Indeed it may be said that the country's modern history centers around the fundamental dichotomy between earlier greatness and more recent political insignificance, a traumatic change that neither the people as a whole nor its leading intellectuals, whether conservative or avant-garde, have thus far managed to overcome. Yet there are other dichotomies as well.

Before 1918 Hungary was a part of the Habsburg monarchy. The country had its own government, parliament, and administration, even a small national army. However, the monarchy conducted its foreign policy from Vienna, and the bulk of its armed forces were anything but national. On the contrary, the so-called Common Army was a purely supranational institution charged with ensuring that none of the eleven nationalities under Habsburg rule—Germans, Hungarians, Czechs, Slovaks, Poles, Ukrainians, Romanians, Slovenes, Serbs, Croats, and Italians—dared to secede. For Hungarians, this policy was particularly crucial: In 1867 Hungary had asserted her special role within the Habsburg empire by forcing the creation of a dual state called Austria-Hungary, yet the legally sovereign Hungarian partner was not empowered to break its ties with the rest of the monarchy. Thus pre-1918 Hungary was both free and unfree, and her inhabitants thought of themselves not only as sovereign and powerful but also in bondage to the Vienna court.

Following the emancipation of the serfs and the enactment of legal equality in 1848, the political leaders of Hungary (*Magyarország*) had insisted that all residents of the country were members of the Hungarian, or Magyar, nation. Those who spoke German, Slovak, Romanian, Croatian, Serbian, Ruthenian (Ukrainian), or Italian were considered simply non-Magyar-speaking Hungarians. Yet in 1900, only about one-half of Hungary's 18 million inhabitants identified Hungarian as their mother tongue (actually a considerable improvement over former periods, when native Hungarian-speakers formed but the largest minority). Thus pre-1918 Hungary was both a national and a multi-national state, a situation subsequently duplicated by the proud "nation-states" created in Central and East-Central Europe following the dissolution of the Habsburg monarchy in 1918.

István Deák studied at the University of Budapest and the Sorbonne in Paris, and received a Ph.D. in 1964 from Columbia University in New York City. He is a professor of history at Columbia, where he also served for 12 years as director of the Institute on East Central Europe. Major publications include *Weimar Germany's Left-wing Intellectuals: A Political History of the Weltbühne and Its Circle* (Berkeley: University of California Press, 1968); *The Lawful Revolution: Louis Kossuth and the Hungarians, 1848-1849* (New York: Columbia University Press, 1979; Hungarian edition, 1983; Austrian edition, 1989); and *Beyond Nationalism: A Social and Political History of the Habsburg Officer Corps, 1848-1918* (New York-Oxford: Oxford University Press, 1990). Deák also has published extensively on the history of Hungary, fascism, anti-Semitism, and Communist Eastern Europe, and is a regular contributor to *The New York Review of Books* and other cultural and political journals.

The kings of Hungary were all Roman Catholics, and it was said that the nation enjoyed the special protection of Holy Mary, the *Patrona Hungariae*. Yet less than two-thirds of the country's inhabitants were Roman Catholics, and Hungarian Protestants could look back to a long tradition of rebellious militancy. In fact, the Calvinist or Reformed variety of Protestantism was considered the preeminently Magyar (non-Habsburg) confession. Moreover, the Jews, a mere 5 percent of the population, constituted the country's most successful element in business, the professions, the patronage of arts, and the arts themselves. These Jews, the vast majority of whom professed to be patriotic Hungarians, were perceived by the others, alternately or even simultaneously, as both harmful intruders and eminent Hungarians.

Hungarian belongs to the family of Finno-Ugric languages, which utterly isolates Hungary among her Indo-European-speaking neighbors, with only such geographically and linguistically distant relatives as the Finns, the Estonians, and a few small ethnic groups in Russia. In fact, English and Russian, for example, have more in common than does Hungarian with the neighboring Germanic, Romance, or Slavic tongues.

The vast majority of Hungarians (as well as the vast majority of Poles, Czechs, Croats, and other East Europeans) have always regarded themselves as full-fledged members of the Western world. However, because of their precarious location on the periphery of Western Europe and their particularly troubled history, Hungarians have had little opportunity to participate fully in the progress of Western civilization. Moreover, some of Hungary's intellectual leaders, both conservative nationalists and revolutionary leftists, have endeavored time and again to persuade the Hungarians that their shining light came not from the West but from the East: from a mythical historical communality of Turkic or "Turanian" peoples (which the ancient Hungarians were not) as a few Hungarian writers and thinkers argued at the turn of the century, or from the great Soviet state as the Stalinists propounded in more recent times.

Hungary's parliamentary system is as old as that of England, and the Hungarian Golden Bull bears nearly the same date as the Magna Carta. The Hungarian nobility, traditionally a large stratum constituting about five percent of the population, was well-versed in the intricacies of political debate and activity, and it managed to achieve a large degree of national and local autonomy even during periods of foreign occupation. But the same nobility granted political rights to non-nobles only during the revolution of 1848. Even in the post-1867 liberal era, suffrage was restricted to one-fourth of the adult male population.

After World War I, parliament dethroned the Habsburg dynasty without electing another king, but Hungary officially remained a kingdom until 1946. During the interwar period Hungary was governed by Miklós Horthy, a former Austro-Hungarian admiral, although it had neither seacoast nor navy. In World War II, Hungary's political leaders generally professed to be pro-British yet went to war alongside Nazi Germany. Clearly, Hungary's avant-garde artists and writers operated in a strange if stimulating milieu.

Nine Hundred Years of Troubled History

It all began with the arrival in the Carpathian basin of an Eastern nomadic tribe, the Hungarians, at the end of the ninth century. They were pagan but by no means primitive, and they easily assumed mastery over the more numerous Slavs, Avars, and other peoples in the region. The natives were generally familiar with farming and Christianity, and their conquerors gradually adopted both practices. In the year 1000, Prince Stephen, later canonized as Hungary's first saint, had himself crowned as a Christian king. The complexity of Hungarian historical and social development stems from this period, which saw the intermingling of conquerors and conquered, and the clashing of tribal tradition with Western and Byzantine influences.

Medieval Hungary was an independent and respected power, expanding toward the Balkans and the Adriatic coast. The economy and society were westernized to a degree, and under Saint Stephen's successors, multi-ethnic Hungarian society gradually divided into a group of free men, or nobles (the theoretical descendants of the early conquerors), a clerical estate, burghers, and a dues-paying peasantry. This too was a decisive development, for alongside an enormous and not invariably wealthy landowning nobility arose an urban middle class of largely Western origin, whose ranks would be repeatedly replenished by continued waves of immigration. Early twentieth century Hungarian society was to display the same traits: a rural nobility proud of its ancient heritage, and a bourgeoisie made up to a large extent of foreigners or the descendants of foreigners — hence the conflict between city and country, which has bedeviled the life of Hungarian intellectuals to the present day.

Hungary lost its native dynasty in 1301, and thereafter foreign princely houses raised conflicting claims to the Hungarian crown, stirring domestic unrest and strengthening the power of the local oligarchy. As a result, the Hungarian nobility gradually separated into two classes — landowning magnates and petty nobility — but the notion of the legal equality of all nobles persisted into the twentieth century.

Seldom did Hungary stand culturally closer to the West than under its native king Mathias Corvinus (reigned 1458-90), whose Renaissance court and great library are legendary. But a few years later, at the Battle of Mohács in 1526, King Louis II (reigned 1516-26), one of Mathias' successors, was killed, and the country succumbed to the Ottoman Turks. This was a turning point in Hungarian history, not so much because of the military defeat, but because two claimants now appeared on the scene, one a Habsburg and the other a native magnate. The final outcome was the division of the country into three parts: western and northern Hungary, which recognized the Habsburg succession; central and southern Hungary, which came under direct Turkish rule; and eastern Hungary, or Transylvania, which became a powerful principality under nominal Ottoman suzerainty. Meanwhile, the Reformation introduced further differentiation, with a largely Catholic, pro-Habsburg, and generally more prosperous West, and a largely Protestant, more independence-minded East.

By the late seventeenth century, Turkish power had greatly declined, and in the last great European crusade, Western armies liberated Hungary, annexing even Transylvania to the Habsburg realm. From that time until 1918, except for brief periods of national revolt, the country was ruled by the House of Austria. The great Turkish wars had left Hungary devastated and depopulated, and the Habsburg authorities responded with an intensive colonization program. The resulting influx of Western European (mostly German) and Balkan (mostly Serbian) peasants, tradesmen, and artisans helped to restore the economy, but it also tipped the ethnic balance in favor of non-Hungarians.

Vienna's attempts at absolute rule and Catholic restoration provoked a revolt early in the eighteenth century, and although this so-called Rákóczi Rebellion ended in defeat, the subsequent peace treaty enabled the Hungarian landed nobility to reaffirm its domestic political supremacy and its right to interpose itself between the state and the peasantry. In the following century and a half, the Habsburg rulers attempted repeatedly to limit the power of the nobility over their serfs, but the peasants continued to be the immediate subjects of their lords and only indirectly subjects of the state.

The eighteenth century brought Hungary domestic peace, a measure of economic success, and the spread of enlightenment and education. It was thus a relatively contented and prosperous nation that confronted the French Revolution and Napoleonic Wars in the 1790s. These events had a profound impact, drawing the attention of the Hungarian educated elite to the country's backward condition and the need to reform language and literature. The aim of these newly conscious intellectuals was to imitate the French example by creating a modern nation in which all citizens would speak the same language and enjoy the benefits of the same culture. During the so-called First Reform Age, customarily dated from 1825 to 1848, Hungarian was transformed into a modern language, literature flourished, and a sense of national identity spread to ever-widening circles of the population. By 1844, Hungarian had replaced Latin as the country's official language. The trouble was that approximately 60 percent of the population was not Hungarian, and these changes were challenged by a simultaneous national awakening among the minority populations and by the centralizing efforts of the Vienna court.

The crisis came to a head in March 1848, when Louis Kossuth and his fellow liberal reformers carried out a bloodless revolution that resulted in their "regaining," as they put it, a constitution. Hungary obtained the right to form its own government, responsible to a popularly elected legislature; feudal dues and services were abolished; and a whole series of legislative measures were introduced to free labor, production, and the distribution of goods. Now all citizens were free, but because the clamor of the ethnic minorities for autonomy was not recognized, the politically conscious among them revolted against the revolutionary Hungarian government. Because the Hungarians insisted on having their own army, finances, and foreign policy, they were drawn into a war with Austria, which the latter won with Russian assistance in the early fall of 1849. Thereafter, Vienna was able to extend its new centralist and absolutist system to Hungary, but the imperial court neither could nor would reverse the social and economic achievements of the year of revolution.

The 1848 revolution was Hungary's greatest historic event. One might well argue, however, that the Hungarians had taken far too great a risk in holding on to Hungary's unconditional right to exist on her own — irrespective of economic backwardness, the nationalist aspirations of the minorities, and the very real possibility of an alliance of the Slavic minorities with both Austria and Russia. It was indeed preeminently in Hungary's interest to continue to be part of the multi-national Habsburg monarchy and to be protected by the imperial-royal army.

In the following two decades, Emperor-King Francis Joseph I, who ruled from 1848 to 1916, attempted unsuccessfully to cope with the passive resistance of the Hungarians. Finally, in the Compromise Agreement of 1867, he guaranteed an equal position to Hungary in what hence was called the Dual Monarchy. From then on, Austria and Hungary were joined only by the person of the ruler, a common foreign service, a common army, a common national bank, and some other arrangements for common finances. Moreover, Hungary obtained the right to organize her own home army, the *honvédség*. The Hungarian political leadership had ultimately won the revolutionary war, without any further bloodshed. The fate of the national minorities and the lower classes was entrusted to the ruling Hungarian aristocracy and gentry.

A Prosperous Partnership: The Dual Monarchy, 1867-1918

The Compromise Agreement of 1867 can be deemed a success to the extent that it allowed the Habsburg dynasty to survive for another 50 years. However, it also alienated the Slavic, Romanian, and Italian majority of the population, thus planting the seeds of the monarchy's ultimate destruction. Hungarian politics over the next five decades were dominated by a continuous struggle between those who accepted the Compromise Agreement and those who strove for even greater independence. In this rather futile struggle, the Hungarian parliament neglected both pressing social issues and the interests of the national minorities.

The emancipation of the peasants in 1848 had brought land ownership to a part of the peasantry only; others now were forced to work as hired hands on the nobles' estates or to move to the cities in search of employment. At the same time, the compensation paid to landlords for their loss of feudal dues and services was beneficial for the most part only to large landowners. Middle-size estates faced a shortage of capital and credit, which drove thousands into bankruptcy.

The distribution of landed property was highly inequitable: In 1900, about one-third of the arable land was owned by fewer than 4,000 proprietors. Two-thirds of the agrarian population consisted of landless peasants, farmhands, and owners of inadequate peasant holdings.

There was a remarkable increase in the size of the Hungarian civil service in the second half of the nineteenth century, largely an accommodation of ruined members of the gentry, who viewed state employment as their inalienable right. The legacy of this situation, which persisted well after 1918, was a state and municipal bureaucracy made up largely of déclassé gentry, dissatisfied with its new condition yet not quite prepared to take part in a capitalist economy.

The problem of rural poverty was considerably alleviated by emigration to the United States and elsewhere, as well as by a transportation, agricultural, and industrial revolution in the second half of the nineteenth century. Economic prosperity continued until the outbreak of the war in 1914, but society was troubled by the increasingly rancorous conflict between the conservative-liberal Independence party (which wanted Hungary to be joined with Austria in a personal union only) and the conservative-liberal Government party of 1867. Moreover, old-style liberalism came under attack from growing antiliberal forces, a motley group comprising romantic anticapitalists, anti-Semitic demagogues, social Darwinist "Great Hungarian" imperialists, Christian populists, bourgeois democrats, radicals, and, last but not least, the Social Democratic party and its trade-union allies. The post-1918 Hungarian political constellation was clearly visible in the ranks of those who opposed the pre-war liberal system. Relations with Austria worsened considerably, while Hungarian nationalists prepared for a showdown with the national minorities and the latter's aggressive foreign supporters — Serbia, Romania, and Russia.

The outbreak of war in 1914 reestablished national unity, at least so far as the Hungarian-speaking population was concerned. The Hungarian government and, for several years, the people proved loyal to the monarchy, but because wartime casualties amounted to 57 percent of those in the armed forces, by 1917 discontent manifested itself in a growing number of desertions, violent peasant resistance to food requisitioning, massive strikes in the war industries, and a sharp increase in socialist trade-union membership. The authorities put down the strikes but were unable to supply the army adequately or to feed the starving population. Nor did the government make plans for the future. As if stricken by blindness, most Hungarian political leaders continued to insist, to the very end, that their country would emerge from the cataclysm politically independent and territorially unchanged.

The front collapsed in October 1918, and the Allies marched on Austria-Hungary from Italy and the Balkans. In the same month, Emperor-King Charles (reigned 1916-18) proclaimed the reorganization of the monarchy along national lines and called for the formation of national councils. The leader of the Independence party, Count Mihály Károlyi, now stepped forward, demanding a separate peace in accordance with the Fourteen Points outlined by President Wilson. Károlyi also demanded political and social reform as well as concessions to the national minorities. Finally, on October 31, revolution broke out in Budapest, against which the Habsburg military and the Hungarian government proved powerless. On the same day, in a last-ditch effort to preserve some of his authority, the king appointed Count Károlyi as prime minister of Hungary. The independence movement had triumphed.

The Revolutions of 1918-1919

Hungary experienced three revolutions between October 31, 1918, and the fall of 1919: a bloodless democratic upheaval at the end of October, a bolshevik takeover on March 21, 1919, and a peasant revolt against the communist regime in the summer of the same year. Ironically, the beneficiaries of the popular uprisings were not the masses, but the counter-revolutionary followers of Admiral Horthy, who filled the power vacuum left by the departing bolsheviks. However, outside actors, such as the Entente (Great Britain, France, and Italy), the Romanians, the Czechs, and the South Slavs played an even greater role in these events than did the domestic forces. Moreover, the prevailing pattern of the period was not so much one of clear-cut progression from one political order to another as one of confusion and chaos.

The Károlyi government embraced the entire moderate left wing in Hungary, none of whose members, with the exception of the social democrats, had a mass base before 1918. The most creative minds in government were the bourgeois radicals, epitomized by the sociologist Oszkár Jászi, a representative of the so-called Second Reform Generation that had rejected the chauvinism of the pre-war ruling elite and called for democracy and sweeping social reform.

The social democratic movement had come into being in 1868, but only in 1890 did it give rise to a modern Marxist party, which was organized along the lines of the German-Austrian model. The strength of the party lay in the trade-union movement with which it was closely allied, but it was also hampered by numerous weaknesses: limited suffrage had prevented the party from sending a single deputy to parliament before 1918; the dogmatism of the party leadership had made it difficult to organize the agricultural proletariat; and differences between the party's mostly radical intellectuals and more moderate leadership consumed valuable energy. All in all, this avowedly revolutionary Marxist party played the role of a democratic opposition before 1918, clamoring for an 8-hour workday, welfare measures, universal suffrage, and secret balloting. During the war, the social democrats gained many new followers, but the party was weakened by the resistance of its left wing to the leadership's patriotic policy.

The Károlyi regime immediately demonstrated its naïveté by proclaiming its intention to participate as an equal partner of the Entente powers in the as yet unformed League of Nations. The government also announced that it would insist on the inviolability of the state's historic boundaries. The rapid demobilization of the Hungarian soldiers returning from the front, however, left the country defenseless against the Czech, Romanian, and South Slav armies, which seized control of vast areas inhabited by a purely Magyar population. Hungary's hopes for Entente protection against her neighbors proved utterly futile.

For a few days, the revolutionary government enjoyed wide popular support, and on November 16, 1918, Károlyi proclaimed Hungary an "independent people's republic." But it soon became apparent that the democratic regime was unable to live up to its promises. Local Entente commanders laid down military demarcation lines that were increasingly unfavorable to Hungary. Democratic parliamentary elections were promised but not held because of the presence of foreign soldiers on what was hoped would remain Hungarian soil. A massive land reform was projected, but the only land distributed among the peasants was a part of President Károlyi's own vast possessions. Meanwhile, industry and transportation stagnated; the cities were poorly supplied; and counter-revolutionaries in high military and bureaucratic circles openly agitated against the regime. Finally, the communists undertook to destroy the republic.

The Hungarian communist movement originated from left-wing social democracy, from various wartime radical organizations, such as the Galilei Circle of young intellectuals *(see Chapter 2)*, and most importantly from the Bolshevik party organized in Russia among Hungarian prisoners of war. The leader of the bolsheviks was Béla Kun, a journalist who, while a prisoner of war in Russia, had become a close associate of Lenin. Kun and his fellow revolutionaries returned to Budapest on November 17, 1918, and a week later they formed the Communist party in Hungary. Their goal was to turn Hungary into a soviet republic and then to join the struggle for a world revolution. In the following months, the communists successfully mobilized thousands of unemployed workers, idle soldiers, and war invalids to demonstrate violently against the government. On February 20, 1919, when the communists wrecked the offices of the main social democratic newspaper in Budapest, causing the death of several people, the government finally decided to arrest the entire communist leadership. But by then it was too late, for the Károlyi regime had lost all popular support.

On March 20, the Entente military representative in Budapest handed over a new note demanding further territorial concessions, which the Hungarian government could not accept. Meanwhile, centrist and left-wing social democrats had visited the communists in prison and decided to unite the two parties, as well as to proclaim Hungary a soviet republic. President Károlyi and his government resigned immediately, and on March 21 a brand-new Socialist party of Hungary took power, with Béla Kun as its most important member. A 133-day experiment in bolshevism, the Republic of Soviets (Councils), or Hungarian Soviet Republic, had begun.

The psychological and political significance of the bolshevik takeover cannot be overstated. It would later serve to legitimize the post-World War II communist regime, even though Kun and most of the other people's commissars were killed in Stalin's purges of the 1930s. On the other hand, the soviet republic's dismal failure allowed the propagandistic repudiation, in the interwar period, of all left-wing movements, including bourgeois liberalism. The latter was decried as a bolshevik ally or as a force that had prepared the way for the likes of Béla Kun, and interwar anti-Semitism gained popularity largely because the counter-revolutionaries identified the Jews with "Godless bolshevism." It mattered little that the overwhelming majority of Hungarian Jews had stayed clear of the bolshevik experiment, or that there had been quite a few Jews in the counter-revolutionary movement.

Like the Károlyi regime, the Hungarian Soviet Republic made a favorable start: for many, its draconian economic measures held out the promise of social justice, and for others the formation of a proletarian army offered the prospect of national reunification. Besides, the new people's commissar for foreign affairs, Béla Kun, promised that the Soviet Red Army would come to the aid of the encircled country. With many former Austro-Hungarian army officers, as well as thousands of factory workers rallying to the colors, the rejuvenated Hungarian army stopped the advancing Romanians and drove back the Czech invaders. At home, however, the alliance of the two working-class parties remained tenuous, with the better organized social democrats slowly gaining the upper hand.

The social welfare legislation and cultural innovations of the new republic at first appeared truly attractive, but the regime's hasty socialist experiments exasperated the bourgeoisie, and antireligious propaganda alienated the rural population. Not only were all banks, mines, factories, and shops declared state property, personal jewelry and family savings were appropriated as well. Worst of all, the government dogmatically nationalized the large estates instead of distributing them among the peasants.

Industrial production and productivity declined rapidly; farmers refused to accept the new currency; and food no longer reached the cities. These developments led to forced requisitioning, which in turn fomented widespread peasant resistance. The repressive countermeasures of the government only increased popular hostility. The Soviet army was unable to break through to the Hungarians; nor was the communist dream of world revolution realized. By July 1919, without having suffered any military reversals, the Kun regime had lost nearly all its power, and at the end of the month the attacking Romanian army met with no resistance.

On August 1, the revolutionary governing council resigned, and Béla Kun and most of the other people's commissars fled abroad. Their place was taken by a social democratic trade-union government, which was overthrown within six days by a rightist coup d'etat. The real power, however, lay in the hands of the Romanian army, which entered Budapest on August 4 and did not leave the capital until November. The only Hungarian force now left in the country was a reactionary political group, the whites, that had established itself in an area of western Hungary not occupied by the Romanian army.

The "National Revolution" and the Conservative Consolidation, 1919-1932

The Hungarian Soviet Republic seemed firmly in power in Budapest when the first counter-revolutionary groups began taking shape in Vienna and two French-occupied cities in southeastern Hungary. One committee was headed by Count István Bethlen, an experienced old-regime politician, and another by Miklós Horthy, the Austro-Hungarian admiral. When the Romanians occupied Budapest and the communists fled abroad, Horthy transferred his headquarters to unoccupied western Hungary, where his small detachments of officers established a white terror, hanging communists, Jews, and poor peasants. On November 16, 1919, after the Romanian army had moved out of the capital, Horthy and his small national army marched into the city. In a public address, the admiral promised a "well-deserved" punishment for Budapest, the "sinful city."

ESTABLISHMENT OF THE COUNTER-REVOLUTIONARY REGIME The newly constituted counter-revolutionary government received quick recognition from the Entente, which had not hesitated to undermine Károlyi's democratic government and had urged the destruction of the bolsheviks. However, since the Entente wanted the entire country to accept the coming peace treaty, it demanded the holding of universal secret elections, the establishment of a representative government, and an end to the white terror. The counter-revolutionaries partially fulfilled these demands, and within a year, order was more or less restored. Elections were held in January 1920, with secret balloting for the first time in Hungarian history. The communists, of course, did not participate, nor did the social democrats, who boycotted the elections because of the white terror. A conservative Christian party and a Smallholders (farmers) party emerged from the elections as victors. The smallholders advocated land reform, a concession that Horthy and his fellows were unwilling to grant.

The victors now proceeded with the establishment of a new state, no easy task since the counter-revolutionaries themselves were divided between radicals with proto-fascist inclinations and conservatives who wished to return at least in part to the pre-war conservative-liberal monarchical system. In March 1920 Horthy, with the active assistance of his officers, put an end to the hesitation by having himself "elected" regent of the country.

Descended from a Protestant gentry family, Horthy was a former adjutant to Francis Joseph I and had been the only successful Austro-Hungarian naval commander during the war. Although he was to wear his Habsburg uniform throughout his career as regent, he was, in reality, a Hungarian nationalist and anti-Semite with little patience for the supranational character, religious tolerance, and political liberalism of the defunct monarchy. In many ways, Horthy was the quintessential expression of the counter-revolutionary dilemma: simultaneously conservative and radical, "European" and truculently chauvinistic.

The person of the regent was to be inviolable; he was the supreme commander and in all other respects enjoyed the rights and prerogatives of a monarch, except for the right to establish a dynasty or to create new nobles. In reality, Horthy did relatively little governing; he insisted only that the prime minister always be the man of his choice. Altogether, the regency proved a great asset in ensuring the stability of the counter-revolution. Under Horthy, the country witnessed several political changes, but the regent was able to head off an increasingly radical rightist tendency in politics by the simple exercise of his prerogatives.

On June 4, 1920, the Hungarians were forced to assent to a devastating peace treaty, signed at the Trianon Palace at Versailles, which reduced the country's territory by two-thirds and its population by nearly 60 percent. The beneficiaries of this territorial truncation were Romania and the newly created Czechoslovakia, Yugoslavia, and the Austrian republic. More than 3.2 million ethnic Hungarians passed under foreign rule, and losses in raw material resources were even greater. None of the other defeated powers, with the possible exception of Turkey, had been so harshly penalized. It is thus really no surprise that territorial revisionism dominated the foreign policy of the new regime. The government was able to justify its less than liberal policies by unceasing calls for national sacrifice and by pointing to the need to prepare for the restoration by conquest of Greater Hungary. The Trianon treaty also effectively prevented the reestablishment of normal relations with Hungary's neighbors, who subsequently set up an alliance system, the Little Entente, for the sole purpose of weakening Hungary even further. The signatories of the Little Entente—Czechoslovakia, Romania, and Yugoslavia—overlooked almost completely the threat of German revisionism and imperialism.

The national ideology of the new Hungarian regime was simple: it emphasized antibolshevism, historical values, "positive Christianity," order, authority, and opposition to "Jewish influence." The intellectual star of the new regime, the historian Gyula Szekfű, argued that there was a direct line of development from nineteenth century liberalism to socialism and, finally, to bolshevism. All of these ideologies, he contended, were alien to the Hungarian mentality, as were the urban businessmen, intellectuals, and workers who cultivated these ideas. In short, fear of foreign influences and antimodernism were the essence of the new regime's ideology. Ironically, the real holders of political power, the military and a number of semiofficial secret societies, consisted of many people who were not native Hungarians. The new Hungarian military command, for example, consisted largely of German and Slavic officers of the former Austro-Hungarian army.

THE JEWISH QUESTION In September 1920, just a few months after the signing of the Trianon treaty that had guaranteed the rights of the national minorities, the Hungarian national assembly adopted a "numerus clausus" law limiting the proportion of Jews in institutions of higher education to 6 percent, equal to their proportion of the general population. Although later rescinded in part, this law drove into exile some of Hungary's most creative scientists and scholars.

The trouble was that much of the pre-1914 economic development had been the work of foreigners, especially Jews and Germans. During the nineteenth century, the number of Jews in Hungary grew rapidly owing to a higher than average birth rate and immigration from both the West and the East. By 1910 there were over 900,000 Jews in Hungary; over 200,000 lived in Budapest, accounting for one-fourth of the city's population.

The success of Jews in business, industry, and even public employment was phenomenal. They dominated industry, mining, banking, and business; they provided one-half of the physicians, journalists, and lawyers; and they owned about 20 percent of the large estates. Jews also served in increasing numbers in the civil service and the army officer corps. Before World War I, one of every five reserve officers in the Common Army was a Jew, and in the Hungarian home army their proportion was even higher.

All of this had made little difference as long as the economy was expanding and political power rested firmly in the hands of liberal politicians recruited mainly from among the aristocracy and the gentry. But after 1918, everything changed. The economy was in ruins and the two left-wing revolutions had demonstrated that non-nobles too could govern. The fact that all the important people's commissars of the soviet republic had been Jews (mostly the rebellious sons of the assimilated, patriotic Jewish bourgeoisie) was never forgotten. Thus, after territorial revisionism, anti-Semitism became the main watchword of the new regime. Nearly unnoticed was the fact that the proportion of Jews in the general population had begun to decline even before the war; that gentiles had begun to take over business and the free professions; or that the Jews had fought at the front in almost the same proportion as other Hungarians.

When contemplating the work of the Hungarian avant-garde between 1908 and 1930, we must remember that a great many of them were Jews. True, their proportion in the arts and sciences varied a great deal: only a few in the fine arts, more in music, the theater, and literature, and even more in sociology, philosophy, mathematics, and physics, as well as in the art trade or patronage of the arts. What counts, however, is that the general public tended to perceive the arts, and most particularly avant-garde art, as the affair of Jews (*see Chapter 2*).

Another factor was the unique nature of Hungarian Jewish assimilation: numerous conversions to Christianity among the social and artistic elite, and the desire even of nonconverts to merge with the gentiles. Patriotic Jews often kept silent about their origins because they felt themselves one with the nation, and left-wing Jews because they considered their membership in the labor movement far more important than their Jewishness. A person's religion was rarely mentioned in educated circles, yet in this small country, such things were always an open secret.

The antisocialist and anti-Semitic measures of the Hungarian government created a poor impression abroad, while at home, the pogroms began to represent a threat to private property and law and order in general. This strengthened the hand of the moderate conservative faction within the counterrevolutionary camp, and they prepared for a takeover, achieved in April 1921, when Horthy appointed Count Bethlen prime minister of Hungary.

THE RETURN OF LIBERAL CONSERVATISM UNDER ISTVÁN BETHLEN The scion of an old Transylvanian family and thus himself a refugee (there were an estimated 350,000 refugees in Hungary), Bethlen was fervently nationalistic, but also cultivated and averse to demagoguery. He saw as his first task the restoration of order, and in that he succeeded amazingly. He neutralized the Smallholders party with a minor land reform and created a vast new unified party, which under various names was to govern Hungary until 1944. Bethlen also came to terms with the socialists in a secret agreement (the Bethlen-Peyer pact), which allowed social democracy and trade-union organizations, restored the freedom of the press, and declared a general amnesty. In return the social democrats promised to restrict their activities to the cities and the trade unions to refrain from agitation among public employees and from organizing political strikes. This agreement would be respected by both sides until practically the last days of the Horthy regime.

Bethlen next abolished the wide suffrage that had been introduced early in 1920 under pressure from the Entente. The new franchise law of 1922 gave the vote to only about one-fourth of the population and reintroduced open balloting in country districts and the smaller towns. Hungary thus returned, in essence, to the mixed liberal-authoritarian policy that had prevailed prior to 1914. Four years later, Bethlen reorganized the upper house of parliament, filling it with representatives of the upper nobility, the highest ecclesiastical dignitaries (including two rabbis), and representatives of rural and municipal councils, the universities, trade, industry, agriculture, and the professions. This conservative chamber of vested interests was to become, during the Hitler years, a bulwark of humane values and opposition to anti-Semitism, national socialism, and German aspirations.

Bethlen's goal was to rebuild the economy,

first by restoring Hungary's international credit. Only then, he believed, would he be able to pursue a policy of territorial revision. However, the Hungarian economy was in dreadful condition. Before the war, 80 percent of Hungary's "foreign" trade was conducted within the Habsburg empire, and her currency, banking, and credit system was intertwined with that of the monarchy. Now, in the place of a single unified economic region, there were seven separate customs zones, each deeply jealous of its prerogatives. How was the economy to recover under such conditions?

Like her neighbors, Hungary instituted strict protectionism and a deliberate inflationary policy, which forced the blue- and white-collar workers to bear the bulk of the costs of reconstruction. In May 1924 one pre-war gold crown was worth 18,400 paper crowns, but by then Bethlen had taken concrete steps toward economic stabilization. In March 1924, Hungary had obtained a substantial League of Nations loan, which allowed the government to put an end to the inflation. Three years later, a new currency, the *pengő*, was introduced; it was to remain stable until World War II.

Hungary's renewed credit standing enabled government and industry to raise more foreign loans, most of them on a short-term basis and at a high rate of interest. By 1929 Hungarian industrial production had surpassed pre-war levels, but two years later, the country owed a total of $860 million to foreign creditors. In the meantime, Hungary managed slowly to improve her international status and domestic conditions. In 1922, she was admitted to the League of Nations, and in 1927 she concluded a treaty of friendship with equally revisionist Italy. Hungary thus was no longer diplomatically isolated. At home, political life had returned to normal; the radical rightists had been mollified with jobs in government service. All would have gone well, had the world economy not been shattered in 1929, and had Hungary been less dependent on foreign credits.

The 1929 crisis devastated the wheat prices on which Hungarian agricultural prosperity depended. A year later, the government began supporting the price of wheat to save the farmers and the big landowners from bankruptcy. In May 1931 the Austrian Creditanstalt bank collapsed and with it the entire Central European credit system. Foreign creditors rushed in to recall their loans, and the Hungarian government was unable to meet their demands. The League of Nations ordered ruthless financial orthodoxy, which led to increased taxation, wage cuts, and massive layoffs in the public sector. The collapse of agricultural prices left the countryside virtually without cash; even landowners with large holdings had to resort to barter. Unemployment among industrial workers and artisans rose from 5 percent in 1928 to 35.9 percent in 1933, and the value of industrial production in 1933 slipped to 61 percent of the 1929 level. Again, as in 1919, there was hunger in the cities, and thousands became homeless. Professionals were no less affected: highly skilled industrial engineers would have been more than content to work as streetcar conductors.

Hoping to return when the crisis was over, Bethlen resigned in August 1931, but his successor, another conservative politician, could offer no new remedies. The result was a wave of strikes and left-wing demonstrations, as well as the far more dangerous emergence of radical rightist sentiments among the agrarian proletariat, unemployed bureaucrats and officers, and jobless university graduates. Giving in to right-wing pressure and frightened by the specter of anarchy, the regent appointed a notorious right-wing radical, General Gyula Gömbös, as prime minister in September 1932. With the appointment of Gömbös, the relatively moderate Bethlen era had come to an end.

From the Great Depression to the Debacle of World War II

Discussions of the Hungarian avant-garde in this publication close with the early 1930s. History, however, continued to shape the life and activity of the avant-garde artists, as well as the developments leading to their belated rediscovery.

MOVE TO THE RIGHT Gyula Gömbös, the new prime minister appointed in 1932, was a fascist ideologist who had groomed himself to become a Hungarian *duce*. He was also an opportunist. Once in power, Gömbös allowed his government to be flooded with conservatives. In the end, he did not abolish parliament, despite his grandiose pronouncements, and because he needed the help of international capital and domestic Jewish industrialists, he soon "extended a friendly hand" toward the Jews. His prime ministry was nevertheless a turning point, for it changed the political atmosphere from one of conservative restraint to one of demagogic posturing and fascist paraphernalia. Gömbös dreamed of a Central Europe divided among Nazi Germany, fascist Italy, and right-wing Hungary. He was the first statesman to pay a visit to Hitler in a fruitless attempt to win the Führer over to his grand plan.

Gömbös's posturing also resulted in a polarization of Hungary's political forces. On the one hand, an unacknowledged and bizarre alliance began to coalesce of all those who feared Nazi German influence: royalists, "Bethlenite" conservative-liberals in the unified party (eventually renamed the Party of National Unity and later the Party of Hungarian Life), the newly created Independent Smallholders party, Jewish capitalists, some anti-Nazi Hungarian populists and racists, bourgeois liberals, social democrats, and trade unionists. On the other hand, there emerged a group made up of déclassé gentry, unemployed university graduates, army officers, and others who expected economic and political recovery to come from a close alliance with the Third Reich. In this new shifting of forces, the right-wing radicalization of the army officer corps was to prove decisive.

Regent Horthy hesitated, as usual, between the two camps, both of which included friends and former counter-revolutionary companions. His desire for territorial revisionism and his personal anti-Semitism drove him toward an alliance with Germany, yet his social conservatism and contempt for the plebeian "Bolsheviks in brown shirts" made him fearful of a Nazi alliance. In the final analysis, he was a conservative officer, not a coarse revolutionary. Of the seven prime ministers Horthy appointed after the death of Gömbös in 1936, only one was a known pro-German at the time of his appointment (in 1944), which was made under Nazi pressure. The others, by contrast, were appointed because of their presumed conservative sympathies and expected ability to fend off German influence.

Yet not even Horthy's prestige could prevent the rise of mass national socialist organizations in the 1930s. The most successful group was the so-called Arrow Cross party led by Ferenc Szálasi, a former major of the Hungarian general staff. Szálasi was an idealist, fanatic, and visionary, whose mystical ideas and comically confused writing style can be explained only by dementia. His quasi-religious message appealed to many groups, however, and in the May 1939 elections, the first nationwide secret balloting since 1920, the national socialists won more than a third of the votes. Local returns and police reports indicated that the Nazis were the most popular among poor peasants and lower-level public employees, but also that they enjoyed significant support among all social groups, including industrial workers.

Despite their electoral success, the Nazis were unable to gain power because the ministry of the interior and the police kept them under tight control. The government had another powerful weapon to use against the right-wing radicals as well: Hungary had begun to recover some of her lost territories, and national socialist agitation against the government thus could be branded as treason. In fact, membership in the National Socialist party began to decline after 1940.

Thanks to the requirements of the German war industry for Hungarian products and raw materials, the country's economy gradually began to recover. By 1938 one-half of Hungary's foreign trade was with Germany, and the value of industrial production well surpassed pre-war levels. In the same year, Hungary too announced a rearmament program, but because modern weapons could be obtained only from Germany, rearmament brought her even closer to the Third Reich. The sharply increased military expenditures did not achieve their goal, however: Hungary was to remain militarily weak throughout the war, even weaker than some of her immediate neighbors. Here, then, was another reason for the Hungarians and their neighbors to court Hitler.

The year 1938 saw the annexation of Austria by Nazi Germany, which thus became Hungary's neighbor. This development worried the Hungarian leadership, especially as the leading German newspapers regularly protested, not wholly without grounds, against the mistreatment of the German minority in Hungary. In an effort to appease the Germans and the domestic national socialists, but also to satisfy their own anti-Semitic inclinations, the Hungarian leadership adopted a series of successively more restrictive Jewish laws in 1938, 1939, and 1941. Opposition to these laws came mainly from the upper house of parliament and the conservatives, who understood that the gradual expropriation of Jewish possessions marked the beginning of a social revolution. As it happened, the execution of these measures was haphazard and sufficiently arbitrary to spare the Jewish elite, and enforcement affected mainly Jewish white-collar workers and young professionals.

Finally, the year 1938 marked the beginning of a series of international crises from which Hungary at first profited, only to fall into an abyss at the end of World War II. Each new crisis presented the government with the same dilemma: how to satisfy Hungary's revisionist ambitions without surrendering independence to Nazi Germany. Ultimately, territorial gains were invariably chosen, though not without desperate efforts to escape the deadly embrace of the Third Reich. In the fall of 1938 Hungary took advantage of the Czechoslovak crisis and Munich agreement to recover southern Slovakia with its overwhelmingly Hungarian population. Less than a year later, the government exploited the dissolution of Czechoslovakia to recover Ruthenia in what used to be the northeastern part of Greater Hungary. In 1940 the government prevailed on Hitler to return one-half of Romanian-held Transylvania, and in the spring of 1941 Hungary shared in the spoils of Yugoslavia following the German lightning campaign against that unfortunate country. Still, Hungary was not at war, even though it was a member of the German alliance system.

A FATAL ALLIANCE War finally came to Hungary in June 1941, when she joined the German campaign against the Soviet Union. This decision was based not on territorial gain but on the arguments of the Hungarian general staff that unless Hungary supported the German campaign she would be left behind in the race for German favor and only the neighboring German satellites (Romania, Slovakia, and Croatia) would benefit. Again, as so often in the past, a great power was able to exploit national antagonisms in the region. Instead of harmonizing their actions, the East-Central European nations attempted to exploit each other's weakness, thereby bringing about their own ruin as well.

On December 7, Great Britain declared war on Hungary, and five days later Hungary declared war on the United States. Now, as Bethlen and other leaders of the anti-German opposition emphasized to Horthy, Hungary would be a loser, whatever the outcome of the war. At the front, only token Hungarian units were used at first, but as things began to go badly for the Germans, the Hungarians consented to send the entire Hungarian Second Army. It was to be utterly destroyed in the Russian winter offensive of 1942-43, and thereafter Hungarian forces were restricted to occupation duty. By then, Hungary again had a conservative prime minister, Miklós Kállay, who hated both the Nazis and the bolsheviks.

In the meantime the Allies had defeated Rommel at El Alamein and landed in North Africa. Both Horthy and Kállay became convinced that Germany had lost the war, and they sought to press secret negotiations with the Western Allies. The April 1943 meeting between Hitler and Horthy ended up in a shouting match, primarily because of Hungary's stubborn reluctance to "solve the Jewish question." In September 1943 a secret agreement was concluded with the British for Hungary's eventual withdrawal from the war.

This was a curious period. Hungary still was officially at war; she also harbored about 875,000 Jews, both Hungarian and refugees from elsewhere, and a considerable number of Polish soldiers and French, British, and American prisoners of war who had escaped from German camps. Government-sponsored newspapers were ordered to comment with moderation on German victories, domestic Nazis were kept under strict control, and the left wing was advised to actively oppose the government. Indeed, Kállay encouraged the formation of an "Independence Front," composed mainly of bourgeois democrats, smallholders, and social democrats. By late 1943 Hungary was for all practical purposes a neutral country; the Allied bombers flying over Hungary were not fired on, nor did they drop bombs. In truth, Hungary would have been happy to surrender but could not do so in the absence of enemy forces on her territory.

In the first months of 1944 the Russian front began to approach the Carpathian mountains, prompting Hitler, who was privy to the Horthy government's secret negotiations, to order an invasion of Hungary on March 19, 1944. The Hungarians offered no armed resistance, and Hitler's plenipotentiary, now Hungary's ruler in fact, prevailed on Horthy to appoint a pro-Nazi general as prime minister. Hungary was no longer a free country.

The new government quickly suppressed the opposition parties, whose leaders along with many anti-Nazi conservative politicians had already been arrested by the Gestapo. A general mobilization was ordered, and steps were taken first to expropriate Jewish holdings and then to deport the Jews themselves. This was to be the greatest human tragedy in Hungarian history: 433,000 Jews were transferred from the countryside to Auschwitz to be gassed or, in smaller numbers, sent to concentration camps in Germany.

The deportations and even the gassings were no secret, and there was a growing outcry from abroad and from the conservatives led by Count Bethlen, who was now in hiding. Finally, Horthy emerged from his semiretirement and in July 1944 resolved to put an end to the deportations. Fearing a fascist coup d'etat, he repelled the Nazis sent to round up the Jews in Budapest. In this way, the regent saved or at least prolonged the lives of the 200,000 Jews in the capital. In August 1944, reasserting himself as head of state, Horthy appointed a new government made up mostly of loyal generals and civil servants. In the same month, Romania turned against Germany, an act which brought the Russian army onto Hungarian soil. Now, for a second time, Hungary attempted to pull out of the war. The Horthy government sought contacts with the leftist "Hungarian Front" (which now included the communists, a small underground movement made up chiefly of intellectuals) and finally began secret negotiations with the Soviet Union.

Following a preliminary agreement concluded in Moscow, Horthy made a radio announcement on October 15 that he had asked the Soviet Union for an armistice. No surrender could have been more inadequately prepared. There were no troops in Budapest to defend the regent; the army commanders were taken by surprise, and few of them could be trusted in any case. On the other hand, the Germans knew perfectly well of Horthy's plans, and on the very day of the radio announcement, German SS units and paratroopers in Budapest arrested Horthy and his commanders and placed the Arrow Cross leader Ferenc Szálasi in power.

Arrow Cross rule was an epilogue to the Horthy regime, yet it also heralded the coming of a new age of fundamental social upheaval. Szálasi's government included a few stalwarts from the Horthy regime but also several new men of lower middle or lower class origin. Parliament continued in session but without the participation of the conservatives, liberals, or left-wing parties. The army and the bureaucracy were required to swear loyalty to Szálasi, the "National Leader." However, the fascists had little time in which to convert their wild ideas into reality. The army fought with less and less enthusiasm, and thousands of Hungarian soldiers surrendered to the Russians. Now the population began to sabotage the war effort: The government's order of total mobilization was quietly ignored, and by mid-November the Red Army was deep in central Hungary.

In September, the resistance groups had united in a national political committee and a military committee. They soon were betrayed, however, and their leaders were arrested by Szálasi's men and tortured; most were executed. Thereafter, small groups engaged in sabotage activities or distributed antifascist leaflets. This resistance movement helped to legitimize both the 1945 antifascist democratic coalition and the later communist takeover.

Arrow Cross rule amounted to the total expropriation of the property of Budapest Jews and a program to carry out their annihilation. The Gestapo reappeared in Hungary in November, and under its direction the Arrow Cross militia began the deportation of the Budapest Jews to the Austrian border. At this time, the Swedish diplomat Raoul Wallenberg, the papal nuncio, the Swiss, Portuguese, and other neutral missions, and some Hungarian officials initiated their humanitarian activity, extending protection to thousands of Hungarian Jews. When the Soviet army reached the outskirts of Budapest, the deportations were stopped; instead, the Jews were driven into a ghetto, only to be liberated by the Red Army in January. Altogether, about 40 percent of the Jews from the Trianon Hungary of 1920-38 survived; this rate of Jewish survival was greater than that in any other European state except for Romania and the Soviet Union.

On December 24, 1944, the Soviet army completely surrounded Budapest. The siege, which lasted until February 13, 1945, resulted in famine, the death of about 25,000 civilians, and wholesale destruction. By the time Budapest was finally liberated, the Red Army had already occupied western Hungary. On April 4, 1945, the last German and Hungarian soldiers left the country. Meanwhile, the Szálasi government, the rump parliament, the remnants of the army and bureaucracy, the gold reserves, and much of the country's rolling stock and industrial equipment had been evacuated to Austria and Germany. Captured by the United States Army at the end of the war, both war criminals and matériel were subsequently returned to the antifascist government in Hungary. Horthy himself was allowed to remain in Western Europe.

While the war was still raging on Hungarian soil, the Red Army ordered the creation of a Hungarian government and parliament at Debrecen in eastern Hungary. On December 21, 1944, a provisional national assembly was convened, consisting of communists, social democrats, smallholders, members of the newly formed Peasant party, and some bourgeois democrats. A day later, a provisional government was established. Incongruously, it included, on the one hand, three Horthy generals, and on the other, representatives of the antifascist parties, among them three communists. Count Bethlen was taken to a Soviet prison where he died two years later.

On December 28, 1944, the provisional government declared war on Germany. A new Hungarian army was organized to fight the Germans, but it never saw action. On March 17, 1945, a decree on land reform was promulgated, and on April 11 the provisional government moved to Budapest. Hungary's reconstruction and social and political transformation could now begin in earnest, even though real power remained firmly in the hands of the Red Army and the Hungarian political police established by the Soviets and the Communist party.

The defeat and destruction created a *tabula rasa* in Hungary. The war cost Trianon Hungary about 600,000 dead. The country's former political and economic elite had been killed or captured or had fled to the West. The leaders of the democratic parties depended for their survival on the good will of the Soviet High Command. The communists, on the other hand, could draw on their Soviet experience and the support of the Red Army. If they did not ask for a greater share in the provisional government, it was only because Stalin insisted, for the time being, on a democratic coalition.

The wartime regulation of the economy and society by the state and the disappearance of owners and managers set the stage for revolution. Unfortunately for Hungary, this revolution was not to come from the nation herself but was imposed from above. By 1947 the state, aided by Soviet occupation forces, had reduced the democratic parties to impotence, and a year or two later, Stalinist terror was established. Not until 1989 did Hungary recover its autonomy, and only in March-April 1990 were democratic elections held, the first since November 1945. Today's parliament is made up of political parties that claim spiritual and political descendance from the moderate democratic groups that tried to rebuild Hungary after World War II.

Hungarian Culture and the Arts and Sciences

The cosmopolitan inclinations of the Hungarian avant-garde were not shared by most Hungarians, who tended toward traditionalism and nationalism. These values were no less important in neighboring nations, which faced nearly identical problems of state building and national identity in the modern period.

SEARCH FOR A MAGYAR IDENTITY At the turn of the century, the public generally expected that Hungarian art, literature, and science should serve a national function and express a specifically Magyar spirit. Bernát Alexander (1850-1927), the neo-Kantian professor of philosophy at Budapest University, saw as his main task the creation of a "truly Hungarian philosophical system"; architect Ödön Lechner (1845-1914) sought to invent a modern Hungarian building style; and composer Béla Bartók (1881-1947) developed a national musical idiom through the study of folk music. One could cite many other examples as well.

The trouble was that no one knew precisely the nature of the Hungarian spirit, this elusive Magyar quality, or what it ought to be, not the least because Hungarians themselves were a thoroughly mixed race. Even the landowning nobility, theoretically a purely Magyar stratum, came from diverse origins, particularly because in pre-modern times the ruling elite had readily received people from any ethnic group, distinguishing between estates but not between nationalities. Moreover, recent converts to Hungarian citizenship were among the fiercest patriots: it is no accident that of the three seekers of Magyar art mentioned above, only Béla Bartók was of Hungarian origin.

One of the most refreshing aspects of the avant-garde movement was its indifference to the issue of national identity. These artists seemed to heed the advice of poet Endre Ady, who could not shed entirely his own peculiarly Magyar idiosyncrasies, to disregard the petty national problems and "to look to higher things, at last." The avant-garde artists entertained social — not national — concerns. Laudable as this vision may have been, it contributed greatly to the episodic role of the avant-garde adventure in Hungary's cultural history.

Nothing better illustrates the desperate search for Magyar national symbols than the figure of the "Turanian horseman," a romantic literary concept created by the leading literary historian Zsolt Beöthy (1848-1922) in 1896, the year when Hungary celebrated, with extraordinary pomp and self-adulation, its millenial existence in the Carpathian basin. Astride his mount in the endless steppe — erect, proud, and magnanimous — Beöthy's horseman was said to embody the unique virtues of a great nation.

After World War I, the theoretical discussion of Magyarness or "Hungarianness" was further clouded by anti-Semitism and xenophobia, but more realistic propositions were advanced as well. In 1940, *Mi a magyar?* [What Is a Hungarian?], edited by the historian Gyula Szekfű, with such prestigious contributors as the composer Zoltán Kodály and the poet Mihály Babits, summed up the debate in a tone of moderation. After World War II, the Stalinists forbade any discussion of national identity, but the debate has resurfaced recently. Again it was no accident that in the 1970s Marxist-trained historians of Jewish origin were the first to complain about "the loss of national identity." Clearly, the practice of assimilation continues in Hungary.

HUNGARY'S CAPITAL The pride and joy of Hungarians was their capital of Budapest, unified in 1873, comprising Pest on the east side of the Danube and Buda and Old Buda on the west. Indeed, much of what has been said about Hungarian progress in the nineteenth century applies more to this beautifully situated metropolis than to the country as a whole.

Buda, once a thriving Renaissance city, and the far more modest Pest and Old Buda were devastated by the Turkish wars of the sixteenth and seventeenth centuries. In 1720 the three towns together comprised only 12,200 residents, most of them artisans and tradesmen of foreign origin. In this respect, the towns followed the pattern of almost all other major urban centers in Hungary, Transylvania, Bohemia, Poland, Russia, and the Balkans. In Hungary, the majority of townspeople were Germans; the rest were Hungarians, Greeks, Serbs, Armenians, and Jews.

The three towns began growing again late in the eighteenth century, and by 1831 they had some 103,000 inhabitants. The German majority increased as well, so what was already the administrative capital of the Hungarian kingdom now possessed a German-speaking theater (but no Hungarian one). However, the Hungarians, both noblemen and peasants, soon began pouring in from the countryside, spurring the German burghers to embrace Hungarian patriotism under an increasingly nationalistic political establishment.

The revolution of 1848 first erupted in Pest. The same year saw completion of construction of the Chain Bridge; conceived by the great Hungarian reformer, Count István Széchenyi, the bridge was the first permanent structure across the Danube. From that time on, there was steady development: the old university was expanded, an academy of sciences was established, and after 1867 a new prosperity manifested itself in the appearance of theaters, schools, publishing houses, galleries, public parks, paved streets, newly laid-out avenues and boulevards, majestic bridges, and cast-iron railroad stations.

In the second half of the nineteenth century, Budapest developed more rapidly than any other European city. With its rise the other Hungarian urban centers gradually declined in importance; none could boast more than 100,000 inhabitants, and only Nagyvárad and Kolozsvár (in present-day Romania) could claim cultural fame. In such areas as housing and literacy Budapest still lagged behind Vienna and Prague, the two other great urban centers of the Habsburg monarchy, but the Hungarian government took pains to catch up with the sister capital of Vienna. Public telephones were introduced in 1881, and the movie theater Ikonograph opened its doors in the year of the millenial celebration, putting Budapest ahead not only of nearby rivals but also of New York and Los Angeles. Continental Europe's first underground railway was also inaugurated there in 1896.

The capital housed a national museum and national library, a museum and academy of fine arts, an academy of music, the national assembly, and all the ministries. The railroad network, proportionally denser than that of France, centered on Budapest, and one of the city's oldest factories, Ganz, delivered the first cars for the London underground railway. The great majority of Hungary's factories and banks were located in Budapest, as were the stock exchange and, especially important for this food-producing country, the grain exchange. Where earlier the landowning aristocrats had tended to winter in Vienna, now they maintained palaces in the capital and the haute bourgeoisie strove to build even greater mansions.

In 1869, soon after the conclusion of the Compromise Agreement, the three towns had 280,000 inhabitants; by 1900 there were 733,000 and by 1910, 880,000. The increase in population was due in part to an extraordinary rate of internal growth but even more to immigration. Hungarian, German, and Slovak peasants, as well as thousands of others, found construction jobs or industrial employment in the city or its suburbs. At the turn of the century, Budapest resembled Chicago in some respects as much as she resembled a traditional European city.

Assimilation was a corollary of urban development: As Budapest became the proud capital of an aggressively expansionist and nationalistic state, both native and immigrant residents of the city began changing their nationality. In 1848 more than half of the city's population spoke primarily German; by 1880 that number had decreased to 34.4 percent, and by 1910 to a mere 9 percent. During the same period, the Hungarian-speaking population had grown to 85.8 percent. Although many of these "conversions" were quite insincere, the process was irreversible, and by the interwar period Budapest had become an entirely Hungarian city.

Urban growth brought with it urban overcrowding. In 1869 the city had 9351 buildings, public and private; by 1910 this number had doubled. Despite this expansion of the housing stock, in 1910 four out of nine people lived in one-room apartments with an average of 4.3 people crowded into each one-room flat. Curiously, the sumptuous abodes of the haute bourgeoisie and the relatively spacious apartments of the middle class were generally situated alongside crowded proletarian flats. In accord with a peculiarly Central European building practice, large showy apartments were located at the front of new residences, while the other three sides were occupied by one-room proletarian flats. The windows of the poorer tenants overlooked hopelessly grim inner courtyards. Despite overcrowding, unsanitary conditions, and squalor, most of the urban proletariat lived better than had their forebears in the countryside, and hygiene, eating habits, clothing, and education generally were improving.

This concentration of the country's resources in one place was acceptable, even if not necessarily wise, so long as this city of nearly 1 million inhabitants was the capital of a kingdom of 18 million people. The capital of the "Hungarian Empire," as the Hungarians officially put it, included the subordinate kingdom of Croatia-Slavonia and a legal claim to other provinces of the monarchy. After Trianon, however, Budapest became the monster capital of a small country.

ARCHITECTURE The majority of architects working in Hungary during the last decades of the nineteenth century were trained in Vienna and brought with them the so-called eclectic style. Under its influence and despite the rapid acceptance of reinforced concrete, cast iron, and glass, the outward appearance of most new private and public buildings reflected some historical style or combination of styles. Eclecticism proved remarkably tenacious: as recently as 1936, a neo-baroque church was built in Budapest with inner vaults of plaster suspended from a frame of reinforced concrete.

The most celebrated and most violently criticized monument to eclecticism was the parliament building along the bank of the Danube, completed in 1904. As if to demonstrate Parkinson's law, this fairy-tale palace was erected only a few years before the dissolution of Greater Hungary. Its architect, Imre Steindl (1839-1902), was strongly influenced by the example of Britain's Westminster palace, but he capped his neo-gothic structure with a somewhat oriental-looking cupola. The Danube-facing front was embellished with rows of arcades, and the lavish decoration of both the interior and exterior reflected a wide variety of oriental and exotic ornamental motifs—all this, of course, to make the building look "Hungarian." Steindl nevertheless succeeded in creating a harmonious structure that has become the touristic symbol of the Hungarian capital. In the new spirit of the late 1980s, the Hungarian government removed from the tip of the highest spire the enormous red star that had disfigured the building for several decades.

The quest for a national character in the arts proved to be an important inspiration for architects and led to the development of a distinctive local variant of the art nouveau movement. Begun in Great Britain, Belgium, and France, art nouveau had conquered Central Europe by the turn of the century. In Hungary it became known as secessionism after the Vienna *Sezession,* a group of artists who had turned their back on the Austrian Academy of Fine Arts in 1898.

Ödön Lechner (1845-1914), regarded as the father of Hungarian secessionist architecture, was the first to turn to folk art for inspiration. For example, he used ornamental motifs of peasant embroideries, having executed them in maiolica, an enameled and decorated faïence, to adorn the exterior of his buildings. After producing several highly regarded buildings, Lechner reduced the façades of his up-to-date concrete structures to simple vertical planes covered with floral ornaments as in his lovely Postal Savings Bank of 1899 in Budapest.

"Floral architecture" proved a great success: town halls, theaters, apartment houses, even churches covered with colorful maiolica ornaments sprung up in many places. Scorned during the following period, these buildings are well regarded today, when the secessionist style is once again in fashion, as valuable witnesses to a fascinating chapter in art history. Béla Lajta (1873-1920), a companion of Lechner, refused to hide the concrete structure of his buildings and placed maiolica ornaments in horizontal bands, thus laying bare the hitherto concealed supporting elements as in the 1912 Rózsavölgyi building in Budapest. Some critics hail Lajta as the first really modern Hungarian architect who anticipated the most important concepts of the Bauhaus revolution, but the public at large rejected his sober style as insufficiently Hungarian.

Another branch of the secessionist movement, folkloristic architecture, was initiated by the Transylvanian architect, painter, and writer Károly Kós (1883-1977). Kós advanced the reasonable proposition that to develop a national architecture from folk art one should turn to peasant buildings. Kós and his followers studied village homes, agricultural buildings, and small rural churches, much as Béla Bartók studied and collected folk songs during this period. This folkloristic trend made the most headway among private urban dwellings, which accepted more readily than did monumental buildings the stylistic motifs of humble rural structures. Nevertheless, its accomplishments include quite a few churches, schools, and other public buildings.

Unlike the floral style, folkloristic architecture survived World War I but with much reduced vigor. Kós himself remained in his native Transylvania, thus becoming a Romanian subject. As a writer and book illustrator he played an important role in the cultural life of Romania's Hungarian minority, but he no longer had much opportunity to practice architecture.

The secessionist building style was in tune with its time and can be called modern art. Except perhaps for the work of Lajta, however, it cannot be related to the avant-garde in architecture, which came to Hungary after the war as the influence of the Weimar (later Dessau) Bauhaus school widened. Several avant-garde artists associated with Walter Gropius and the Bauhaus movement were Hungarians who had gone to Germany following the collapse of the Hungarian Soviet Republic. Hence, one might say that their art had "returned" to the homeland. The returning avant-garde was quickly tamed, however, partly by the conservative taste of the public and partly by the poverty of defeated and truncated Hungary. *(See Chapter 2.)*

During the interwar period the still popular and pretentious neo-baroque mannerism, the sober and dry modern fashion inspired by Bauhaus, and the somewhat romantic populist tendency coexisted quite successfully, with Bauhaus adherents gradually gaining the upper hand. Firmly entrenched at the Budapest Technological University, Bauhaus followers in the early 1940s instituted a virtual dictatorship, interrupted only briefly by the Stalinist neoclassicism of the late 1940s and early 1950s. That the adherents of this rigid "cubic" building style enjoyed an unusually long ascendancy in Hungary may explain the surprising violence of "postmodernist" attacks on them in the 1970s and the subsequent rediscovery by the postmodernists of their secessionist antecedents.

LITERATURE The last years of the nineteenth century witnessed intense literary activity in Hungary. In Budapest alone, 22 newspapers regularly printed poems, short stories, and critical reviews. Scores of literary magazines appeared and disappeared in turn, and dramatic plays were performed in at least six Budapest theaters. Publishers reaped handsome profits with gorgeous editions of foreign and native classics as well as with translations of contemporary foreign authors. Underlying all the activity, however, was stagnation, largely because the suddenly swollen urban public contented itself with traditional styles and themes. The poets and writers who had attempted in the 1880s to throw off the shackles of traditionalist epigonism were silenced by indifferent readers and hostile critics. None of the great figures of this "lost generation" — Jenő Komjáthy (1858-95), Gyula Reviczky (1855-89), and Zsigmond Justh (1863-94) — lived to see the new century.

In poetry, the ruling norm was still the national classicism of János Arany (1822-82), who had been a populist and near-revolutionary poet in the 1840s but later turned to the Hungarian past. Arany made monumental though abortive efforts to re-create a nonexistent national "naive epic," something akin to the Germanic *Edda* or the Finnish *Kalevala*. With his incomparable mastery of language and poetic forms, Arany remains a father figure for many Hungarian poets, but his unconcern for contemporary life, vulgarized by numerous epigones, contributed to a rigid academicism in the poetic trends of his day.

The most important prose author of the period, probably of all Hungarian literature, was Mór Jókai (1825-1904). In most respects Jókai was Arany's polar opposite, producing during his long and active life hundreds of novels portraying Hungary's past and present in a romantic glow. Jókai's extraordinary popularity transformed indifferent masses into readers, readers into subscribers, and Budapest's mainly German-speaking middle classes into fervent Hungarians. He did not shrink from depicting contemporary life — the stock exchange, city life, the industrial revolution, even social problems — but these themes appeared as romantic fairy tales with little bearing on reality. Thus Jókai too bore a share of responsibility for the failure of turn-of-the-century Hungarian literature to reflect the economic upheavals and social tensions caused by rapid industrialization and urbanization.

Kálmán Mikszáth (1849-1910), an imitator of Jókai's narrative style, was a keen realist, but he had eyes only for his own caste, the gentry. As a member of parliament, he belonged to the establishment, and although a most popular writer he was unable to infuse the sclerotic literary life with fresh vigor. Nor was any such inspiration provided by the theater. Hungarian theaters regularly presented French, English, and German plays, but the native product was limited largely to romantic historical drama or the immensely popular folk play. The only late nineteenth century playwright of significance, Gergely Csíky (1842-91), attempted to present contemporary urban life on the stage but was unable to go beyond the merely anecdotal.

At the turn of the century, two literary weeklies competed for the favor of the public: *A Hét* [The Week], founded in 1890 with the goal of offering a forum to "modern urban" trends, and *Új Idők* [New Times], founded in 1895 as a conservative, nationalist reply to *A Hét*. Appropriately enough for the mixed ethnic background of the Hungarian intelligentsia, the editor of *A Hét* was the Jewish poet József Kiss (1843-1921), and the editor of *Új Idők*, Ferenc Herczeg (1863-1954), was a novelist of German origin who had begun his career uncertain as to whether he wished to become a German or a Hungarian writer. Neither editor was born in Budapest.

Kiss followed in the poetic tradition of János Arany, but scenes of rural Jewish life also appeared among the themes of his ballads and epic poems. Herczeg, who imitated Kálmán Mikszáth, earned much acclaim with his often delightfully humorous novels on the country gentry and after World War I became a leading supporter of the Horthy regime. *A Hét* was unable to free itself from the Arany literary tradition, but it nevertheless helped to prepare for the cultural revolution of the early twentieth century. *Új Idők* reflected the tastes of its subscribers, recruited mainly from the countryside; it attracted only a few talents and gradually degenerated into a high-level magazine of social gossip.

The contest between traditional and modern literary trends became increasingly political, not in terms of party politics but in the modernist writers' acerbic rejection of the political establishment, its political parties, parliamentary infighting, and nationalist slogans. Believing that Hungary was heading toward catastrophe, the modernists demanded radical change.

In 1900 when the Sociological Society and its journal *Huszadik Század* [Twentieth Century] were founded, the circle of cultural-political polemics widened, but, without support, the radical scholars, artists, and journalists who wrote for the journal could not initiate an upheaval. Politics came to their aid in the form of ever more volatile (occasionally even physically violent) parliamentary struggles, unrest among the industrial and agricultural proletariat, and the repercussions of the 1905 Russian revolution, which among other things brought a delegation of rebellious sailors from the cruiser Potemkin to Budapest in July of that year.

Modernist trends became apparent in all branches of art, especially painting. In literary theory, the struggle for renewal was led by Ignotus (Hugó Veigelsberg, 1869-1949), the courageous and witty critic of *A Hét*, but theory was not enough. A creative writer was needed as well, and he appeared in 1906 with a small volume entitled *Új versek* [New Poems]. He was Endre Ady (1877-1919), the originator of a literary and cultural revolution in Hungary.

Only 29 at the time, Ady was by no means a beginner. For ten years he had been a journalist at Nagyvárad (today Oradea, Romania), where he had developed an implacably critical eye for the ills of state and society. He had already published two volumes of poetry revealing the main influences that helped to shape his own style: the poets of the Hungarian "lost generation," the French symbolists, the French poet Charles-Pierre Baudelaire, and the German philosopher Friedrich Wilhelm Nietzsche. Ady's *New Poems* had an immediate and breathtaking impact, dividing educated society and moving nearly everyone who read newspapers to take sides. What made this miracle possible?

In Hungary, the tradition and concept of a "national poet" were always taken seriously; he was seen less as a critic and entertainer than as a secular prophet or shaman who could express the people's collective consciousness. This was perfectly understandable in a country whose political leaders had so often been tragic failures. Ady brazenly asserted, and convinced his readers with the power of his words, that he was the very incarnation of the Magyar people. And perhaps he was: the scion of a family proud of its ancient nobility but utterly impoverished; born in a region inhabited by Romanian, Hungarian, and German peasants; and growing up in devout Protestant surroundings but sent to study in a Catholic school and later to Nagyvárad. In Nagyvárad Ady became acquainted with corrupt provincial politics and joined the city's partly Jewish radical intelligentsia. Indeed, nothing could be more Hungarian than Ady's multiconfessional, interclass, and multi-ethnic experiences. The power of his language was drawn from old Hungarian literature, especially the late sixteenth century Protestant translation of the Bible.

Ady was not so much a political poet as a prophet. He called for total revolution, castigating cultural backwardness, provincialism, the corruption of the powerful, the cowardice of the oppressed, hypocritical sexual mores, and sanctimonious religiosity. He boldly dismissed self-satisfied claims to national superiority and proclaimed the fraternity of all the nationalities in Hungary. Through such powerful verbal symbols as "the Hungarian fallow," "the horseman who lost his way" (an allusion to Beöthy's Turanian horseman), and "the pig-headed lord," to cite some of the translatable ones, he proferred his ideas directly, without need for theory or ideology.

It would be hard to find a more convincing demonstration of Ady's sweeping influence on his contemporaries than the case of György Lukács (1885-1971). Later a dogmatic Marxist-Leninist, Lukács by his own account was won over to Hungarian literature by the poems of Ady. Until that time, he had been totally submerged in German philosophy. Unfortunately, however, Lukács never really mastered Hungarian style, and the works he wrote in Hungarian make for even more difficult reading than those translated from the original German.

Under Ady's banner, young Hungarian literature now began to assert itself. In 1908 the monthly *Nyugat* [West] appeared, headed by Ernő Osváth (1877-1920), who brought together an unparalleled team of talented writers. The title of the journal spelled out its orientation, but it was by no means the organ of a single group or trend. Among its most prestigious contributors were the *parnassien* poet Mihály Babits (1883-1941), who took over the editorship after Osváth's death; the incomparably witty and philosophical "urban" satirist Frigyes Karinthy (1887-1938); the naturalist Zsigmond Móricz (1879-1942), who brought into novel literature the figure of the peasant as he really was; and Géza Csáth (1887-1919), the author of morbid psychoanalytical short stories. In brief, *Nyugat* represented the best in Hungarian literature.

Though radical innovators of language and style, Ady and the rest of the *Nyugat* team cannot be called avant-gardists in the formal sense. The first writer to do away with rhyme and metric form and to experiment with syntax, Lajos Kassák (1887-1967), came from the working class. Kassák was still an apprentice locksmith when he began publishing poems under Ady's influence. Later, in the ancient tradition of wandering artisans, he traveled across Europe on foot and learned to admire the Belgian Verhaeren as well as Walt Whitman. Returning to Hungary shortly before the outbreak of World War I, Kassák became the father of Hungarian avant-garde literature and art. In contrast to Western writing, however, his work was profoundly imbued with leftist politics and thus closely resembled the poetry of the Russian avant-garde.

During the war, Kassák founded the literary journal *A Tett* [The Deed], and when it was suppressed by the authorities, he tried again in 1916 by founding *Ma* [Today], which managed to survive for a decade. To make his political message less conspicuous, Kassák devoted much space in his journal to art and discovered in himself the painter he had always wanted to be. Under the Republic of Soviets in 1919, he was among the first to discover that the Marxist authorities had ideas about progressive art quite different from those of the progressive artists themselves. *Ma* was suppressed, ostensibly due to a lack of paper, and Kassák was told by no less a person than Béla Kun that proletarian literature "will certainly not be that of *Ma*." (*See Chapter 2.*)

Following the collapse of the bolshevik regime, Kassák went to Vienna where he published *Ma* until his return to Hungary in 1925. Without formal links to either the leftist emigration or legal social democracy, he gathered a strong enough group of followers to publish a leftist avant-garde journal, *Munka* [Work], between 1928 and 1939. After World War II, Kassák again fell out with the communist authorities. Only after 1956 was he rehabilitated and recognized at last as a great poet and painter.

The revolutionary euphoria of 1918-19 brought many of the *Nyugat* writers and poets over to the bolshevik regime. A notable exception was Dezső Szabó (1879-1944), who in his 1918 novel *Az elsodort falu* [The Village That Was Swept Away] preached a return to the "healthy" roots of the nation: peasant culture and blood. His book had a tremendous impact on the public and the next generation of writers, but it soon was outdated because of its mannerism and extravagant style. Its message, subsequently vulgarized and distorted, contributed much to the racism of the interwar period, which saw assimilation, especially Jewish assimilation, as the source of all evil. Szabó's writings also facilitated the schism in the late 1920s between populist and urbanist literatures.

The undoubted literary giant of the interwar years was Attila József (1905-1937). Of poor peasant origin, raised in utter misery in the countryside by his step-parents, József succeeded in creating an original poetic language and new poetic forms, fusing elements of surrealism and folk verse with traditional Hungarian poetry. A devout communist, József tried to reconcile Freudianism and Marxism, but was anathemized by the illegal Communist party. Suffering from bouts of schizophrenia, József committed suicide in 1937. His poems became truly popular only after his death, and he is now counted among Hungary's greatest poets, alongside Sándor Petőfi and Endre Ady.

MUSIC Hungarian painting also went through its

classicist, nationalist, populist, modernist, and avant-garde phases, as discussed at length in other chapters of this publication. Unlike painting and architecture, Hungarian music knew something of a national style, at least from the end of the eighteenth century when military recruiting dances became popular. The characteristic *rubato* rhythm and original melodies of these dances gave birth to a new musical idiom, the *verbunkos* (from the German *Werbung* meaning military recruitment). The *verbunkos* was not high art but light music for entertainment. However, it was characterized rightly as "national" because the whole nation, from the high nobility to the peasantry, accepted and enjoyed it and because it was immediately recognized abroad as a distinctly Hungarian style.

CLASSICAL MUSIC Fascinated by the *verbunkos*, Franz Liszt (1811-86) was among the first to elevate it to the level of concert music in his Hungarian rhapsodies. He mistook it, incidentally, for gypsy music because it was usually performed by gypsy bands. Later research has shown that the gypsies, whose own folk music is quite different from the "Hungarian" tunes they play for their audiences, contributed relatively little to the *verbunkos* style and content.

Most of the *verbunkos* dances and songs were composed by Hungarian amateur musicians. During the nineteenth century, however, Hungarian composers made diligent efforts to develop operatic and orchestral music from the *verbunkos* style. Ferenc Erkel (1810-93) fused it with Italian and, later, Wagnerian themes to create a national opera. Mihály Mosonyi (1815-70) composed music and wrote theoretical essays, mainly under the influence of Liszt. But by the end of the century, this movement too had faded, as had the national classicist literary style and academic historical painting.

In the meantime, Budapest could boast of a buoyant musical life. Its music academy, founded in 1875 with Franz Liszt as its first president, has turned out fine performers and composers ever since. The Royal Opera House (established in 1884) and other concert halls regularly hosted international stars. Unfortunately, good music did not attract sufficiently large audiences to relieve the opera house of dependency on state subsidies and, therefore, vulnerability to the unceasing clamor for

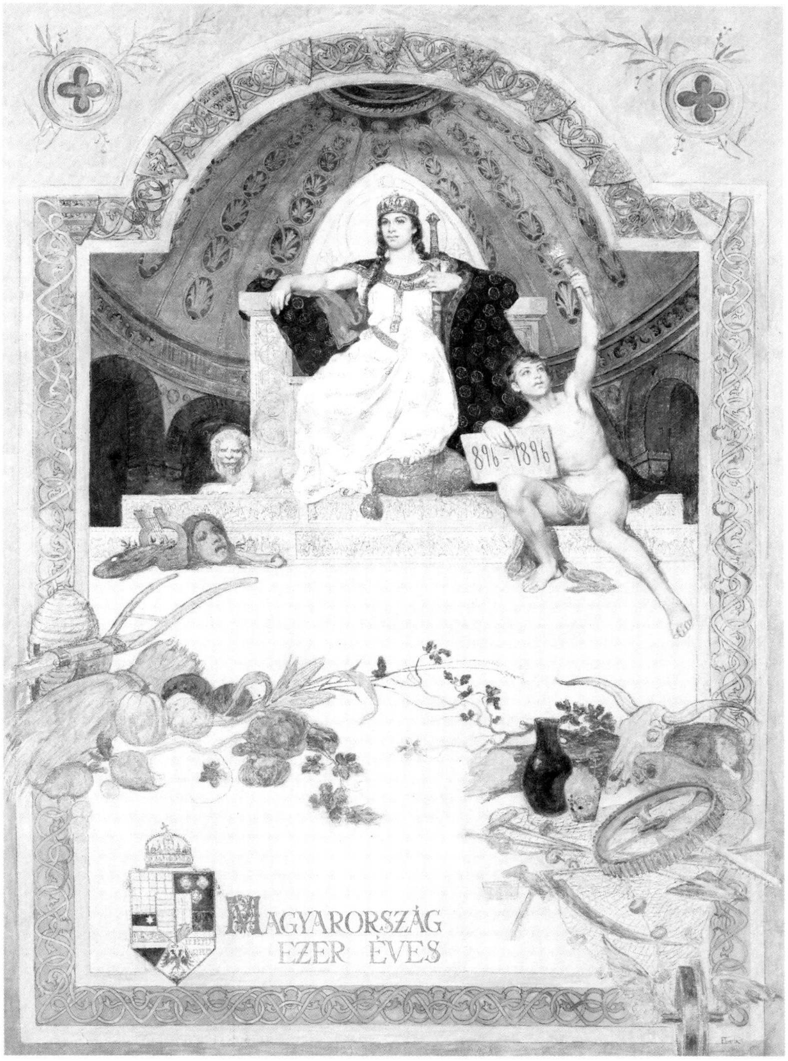

36. LAJOS DEÁK-ÉBNER, Hungaria, 1896

"national" art. Given the lack of suitable and willing artists, press campaigns and parliamentary speeches were of no avail, except to make life difficult for the eminent foreign musicians hired as concertmasters or artistic directors. Perhaps the most painful experience was that of Gustav Mahler, who was engaged as artistic director by the opera house in 1888 on a ten-year contract only to quit in disgust after three years.

Just how strongly the idea of national art held the best educated and most brilliant minds in thrall can be measured by the quest of the young Béla Bartók (1881-1947). Following the resounding success in 1903 of his first major work, the Kossuth symphony, which was influenced by Liszt and Richard Strauss, Bartók became dissatisfied and resolved to dig deeper. With his close friend Zoltán Kodály (1882-1967) he initiated a vast program of collecting peasant music. Together they sought out remote villages where old traditions were most likely to persist and recorded their findings with the aid of the newly invented phonograph.

Bartók and Kodály soon found that the oldest original Hungarian folk music bore little resemblance to later "Magyar" styles. Its chief features were a pentatonic scale and a fifth construction in which each line was repeated one fifth lower. The same features characterized the folk music of some Uralic tribes speaking languages related to Hungarian. Clearly, all these peoples had once lived together but had separated two or three thousand years before.

Aside from the amazing discovery that a thing as airy and fragile as a melody can survive for thousands of years, the two musicians soon found that the educated public, although enamored with folk culture and the pseudopeasant songs of the *verbunkos* style, found the melodies published by Bartók and Kodály alien and exotic. This second discovery made the two musicians natural allies of the modern writers and poets gathered under the banner of Endre Ady.

Bartók's and Kodály's musical discoveries were first announced in the foreword to a collection of 20 peasant songs with piano accompaniment published in 1906, the same year that *New Poems* appeared. In the following years, the two masters, while continuing their scientific research, began to construct their own works on this new basis, proceeding from simple adaptations of folk melodies to autonomous compositions. Of the two, Bartók made freer use of the elements of folk music and produced within a few years a whole series of major compositions that won him international recognition as a member of the musical avant-garde. The attitude of the Hungarian public gradually changed from violent rejection to sympathetic interest, and Bartók's ballet, *The Wooden Prince*, was a resounding success in the Royal Opera House in 1917. Kodály, on the other hand, was more inclined to hold on to folkloristic roots. He gradually waxed into the role of national cultural leader with such works as the oratorio *Psalmus Hungaricus* first performed in 1923, and with his tenacious fight for the reform of musical education. The latter effort bore fruit, however, mainly after 1945.

Under the Hungarian Soviet Republic both masters sat in the official "musical directorium" and therefore suffered some difficulties afterward. Nevertheless, they soon regained their chairs at the Academy of Music and exerted a decisive influence on Hungarian musical life. This influence was no longer confined to concert podiums: through the novel instrument of radio, the newly discovered folk songs reached the public at large and were fervently embraced by young people and ironically by urban, often Jewish, intellectuals.

LIGHT MUSIC The popular form of musical entertainment in the late nineteenth century also derived from the *verbunkos* style, but in a vulgar and mannerist form: the *magyar nóta* (Hungarian tune), sung to the accompaniment of a gypsy band. *Magyar nóta* is still highly popular in the countryside, often besting rock music and other competing musical idioms. The folk tune style also conquered the stage in the form of the *népszínmű* (folk play), a kind of musical comedy in rural setting that idealized the life of the gentry and peasantry. Earlier, in the romantic period, these plays had found their place in the national theater and attracted their audience from among the educated classes. By the end of the nineteenth century, however, both their literary and musical content had degenerated into shallow vulgarity.

Folk plays quietly disappeared from the major stages to be replaced by operetta, the new urban form of musical comedy. Imported from Vienna, the operetta was given new life by a host of brilliant composers, mostly trained at the Budapest Academy of Music, who for a time turned the Hungarian capital into the operetta capital of the world. To endear their work to Hungarians and provide some exotic *couleur locale* for foreign audiences, these composers spiced their music with *verbunkos* elements. *Csárdás Queen* by Imre Kálmán (1882-1953) became the most successful piece of this genre performed on countless occasions in many countries. Again, typically for the Hungarian arts, Kálmán was of Jewish origin as were other masters of the Magyar national operetta style. Other successful operetta composers were Ferenc Lehár (1870-1948), Victor Jacobi (1883-1921), and, last but not least, Sigmund Romberg (1887-1951), who emigrated to the United States in 1910 and is well remembered for *Maytime* and *The Student Prince*.

In the 1920s, a new type of music hall song captured the streets of Budapest, recalling the novel features of urban life with such titles as "Let's go to the movies!," "On top of the streetcar at night," and "If only I earned 200 *pengős* a month." Simple, unpretentious, and more funny than sentimental, these tunes were certainly in better taste than the earlier pseudo-folk songs.

SCIENCE The world knows Hungary primarily for its émigré scholars and scientists, the great pride of the nation: mathematicians, physicists, medical researchers, psychoanalysts, sociologists, and economists who achieved their greatest fame in the West. Consider the sociologist Karl Mannheim, the economist Sir Thomas Balogh, and the mathematicians, biologists, or physicists Albert Szent-Györgyi, Eugene Wigner, George Békésy, Leó Szilárd, Theodore von Kármán, Lipót Fejér, Georg de Hevesy, and Edward Teller! There are several Nobel Prize winners among them, but only Albert Szent-Györgyi (1893-1987), one of the founders of molecular biology, received the prestigious award for research done in his native country. Later, even Szent-Györgyi emigrated to the United States, where he worked for many decades. Only the briefest mention can be made here of the training and social and ethnic background of this gifted pleiad. [For a fine treatment of the subject, see John Lukács, *Budapest 1900: A Historical Portrait of a City and Its Culture* (New York: Weidenfeld and

19. SÁNDOR BORTNYIK, Geometric Form in Space, 1923

Nicolson, 1988).]

The international success of Hungarian scientists must be attributed to the country's educational system, created in the 1870s by such liberal reformers as Minister of Education Baron József Eötvös. Emphasizing the "discipline of brainwork" over character building, this system was also tolerant of different religions to a degree almost unmatched anywhere. Tolerance extended to the nation's private schools, with the result that some of the greatest Jewish scientists, all sons of successful businessmen, received their training in Budapest at Lutheran and other Christian high schools. The overwhelming fact of Hungarian scientific life is that, with a few exceptions such as Albert Szent-Györgyi, these Hungarian scientists were Jews, and whereas the tolerant atmosphere of pre-World War I years allowed them to develop their extraordinary talents, the poverty and not inconsiderable anti-Semitism of the interwar period led them to emigrate and thus to world recognition.

Scientific life in Hungary centered around the universities in Budapest (the Péter Pázmány University and the Palatine Joseph Technological University) and Kolozsvár University in Transylvania, which had grown out of a theological and legal academy founded by Jesuits in 1579. After Romania seized Transylvania at the end of World War I, Kolozsvár University moved to the southern Hungarian city of Szeged.

The financial and technological means of these institutions were rather modest when compared with those of Western Europe or with the needs of the country. As late as 1910, more Hungarians studied medicine in Vienna than in Budapest and Kolozsvár. Thanks to a host of brilliant scholars, however, the standard of education was exceptionally high in Hungary as well.

In theoretical physics it was Baron Lóránd Eötvös (1848-1918), the famous geophysicist and son of József Eötvös, who laid the foundations of a school of thought that produced such scientific giants as Leó Szilárd, Theodore von Kármán, and Edward Teller. They and other Hungarians later played a crucial role in the development of the Manhattan Project.

As minister of education in the 1890s Eötvös also initiated the Society of Mathematics and Physics and *Mathematikai és Physikai Lapok* [Journal of Mathematics and Physics]. The real upswing, however, began at Kolozsvár University in 1905 when Lipót Fejér (1880-1959) inaugurated his lectures on the theory of analysis and Fourier series. In 1911, Fejér moved to the Péter Pázmány University in Budapest. His chair at Kolozsvár was taken by Frigyes Riesz (1880-1956), the founder of functional analysis, who later continued working at the University of Szeged. It is mostly to the credit of these two great scholars that Hungary today boasts such a strong tradition in mathematics and that more recent Hungarian mathematicians such as Gábor Szegő, György Pólya, John von Neumann, and Pál Erdős have achieved world renown.

INTO THE INTERNATIONAL ARENA The loss of Hungary's brilliant scholars since World War I has been the gain of the international scientific community. Yet even without the trauma of two lost wars and the terrors of left- and right-wing political radicalism, it is difficult to imagine what might have persuaded such scientists, particularly the mathematicians who spoke an international language, to remain in that small country. The same can be said of such talented individuals as the musicians Joseph Szigeti, George Szell, and Eugene Ormandy; the moviemakers Alexander Korda and Joe Pasternak; the photographers Brassaï and André Kertész; the designers László Moholy-Nagy and Marcel Breuer; the playwrights Ferenc Molnár and Melchior Lengyel; the journalists Theodor Herzl and Arthur Koestler; and philosophers Michael Polányi, Karl Kerényi, and György Lukács. Perhaps it is not only a boon but a contradiction for a small country to possess an excellent educational system, a vigorous culture, and a stimulating intellectual life.

Hungary's extraordinary contribution to culture and science presents a fascinating enigma. What explains such a flourishing: the political strength, prosperity, and religious and political tolerance of pre-World War I Greater Hungary, or the political impotence, poverty, and growing anti-Semitism that characterized "rump Hungary" after World War I? The answer is that the conditions of both periods have played a role. What has remained unchanged throughout the country's troubled modern history is an intense preoccupation with past failures and successes, with questions of "what went wrong" and why. Out of a national history of failed

43. GYULA DERKOVITS, Dózsa on the Ramparts [V]

politics and politicians and from the trauma and suffering brought about by so many wars and revolutions there has emerged an intense and persistent belief that creative intellectuals and artists alone have the power and wisdom to interpret the past and point the way to the future. The respect paid to creative talent may explain why this small country has been able to produce such musical giants of international stature as Franz Liszt, Zoltán Kodály, and Béla Bartók, and such heroes of science as Hungary's many Nobel Prize winners. It may also explain why during the uprising of 1956 and the bloodless revolution of 1989-90, intellectuals were once again in the vanguard of all political activity.

Acknowledgments
I am profoundly indebted to my brother-in-law, Mr. Pál Veress of Budapest, for having helped me write the difficult section on Hungarian culture and the arts. Mr. Veress is both an experienced journalist and a well-known avant-garde painter.

revolutionary engagements: THE HUNGARIAN AVANT-GARDE

S. A. MANSBACH

The history of early twentieth century art can be interpreted as a succession of artistic movements that shared a profound belief in the authority of art to shape the very character and destiny of mankind. Thus, whether expressionist or constructivist, futurist or surrealist, all regarded the creation and comprehension of modern art as a political and social act. To make art was to comment, usually negatively, on inherited norms and mores, and to project an alternative system that was at once ethical and aesthetic. Most of the modernist movements and their supporters favored radical changes in both art and society to allow the emergence of powerfully new and creative relationships within individual and social life. No better model of modernist idealism and dissolution exists than that of the Hungarian avant-garde, which between 1908 and 1930 expressed the aspirations, achieved the successes, and experienced the failures of the modern movement as a whole.

The story of the Hungarian avant-garde provides an instructive example of how a group of artists forced their way from the periphery of modern Europe into the very core of European creativity and consciousness, only to retreat into relative historical obscurity at the end of the 1920s. Owing to a recent burst of scholarly attention to this subject, the Hungarian avant-garde is emerging from the shadows of neglect, from an isolation seemingly abetted until recent years by restrictive tendencies in Eastern European scholarship, and by a formidable language barrier. Now freely investigated by art and cultural historians and with a considerable literature available in translation,[1] the Hungarian avant-garde warrants further attention, especially by Western scholars, who necessarily bring to this rich subject alternative perspectives and somewhat different historiographical traditions.

This essay presents a general interpretive reading of the Hungarian component in the collective effort to assess the "new vision" that lay at the heart of modernist art. The assessment focuses on the events and activities that fall roughly into the decade 1918-28. It is important, however, to examine the artistic environment of the preceding decade to appreciate the suggestive historical continuities as well as the noteworthy ruptures that characterize the entire sweep of Hungarian avant-garde activity. (*See also Chapter 3.*) There also are implications here for a general understanding of the emergence of modern art and progressive aesthetics in the relatively backward societies of East-Central Europe.[2]

S. A. MANSBACH has published widely on the avant-garde movements of Central, Eastern, and Western Europe. Currently an Alexander von Humboldt Fellow and guest professor at the Freie Universität Berlin, Mansbach has been a professor of art history at several American universities and served as associate dean of the Center for Advanced Study in the Visual Arts at the National Gallery of Art, Washington, D.C.

3. RÓBERT BERÉNY, To Arms! To Arms!, 1919

Fig. 2-1 JÓZSEF RIPPL-RÓNAI, *Nudes*, Hungarian National Gallery, Budapest.

Fig. 2-2 KÁROLY FERENCZY, *Morning Sunshine*, 1905, Hungarian National Gallery, Budapest.

1. RÓBERT BERÉNY, Self-portrait with Straw Hat, 1906

Artistic Prelude

Although there had been serious interest in contemporary art among Hungarian intellectuals since the mid-nineteenth century,[3] it was not until 1896 that this interest assumed a trait that would characterize all subsequent progressive art: namely, an appropriation of what was most progressive in European art and a recasting of those innovative elements into an expression that was distinctly "magyar" and simultaneously international. For artists to effect this innovative synthesis required not only an openness to a variety of styles, often embraced concurrently, but also an acceptance of subject matter that did not always accord with the expectations of the tradition-minded aristocracy and court.

Before 1896, artists from the vast territories dominated by the Hungarian half of the Dual Monarchy, seeking an education in the fine arts, traveled in significant numbers to Germany, particularly to Munich, but also in considerable profusion to Düsseldorf and Vienna. These students, like many young American painters, perceived the academies in Munich and Düsseldorf as affording a firm foundation in the tenets of realism and naturalism with special attention paid to capturing naturalistic landscape effects. For the Hungarians, however, Munich held an added attraction: among the prominent academicians established there were Hungarians, particularly Simon Hollósy who welcomed his fellow countrymen into his private studio.

By the mid-1890s there nevertheless was increasing dissatisfaction among the younger generation with the formal training available in Munich. Indeed, the very emphasis on naturalism that encouraged so many German art students to retreat literally into nature as a way to affirm one's connection to *natura* also stimulated the longing of Hungarians to discover their own nature. Thus, in 1896, with the aid of other foreign-trained artists, Hollósy established the artists' colony at Nagybánya in Transylvania (today Baie Mare, Romania), which sought to introduce into Hungary the most progres-

Fig. 2-3 JÁNOS VASZARY, *The Golden Age*, Hungarian National Gallery, Budapest.

167. SÁNDOR ZIFFER, Nagybánya Winter, 1910

sive Western styles of painting. Eschewing the formality and restrictiveness of the German academic tradition, Hollósy, István Réti, and their colleagues effected a new style in Hungarian art that would have a significant impact over the next two decades.

In its affirmation of the value of the impressionist *plein airisme* of contemporary France, the Nagybánya school represented a fundamental shift in the emphasis in Hungarian painting toward an unfettered naturalism. With its distinguished "teachers" and the promise of free artistic development in the newest styles, Nagybánya attracted numerous aspiring artists from all over the Austro-Hungarian empire and beyond. Among them were József Rippl-Rónai (FIG. 2-1), who brought to Hungary the style of the Nabis with whom he had been working and exhibiting in Paris, and Károly Ferenczy (FIG. 2-2), whose work from this period marks the artistic high point of impressionism in East-Central Europe.

While French art of the late nineteenth century was actively emulated and enthusiastically received by artists, critics, and the growing class of collectors in Budapest, the 1896 celebrations to commemorate one thousand years of the Hungarian nation prompted many Hungarian artists to turn to an art style that blended progressive formal trends with more traditional iconography. In the years immediately following the 1896 millennial, advanced Hungarian artists were self-consciously aware of the singularity of their historical position: they were looking increasingly toward the West for inspiration and innovation, while celebrating their traditional ties to the East. To some extent, one can recognize this apparent contradiction as a first act in an aesthetic epic that would be replayed throughout the history of Hungarian modernism.

Many Hungarian painters such as János Vaszary responded to this challenge by embracing symbolism (FIG. 2-3), which acknowledged the growing sympathy for contemporary French styles and at the same time satisfied the more tradition-minded patron class (including the state itself) with identifiable, often patriotic, subject matter. Thus, the naturalist-impressionist current so popular with the influential urban middle class flourished alongside the symbolist trend embraced enthusiastically by other powerful segments of the society. This tolerance and encouragement of various competing progressive styles was to become a fundamental characteristic of Hungarian art itself, as well as the social history of Hungarian modernism, dur-

26. DEZSŐ CZIGÁNY, Hay Stacks, 1909

29. DEZSŐ CZIGÁNY, Self-Portrait, c1912

ing the next quarter century.

The embrace of French Impressionism by the Nagybánya painters, the acceptance of symbolism by many Budapest-based artists, and the passionate adoption of art nouveau throughout Greater Hungary[4] prepared the way for the enthusiastic reception of the next wave of Western art. As early as 1905 at Nagybánya younger Hungarian painters such as Béla Czóbel, Lajos Tihanyi, and Sándor Galimberti sensed in the work of Cézanne a new path that Hungarian art might productively follow. Believing that Cézanne's art heralded the beginning of a new aesthetic era, they and others separated themselves from the *plein airisme* of their teachers and assumed the name of "Neo-Impressionists" under which they strove to promote a modern Hungarian art that might assume contemporary aesthetic and social responsibilities.

Admittedly, the social platform of the "Neos" was naive and overly ambitious. It affirmed ever more emphatically a return to a freer and at times even "primitive" style of art and life that betrays stylistic affinity with French Fauvism and philosophical kinship with the emerging German Expressionism, especially that of Munich.[5] Since the teaching at Nagybánya had itself extolled the importance of expressing the "natural" in life and art, the Neos' break with the past was hardly absolute. Nevertheless, increasing identification with French models persuaded many Hungarian artists that the only effective way to introduce into Hungary the modernism they sought was to absorb it at the source.

Thus, between 1905 and 1907 there was a virtual flood of young Hungarian painters into Paris, many by way of Munich: Béla Czóbel, Ödön Márffy, Dezső Czigány, Sándor Galimberti, Valéria Dénes, Róbert Berény, János Máttis Teutsch, and Károly Kernstok, to name the most prominent. Although important for introducing post-impressionism and later French styles into Hungary,[6] this group of artistic francophiles is significant less for what they created before 1907 than for what many of them would soon become: the first truly modern Hungarian movement, later known as The Eight.

27. DEZSŐ CZIGÁNY, Funeral of a Child, 1910

Emergence of Hungarian Modernism

Beginning in about 1907, a succession of radical artistic groups appeared in Hungary, primarily in Budapest. Increasingly leftward in their social ideology and drawing intellectual nourishment from the various loose associations of poets, philosophers, composers, and left-leaning intellectuals, all ultimately were attracted to the bourgeois radicalism of the several "circles" that gathered around such young radical thinkers as György Lukács.[7] For the (slightly later) "Sunday Circle," which Lukács had joined at its inception and in which most of the leading Hungarian cultural figures participated, Cézanne was the symbolic embodiment of a new idealism for which they might serve as evangelists.[8]

Lajos Fülep, arguably the most important Hungarian art historian of an impressive generation of Hungarian scholars,[9] best summarized the role the Sunday Circle assigned Cézanne. Cézanne, said Fülep, was a new Giotto whose art was:

the most decisive affirmation of the reality of the real world.... [His] world view, like those of the Middle Ages, is a dualism which strives for monism and attains it, not by the dissolution of material but through its spiritualization.[10]

Frederick Antal also saw in Cézanne the simultaneous merging of subjectivism and objectivity into a profound synthesis that established a new reality.[11] Stimulated by the belief that this new visual reality had significance for the creation of new social syntheses, the young artists were supported not only by the Sunday Circle but by two earlier events that gave impetus to their own emerging social theories.

147. LAJOS TIHANYI, Working Class Family, 1921

The Eight

In 1908 the National Salon [*Nemzeti Szalon*] held an extraordinarily influential exhibition of the "Hungarian Impressionists and Naturalists," an umbrella term under which artists of every anti-traditional style and temperament banded together in a joint display of anti-establishment art. Rejecting the inherited tradition that art served the wishes and complimented the taste of the patron, eight of the exhibiting painters decided to band together in a common effort to champion a new, politically engaged aesthetic.[12] Known as The Eight, they were Róbert Berény, Béla Czóbel, Dezső Czigány, Károly Kernstok, Ödön Márffy, Dezső Orbán, Bertalan Pór, and Lajos Tihanyi.

Believing that art could spearhead the assault on society's conventions, thereby helping to manifest a new, heightened reality, The Eight came under the influence of several university students who formed a section of the Union of Freethinkers, soon renamed the Galilei Circle. This circle of young radicals served as an important nexus for progressive intellectuals throughout Hungary, and from this association issued the intellectual and social theories that served as the ideological foundation of The Eight's opposition to the prevailing political and social systems.[13]

Encouraged by Galilei Circle discussions and stimulated indirectly by Lukács, The Eight engaged their art in a social and aesthetic rebellion against what they perceived as the decadence of the prevailing culture, especially its bourgeois values. Like others of their generation, they proclaimed themselves victims of society and denounced industrial capitalism, which had only recently come to Hungary, as the enemy of true social integration and cultural creativity. In this conviction, as naive as it was passionate, The Eight was spiritually akin to many contemporary groups throughout Europe who also understood themselves, romantically, as revolutionaries in the just cause of social reconstruction.

Lukács and other activist intellectuals of the Galilei and Sunday circles prodded the artists to think of their painting as a vehicle through which to articulate a new system of values. Artists such as Károly Kernstok, the leader of The Eight, therefore demanded that the modern painter also assume profound social responsibilities in an attempt to mold

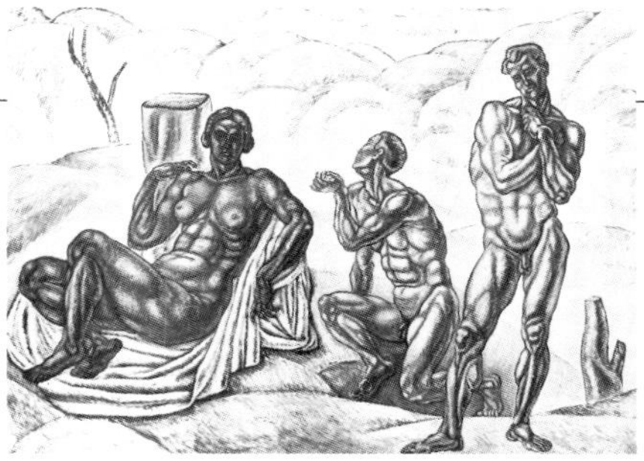

Fig. 2-4 BERTALAN PÓR, *Longing for Pure Love*, 1911, Janus Pannonius Museum, Pécs.

117. DEZSŐ ORBÁN, Church Yard, c1908

the visual character of the modern age. To exalt the social role of art, the artists would necessarily have to transform the structure and form of visual expression. Realization of such a transformation was indeed the greatest challenge. To meet it, The Eight seized on a variety of pictorial solutions by combining an amalgam of "Cézanneism," fauvism, and cubism with traditional genre types (still lifes, nudes, portraits, and landscapes). Such a synthesis produced striking results, especially during The Eight's mature years, 1911-12 (FIG. 2-4).[14]

The originality of their work was immediately celebrated in a review by Lukács himself, who proclaimed The Eight's first public exhibition a declaration of war "on all Impressionism, all sensation and mood, all disorder and denial of values...and [all] art which writes 'I' as its first and last word." His review continues:

...the greatest significance of Károly Kernstok and his friends is that they are the ones who up to now have given the clearest, most forceful and most artistic expression to this [new] mode of feeling and seeing things.... This [new]

125. BERTALAN PÓR, The Family, 1909

art of order must destroy all the anarchy of sensation and mood. The mere appearance and existence of this art is a declaration of war.[15]

Betraying an exaggerated estimation of their social role, Kernstok desired a complete restructuring of social relations in which the artist would "stand on the highest rung of the social ladder, where even if he will not enter into discussion with the gods, he will direct the spirit of the masses."[16] Thus, the artist in Kernstok's vision would move from the periphery of society to its center, from being the servant of the ruling powers to arrogating the authority of intellectual director. Just how this program was to be effected was never made clear.

For The Eight it was sufficient to make compelling visual statements and to leave the details to others. The Eight were hardly systematic thinkers or serious scholars, and much of their philosophy of art and life was borrowed from what they heard discussed (and often failed to understand fully) by the bourgeois radicals of the university and the Galilei Circle. Dwelling mostly on the problems of the past and present, The Eight did not address the consolidation or systematization of an ultimate solution beyond pontificating in favor of a bourgeois republic.[17] Despite the naiveté of their social *Weltanschauung,* The Eight achieved in their art an elegant and powerful expression of a radically new perspective. Moreover, it was this closely held belief in the obligation of modern art to transfigure contemporary reality that inspired the next and most fertile Hungarian avant-garde movement.

91. ÖDÖN MÁRFFY, Constructivist Self Portrait, 1914

12. SÁNDOR BORTNYIK, Composition with Six Figures, 1918

The Activists

As the artistic influence of The Eight began to diminish between 1913 and 1915, a new and far more radical band of artists emerged. Based in Budapest and calling themselves "Activists," these cultural revolutionaries took the social engagement of The Eight to a higher plane of aesthetic activity, embracing contemporary literature, music, and the arts as the hallmarks of a new age. Inspired by the socialist engagement of The Eight, the Activists erected their new vision of Hungarian culture on a more radical foundation.

Unlike The Eight, many of the Activists came from lower or the lower middle classes. Thus, their identification with the interests of the masses was perhaps more genuine, if not less romantic, than that of earlier Hungarian artistic movements that had laid claim to socialism.[18] What the Activists lacked in formal education they sought to gain through attendance at various discussion groups; and it was from impassioned university thinkers that they, like The Eight, ultimately received their ideological education. Debates held by the Galilei Circle persuaded the Activists that each creation of the modern artist was a political as well as an aesthetic act. Thus, they asserted that the "poet and artist should go out and stand in the tempest" of current events. In attempting to unite the political and the artistic as a means of galvanizing the masses, these painters and their apologists, not surprisingly, seized on new forms and media of expression.

To gather the artists around him, Lajos Kassák (1887-1967), leader of the Activists, founded a cultural periodical in 1915 with the ringing title *A Tett* [The Deed]. Modeled after Franz Pfemfert's Berlin journal *Die Aktion*, *A Tett* sought more than a renewal of national culture: It strove for a comprehensive restructuring of the universal political order, beyond the borders of Hungary and East-Central Europe.

Kassák was primarily concerned with the broadest issues of culture and its ethical dimensions, and at this time he was not an artist in his own right nor was he particularly impressed by the stylistic debates held within artist circles.[19] Thus *A Tett* never championed an exclusive formal vocabulary or style during its brief life. The use of expressionist-derived graphics and the publication of articles on the visual arts suggest that *A Tett* endorsed the stylistic trends currently embraced by young Hungarian artists, which were variously expressionist, cubist, and (vaguely) futurist, though with an evident visual debt still owed Cézanne. What truly engaged Kassák's passion, however, was an uncompromising opposition to Hungary's participation in World War I. Like Pfemfert in Berlin, Kassák was fundamentally a pacifist; unlike many other cultural radicals from England, France, Germany, Italy, and elsewhere, he could marshal no patriotic enthusiasm for his country's participation in the savage conflict.

Kassák's opposition to the war, and his sponsorship of exhibitions of progressive art by socialist-minded painters, lectures by left-leaning intellectuals, and radical artist gatherings fell afoul of Austro-Hungary's wartime censorship. Not surprisingly, *A Tett* was proscribed by the authorities on October 2, 1916, less than a year after its initial appearance.[20] Undaunted, indeed even stimulated in his increasingly visible role as opponent of the prevailing regime, Kassák launched the Activist journal *Ma* [Today] within weeks of the demise of *A Tett*.

The various phases of *Ma* correspond roughly to the early and middle periods of avant-garde activity, and to an extent the journal chronicles the mature period of Hungarian modernism.[21] Taking care to skirt the censorship laws, Kassák initially guided his new publication more emphatically toward the fine arts, devoting proportionally less space (at least in the first year and a half) to overtly political commentary. By no means had Kassák forsaken his agitational politics, however; indeed, in the first issue of *Ma* he contributed an essay of signal importance to the later creativity of the avant-garde.

In "The Poster and the New Painting,"[22] Kassák urges artists to embrace the poster "in the spirit of radicalism" since the poster has "by its very nature...the properties of an agitator." Without compromising its exhortatory mission, the poster carries "all the values hitherto seen in painting, indeed it may add new values to it much more easily than any 'artistically' created picture." Further, the new trends of futurism, cubism, expressionism, and "simultanism," to use Kassák's terms, are readily adaptable to the poster, through which artists become the warriors for and "the signposts of a century in travail." By its very nature this new Activist genre supposedly was incapable of promoting the merely decorative and was compelled to function as "living interrogation marks and exclamations, each one of them [intended] for the intellectual masses." Thus, Kassák exclaims, "The new painter is a moral individual....And his pictures are weapons of War!"

Kassák's article conveys no preference for any single style but rather a blanket acceptance of the social utility of various modernist idioms. In this broad endorsement of contemporary art, he embraces the stylistic diversity that was characteristic of The Eight and continued until the close of the avant-garde era. Following the example of Pfemfert and Herwarth Walden in Berlin, Kassák promoted under *Ma*'s aegis various currents of modern art through mounting exhibitions, publishing pamphlets, and organizing lectures. All these enterprises he intended as collective means of furthering "continual action for the revolution of the individual, for the destruction of all the forms of government and all forms of dictatorship." [23]

Believing that the Activists were witnessing the "beginning of a new epoch in the development of mankind,"[24] Kassák and his editors increasingly committed *Ma* to supporting the newest artistic and social manifestations of the international avant-garde. By 1917 *Ma* was publishing the work of the most progressive artists from Russia to Holland, promoting Béla Bartók and the "new music," founding one of Europe's most innovative theaters under János Mácza[25] (*see Chapter 4*), and conducting through its pages the most elevated intellectual discourse in East-Central Europe. By July 1918 the journal had attracted to the Activist cause most of the left-leaning Hungarian intelligentsia as contributors or supporters, and thus went beyond the more restricted audience of The Eight.

Ma's success is largely attributable to Kassák's talents as an intellectual impresario of the first rank. He recognized that the bourgeois radicalism espoused by The Eight (and by several of the Activists) was out of step with the mood and needs of the

10. MIHÁLY BIRÓ, Farewell Requiem for the Austro-Hungarian Monarchy, 1919

11. MIHÁLY BIRÓ, May 1, 1919, 1919

collapsing Habsburg empire. Accordingly, in 1918, he steered the Ma group of artists, philosophers, and literary radicals to an idealized view of the proletariat as the bearer of a new culture. On behalf of their new vision, Ma Activists demanded a social revolution of the proletariat, which the artists themselves would help precipitate and of which they would become, ironically, among the first victims.

Art and Revolution

From October 1917 to October 1918, the Ma Activists increased their visibility through published articles and the numerous exhibitions held under their aegis, particularly those presenting the radical aesthetics of Béla Uitz, Sándor Bortnyik, and János Máttis Teutsch. The government that had successfully closed *A Tett* now was unable to censor *Ma* effectively, prompting the Activists to engage in further agitation against the social and artistic precepts of the regime. At the end of October 1918, the monarchy finally capitulated to a Hungarian national council of mostly socialist intellectuals, many from *Ma*'s readership.

This October "Chrysanthemum" revolution was hailed as a great triumph for the workers and soldiers of Budapest,[26] and many in the countryside hoped that social justice and peace would be the fruits of the new order. Artists, too, rallied to the cause of the new national council government. Members of the former Eight and Activists, as well as painters and poets who had previously not been affiliated closely with either, readily took up brushes and pens on behalf of the new government, especially after Hungary was declared a republic in mid-November 1918.[27] Kernstok, who had once led The Eight and later radicalized the artists' colony in Nyergesújfalu,[28] accepted an official cultural position with the new government of Count Mihály Károlyi (1875-1955). Kassák brought out special supplements to *Ma* to celebrate the new social possibilities and to encourage liberal officials to follow the path he was charting. The publication of excerpts from Lenin's essay "The State and Revolution" and of the politically charged etchings by

126. BERTALAN PÓR, Workers of the World, Unite!, 1919

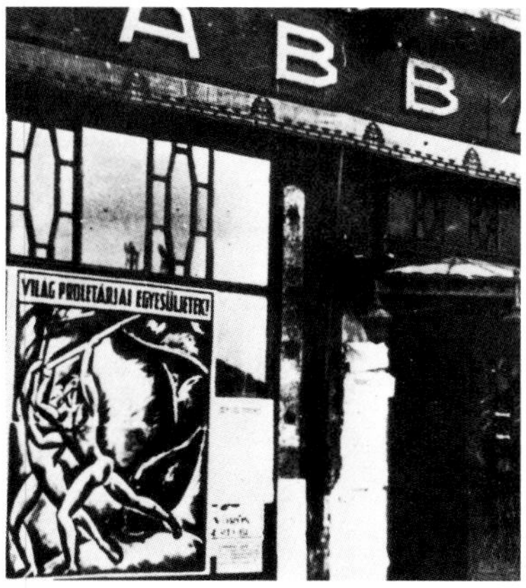

Fig. 2-5 BERTALAN PÓR posters on Budapest street by the Cafe Abbazzia in 1919.

Bortnyik indicate the revolutionary nature of *Ma*'s editorial impetus.

Despite increased avant-garde activity on behalf of the new regime, many of the more radical painters felt frustrated. The Károlyi government was fundamentally a bourgeois republic that had the support of the middle classes against whose taste and culture the Activists were rebelling. By 1918 the form of social revolution for which the leftist painters, poets, and their adherents had been clamoring was more in the bolshevik vein. Moreover, these artists could see in nearby Russia the realization of what they perceived to be a "truer" revolution, one that came into power only through toppling a liberal (Kerensky) regime that was very similar to that in Hungary.

Exacerbating the artists' disappointment was Károlyi's reluctance to invite their participation in a restructuring of society. Given the disastrous state of the nation, Károlyi was hardly in a position to allow groups of utopian-minded artists to introduce a comprehensive, costly, and most likely impractical cultural restructuring of Hungarian society. By this time, however, the majority of the avant-garde had already been swept up in the popular sympathy for Béla Kun's communist alternative to Károlyi's bourgeois radicalism.

The Communist party of Hungary, founded a month after Count Károlyi assumed authority, never attained the cohesion or ideological discipline of its Russian model. This may, in part, help to explain its popularity among the mostly urbanized Jewish middle class in Budapest: The party not only appeared to be tolerant of disparate viewpoints, it actively promoted access to government by national minorities that traditionally had been excluded from the higher levels of statecraft. Moreover, Béla Kun successfully exploited the numerous shortcomings of the Károlyi government, thereby contributing to the growing disenchantment with liberalism.

The day after Károlyi's resignation in March 1919 the Hungarian October revolution collapsed, and the communists immediately and bloodlessly proclaimed a dictatorship of the proletariat with Béla Kun as *de facto* head of government.[29] Many of the intelligentsia learned of the new Republic of Soviets (Councils), or Hungarian Soviet Republic, in a lecture, "Culture: Old and New," delivered that very day by György Lukács to radical artists. This fortuitous coincidence of politics and culture presaged the close connection that would develop between Kun's communist regime and the Hungarian avant-garde.

Sympathy for the new republic on the part of radical artists was both immediate and genuine. For the first time, the profound social reconstruction for which they had clamored on their canvases and in their writings appeared within reach. In addition, they were offered a direct role by the communist government in shaping the culture of the new society. Hungarian modernist artists were well positioned to exploit this opportunity: They had been experimenting with visual forms of expression by which to unify society and foster "the spirit of the masses." Kun gave them further encouragement when he appointed as people's deputy commissar for culture and education none other than György Lukács, who had exerted a preeminent influence on the intellectual development of the progressive artists and defended the early experimentation of Kernstok and The Eight.

Such support in official circles stimulated the Hungarian avant-garde to heightened productivity and engagement. The central board of a new directorate for arts and museums included Róbert Berény, a member of The Eight and of the Activists. The directorate was charged with a variety of tasks, all of which affected the avant-garde favorably. Radical academies were founded for the reform of

154. BÉLA UITZ, Red Soldiers, Forward!, 1919

art education, often with the active participation of Eight and Activist painters, such as Márffy, Pór, Czigány, Orbán, and Tihany at the "artists' city" of Balatonfüred, and Uitz and Berény at the Workshop for Proletarian Art. Kernstok, who had once served Károlyi, founded a free school for young artists of proletarian origin, and Nemes Lampérth was active in an art center for workers.[30] Even summer "art camps" for proletarian youth were to be organized by members of the Hungarian avant-garde.[31]

Within months of its bloodless assumption of power, the Kun government increasingly had alienated the general populace; invading armies of Romanians, Czechs, and Serbs made further advances; and Entente hostility escalated.[32] Pushed to the brink of collapse, the government turned directly to the artistic avant-garde to galvanize popular allegiance. This gambit was to afford the radical artists some of their greatest triumphs; for a limited time, the avant-garde realized Kernstok's ideal of the modern artist standing at the very center of society. To inspire support for the embattled republic, the artists created some of their most potent imagery, much of which was expressed through the medium of poster art.[33]

The perilous condition of the country left little room for subtle expression, and the artists often acceded to the need for straightforward propaganda on behalf of the communist regime, although in styles that allowed them to be both artistically modern and socially engaged. Bertalan Pór, for example,

Fig. 2-6 BÉLA UITZ posters on Budapest street in 1919. Heroic scale of posters can be seen from size of children standing by them.

Fig. 2-7 SÁNDOR BORTNYIK, *Red Locomotive (Train Leaving Tunnel)*, 1918. Yale University Art Gallery, New Haven. Gift of Collection Société Anonyme.

combined futurist and expressionist elements with an easily understood exhortatory message in his *Világ Proletárjai Egyesüljetek!* [Workers of the World, Unite!]. Drawing on his familiarity with the Cézannesque heroic figure from his days as a member of The Eight and his command of expressionism from his early work as an Activist, Pór here substitutes for the arcadia of the past a dynamically charged environment of the eternal present. Heroically scaled nudes bearing elongated red banners stride forward, creating a compositional vortex, its powerfully affecting movement enhanced by the thick contours and roughly defined surfaces. Style and iconography unite to goad to action any spectator who might have seen this poster affixed to shop windows, walls, and kiosks (FIG. 2-5).

Béla Uitz's *Vörös Katonák, Előre!* [Red Soldiers, Forward!] was among the most effective of the posters intended to stimulate public support for the embattled regime (FIG. 2-6). It also demonstrates the stylistic compromises demanded by a mass audience. While Uitz capitalizes on expressionist drawing to simplify the forms, he is careful to ensure that the advancing figures are easily recognizable. He "standardizes" the soldiers' bodies and reduces the individuality of the physiognomies. The composition is poorly resolved, however, in the relation between the four figures in the foreground and the seemingly endless procession of background figures. Uitz employs bold red letters in the lower register of the poster to emphasize verbally the message that is only partially realized visually.

Easel art, too, was enlisted in the service of revolutionary politics and aesthetics, as exemplified by Sándor Bortnyik's *Vörös Mozdony* [Red Locomotive] (FIG. 2-7).[34] Emerging from a cubist-derived landscape of factories and industrial sheds, the red locomotive, with its forceful frontal geometry, has just been given clearance by the signalman on the left to burst through the picture plane into the spectator's space. Behind the advancing engine, a trailing diminutive train car, seen laterally, affirms the picture plane. Animating the complex composition is a succession of cylindrical forms suggesting factory smokestacks and echoing the shape of the locomotive smokestack. The repeated oblong forms, as well as the reiterated circles of lights and puffs of smoke, establish an arrhythmic concatenation of geometrical planes that invigorates the picture surface.

An active image, both formal and iconographic, was exactly what Bortnyik deemed necessary to meet the social demands of the time. His choice of the locomotive imagery was itself deliberate, for in Hungary—even more than in the industrialized Western countries—the railroad had served for decades as a proud emblem of a dynamic new industrial development in an otherwise backward society.[35] The color red reinforces the political nature of the image: it is the motor force of the communist culture about to burst through the frame of art into the presence of the spectator. In the

41. GYULA DERKOVITS, Fleeing the Storm, 1926

turbulence of the revolutionary era, this was both a powerful and prescient theme.

Ironically, as the embattled Hungarian Soviet Republic drew more and more on the modern artist for support, the leading figure of the avant-garde not only rejected government overtures but actively opposed the regime. Kassák's opposition did not imply abandonment of his socialist commitment or of his desire to introduce art and artists into the social nexus. Rather, there were a number of strategic reasons for his rejection of Kun. First, Kassák always relished being in an oppositional position. Even when he applauded specific policies of the monarchical, liberal bourgeois, and radical regimes, he remained very much an outsider and felt free to criticize successive governments for their shortcomings.[36] Kassák thus was the consummate gadfly and rebel, always refusing to fall into line.

There were other reasons for Kassák's active disapproval. Although he published several articles that appear to be communist, Kassák remained closer to the social democrats than to the bolsheviks. Moreover, his party politics were always subordinated to his general belief in the consummate importance of art as the vehicle for social regeneration and integration. Thus, he could oppose the doctrinaire art policies of any government, writing that, "We want a socialist art; however, we emphasize renewal. We put before us no external patronizing."[37]

Kassák insisted on the independence of the artist and vociferously rejected any suggestion, much less a mandate, to pursue a particular style, subject matter, or purpose. He wanted to be revolutionary but without accepting unquestioningly the validity of any specific revolution. As necessity pressed the Kun government to become increasingly doctrinaire in its policies, including those affecting art, Kassák reproved the regime. Indeed, he acted in direct opposition to the exhortations of the leading communist politicians: Not only did he enhance the international flavor of *Ma* by increasing the number of illustrations of Western art and articles by foreigners, he also attacked Kun directly. In his "Letter to Béla Kun in the Name of Art" (*Ma* 4, no. 7, 1919), Kassák wrote:

I honor you as one of the greatest political leaders, but allow me to express doubts about your understanding of art.... Your superficial criticisms harm...the fulfillment of the revolution.[38]

Kun's outraged response was to label *Ma* "an excrescence of bourgeois decadence," and citing the acute shortage of paper he had *Ma* closed.[39]

Kassák's opposition to Kun was not shared by the majority of the avant-garde; in fact, it was not endorsed by all the Activists. Uitz, who was an editor of *Ma*, was a strong advocate of the Republic of Soviets and continued to serve it well. Others felt obliged to support the regime, if not entirely for ideological reasons then at least partly for nationalistic ones. Despite heroic artistic efforts, however, nothing could save the Kun government, either militarily or among the populace. On August 1, 1919, 133 days after it seized power in a nonviolent revolution, the Republic of Soviets collapsed as royal Romanian troops entered the outskirts of Budapest. (*See Chapter 1.*) That very day, Hungarian avant-garde culture was to begin its next phase of development: in exile.

Art in Exile

Soon after the fall of the soviet republic, a series of conservative figures served successively as prime minister, all of whom attempted to overturn the revolutionary changes promulgated under the Kun regime. By the time Admiral Miklós Horthy became regent in March 1920, a wave of vicious political reprisals had been unleashed, primarily by troops under Horthy's command. The Jewish community bore the brunt of this "white terrorism." Also assaulted, arrested, and sometimes executed were Hungarians who had served in the revolutionary governments under both Károlyi and Kun, as well as some members of the artistic avant-garde.[40]

Kassák was imprisoned for several months before escaping in 1920.[41] Other artists, including those who had taken no active role in the revolutionary regimes but had embraced modern styles, recognized the danger of remaining in Budapest,[42] and between the summer of 1919 and the end of 1920 almost the entire corps of modern artists fled the capital, most electing to emigrate to Vienna, Berlin, or shortly later to the Weimar Bauhaus.[43] (*See also Chapters 4 and 5.*)

162. BÉLA UITZ, White Terror (XIV)

VIENNA Vienna was a logical refuge for the emigrant Hungarians, and along with other German centers (Berlin, Weimar, and Dessau), it played a signal role in the history of the Hungarian avant-garde.[44] Like Budapest, Vienna was the capital of a greatly diminished country. Although the political ties between the two countries had been severed with the collapse of the Austro-Hungarian empire, Hungarians still had an emotional association with the former imperial capital. Jewish emigrants had an especially strong attachment to Vienna's large and relatively secure Jewish community, where they hoped to find hospitality and solace as they fled from the virulently anti-Semitic white terror that ensued in Hungary on Kun's departure.[45] (*See Chapter 1.*) Furthermore, many middle-class Hungarian Jews spoke German at home, and this facility with the language would be an advantage in reestablishing themselves. Vienna also appealed politically to the predominantly liberal-minded Jews from Budapest. Unlike Hungary, the new

160. BÉLA UITZ, Captain Nottingham (VII)

161. BÉLA UITZ, General Ludd (XII)

33. BÉLA CZÓBEL, Berlin Street, c1920

Fig. 2-8 MIHALY BIRÓ, *"Horthy: We haven't heard a single complaint,"* from the *Horthy Portfolio*, 1920. Hungarian National Gallery, Budapest.

Austrian republic had a socialist government that did not turn away the refugees even if it did not welcome them with open arms.

For artists, the appeal of Vienna was immense. An impressive number of them were Jewish or of Jewish background, and they undoubtedly shared expectations similar to those of the Jewish middle-class émigrés who had been their patrons and apologists in Budapest. Some of the avant-garde were familiar with Vienna, having studied or lived in the city in their youth. Moreover, Austria had recently been an active center of progressive art, but by 1920, Schiele, Klimt, and many other members of the Viennese Sezession and expressionist movements were dead and their mantle had not been assumed by others. Thus, a vacuum was left by these artists whose works had been exhibited early in Budapest under the aegis of Hungarian progressive art associations. The Hungarians might have hoped to exploit this opportunity, establishing themselves as leaders of the new art in a major European capital without competition from an indigenous avant-garde.

Finally, Vienna offered the promise of artistic freedom. In Austria there was no governmental insistence on the form, subject matter, and purposes of art as there had been under Kun and his commissar Lukács. This was particularly appealing not only to individuals like Kassák, who almost intentionally had run afoul of governmental policies on the arts, but also to artists who had been uncomfortable with the political engagement that was heralded as the hallmark of modernism.

Whatever their expectations, Hungarian artists found life in Vienna extraordinarily difficult and frustrating. The economy was in shambles and the Viennese themselves were completely indifferent to the Hungarian modernists and their attempt to establish an international avant-garde culture.[46] However, the initial disappointments of Hungarian avant-garde artists in Vienna were, to a large degree, of their own making. Their primary focus was Hungary, not Vienna or the West. Especially during the first six months of exile, the artists remained obsessed with contemporary events in their homeland. When asked why he reestablished *Ma* in Vienna (May 1920), Kassák admitted, "I did it for Hungary, so the door which had been opened to international life would not again be closed. Thanks to this journal, the modern spirit arrived in Hungary."[47]

Biró created a series of politically pointed prints, the *Horthy Portfolio,* through which he commented tendentiously on the savagery of the conservative government in Hungary (FIG. 2-8). Other avant-garde veterans of the Republic of Soviets continued to compose striking political posters through which to galvanize the anti-Horthy opposition. The majority of these works never circulated widely in Hungary but were destined from the outset to convey their fiery message through the pages of exile periodicals such as Vienna's Hungarian newspaper, *Bécsi Magyar Újság*. When the Activists met, usually at the Schloss Café near the Schönbrunn palace, they worried over the distribution of their journal (and art) not in Vienna but in Budapest,[48] and they often engaged in a passionate, characteristically Hungarian, debate over the "minority nationalities" question.

Despite the call "to artists of all lands," the early Viennese issues of *Ma* addressed primarily those confederates who remained in Hungary and in the former Hungarian lands incorporated into Czechoslovakia, Romania, and Yugoslavia that lay beyond the reach of Horthy's white terror. Kassák continued to employ his journal as a weapon to discredit Horthy and to consolidate his own role as the leading social and political critic of conservatism. Thus, he could announce from exile that "the revolution lives in us and through us continuously."[49] No wonder that it was difficult for the Hungarian avant-garde to integrate themselves into Viennese culture: they were still living spiritually in Hungary, while physically isolated in Vienna. By the end of the year, many had begun to tire of their divided existence and elected to leave for Berlin.

Contributing to the migration from Austria to Germany was the growing internecine antagonism among the Hungarian artists living in Vienna. Long-standing differences within the avant-garde had been consciously downplayed in Hungary as the artists attempted to appear united in their relations with the prevailing government. During 1921, however, these schisms resurfaced in Vienna. In exile, the artists lacked a common cause around which to rally and thereby transcend their internal disagreements. Hence, disputes over social ideology, the issue of nationalities, and the proper role of the avant-garde within the international community of progressive artists were expressed without restraint.

At the center of these controversies was Lajos Kassák, who seemed to relish his role as agitator within the twin spheres of politics and art. Once the editor of *Ma* determined to take up the brush in addition to the pen in the service of progressive art, the internal disputes among the exiled artists were fueled to the boiling point.

KASSÁK AS ARTIST AND AGITATOR Kassák seemingly had been satisfied with his role as poet and impresario of the Hungarian avant-garde. In late 1920 or early 1921, however, he decided to become an artist in his own right. What might have prompted him to embrace advanced painting (and the graphic arts) as a practitioner as well as an apologist is unclear. Perhaps he was stimulated by his increasing contacts with such figures as Theo van Doesburg who expertly combined editorial, organizational, and artistic activities.[50] Or maybe he was prodded by his enhanced familiarity with the many-sided talents of the young generation of Russian abstractionists.[51] In any case, he embarked on his career as an artist with the same passion and social commitment that characterized his editorial activities.

Significantly, Kassák's visual artistic work was from almost the first moment (in Vienna) fundamentally "constructivist," and in 1921 this separated him from most of his compatriots who were still working in an essentially expressionist-derived idiom.[52] For Kassák, expressionism was not a style that any longer held appeal.[53] By late 1920, expressionism was perceived as "philosophically" too spiritual for the progressive thinker who had emphatically renounced the metaphysical and affirmed the material, however romanticized. Moreover, expressionism, even with its distortions, was visually too close to naturalism, which (with its corollary, subjectivism) the Activists had opposed since *Ma* first appeared in 1916.

Kassák also must have realized that without the slightest training in art, he could hardly "compete" favorably in an expressionist style that others had mastered only after prolonged effort. As a rebel against prevailing views and as an untiring promoter of whatever was both progressive and socially committed, Kassák must have been captivated by the visual power and novelty, as well as the ethical possibilities, of constructivism. Consequently, he turned his energies toward furthering its development and application.

Kassák's embrace of constructivism fitted into a life-long pattern of reconciling new visual forms and styles with his unwavering belief in socialist idealism, and it is this contribution to international constructivism that constitutes the greatest achievement of his years of exile.[54] On the second anniversary of the Hungarian communist revolution, Kassák published on the cover of *Ma* (March 1921)

70. LAJOS KASSÁK, Bildarchitektur, 1921-26

Fig. 2-9 *MA* cover by LAJOS KASSÁK, 1921.

a geometrically abstract linocut (FIG. 2-9).[55] This image might be considered his first important attempt at constructivism. An experiment in contrasts of geometrical forms, voids and solids, and spatial interpenetration, the image is relatively primitive, especially when compared to contemporary Russian suprematist and early constructivist examples.[56] Nonetheless, this work marks a major step in Kassák's new orientation, for it was not only an early experiment in constructivism but was among his first artistic endeavors.

Within six months Kassák was sufficiently confident of his mastery of constructivism to publish a booklet that contained not only eight new constructivist linocuts but the most eloquent statement of his constructivist principles. Written in the characteristic avant-garde declamatory format, Kassák's manifesto *Bildarchitektur* [Architecture of the Picture, or Pictorial Architecture] reveals his debt to various contemporary currents in the international avant-garde. Retaining his practice of adapting the thought of others to his own purposes, here Kassák insists on the absolutist nature of art by which "there is no new art and no old art; there is only art...." And again, "Now we can see clearly that art is Art, and no more and no less than this."[57]

Kassák thus maintained that the artist can never serve merely as the advocate of any one class, nation, or group. Rather, he is compelled to express a world view, for Kassák an essentially socialist one, that is universal and intrinsically valid. Art, then, necessarily becomes the very foundation for construction, especially social reconstruction: "Art transforms us; and we become capable of transforming our surroundings." Nevertheless, in its emphasis on the independence of the artist and the autonomy of art, the manifesto betrays fundamental differences with the Russian constructivist programs for communist art by committed "party artists" in the service of proletariat.[58]

Kassák's refusal to subordinate art to the programs of the communist party engendered great controversy among the emigrant Hungarians, just as it had during the days of Béla Kun's soviets. Many of the avant-garde painters believed dogmatically in the obligation of progressive artists to serve the needs and further the interests of the proletariat by acting in concert with the communist party.[59] Both Bortnyik and Uitz held this view despite their intimate Activist association with Kassák for many years. Kassák recognized Bildarchitektur as world feeling manifested materially. Bortnyik, on the other hand, held that the concept signaled merely a requirement for pictorial harmony, not unlike that demanded in progressive architecture, and therefore was in itself insufficient to accommodate the degree of ideological commitment that he and Uitz believed necessary. Both artists, therefore, augmented their own "pictorial architecture" with either agitprop representational work or explicit political imagery.[60] Equally significant, both abjured Kassák's *Ma*, which since its founding had been the rallying point of Hungarian Activism.

In May 1922, Uitz, previously a co-editor of *Ma* in Vienna, joined former *Ma* poet and long-time Kassák associate Aladár Komját in establishing a rival journal, *Egység* [Unity].[61] *Egység* immediately identified itself with the proletkult movement, which Uitz must have encountered in Moscow and which was endorsed by fellow activists within the German Communist party.[62] Moreover, in the fifth issue of *Egység*, Uitz published the various Russian suprematist, productivist, and realist art manifestoes that he had brought back with him to Vienna and was either unwilling or unable to publish in *Ma*.[63]

Egység's existence confirmed the rift among the Hungarian avant-garde in exile.[64] At the same time, Kassák himself placed less attention than before on events in Hungary, which had always served to bring together the Hungarian exiles, and became increasingly engaged in cultivating his contacts with the international avant-garde. By this time, however, many former *Ma* associates had already abandoned Kassák and Vienna for Germany.

BERLIN The tens of thousands of Hungarian émigrés constituted one of the largest minorities in Berlin. Prominent among them was the Hungarian avant-garde, including members of The Eight, Activists, and independent expressionists such as Hugó Scheiber and Béla Kádár, who hoped to find fertile ground for their socialist idealism in Germany's major city.[65] Most found an active cultural life in which they eagerly sought to participate. In fact, it was the opportunity to interact with other artists, to exhibit, and to find work in a truly dynamic world city that attracted many of the Hungarian artists from Vienna to Berlin.[66]

By removing themselves to Berlin, Hungarian artists did not elude the political contention within their movement over the function of modern art and the responsibilities of the progressive artist. In fact, the highly charged atmosphere of Berlin encouraged just such debate. Moholy-Nagy, who had journeyed from Vienna to Berlin in 1920 and soon thereafter became the German correspondent for *Ma*, presently joined his powerful voice (and art) to the fray. He published in the May 1922 issue his own polemical statement ("Constructivism and the Proletariat") regarding the proper focus of the new constructivist art. Advocating a position similar to that of Kassák in his manifesto on Bildarchitektur, and opposed to the proletkult partisanship of Uitz and Bortnyik, Moholy-Nagy affirmed that:

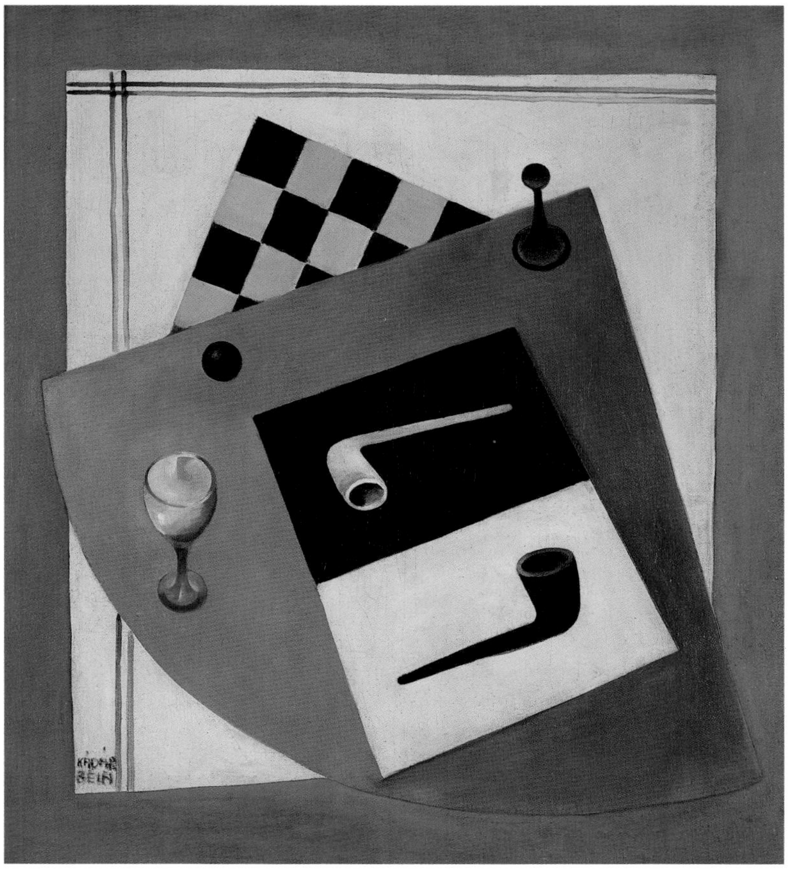

64. BÉLA KÁDÁR, Still Life with Chessboard and Pipe, c1920

Fig. 2-10 *MA* cover reproducing MOHOLY-NAGY, *Glass Architecture*, 1922.

Fig. 2-11 LÁSZLO PÉRI, *Painted Relief*, 1920-21.
Hungarian National Gallery, Budapest.

Constructivism is neither proletarian nor capitalist. Constructivism is primordial, without class and without ancestor. It expresses the pure form of nature... not distorted by utilitarian motifs. The new world of the proletariat needs Constructivism.... It is the socialism of vision — the common property of all men. Only the today is important for the Constructivist. He cannot indulge in the luxurious speculations of either the Utopian Communist who dreams of a future world domination, or of the bourgeois artist who lives in splendid isolation.

Although valiantly steering an ideological course somewhat between *Ma* and *Egység* or Barta's *Akasztott Ember* (*see note 64*), Moholy-Nagy professed strong support for constructivism without ever becoming dogmatic.[67] His constructivist kinship with Kassák, Bortnyik, and other committed members of the avant-garde is perhaps best demonstrated in his "glass architecture" declarations. Articulated and presented visually in 1922, glass architecture dealt forthrightly with the concept of transparency, a frequently employed artistic metaphor of utopian aspiration. For Moholy-Nagy, glass architecture was an idealist symbol that materially expressed his aspiration to redeem the world through the creation of transparent objects.[68]

As is evident in his *Glass Architecture III* (FIG. 2-10), Moholy-Nagy is deeply indebted to the Bildarchitektur concepts of Kassák and Bortnyik. Not only does he use the term *architecture* in the title, thereby attesting to the idealistic dimension of constructivism,[69] but his pictorial exploration of abstract geometry, spatial relationships, and color interaction, although far more dynamic, is strikingly similar to the visual concerns of his Hungarian constructivist colleagues. Kassák himself noted the compatibility of Moholy-Nagy's work with his own, for he reproduced *Glass Architecture III* (though with different colors) on the cover of *Ma* (May 1, 1922). It is not known whether by so doing Kassák wanted to stress the revolutionary nature of Moholy-Nagy's work and, by extension, of his own concept of "pictorial architecture."

Just three months before *Glass Architecture III* appeared on the cover of *Ma*, Moholy-Nagy was given an exhibition at Herwarth Walden's Der Sturm gallery. That his work was shown along with that of László Péri reveals the inroads that constructivism — particularly the Hungarian "architectural" variant — was making in Berlin. It was also at this exhibition that Walter Gropius encountered Moholy-Nagy's constructivist paintings, most likely for the first time.

Herwarth Walden had been active in promoting Hungarian expressionists since at least 1918.

Although by the early 1920s his prominent position as a leading commercial advocate of the avant-garde was in decline, Walden continued to exhibit Hungarian expressionists, especially the work of Scheiber and Kádár, throughout the decade. To regain his former status, or as a result of a genuine interest in the newest art coming out of Eastern Europe, Walden began to exhibit constructivist painters and designers.[70]

Before the great First Russian Exhibition at the end of 1922, there was very little Russian abstract work available in Berlin, and essentially no Russian constructivism at all. The Hungarians, then, must have represented to Walden an excellent alternative. For not only did Der Sturm gallery mount a two-man exhibition for Moholy-Nagy and Péri in 1922, it also presented the work of Bortnyik that December. In addition, *Der Sturm* published works on Hungarian constructivism. In February 1924, demonstrating either an unusual degree of stylistic eclecticism or a distinctive "marketing" strategy, Walden devoted gallery space to the work of Scheiber and Moholy-Nagy.

Walden's enthusiasm for constructivism was accompanied by a commensurate interest in politics, particularly radical left-wing politics.[71] As one who had long associated with the Jewish socialist intelligentsia, Walden must have been open to the influence of László Péri (1899-1967), a young Hungarian painter of Jewish background. Péri not only helped Der Sturm become one of the first commercial galleries to display constructivism, but also introduced Walden to communist politics.

A student at the radical Workshop for Proletarian Art under Uitz during the Hungarian Soviet Republic and later a member of the *Ma*-sponsored theater group under Mácza, Péri was on tour in Czechoslovakia when the Kun regime collapsed. After a brief stop in Vienna, he went directly to Paris, from which he was expelled for his anti-Horthy activities.[72] Forced to leave France, Péri traveled to Berlin where he found sympathetic ground to develop both his art and politics. He shared an interest in communism with the Berlin-based Hungarian critic Alfréd Kemény, who later wrote the introduction to Péri's 1923 album of abstract linocuts, which Walden published. With the recently arrived Moholy-Nagy, Péri was able to explore the new artistic territory of constructivism.

What must have enhanced the appeal of advanced Russian art for Péri was the prominent role played by the theater in the art and politics of the Russian avant-garde. His own work (FIG. 2-11), such as the painted reliefs and his later design for a series of monumental wall abstractions, reveals a debt to the abstract stage, as well as a kinship with the constructed reliefs of Bortnyik's variant of Bildarchitektur. Péri's forms bring the geometric planes into depth—illusionistically or literally—thereby constructing an "architectural" space (what Péri called *Raumkonstruktion*) that corresponds to the general concept of Bildarchitektur advocated by Kassák, Bortnyik, Uitz, and Moholy-Nagy in their polemical writing and committed designs.

Despite the great promise of his constructivist work and the strong backing of Walden, Péri gravitated increasingly toward politics.[73] By 1924, he joined Kemény as an active member of Berlin's Rote Gruppe, a communist association of artists, many of whom abjured abstraction in favor of a representational art that the proletariat might better understand. Persuaded by this or similar arguments that denounced non-objective art as "bourgeois" decadence, Péri gave up constructivism in 1925. By this time, however, a large contingent of the Hungarian avant-garde had taken up residence at Walter Gropius's Bauhaus.

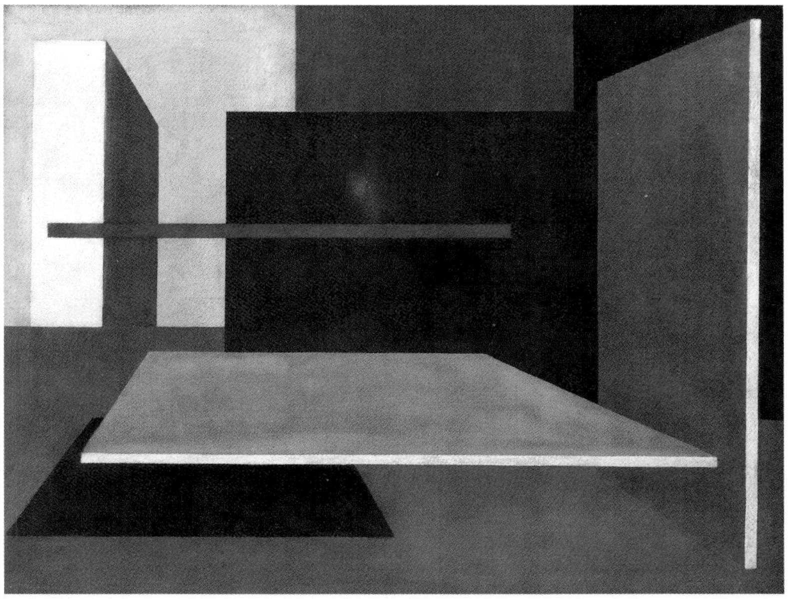

20. SÁNDOR BORTNYIK, Geometric Forms in Space, 1923

165. ANDOR WEININGER, Composition, 1922-62

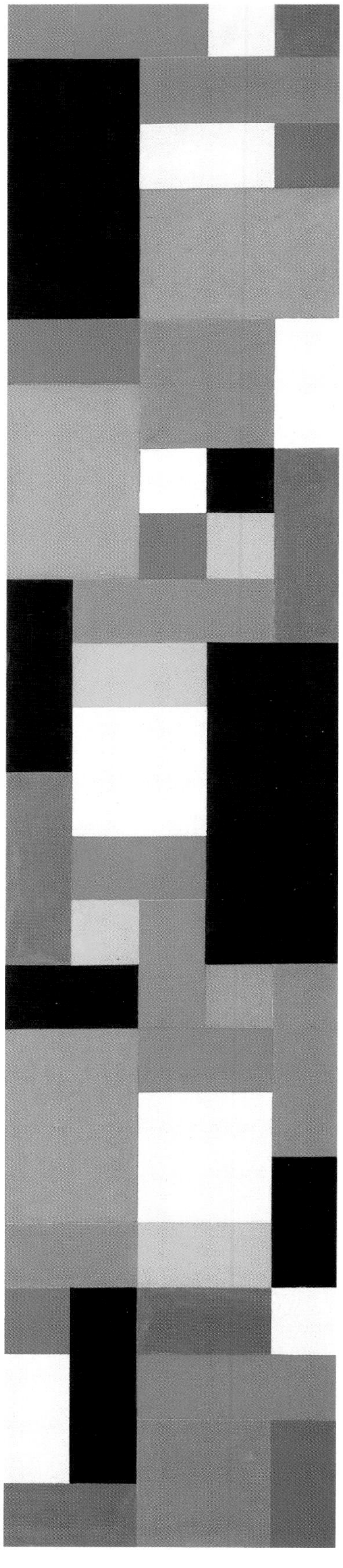

166. ANDOR WEININGER, De Stijl Composition, 1922

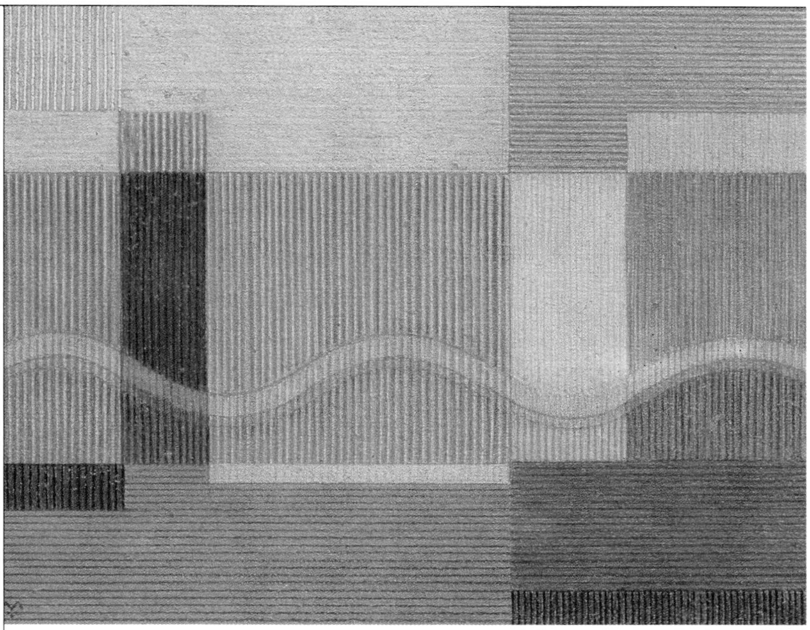

56. ALFRÉD FORBÁT, Composition, 1923

WEIMAR: THE BAUHAUS The prominence of Hungarians at the Bauhaus, both as masters and students, is well known. Hungarian contributions to Bauhaus pedagogy, theater, architecture, and design, indeed to every facet of Bauhaus creativity and daily life, were as far reaching as they were significant. Moholy-Nagy, Breuer, Molnár, Weininger, Forbát, d'Ébneth, Pap, and more than a dozen others from Hungary shaped the character and set the tone of Gropius's great experiment in Weimar and Dessau. Later, several would play a signal role in transmitting the Bauhaus philosophy of education and life to the United States and Eastern Europe.[74]

In addition to those formally associated with the Weimar Bauhaus, Sándor Bortnyik, who like Theo van Doesburg had moved to Weimar in 1922, exercised a constructivist influence on the still-dominant expressionist character of the Bauhaus. Although impressed by the workshop system and with Gropius's creative fusion of art and industry, Bortnyik was disturbed by the absence of an ideological commitment to architecture.[75] As it soon became for Moholy-Nagy and was already for Gropius himself, architecture was in Bortnyik's mind the essential pathway toward social reconstruction, a view that was in complete accord with his own Bildarchitektur concepts. Indeed, the paintings he made during his Weimar period are his most architectural.

Perhaps no juxtaposition of Bortnyik's paintings is more suggestive of his views than *The New Adam* (1924) and *Portrait of Fréd Forbát and His Wife* (1924). In *The New Adam* a foppishly dressed man of the middle class, straw hat in one hand and cane in the other, is caricatured as a fashionable mechanized mannikin. The gears on the free-standing wall behind him strongly suggest that he stands on a motor that revolves in circles. Here is the parodied emblem of the "new man" of the Bauhaus who lacks the ideological commitment to make him fully human. Moreover, he stands preciously poised, as if on display in a shop window, separated by the transparent plane to his right (and an opaque wall behind him) from a constructed world of pure relationships. The "pictorial architectural" elements of the ideal world operate on an entirely different plane, defying gravity's limitations to float freely in space.

49. LAJOS D'ÉBNETH, Composition, 1927

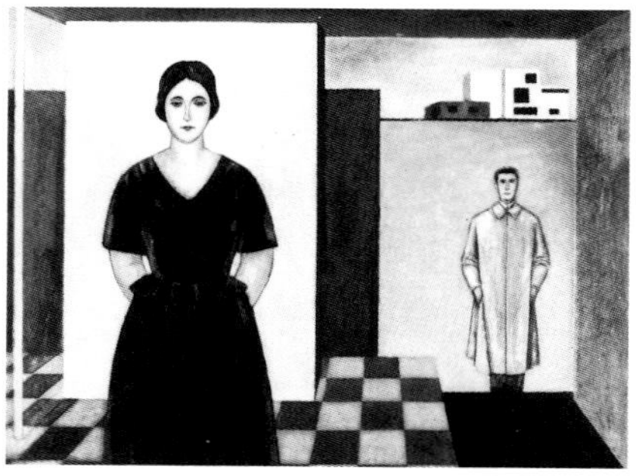

Fig. 2-12 SÁNDOR BORTNYIK, *Portrait of Fréd Forbat and his Wife*, 1924.

IF *The New Adam* CAN BE UNDERSTOOD as Bortnyik's comment on the potential of the Bauhaus to construct an ideal environment of the future but its inability to create a new man to inhabit it, *Portrait of Fréd Forbát and His Wife* might function figuratively as its ideological pendant (FIG. 2-12). Here too we find Bortnyik's combination of representation and constructivist (semi-) abstraction. In place of the stylish mannikin rotating mechanically on his platform, we find a portrait of the Hungarian architect, Fréd Forbát, a principal designer in Gropius's own Weimar practice,[76] and one of the few architects employed by a Bauhaus organization during the period of Bortnyik's presence. A friend of Bortnyik, Forbát was a productive architect who had demonstrated his commitment to constructivism.

Standing beneath a model of a villa (designed by Forbát in 1923 as a two-family house in Weimar) reminiscent of the floating architecture of *The New Adam*, the architect and his wife are enclosed within the dynamic space of "pictorial architecture." The spatial recession is somewhat irrational, but Bortnyik is attempting here to realize pictorially the same spatial disjunction that one finds in *The New Adam*.[77] Although Forbát served Bortnyik ideally as a model of the new constructive man, the Bauhaus (and its numerous Hungarian affiliates) failed to meet the painter's expectations of an ideal creative community. In 1925, he returned to Hungary, there to attempt to improve on Gropius's model.[78]

REPATRIATION AND THE FINAL PHASE Bortnyik's return to his homeland in the mid-1920s was hardly an isolated event. Beginning as a trickle in 1921-22 and increasing to a flood in 1925-26, Hungarian avant-garde painters and poets returned to Hungary to face an uncertain future. Not every Hungarian adherent of modern art (and socialist aesthetics) chose to return to a "rump" Hungary that was under the firm control of the ultraconservative Horthy. However, the list below (incomplete) of avant-garde figures suggests that a majority of progressive painters and critics did return, though several committed communists came back only after long sojourns in the Soviet Union. Still others left Hungary when the government moved closer to the fascist politics of Italy and Germany.

Repatriation of Hungarian Avant-Garde Artists and Critics

ARTISTS

RÓBERT BERÉNY (1887-1953),
also active as a composer while in Berlin, returned in 1926

AURÉL BERNÁTH (1895-1982),
from Berlin in 1926

MIHÁLY BIRÓ (1886-1948),
not until 1947

DEZSŐ BOKROS BIRMAN (1889-1965),
sculptor, from Berlin in 1921

SÁNDOR BORTNYIK (1893-1976),
from Germany in 1925

MARCEL BREUER (1902-1981),
never repatriated

DEZSŐ CZIGÁNY (1883-1937),
from Paris ca. 1927

BÉLA CZÓBEL (1883-1976),
from Berlin and Paris at the end of the 1930s

LAJOS D'ÉBNETH (1902-1982),
never repatriated

GYULA DERKOVITS (1894-1934),
from Vienna ca. 1927

SÁNDOR ÉK (1902-1975),
from the USSR not until 1945

BÉNI FERENCZY (1890-1967),
sculptor, from the USSR in 1935

NOÉMI FERENCZY (1890-1957),
from Berlin in 1932

FRÉD FORBÁT (1897-1972),
never repatriated

BÉLA KÁDÁR (1877-1956),
from Germany about 1932

LAJOS KASSÁK (1887-1967),
from Vienna in 1926

KÁROLY KERNSTOK (1873-1940),
from Berlin in 1926

LÁSZLÓ MOHOLY-NAGY (1895-1946),
never repatriated

FARKAS MOLNÁR (1898-1944),
from Germany in 1925

JÓZSEF NEMES LAMPÉRTH (1891-1923),
from Berlin in 1922

GYULA PAP (1899-1984),
from Germany in 1934

LÁSZLÓ PÉRI (1899-1967),
never repatriated

HUGÓ SCHEIBER (1873-1950),
from Berlin in 1934

LAJOS TIHANYI (1885-1938),
never repatriated

BÉLA UITZ (1887-1972),
from the USSR not until 1970

ANDOR WEININGER (1899-1986),
never repatriated

CRITICS

BÉLA BALÁZS (1884-1949),
from the USSR not until 1945

ERNŐ KÁLLAI (1890-1954),
from Germany in 1935

ALFRÉD KEMÉNY (1895-1945),
from the USSR (as a Red army soldier) in 1945

55. ALFRÉD FORBÁT, Abstract Composition, c1925

23. SÁNDOR BORTNYIK, The New Adam, 1924

54. ALFRÉD FORBÁT, Abstract Composition, 1921

This massive repatriation has yet to be explained convincingly. Why would so many Hungarian progressive artists decide to return to a country that was still in the grip of an ultraconservative regime, whose head of state was largely responsible for their initial flight following the collapse of the Hungarian Soviet Republic? What did the avant-garde expect to accomplish when their return necessarily meant that they would have to moderate, if not surrender entirely, the very ideologies that informed their art? Although it is not possible to answer these questions for each artist, there are a few hypotheses that might apply generally to the majority.

With a few notable exceptions — Moholy-Nagy, Breuer, several other Bauhäusler, and Tihanyi — the Hungarian avant-garde artists were rarely more than superficially integrated into the cultural or social mainstream of their respective "host" cities. The major cities in Germany and Austria do not appear to have made any special official effort to welcome or aid the Hungarian refugees, although some private and religious agencies did provide a modest measure of support. Moreover, many members of the avant-garde, not just Hungarian artists, were extraordinarily peripatetic in the decade following World War I, and their choice of residence often was determined by political considerations as well as artistic opportunities.

The attempt to establish a spiritual center where East and West would meet, with the Hungarians themselves at the hub, was never effectively realized. Indeed, whenever the Activists in Vienna or Berlin held their occasional "*Ma*-Abende" [*Ma* Evenings], very few non-Hungarians attended. Attendance by non-Hungarian speakers at Kassák's *Ma* Evenings in particular may have been discouraged by his inability to speak any foreign language.[79]

72. LAJOS KASSÁK, Bildarchitektur, 1923

On the whole, the Hungarian artists were not successful commercially. They had been given very few exhibitions and received almost no private or governmental patronage. Nemes Lampérth, although finding no commercial gallery with which to exhibit, was unusually fortunate in discovering a Swedish collector who purchased a great number of his paintings.[80] The Hungarians also were reluctant and generally not able to establish themselves as independent product designers in the profitable world of commercial manufacturers and distributors.

CLEARLY, THERE WERE FEW STRONG ATTACHMENTS that bound the artists securely to their places of refuge. At the same time, their attachment to Hungary had never seriously wavered for long. The innovative journals that were the major vehicles for avant-garde activities — *Ma*, *Egység*, *Akasztott Ember*, and *Ék* [The Wedge] — were geared as much to an audience in Hungary as they were oriented to Hungarians abroad.[81] Thus, with their initial great expectations of social revolution, individual artistic success, and personal satisfaction largely unfulfilled, most of the avant-garde took advantage of improving conditions in Hungary to return.

To return to Hungary under Horthy's regency must have been chastening. The government, perhaps rightly, was suspicious of the returned veterans of the revolutionary soviet regime, because most had continued their political activities while abroad.[82] In addition, the artistic style of the repatriates, whether essentially constructivist or expressionist, was not in accord with the conservative tastes of officialdom nor of the large middle class.[83] With scant freedom to engage in political agitation and with little likelihood of selling enough of their progressive paintings to support themselves, the avant-garde faced enormous difficulties. They responded to this challenge initially by focusing their efforts on publishing, teaching, or artistic accommodation, in some cases successfully penetrating the commercial advertising field. To all these undertakings they brought their considerable experience as artists in exile.

In 1926 Kassák returned from Vienna to Budapest, having been forced to close *Ma* for financial reasons. Once back in Hungary, he founded yet another journal through which to conduct his campaign for an ideal world of social, aesthetic, and ethical integration. From December 1926 through May 1927 he published *Dokumentum* in which he continued to champion international constructivism, apparently oblivious to the changed social environment.

The intellectual climate of Horthy's Hungary was no longer interested in modernism, and it showed little patience for artists who still championed revolutionary aesthetics. Within a matter of months, Kassák was forced to suspend the publication of his journal, noting (*Dokumentum* 2, no. 5, 1927):

After six months of editing we realized that the situation had changed considerably in Hungary since 1919, and that we would have to continue our fight basically with other means, on different grounds, and with other individuals.

To garner potential readers Kassák had to forsake his personal commitment to internationalism, and in 1928 he brought out *Munka* [Work], which assiduously focused realistically on local topics and events. Perhaps as a wistful gesture to lingering dreams from the past or to compensate for the compromises he felt compelled to make, Kassák formed the *Munka* Circle as an Activist adjunct to the journal. He envisioned a socially engaged union of leftist intellectuals and young workers just as he had hoped to do years before with the artists and intellectuals whom he gathered around *Ma*. However, this venture generated little interest among either workers or artists. Discouraged, Kassák devoted less and less attention to art and more diligence to the realistic journalism of *Munka*, which absorbed his energies until it ceased publication in 1939.[84] Kassák's distinctive contributions to the avant-garde, however, had concluded nearly a decade earlier.

Bortnyik returned to Budapest and almost immediately tried to transmit to Hungary the innovative pedagogy he had found at the Bauhaus. Overlooking his personal enmity toward Moholy-Nagy, he embraced the educational reforms and philosophy that the latter had brought to Weimar in 1923. Following Moholy-Nagy's lead, Bortnyik

Fig. 2-13 LAJOS KASSAK, *Steyer Auto Poster*, 1922, László Collection, Basel.

acknowledged the importance of mass production and the necessity of moderating through artistic education the degradation occasioned by mechanization.

The principles of Bortnyik's *Műhely* [Workshop] school betray his emphasis on architecture and applied graphics: the dimensions of creative activity that affect most immediately and profoundly the face of society. Unfortunately, before he had time to implement fully his "Hungarian Bauhaus" program, economic and health considerations forced him to limit his work to a very few areas.[85] The field in which he achieved his greatest results, applied graphics in the service of commercial sponsors, was the very one in which Kassák, Moholy-Nagy, and much of the Hungarian avant-garde had labored with only limited success as early as the first years of exile.

As the economy began to stabilize in Central Europe between 1923 and the end of the decade, many artists of the avant-garde turned their attention to advertising. This strategem was not merely pecuniary: It accorded well with the constructivist concern with creating a modern mass culture, of appealing directly to the populace with clear, rational, and dynamic designs. In addition, during the 1920s, advertising and the mass media in general were seen as value-neutral, and thus were perceived by painters and commercial patrons alike as a legitimate means to be exploited by progressive artists to heighten the social consciousness and artistic awareness of the general population.[86]

As early as 1921-22, Lajos Kassák had adapted his utopian Bildarchitektur to promoting the products of capitalistic industry. In a 1922 design for Steyr-Auto (FIG. 2-13), Kassák produced an advertisement that makes consummate use of his newfound interest in constructivist design. Moreover, he joined the abstract design with photography,

144. JÁNOS TÁBOR , Meinl Tea, 1930

Fig. 2-14 LAJOS KASSÁK, *Advertising Kiosk*, 1922, Kunsthalle, Nürnberg.

thereby creating a striking photomontage that reveals his debt to such dada figures as Kurt Schwitters, whose innovative graphic work Kassák championed in the pages of *Ma*. With the angle of the racing car and the suspended tire seemingly penetrating the viewer's space, Kassák suggests the dynamism as well as three dimensionality he had advocated in his "pictorial architecture" theory.

In a sketch for an advertising kiosk, also from 1922, he created on paper a brilliant example of what he hoped to achieve in physical space (FIG. 2-14). Combining many of the functions and services of urban society—posting box, newspaper stand, advertising or placard surfaces, among others—Kassák's design graphically demonstrates how he planned to translate "pictorial" theories into the architecture of modern life.[87] The various quadratic planes "construct" the architectural program of the composite structure, as well as constitute visually an elegant abstract design. Thus, "pictorial architecture" might function simultaneously as constructivist "picture" and "architecture." Similarly, Moholy-Nagy, Pór, Biró, Péri, Berény, Bortnyik, and many others adapted Hungarian modernist art to the demands of advertising, conceiving masterful progressive designs for newspapers, department stores, tire manufacturers, and shoe sole manufacturers, among others. Probably the most accomplished series of graphic designs that the Hungarian avant-garde ever created, and one that promoted not the revolutionary initiatives of a socialist state but the product of a private concern, was the series of posters for Modiano.

Modiano was an Italian firm that specialized in the manufacture and sale of cigarette papers, particularly in Hungary. The company devoted significant resources to promoting its product, and to this end it retained the services of many of the recently returned avant-garde artists. Among those "revolutionary" artists who designed advertising posters for Modiano was Bortnyik, whose *Műhely* school included applied graphics in its curriculum.

Bortnyik's first designs for Modiano date about 1926. In an early poster, the artist effectively employs the geometry he had previously embraced in his constructivist "pictorial architecture" works of the early 1920s. An abstract man in the lower right, not unrelated to the well-dressed New Adam of 1924, stands smoking while contemplating a kiosk on which is prominently displayed a Modiano poster also designed by Bortnyik earlier in the year. Behind the kiosk a large monochromatic circle helps

4. RÓBERT BERÉNY, Flóra Terpentine Soap, 1927

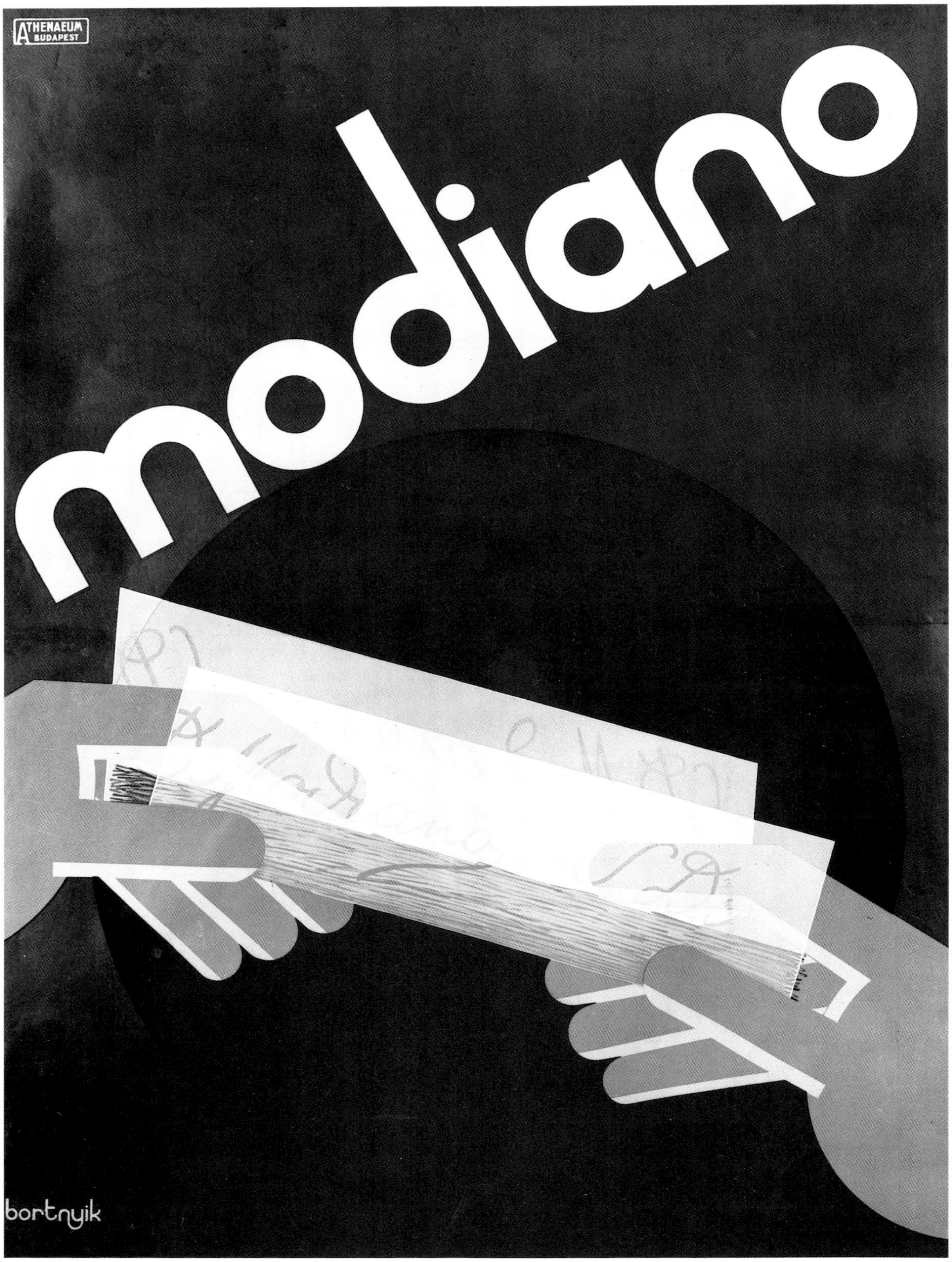

24. SÁNDOR BORTNYIK, Modiano, 1928

Fig. 2-15 SÁNDOR BORTNYIK, Modiano Poster, c. 1928, Hungarian National Gallery, Budapest.

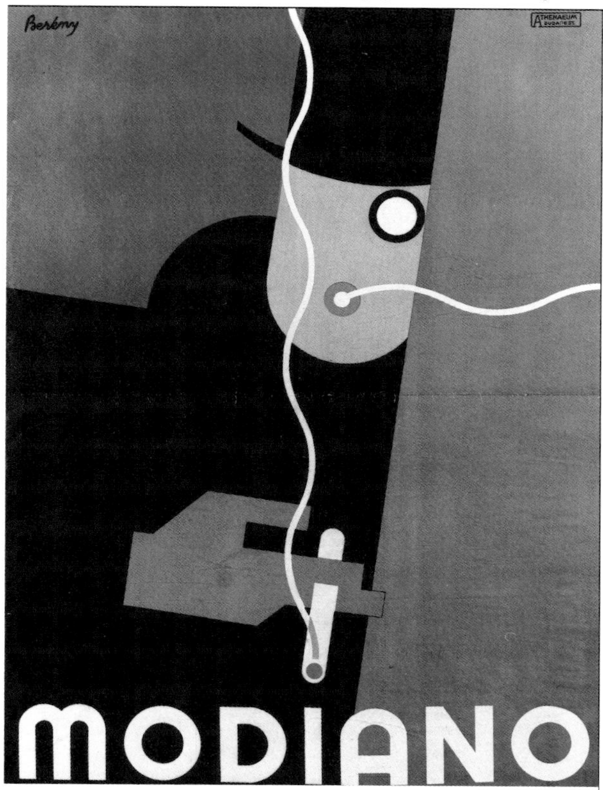

5. RÓBERT BERÉNY, Modiano, c1927

to focus attention on the kiosk and to suggest the risen sun of the day. The concatenation of circular disks is utilized convincingly to unite pictorially the various spatial planes, as well as to tie visually the geometry of the image to the orthography of the "O"s in the brand name.

Within two years, Bortnyik conceived posters for Modiano that reveal a more mature command of modernist design. The rounded letters used for the manufacturer's name affirm the artist's mastery of contemporary experiments in typography and design.[88] In another poster his diagonal placement of the brand name betrays his debt to van Doesburg, whom Bortnyik knew from Weimar and whose theory of elementarism interested the Hungarian greatly. Even if Bortnyik was reluctant to introduce photography directly into his composition, the prominent exploitation of transparency, apparent in the handling of the cigarette paper, demonstrates his proficiency in capitalizing on Moholy-Nagy's transparent photograms (FIG. 2-15).

Bortnyik's graphic work for Modiano may well exemplify the consummation of Hungarian avant-garde art. Like the intrepid artists of The Eight early in the century, Bortnyik adapted to the contemporary circumstances of Hungary the progressive artistic forms he learned in the West. Furthermore, he successfully projected the aesthetics of modern life into a country that held tenaciously to the social structures of the past. If, in the late 1920s, this was no longer revolutionary, it was still innovative, and it helped prolong the era of aesthetic experimentation until the end of the decade. By the early 1930s, however, increasingly draconian social and political conditions altered the climate for creating the array of progressive art that the Hungarian avant-garde had epitomized.[89] With the consolidation of totalitarianism in Central and Eastern Europe, the environment was no longer accommodating to those idealistic artists who sought to lead mankind into a perfect future. The Hungarian avant-garde, whose talented and committed adherents had yearned to "stand in the tempest of current events," was destined to be inundated by the turbulence of contemporary political realities.

Acknowledgments

I wish to thank the Alexander von Humboldt-Stiftung (Bonn), which enabled me to research and write this article while a *Stipendiat* in Berlin. I would also like to acknowledge the hospitality of the Kunsthistorisches Institut of the Freie Universität Berlin and the friendly encouragement of Professor Thomas Gaehtgens.

Notes

Frequently cited works are identified by author, editor, or sponsoring organization and abbreviated title; journal articles, essays, and chapters in larger works are enclosed in quotation marks, and book titles are set in italics. Interested readers are referred to the comprehensive Select Bibliography at the end of this volume for full details of publication.

1. Examination of the Hungarian avant-garde has benefited greatly from several recent studies. Among the most notable in Western languages are: C. Dautrey and J.-C. Guerlain, eds., *L'Activisme hongrois;* The Arts Council of Great Britain (cited as Arts Council), *The Hungarian Avant-Garde: The Eight and the Activists*, and the slightly different French version, *L'art en Hongrie 1905-1930, art et révolution*; Éva Körner, *Die ungarische Kunst zwischen den beiden Weltkriegen* [Hungarian Art between the Two World Wars]; Éva Körner, *Ungarische Avantgarde, 1909-1930;* Esther Levinger, "The Theory of Hungarian Constructivism"; Esther Levinger, "Lajos Kassák, *Ma* and the New Artist, 1916-1925"; Hubertus Gassner, ed., *Wechselwirkungen, ungarische Avantgarde in der Weimar Republik*; S. A. Mansbach, "Revolutionary Events, Revolutionary Artists: The Hungarian Avant-Garde until 1920"; and S. A. Mansbach, "Confrontation and Accommodation in the Hungarian Avant-Garde."

The first significant retrospective exhibition of the avant-garde took place in Hungary only in 1981 (Éva Bajkay-Rosch, *Die ungarische Avantgarde-Kunst in Wiener Exil, 1920-1925*, p. 34). However, serious study of this period by Hungarian scholars began in the early 1960s. Two reference works remain standard: Júlia Szabó, *A magyar Aktivizmus művészete* [The Art of Hungarian Activism], *1915-1927*; and Krisztina Passuth, *Magyar művészek az európai avantgarde-ban* [Hungarian Artists in the European Avant-Garde], *1919-1925*.

2. For an assessment of the avant-gardes of East-Central and Eastern Europe during the first third of this century, see the special issue of *Art Journal*, "From Leningrad to Ljubljana: The Suppressed Avant-Gardes of East-Central and Eastern Europe during the Early Twentieth Century," edited by S. A. Mansbach.

3. Many aristocratic families possessed impressive collections of European paintings; however, they were far less active in the acquisition of contemporary art than were members of the large Budapest-based bourgeoisie. For an excellent examination of the rise, character, and interests of the bourgeoisie in late nineteenth century Hungary, especially Budapest, see Andrew C. János, *The Politics of Backwardness in Hungary, 1825-1945*.

4. For a discussion of the artistic accomplishments of Hungarian art nouveau and an assessment of its political, social, and philosophical implications, see Gyöngyi Éri and Zsuzsa O. Jobbágyi, eds., *Lélek és forma: Magyar művészet*, [Form and Spirit].

5. The relationships between the Hungarian artist colonies and the artistic and theoretical activities in and around Munich are best exemplified by János Máttis Teutsch (1884-1960), a German-speaking artist from Hungarian Transylvania. Máttis Teutsch participated with Marc, Campendonk, and others in formulating the idealist theories that would infuse idealism into expressionism (Der Blaue Reiter). He became a major figure in the international avant-garde as a member of the Ma circle, the Munich expressionists, the Berlin Der Sturm group, and, after 1930 especially, as a principal teacher and author in the Romanian avant-garde. Although affiliated with many major avant-garde groups, Máttis Teutsch remained aloof and continued to develop the spiritual dimension of his own art and philosophy. The foundation of his pedagogy, *Kunstideologie*, was published in 1931. See Júlia Szabó, *Máttis Teutsch János*; Mircea Deac, *Máttis Teutsch, si realismul constructiv und der konstruktive Realismus* [His Constructive Realism and Konstruktive Realismus]; and Gheorghe Vida, "Hans Máttis Teutsch and the European Dialogue of Forms."

6. Upon their return, these artists swelled the interest in up-to-date Western art. As early as May 1907, major exhibitions of the work of Cézanne, Gauguin, and the post-impressionists were organized in Budapest. Especially important for the later history of Hungarian art were the exhibitions held at the National Salon under private sponsorship. See Júlia Szabó "The Exhibitions of the International Avant-Garde in Budapest, Vienna, and Berlin and Their Influence on the History of the Hungarian Avant-Garde Movements."

7. For an excellent discussion in English of the intellectual climate in Hungary at this time, particularly as it affected the leftist

intelligentsia, see Mary Gluck, *George Lukács and His Generation, 1900-1918*. See also Anna Wessely, "Der Diskurs über die Kunst im Sonntagskreis" [Discussion on Art in the Sunday Circle], and Éva Karádi, "Der 'Sonntagskreis' und die Weimarer Kultur."

8. See Lee Congdon, *The Young Lukács*, pp. 118-44. Founded in December 1915 by Béla Balázs (1884-1945), poet, librettist for Bartók, and later renowned film "aesthetician," the Sunday Circle met in Balázs's Biedermeier apartment on Sunday afternoons. In addition to Lukács and Balázs, earliest members were Károly Mannheim, Arnold Hauser, Frederick Antal, Béla Fogarasi, Károly Tolnay, Anna Lesznai, and Lajos Fülep. Later they were joined by János Wilde, József Nemes Lampérth, Zoltán Kodály, Béla Bartók, and other leading figures of Hungarian arts and letters.

After the collapse of the Hungarian Soviet Republic, the Sunday Circle continued in Vienna until 1926, although without the participation of Fülep and Lukács, and with Antal or Karl Mannheim only rarely present. Hauser had withdrawn because of internal disagreements about the degree of political engagement and identification with the Communist party.

9. Lajos Fülep (1885-1970), a major art historian and scholar, is too little known in the West. His prolific writings have not been translated, and he elected internal exile rather than emigration. Thus, both the man and his work have been cut off from the West, unlike his contemporaries, all of whom recognized in Fülep an innovative and profound mind and a signal influence on the younger generation of Hungarian artists and scholars.

10. "Cézannes Kunst ist die entschiedenste Affirmation der Realität der realen Welt, so wie die Michelangelos war. Ein Realismus, der nicht neu ist, sondern uralt, im Grunde derselbe, wie der des Mittelalters...Der orthodoxe Cézanne mit seinem Realismus vertritt ein Stück mittelalterlicher Weltanschauung in der impressionistischen Umgebung: ...seine Weltanschauung, wie die des Mittelalters, ist ein Dualismus, der nach Monismus strebt und dies nicht mit der Auflösung der Materie, sondern mit deren Vergeistigung erreicht." Quoted by Wessely, "Der Diskurs," p. 545; see also Károly Tolnay, "Les écrits de Lajos Fülep sur Cézanne [Lajos Fülep's Writings on Cézanne], *Acta Historiae Artium* XX (1974), pp. 103-106. All text quotations have been translated into English by the author.

11. See Wessely, "Der Diskurs," and Éva Karádi and E. Vezér, *György Lukács, Karl Mannheim, und der Sonntagskreis*, p. 285. Regarding Tolnay's similar attitudes toward Cézanne see Éva Karádi and E. Vezér, *A Vasárnapi Kör* (Budapest: 1980), pp. 334ff.

12. By the summer of 1909, these painters, who had originally called themselves "The Seekers," had exchanged their symbolist appellation for the more neutral designation "The Eight," a number that often was exceeded in later years.

13. As early as December 1908, Lukács was invited to participate in the Galilei Circle's discussion on "What is scientific and artistic truth?" Thereafter, he periodically addressed Galilei members on cultural themes. His interest in modern Hungarian painting may have stemmed in part from his family's patronage. His father József, a director of the English-Austrian Bank, sat to Károly Ferenczy for his portrait and purchased Kernstok's large painting of the *Solitary Rider*, which hung in the well-appointed living room of the family apartment.

Tomáš Straus infers (*Kassák: A Hungarian Contribution to Constructivism*, p. 25) that Lajos Kassák attended at least some of the 1908 discussions of the Galilei Circle; and "although many of their ideas and thoughts were incomprehensible to Kassák, they still fell on fertile ground."

14. By 1912 The Eight were able to exploit the pictorial innovations of the cubists and futurists whose works they had seen first-hand in Budapest. In April and May 1910, Picasso exhibited four works, including his *Woman with Mandolin* (1909), in a group exhibition at the Budapest Művészház (House of Arts). By the end of 1912, the exhibition of futurist painters, which had begun in Paris at Bernheim-Jeune and included Boccioni, Carrà, Russolo, and Severini, had traveled to Budapest. During the same year, it also was presented in one form or another at London's Sackville Gallery (March), the Berlin Tiergartenstrasse Galerie, sponsored by *Der Sturm* (April and May), and Galerie Georges Girous in Brussels (May and June), and then at galleries in The Hague, Amsterdam, Cologne, and Munich.

15. From "The Ways Have Parted," translated by George Cushing in Arts Council, pp. 106-108. Kernstok's programmatic lecture of January 9, 1910, to the Galilei Circle later was published as "Art as Exploration" in *Nyugat.* The lecture is discussed by Júlia Szabó, "Ideas and Programmes: The Philosophical Background of the Hungarian Avant-Garde," in Arts Council, p. 12. In 1909 Leo Popper, also affiliated with the Sunday Circle, wrote from Paris in a vein similar to that of Lukács endorsing the necessity of breaking "out of the stylistic chaos of Impressionism toward the solidity of still life, which, no matter what form it takes...it will bear the mark of the same inner certitude and simplicity of which architecture is the embodiment." Quoted in Gluck, *Georg Lukács*, p. 19.

16. Kernstok, "The Social Role of the Artist," quoted in Szabó, "Ideas and Programmes."

17. In 1913 Kernstok affirmed that *Die Ereignisse sind ausserhalb wie auch innerhalb Ungarns so sehr vorangeschritten, dass die radikale Umwälzung des feudalen Staates bald zu erwarten ist. Die politische Situation im Ausland und die Nachrichten, die hierüber im Umlauf sind, beweisen, dass die bürgerliche Republik in Ungarn nicht nur ein Wunsch, sondern auch eine Notwendigkeit ist. [The achievements are, both outside and inside Hungary, so advanced that a radical change of the feudal state is soon to be expected. The political situation abroad and the news circulating about it all prove that in Hungary a bourgeois republic is not a mere wish, but a necessity.]*
Quoted by Krisztina Passuth, "Autonomie der Kunst und sozialistische Ideologie in der ungarischen Avantgardekunst" [The Autonomy of Art and Socialist Ideology in the Hungarian Avant-Garde], p.12.

18. Lajos Kassák, the impresario of the avant-garde from 1915 until about 1928, was from the lower classes. He dropped out of school at age 12 and soon became a locksmith's apprentice, and later, at 14, an ironworker. In 1909 he walked from Budapest to Paris (and back). In Paris he may have "met Apollinaire, Cendrars, Picasso, Modigliani—all those who with pen or brush were setting out to storm the ramparts of fame," as he boldly claimed in his 1963 "Sketch for a Self-Portrait." Whether Kassák's declaration is inflated, it is not likely that his interest in art at the time was as developed as that of other Hungarians who journeyed to Paris in 1905-1907.

19. Kassák now was beginning to establish a reputation as a poet and essayist of note. Aided by his frequent *engagé* contributions to his own journals, he developed consummate skill as a polemicist. Moreover, the increasingly novel use of vocabulary and syntax in his poetry would become a significant influence in modern Hungarian letters, reaching its acme in his *Bildgedichte* [Picture Poems] of the early 1920s. (See János Brendel, "The *Bildgedichte* of Lajos Kassák:

Constructivism in Hungarian Avant-Garde Poetry"; and Sylvia Bakos, "The Synthesis of the Arts and the Desire for Cosmic Unity: The Hungarian Literary Avant-Garde, 1915-1925.") Despite his extensive contacts and correspondence with leading figures of the international avant-garde, and years of exile in Vienna, Kassák never learned a foreign language. Much of his "critical" writing, especially essays on art and culture, was, however, published in German, but most of his literary works have yet to be translated.

20. Only 17 issues were published before *A Tett* was banned by the ministry of the interior for "undermining public morale" and compromising the war effort, largely as a result of its commitment to internationalism. Rather than celebrating the eminence of Hungarian culture, Kassák published progressive French writers, among them Apollinaire. Kassák also encouraged non-Hungarian authors to submit articles on such subjects as Karl Liebknecht. The circulation of this important journal was never great. The first number was published in an edition of only 500; and subsequent editions rarely exceeded 1000. (See Štraus, *Kassák*, p. 31, and Levinger, "The Theory of Hungarian Constructivism," p. 456, n. 9.)

21. Hungary's posture toward modern art following World War II also is reflected in a critical attitude toward *Ma*. Levinger points out ("Lajos Kassák, *Ma*, and the New Artists, 1916-1925," n. 1) that for many years after 1949, if mentioned at all by art historians and cultural figures, *Ma* was discredited for its bourgeois decadence (despite the journal's leftist sympathy). Even when addressing a foreign reading public, art historian Lajos Németh (*Modern Hungarian Art*) devoted less than two pages to Kassák and his circle, and provided no illustrations of Kassák's works. (Cf. Anna Zádor, ed., *Magyar Művészet 1800-1945*, pp. 359 and 453.)

22. *Ma*, vol. I, no. 1, available in an English translation in Arts Council, pp. 112-13

23. From a lecture in February 1919 announcing the formation of a Budapest section of the Activists, as quoted in Levinger, "Lajos Kassák, *Ma*, and the New Artist," p. 79; Levinger points out (n. 7) the changes in the journal's subtitle between November 1916 and January 1919, and February 1919 and October 1922.

24. Kassák, "Programs," *A Tett*, 2, no. 10 (1916), p. 153.

25. János Mácza (1893-1974) was charged by Kassák in 1917 with developing a Ma theater and drama studio through which progressive theater might enter Hungarian cultural life. Having taken part in the 1919 soviet republic, Mácza remained in Czechoslovakia, where he was on tour, after the republic's collapse. In 1922 he moved to Vienna where Kassák had reestablished *Ma*. In 1923 he emigrated permanently to the USSR, where he wrote on the theater and taught.

26. For a summary of the national council program, see István Deák, "The Decline and Fall of the Habsburg Monarchy, 1914-1918." See also Mansbach, "Revolutionary Events, Revolutionary Artists," pp. 42-47.

27. Even without a change in government, artistic activity would have increased once Hungary's participation in World War I had ended, although the shortage of supplies that characterized the war years grew more acute during the postwar period. (See note 39.) Nevertheless, opposition to the Dual Monarchy united all the leftist artistic groups and individuals, fostering a profound sympathy for first a bourgeois democracy and later a more radical socialist state.

28. According to Passuth ("Autonomie der Kunst," p. 12), Kernstok was captivated by the success of the Russian Bolshevik Revolution several months earlier and even tried to establish a village soviet along the Russian model. Passuth also notes that Pór, Tihanyi, and Kernstok belonged to a small communist cell allied to the radical press.

29. Károlyi genuinely wanted to avoid the bloody revolution he believed contending leftist parties were promoting, and he resigned in favor of a communist-dominated revolutionary governing council under the presidency of Sándor Garbai. Not until early April 1919 was an election held for a national congress of soviets. Although Kun was officially only one of 34 commissars, he executed effective government leadership from the beginning of the revolutionary governing council until the final collapse of the soviet republic.

30. See Passuth, "Autonomie der Kunst," pp. 13ff.

31. The brief duration of the new republic did not allow realization of these ambitious plans to any significant degree. In the same period, however, members of the avant-garde managed to produce a rich body of artistic work, many finding sufficient time to devote to radical pedagogy as well.

32. See Mansbach, "Revolutionary Events, Revolutionary Artists," pp. 48-54, and Frank Eckelt, "The Internal Policies of the Hungarian Soviet Republic." On April 17, 1919, the Entente actively began their military intervention against the Hungarian republic. In response, György Lukács published in the party newspaper an exhortation to the citizens of Budapest to join the Red Army. The title of his article, "Be a Vörös Hadseregbe," was translated by painters Kmetty and Nemes Lampérth into one of the great propagandistic posters of the age, *Be!* (Forward!).

33. See also Iván Hevesy, "The New Poster," *Ma*, 4, no. 5 (May 1919); and Levinger, "Lajos Kassák, *Ma*, and the New Artist," p. 81. The political and visual dynamism of these posters carried over into the various "decorative" projects assigned by the government to the avant-garde painters. Bertalan Pór received, but regrettably was unable to execute, a commission to create vast panels and frescoes for the 1919 May Day celebrations. Revolutionary street decorations by Bortnyik, Uitz, and other Activists suggest the stylistic environment in which Pór's project might have been seen. The impressive scope of these "decorative" projects is significant, for it demonstrates convincingly the avant-garde's considerable government support despite Lukács's own profound reservations regarding abstract and most non-realist art, and Kun's personal preference for the classical tradition.

34. Bortnyik was quite serious about the social relevance this image carried, as well as being intrigued by the potential of the vaguely constructivist formal language. Several months later, he painted a smaller version (44 x 34 cm) of the same theme, one that reveals an enhanced handling of "constructivist" forms. Now in the collection of Budapest's National Museum of Contemporary History, this second version of the *Red Locomotive* eliminates the signalman and the train cars, introducing in their place flat planes of color organized along diagonals. Significantly, Bortnyik eliminated the industrial background, substituting an abstract "landscape" of overlapping planes. In the upper left corner, he inserted an abstract reference to a steel or iron railroad bridge. This bridge imagery resurfaces in the early abstract work of Moholy-Nagy of about 1920-21. Cf. plates 30 and 31 in Passuth, *Moholy-Nagy*.

35. Ever since the 1880s, when Hungary had achieved a leading position in engine manufacture and railroad construction, Hungarians had used railroad imagery as a symbol of industrial achievement. For further discussion of the role of railroads in Hungarian culture, see Iván T. Berend, "From the Millennium to the Republic of Councils."

36. In 1918 (*Ma*, no. 12, p. 183) Kassák announced, characteristically, his disappointment with the bourgeois revolution he previously had desired: "For us the revolution has run aground before it developed anything productive at all. It lacks true revolutionary consciousness and the willpower of the people; and without that basis, the construction of a new society is not possible. The...Russian Revolution, which was released through the catastrophe of world war, developed its power and through it was able to change the face of the world; [it has now] reduced itself to the [mere] education of the masses." (See Passuth, "Autonomie der Kunst," p. 15.)

37. Kassák, "Verfolgen wir unseren Weg!" [Let us go our own way!], *Ma*, no. 12 (1918), p. 183; quoted in Passuth, "Autonomie der Kunst," p. 15. Kassák persisted in his oppositional stance for the remainder of his life, successively criticizing each respective government regardless of its ideological character. Naturally, this posture endeared him to few politicians, regardless of shared ideological assumptions. Not until the mid-1960s did his importance begin to be accepted by Hungarian officialdom, heralded by an interview published in the (then) officially approved *The New Hungarian Quarterly* (Winter, 1964). Only in 1987 was he given a comprehensive retrospective exhibition at the Hungarian National Gallery in Budapest.

38. Reprinted in German in *Wechselwirkungen* (Dokument 6), pp. 32-34. See also Mózes Kahána, "Zu den wiederholten Angriffen gegen *Ma*," [To the repeated attacks against *Ma*], *Ma*, 1919, pp 141-43 (in Hungarian) and excerpted in Passuth, "Autonomie der Kunst," p. 16. For an interpretation of Lukács's attitude toward Kassák and *Ma* at this time, see Lee Congdon, *The Young Lukács*, pp. 159-61 See also Lukács's article, "Zur Klarstellung," in *Wechselwirkungen* (Dokument 5), pp. 31-32.

39. According to Levinger ("Lajos Kassák, *Ma*, and the New Artist," n. 20), the exact reasons for the closing of *Ma* in July 1919 are still unknown. Passuth and Szabó accept Kassák's own claim that the journal was suppressed on account of its ideological opposition to Kun's government. Levinger reports that József Farkas ["Révolution du prolétariat, avant-garde et culture de masse" (Proletarian Revolution, Avant-Garde, and Mass Culture), in Dautrey and Guerlain, eds., pp. 53-53] suggests that *Ma* and a variety of other periodicals were forced to stop publication as a result of an acute paper shortage, or that the paper shortage provided a reason for interdicting certain publications.

40. See János, pp. 201ff. According to the figures that János cites (p. 202, n. 1), approximately four times as many people perished in the white terror than in the preceding red terror.

41. Efforts by Béla Bartók, Zoltán Kodály, and others to secure his release were unsuccessful. According to Paul Kövesdy in his introduction to *Lajos Kassák 1887-1967* (New York, 1984), p. 3, Kassák was able to escape confinement in 1920 and was smuggled from Budapest to Vienna in a trunk aboard a cargo vessel.

42. See Éva Bajkay-Rosch, "Die ungarische Avantgard-Kunst im Wiener Exil, 1920-1925" [The Hungarian Avant-Garde in Viennese Exile], p. 34, and "Künstler im Exil" [Artists in Exile]. The "nonpolitical" artists who chose to go into exile included Hugó Scheiber, Anna Lesznai, and Béla Kádár, as well as Aurél Bernáth, Vilmos Perlrott Csaba, and Lajos Tihanyi who were not active supporters of Kun. Passuth (*Moholy-Nagy*, p.16) points out that Moholy-Nagy, who left for Vienna in December 1919, had previously taken no part in the revolutions in Hungary: "he exercised no function and was assigned no role."

43. This essay focuses primarily on artists who went into exile in Germany and Austria. Many others, however, went directly (or by circuitous routes) to other places of refuge.

44. In one of history's ironies, the emigration of Hungary's "revolutionary" intelligentsia, primarily from Budapest, to Vienna in 1919 and 1920 was almost a reprise of a similar "leftist" political exodus 70 years before. Following the failed Hungarian revolution of the mid-nineteenth century, a large portion of the liberal aristocracy and a significant number of liberal artists fled to Vienna for safety. Political leaders of Hungary's war of independence (1848-49) such as Lajos Kossuth and György Klapka, and painters such as Mihály Kovács, Antal Ligeti, Mór Than, and Soma Orlai Petrich, found in the imperial capital a sanctuary from the political reaction in their native land.

45. Kun was Jewish, as were significant numbers of his government and communist party senior members, and conservative opposition in the Christian and Agrarian Smallholders' party did not hesitate to identify the Hungarian Jewish population of Budapest with communism. According to János (p. 222), "While the revolutionaries attacked entrepreneurs as 'bourgeois exploiters', the counter-revolutionaries harassed them as Jews, leaving them demoralized and fearful not only for the safety of their assets, but also of their lives and limbs." For the place of Jews in Hungarian society during the mid-1920s, see János, pp. 225-28.

46. Tihanyi was one of the few Hungarian artists to attain financial security. The least connected to Vienna, he left for Berlin after only ten months. Before he departed, however, the Moderne Galerie exhibited his work with considerable critical success. *Ma* did not review Tihanyi's exhibition, a failure that could only have been intentional. Moholy-Nagy mentioned in a letter from Berlin to Iván Hevesy that he thought Tihanyi's "circumstances of life in Vienna thoroughly positive, since except for Kokoschka, the Germans had no other good painters" (quoted in Passuth, "Autonomie der Kunst," p. 20).

47. Quoted by Passuth ("Autonomie der Kunst," p. 19).

48. As Kassák wrote, "My wife traveled regularly to Hungary where she was not followed by the authorities. Often she spoke in party locales or in cultural establishments. She organized more than once illegal '*Ma* Evenings' and introduced works of Hungarian and foreign avant-garde artists." See Passuth, p. 19.

49. Kassák, "An die Künstler aller Länder," *Ma*, 1, no. 2 (1920), p. 2. By "revolution" Kassák did not mean specifically the revolutionary politics of Béla Kun but implied a more generalized revolutionary cultural politics.

50. Kassák devoted increasing amounts of space and attention to the international avant-garde beginning with the January 1921 issue of *Ma* which was devoted to Kurt Schwitters. Subsequent issues focused on Archipenko, Arp, Grosz, Puni, Picabia, van Doesburg, El Lissitzky, and a host of other prominent avant-garde figures. The conspicuous attention paid to dadaism still needs to be examined; however, it may be understood as a consequence of Kassák's own contemporaneous activity as a "dada" poet (and "artist"). Much to the disapproval of Uitz, who had been for many years his coeditor at *Ma*, Kassák was devoting considerable attention to completing his epic dada poem, "The Horse Dies and the Birds Fly Away." (See n. 53.) Equally significantly, Kassák had put on the cover of *Ma* (6 no. 3) a dada work of his own invention (bearing a date of 1920), indeed, the first work that Kassák had ever published. To Kassák, van Doesburg must have been an inspiring example of an impresario of modernism who could simultaneously paint geometrically abstract canvases, edit several progressive journals (of varying tendencies), and write and perform dada poetry, while effectively articulating the social responsibilities of the modern

artist. (See Mansbach, *Visions of Totality*, passim; cf. Levinger, "Lajos Kassák, *Ma*, and the New Artist," n. 8; and Passuth, "Contacts between the Hungarian and Russian Avant-Garde in the 1920s.")

51. Kassák had only a vague awareness of recent developments in Russian art before he fled Hungary. (Cf. Levinger, "Lajos Kassák, *Ma*, and the New Artist," p. 82, and n. 21; Passuth, "Contacts between the Hungarian and the Russian Avant-Garde in the 1920s," p. 48.) While in Vienna, he organized several events that focused on the newest currents in international avant-garde art, including an evening specially devoted to Russian Modernism. On November 13, 1920, Konstantin Umansky, a *Tass* correspondent who acted as a self-annointed ambassador for the new Russian Soviet regime's culture while studying art history at the University in Vienna, was invited by the Ma circle to show and discuss his slides of the work of Kandinsky, Malevich, Falk, Goncharova, Tatlin, and other modernist Russians. Significantly, this was among the very first occasions for "Westerners" to see the new art being created in Soviet Russia. As Bowlt points out ("Lajos Kassák: The Wolf Outside the Cage," p. 10), it is remarkable how readily Kassák and the Hungarian critics such as Ernő Kállai understood modern Russian art. Most of the Russians who had emigrated to Berlin after the revolutions were not sympathetic to the new art, and it was only in November 1922, with the First Russian Art Exhibition at the Van Diemen Gallery, that the Berlin public could see a rich sampling of contemporary Russian art. By the end of the same year, the Hungarian avant-garde was already quite familiar with Russian Suprematism and Constructivism. Not only had Umansky come to Vienna, but from late January until the fall of 1921 Béla Uitz was in the USSR as a guest of the Third Comintern. There he met El Lissitzky, Rodchenko, and other prominent members of the various branches of Russian Constructivism; and he returned to Vienna with numerous photographs, documents, and even a copy of *The Realist Manifesto* (see Levinger, "The Theory of Hungarian Constructivism," p. 457; and H. Gassner, "'Ersehnte Einheit' oder 'erpresste Versöhnung'" [Desired Unity or Forced Conciliation] p. 197.)

52. Even Tihanyi, whose now lost *Seated Woman* was exhibited successfully in Vienna the previous year (see note 46), worked in a rather "retardataire" style at the time, drawing heavily on working methods The Eight had used a full decade earlier. Moholy-Nagy, who had been profoundly influenced by Kassák's attitudes toward art and society and served as the Berlin correspondent for *Ma*, also began working in a constructivist vein at almost the same moment (Passuth, *Moholy-Nagy*, pp. 20-25). For further discussion of constructivism among the Hungarian artists of Vienna and Germany, see Gassner, pp. 158-284; Eva Forgács, "Der Konstruktivismus von Ernő Kállai"; János Brendel, "Der deutsche Einfluss von Scheerbart und Wilhelm Ostwald auf die ungarische Konstruktivismustheorie" [The German Influence of Scheerbart and Wilhelm Ostwald on the Hungarian theory of Constructivism]; Gassner, "'Ersehnte Einheit' oder 'erpresste Versöhnung'"; Bajkay-Rosch, "Die KURI Gruppe," Wolfgang Kunde, "Abstraktion als Notwehr"; and Oliver A.I. Botar, "Constructed Reliefs in the Art of the Hungarian Avant-Garde: Kassák, Bortnyik, Uitz, and Moholy-Nagy, 1921-1926."

53. *Ma* had published articles in which expressionism was endorsed as a legitimately progressive form, especially during the journal's Hungarian phase, when many of the German author/poets who were published came from the expressionist circle around Pfemfert's *Die Aktion*. (See Levinger, "Lajos Kassák, *Ma*, and the New Artists," p 82.) For a time after 1916, *Ma* was the sales representative in Hungary for expressionist works in Herwarth Walden's Der Sturm gallery. While deprecating expressionism during their first years in Vienna, the Activists cherished their commercial connection to Walden's predominantly expressionist-oriented gallery and journal, which had first exhibited and published a work by a member of the Hungarian avant-garde (Máttis Teutsch) as early as 1918. It was in Walden's Der Sturm gallery that Kassák held his *Ma* literary evening on November 21, 1922, during his only visit to Berlin (November 12-25). So impressed was Walden with the many-sided artistic talents of Kassák that, in 1924 in a special *Ma-Buch*, *Der Sturm* published a German translation of the Hungarian's epic dada poem, "Das Pferd stirbt und die Vögel fliegen hinaus" [The Horse Dies and the Birds Fly Away] (trans. Endre Gáspár), and other dada works, as well as four of Kassák's constructivist linocuts. See Ferenc Csaplár, "Lajos Kassák in Berlin," pp. 20-22. Kassák's poem, translated into English by Kenneth McRobbie and Mária Körösy, is included in a volume of writings by and about Kassák, *Kassák 1887-1967* in the series "Arion, Nemzetközi Költôi Almanach" [International Almanac of Poetry], no. 16, (Budapest: Corvina, 1988), pp. 100-10, edited by György Somlyó. The original Hungarian version of the poem was first published in 1922 in the premier (and only) issue of *2x2*, which Kassák edited.

54. See Levinger, "The Theory of Hungarian Constructivism," especially pp. 456-59.

55. This issue of *Ma* could hardly be said to celebrate the communist revolution. As Passuth has pointed out ("Autonomie der Kunst," p. 25) only a single page was devoted to the occasion, and it was more a critique than a glorification. This issue is remarkable also for publishing for the first time a work by Moholy-Nagy.

56. Levinger ("The Theory of Hungarian Constructivism," p. 456) suggests that Kassák originally might have intended to use color but did not do so because of the high cost of color reproduction. A comparison of this work with several of his color prints of late 1921-22 demonstrates how effectively color might have strengthened the compositional unity and overall visual authority of this linocut.

57. For English translations of the *Manifesto*, see Arts Council 114-17 (trans. George Cushing); and *The Structurist*, no. 25-26 (1986), pp. 96-98 (trans. Oliver A.I. Botar). A German translation can be found (Dokument 46) in *Wechselwirkungen*, pp. 179-82. Kassák's first use of the term *Bildarchitektur* (*kép-architektura* in Hungarian), or "pictorial architecture," may have been in his introduction to a 1921 portfolio of six prints by Bortnyik. (See Kassák, "Sándor Bortnyik.")

58. See Levinger, "The Theory of Hungarian Constructivism," pp. 456, 458.

59. In any discussion of the Hungarian artist's responsibility to society, the role of the critics, especially Alfréd Kemény and Ernő Kállai, cannot be underestimated. Both were more than authors of reviews; they were important thinkers and writers on the nature, purposes, and implications of modern art, and especially on its social dimensions. Their critical writings provide the most articulate statements of the ideological obligations of the modern artist. These forceful arguments exerted considerable influence among the avant-garde painters. A selection of their writings is included in the Dokumente sections of *Wechselwirkungen*. See also Botar, "Ernő Kállai and the Hidden Face of Nature"; and Forgács, "Die Konstruktivismus von Ernő Kállai" and "Ernő Kállai: Art Critic of a Changing Age."

60. Ironically, neither Bortnyik nor Uitz demonstrated any reluctance to exploit the constructivist vocabulary of Kassák's Bildarchitektur philosophy in their work. This inclination may have derived in part from their familiarity with the stylistically similar constructivism practiced by progressive Russian artists, many of whom Utiz knew from his recent visit to Moscow. Although the debate over "pictorial architecture" lay at the heart of the rupture among the Vienna-based artists

of the early 1920s, not all members of the Hungarian avant-garde understood the concept or its implications for the future of visual culture. For example, Iván Hevesy, one of the most perceptive critics, saw it only as an exalted form of decoration.

61. Uitz and Komját were joint editors for the first three numbers, which were published in Vienna (May, June, and September 1922). Two later issues were published in Berlin under the sole editorship of Komját, who had been active in Kassák's first journal, *A Tett*.

62. In the words of Komját and Uitz ("Der Weg und das Arbeitsprogramm der Egység," *Egység*, Vienna 1922):
Egység *ist ein kommunistisches Kulturorgan.* Egység *ist keine "neue Tendenz," keine "manifeste Schule," sondern unmittelbarer Bestandteil der Revolution des Proletariats, ein Prozess, im dem sich das Proletariat zur Klasse organisiert. Diese Unteilbarkeit und Einheitlichkeit drückt auch der Name dieses Blattes aus.* Egység *hat ideologische Bedeutung, weil die Grundlage des Blattes das Klassenbewusstsein des Proletariats ist, das Bewusstsein seiner geschichtlichen Bestimmung; methodische Bedeutung hat es deshalb, weil im seinen theoretischen Untersuchungen die marxistische Dialektik seine Richtlinie ist; und politische Bedeutung hat es insofern, als das Blatt wie auch seine Mitarbeiter aktive Teilnehmer am proletarischen Klassenkampf sind: absolut konsequente Kommunisten....*
*[*Egység *is a communist cultural organ.* Egység *is not a "new trend," it is not a "manifest of a new school"; but it is directly connected to the proletarian revolution; it is a process in which the proletariat is organizing itself into a social class. This close connection and unity is expressed also by the name of the journal.* Egység *[Unity] has an ideological significance, because the journal is based on the class consciousness of the proletariat; on the consciousness of its historic mission; it has a methodical implication too, because Marxist dialectics give the guideline in its theoretical pursuits; and, furthermore, it has a political meaning as well, inasmuch as the journal and its editors and authors are active participants of the proletarian class struggle: they are absolutely....]* The author-editors go on to list four objectives, the last of which is to introduce Proletkult into Hungary itself.

Egység and two journals edited by Barta (see note 64) monitored events in Hungary and often oriented their polemic to appeal to leftist supporters still in Budapest. Attention to the homeland was prompted by more than mere emotions. The Bethlen-Peyer Pact of December 22, 1921 (see Chapter 1) provided for government concessions in exchange for agreement by the adherents to social democratic politics, among other things, to sever their ties with émigrés of the Hungarian Soviet Republic. (See János, *The Politics of Backwardness*, pp. 234-35.) Perhaps the avant-gardists in exile sought to counter the concessions, made by their confederates in Hungary, especially the severance of ties.

63. That Kassák might have refused to publish these documents in *Ma* is plausible; he had vehemently condemned Russian Constructivism and Productivism in his review of the 1922 First Russian Art Exhibition in Berlin (*Ma*, 8, December 1922). For a contrasting view of this exhibition, see Alfréd Kemény, "Bemerkungen zur Ausstellung der russichen Künstler in Berlin" [Notes to the Exhibition of Russian Artists in Berlin]. Bajkay-Rosch claims ("Die ungarische Avantgarde-Kunst im Wiener Exil," p. 37) that the publication of these important Russian documents in *Egység* marks the first occasion that they appeared in a foreign language. Uitz left Moscow in the fall of 1921 and returned to Vienna via Germany; his discussions in Berlin with Kállai and Moholy-Nagy over the merits of the new constructivist art may constitute the first "Western" debate concerning Russian constructivism. (See Botar, "Constructed Reliefs," p. 92.)

64. Also in 1922, the disaffected *Ma* literary figure Sándor Barta founded in Vienna a journal in opposition to Kassák. Barta's *Akasztott Ember* [Hanged Man] and its 1923 successor *Ék* [The Wedge] were strongly ideological and took a position close to that of the Soviet Communist party. See Amalie Maria Lindner, "Tendenzen der ungarischen Avantgarde im Spiegel der Zeitschriften von 1915-1933," [Trends of the Hungarian Avant-Garde as Reflected in Periodicals of 1915-1953].

65. *Wechselwirkungen* (H. Gassner, ed.) is an indispensable resource for understanding the activities of the Hungarian avant-garde in Weimar Germany. It includes a selection of original documents (in German translation) and numerous interpretive essays. (See also Nóra Aradi, Berlin-Budapest, in Klaus Kändler and Helga Karolewski and Ilse Siebert, eds., *Berlin Bewegnungen: Ausländerische Künstler in Berlin 1918 bis 1933*, [East] Berlin: Dietz Verlag, 1987, pp. 219-38.)

66. This is not to suggest that Hungarians living in Berlin were not preoccupied with their homeland. It was in Berlin, after all, that Kernstok painted a version of his *Last Supper*, a powerfully nostalgic image that uses Christian iconography to affirm the "religious" importance of the Hungarian revolution(s). Nevertheless, almost immediately upon their arrival the painters sought integration into the large artists' community and active gallery and commercial network. Berlin-based Hungarians rarely stood aloof from other artist groups and institutions, as had happened in Vienna. Kernstok could even remark that in Berlin he and his colleagues found a "seelisch-psychisch-geistige-soziale Atmosphäre" [a social atmosphere for the soul, the psyche, and the spirit]. For others, however, such as Nemes Lampérth who was neither expressionist nor constructivist, life in Berlin could be depressing even if one made artistic progress. (See Nemes Lampérth, "Letter from Berlin" (1920).)

67. Passuth states (*Moholy-Nagy*, p. 28) that Moholy-Nagy "adopted the ideas of Constructivism without the necessary basis of a socio-political background." In a larger context, Moholy's attitudes toward constructivism may be understood as a necessary aspect of his views toward education, science, and society (Mansbach, *Visions of Totality*). Moholy-Nagy did attempt, with limited success, to placate both the Kassák and the proletkult factions of the Hungarian avant-garde. In 1922, he published an article in Barta's *Akasztott Ember* (no. 3-4, p. 3). In 1923 he joined Kállai, Kemény, and Péri, who were all active in Communist party organizations, in signing a manifesto to be published in *Egység* (no. 4, p. 51). This manifesto distinguished between the destructive "aestheticism of bourgeois constructivists," by which the authors meant the Dutch De Stijl and Russian OBMOKhU groups, and the constructivists whose "constructive potentialities...can be fully realized only within the framework of communist society." Both articles are reprinted in Passuth, *Moholy-Nagy*, pp. 286-89.

68. Cf. Naum Gabo's similar intention expressed in his sculpture. See Mansbach, "Gabo's Template for Utopia: *Linear Construction in Space No. 1*."

69. See Botar, "Constructed Reliefs," p. 88 and n. 5; and Mansbach, *Visions of Totality*, pp. 105-23.

70. See Miklos von Bartha and Carl László, *Die ungarischen Künstler am Sturm Berlin 1913-1932* [Hungarian Artists at Sturm in Berlin]; Passuth, " 'Der Sturm' der Ungarn"; Ildiko Hajnal-Neukäter, "Herwarth Walden und Lajos Kassák—ein Porträt" and Lindner, "Tendenzen der ungarischen Avantgarde im Spiegel der Zeitschriften."

71. Hajnal-Neukäter notes (p. 62) that there is some controversy regarding the onset of Walden's passionate interest in left-wing politics. His second wife Nell asserted that before 1923 Walden had no interest in politics; how-

ever, Hajnal-Neukäter suggests that his interest was already apparent by 1919.

72. See Gassner, "Ersehnte Einheit," p. 205. The French had occupied the southern part of Hungary since the end of World War I; from their base at Szeged, they now gave considerable support to Admiral Horthy and refused to tolerate anti-Horthy activities among Hungarian émigrés in Paris.

73. About the time Péri withdrew from Der Sturm, the gallery was in decline despite its worldwide reputation. Many of Der Sturm's Hungarian artists had left Berlin, and a number of others had given up art. Walden himself devoted increasing attention to political affairs, primarily in behalf of communism and its causes. In 1932, he closed the gallery and moved to Moscow to continue his own literary activities. In 1941, he perished under Stalin. (See Hajnal-Neukäter,"Herwarth Walden und Lajos Kassák," p. 62.)

74. The exact number of Hungarians officially associated with the Bauhaus is difficult to determine. Bajkay-Rosch's ("Die KURI Gruppe") suggestion of 19 students, in addition to Moholy-Nagy and Breuer, seems most reliable.

75. Bortnyik provided a surprisingly objective account of his activities in Weimar in an essay "Etwas über das Bauhaus" [Something on the Bauhaus], excerpts of which are reprinted in Eckhard Neumann, ed., *Bauhaus and Bauhaus People*, pp. 69-72. Bortnyik acknowledged that "everything I found there was for me really new, interesting, and instructive." He was frustrated when finally he was able to speak with Gropius, however. Bortnyik believed that the profound influence of Klee, Kandinsky, and Feininger encouraged originality through subjectivity, when what was needed in Bortnyik's view was a pathway out of the subjective chaos of contemporary art. The direction he suggested was along the collective lines of Mondrian and van Doesburg's "neo-plasticism," ironically, the very type of constructivism censured as bourgeois "aestheticism" in the *Egység* manifesto signed by Bortnyik's colleagues Kállai, Kemény, Moholy-Nagy and Péri.

76. Once at Weimar, Forbát was immediately hired by Gropius to work in his "Baubüro." Between 1922 and 1924 he was employed by the Bauhaussiedlung GmbH, which was under Gropius's direct supervision and had also retained the services of the Hungarian designer Farkas Molnár. See Ottó Mezei, "Ungarische Architekten am Bauhaus" [Hungarian Architects at the Bauhaus]. In an autobiographical article, Forbát admits that there was some residual strife among the Hungarians resident in Weimar, most likely a carryover from their days in Berlin. According to Forbát, Moholy-Nagy was still "little loved and his art not taken seriously" by a number of his fellow Hungarian artists. See Forbát, "Ungarische Künstler in Berlin und am Bauhaus."

77. This was an effective compositional means of introducing into his work the "dynamic-constructive system of forces" that had been debated by the Hungarian artists in Berlin. Cf. L. Moholy-Nagy and A. Kemény, "Dynamisch-konstruktives Kraftsystem" (*Der Sturm* no. 12, 1922) reprinted in Passuth, *Moholy-Nagy*, p. 290: "Translated into art, *today*, this means the activation of space by means of dynamic-constructive systems of forces, that is, construction of forces within one another that are actually at tension in physical space and their construction within space, also active as force (tensions)."

78. See Bortnyik, "Programm des ungarischen Bauhauses. Neue Wege des 'Kunstgewerbe'-Unterrichts" (1928).

79. For a positive review of the November 21, 1922 *Ma* evening in Berlin, see the November 26, 1926 issue of *Bécsi Magyar Újság* [Viennese Hungarian Journal], quoted by Csaplár, "Lajos Kassák in Berlin," p. 21.

80. See Éva Forgács, "József Nemes Lampérth."

81. Since most of the articles were published in Hungarian, it is unlikely that the editors intended that their respective journals would have a large circulation among the international "foreign" avant-garde. The limited printing runs of the journals appear to bear this out. With so few opportunities to exhibit their work, many artists took advantage of the "little reviews" to put their art before the "public." The importance of these journals in the life of the avant-garde may have encouraged the artists to create graphic series for publication either within the journals or as special supplements. The prominent place of typographical innovation within the Hungarians' creative activities also may be related loosely to the position these magazines occupied in the exiles' lives.

82. For example, immediately upon his arrival in Budapest in 1926, Kassák was summoned to appear before a court of inquest accused of "distributing" and promoting communist literature. The legal case was not dropped until October 1930. In 1932, he was summoned again before the courts and charged with inciting revolution due to the appearance of several poems in a *Munka* [Work] publication. In 1936, he was convicted and sentenced to a year's imprisonment for his previous "revolutionary" activities. Only the intercession of prominent figures from PEN was able to persuade the Horthy courts to suspend sentence. However, two years later, Kassák did serve three months in prison for his (mostly earlier) agitational activities. See Štraus, *Kassák*, pp. 103-105.

83. To stimulate the economy, which was so dependent on largely Jewish professional, financial, and industrial enterprises, Count István Bethlen, the consummately adroit prime minister during the period 1921-31, convinced Horthy to ameliorate the anti-Semitism that had flourished in post-Kun Hungary. Nevertheless, the Jewish middle class of Budapest that had once lent support to the avant-garde was no longer interested by the mid-1920s in patronizing the activities of the returning artists. For example, in 1928 Kassák's modest exhibition in the Budapest bookshop of Mentor garnered negative public criticism; even *Nyugat*, the historically progressive journal that first published Kassák before World War I, reproached the artist for the incomprehensibility of his work. Group exhibitions of the work of the avant-garde held in 1929 and 1930 also drew quite negative reaction from the popular and art press. See Štraus, *Kassák*, pp. 105-107; János, *The Politics of Backwardness*, pp. 201ff.; and Zsuzsa Nagy, "The Secret Papers of István Bethlen," in *The New Hungarian Quarterly*, vol XIV, no. 49, pp. 171-176.

84. Twenty years passed before Kassák took up painting again, and then he embraced a lyrical abstraction that eschewed the idealist social goals of his youth. Enjoying only a brief two years of renewed recognition, between the end of World War II and the communist seizure of power, he again endured official neglect until the end of his life. Kassák was awarded the Kossuth Prize in 1965; however, the honor was granted in appreciation of his late poetry and not in recognition for his decades of innovation as a visual artist and impresario of the avant-garde. See Éva Körner, "Kassák, The Artist," in *Lajos Kassák 1887-1967*, (New York: 1984), p. 15; and Ferenc Csaplár, "Nach meinem eigenen Gesetz: Porträtskizze Lajos Kassák," in *Lajos Kassák 1887-1967*, (East Berlin), p. 12.

85. See S. Bortnyik, "Programm des ungarischen Bauhauses" [Program of the Hungarian Bauhaus].
Nach zwölf Jahren mußte ich diese Arbeit wegen einer schweren Erkrankung aufgeben. In diesem Zeitraum hatte das "Műhely" ungefähr 120 Studenten. Viele von ihnen arbeiten in Budapest und mehrere in Ausland. Auch durch sie werden die Impulse des Bauhauses weitergetragen.

[After twelve years, I had to give up this work on account of a serious illness. During this period, the "Műhely" [Workshop] had about 120 students. Many of them work [now] in Budapest and more abroad, and through them the impulse of the Bauhaus is carried forth.]
(From Neumann, ed., *Bauhaus und Bauhäusler*, and excerpted in *Wechselwirkungen*, p. 376.)

86. See Heidrun Schröder-Kehler, "Künstler erobern die Warenwelt: Neue Typographie in der Werbegestaltung" [Artists Conquer the World of Goods: New Typography in Applied Design] in *Wechselwirkungen*; and Esther Levinger, "Hungarian Avant-Garde Typography and Posters," in John Kish, ed., p. 112-22.

87. The affinity with the contemporary architectural designs of the De Stijl group should not be discounted. In 1922, Kassák was actively cultivating his contacts with the Dutch artists, and by then he was familiar with the various architectural projects (by De Stijl architects and other modernists) that had been published in *De Stijl*.

88. Schröder-Kehler points out ("Künstler erobern die Warenwelt," p. 398) that Bortnyik's poster suggests his familiarity with Herbert Bayer's 1926 concept of a universal typographical alphabet.

89. Paradoxically, it was in 1933 that Hugó Scheiber reached the critical acme of his career. Having abandoned Berlin when Hitler assumed power (and after Herwarth Walden emigrated to the Soviet Union), Scheiber as a Jewish socialist faced bleak prospects in Budapest. Upon returning to Horthy's Hungary, he was approached by F. T. Marinetti with an invitation to participate in the immense futurist exhibition to be held in Rome under the patronage of Mussolini's fascist party. There his work received lavish praise, the last time he would be celebrated in his lifetime. From 1934 until his death in 1950 Scheiber endured the indifference of his fellow artists and suffered the pecuniary consequences of official neglect from successive Hungarian fascist and communist regimes.

JÚLIA SZABÓ

COLOR, LIGHT, FORM, & STRUCTURE:

new experiences in hungarian painting, 1890-1930

Painting in nineteenth century Hungary was not a pure visual art form but visualized national history. During the 1800s, Hungary fought for national sovereignty and civil rights. Revolution and a war of independence (1848-49), the absolute rule (1850-67) of the Austrian emperor, and a compromise agreement (1867) formed the historical background of a national art that was at once neoclassical, romantic, and historical (see Chapter 1). Hungarian critics and the public wanted to see a national architecture and portrayal of native landscapes, national historic events, past and contemporary heroes, and the life of the people, permeated at times by a kind of national mythology.

The Nineteenth Century Heritage

Gustave Courbet's realism, together with a certain informality and preoccupation with the immanent problems of painting, marked the orientation of only a handful of young Hungarian painters. Beginning in 1870-73, considered the inception of modern painting in Hungary, painters concerned themselves with the autonomous fields of art and with new ways of capturing nature on canvas. Artists of the age sought to create a new style out of the inherent pictorial elements of painting: bright color, light, expressive line, and form. At the same time, they strove to capture individual as well as collective stylistic qualities in their own works.

PÁL SZINYEI MERSE: PIONEER OF PURE VISUAL ART

The great colorist Pál Szinyei Merse (1845-1920) broke the ice in 1873 in Munich. His main interests were landscapes devoid of historical motifs and nonnarrative genre paintings in which he experimented with clear bright colors and natural, or *plein air*, lighting. He painted *Picnic in May* (FIG. 3-1), the first masterpiece of modern Hungarian painting, during the winter and spring of 1872-73.[1] A gathering of artists, connoisseurs, and models for a picnic in a hilly landscape provided a personal experience for the painter, who had discovered the joy of nature, transferred to the canvas by Manet and Monet and traceable in its iconography back to the

Júlia Szabó (Marosi) is a widely published art historian and a staff member of the Research Institute of Art History, Hungarian Academy of Sciences. Formerly in the Department of Prints and Drawings of the Hungarian National Gallery, Budapest, she participated in the CIHA international congresses in Vienna (1983) and Strasbourg (1989). Many of her books, journal articles, and essays are cited in the comprehensive bibliography at the end of this volume.

Renaissance. Like Monet in his large *Déjeuner sur l'herbe* (1866), Szinyei painted his figures from models in his atelier.

Though he was a pupil of Carl Theodor von Piloty at the academy in Munich, Szinyei Merse preferred Courbet's simple and monumental experience of nature, the powerful intensity of color in Arnold Böcklin's pictures, and the classical persiflage and scandalously "ordinary" compositions of Manet and Monet. He himself was a master of the fresh harmonies of bright and shadowy color. As we know from one of his sketches, he painted the walls of his atelier red, and in the spirit of the Japonisme of the period, he drew kimono-clad figures on the wall, with a deep blue sky and feathery clouds above them. The contrast of blue, red, and green also is present in *Picnic in May*, which can be seen on the easel in Szinyei's *Atelier* (1873).

Lajos Fülep, the outstanding Hungarian critic, later observed:

Szinyei is a spectator of nature.... he perceives the sky as color and distance, sees trees, grass and bushes as form and

Fig. 3-1 PÁL SZINYEI MERSE, *Picnic in May*, 1873, Hungarian National Gallery, Budapest.

61. BÉLA IVÁNYI GRÜNWALD, Nagybánya Landscape, 1900

material, and air and sunshine as color... Szinyei is more interested in valeur *than in tone, in color than in analysis. That is why he sees light green, red, or brown as homogeneous, dispersed color. He discovers formerly unknown beauties in nature. He realizes his discovery with the power of genius. He comprehends all the beauty in the marvelous green of grass, in the bright sunshine of May, in the effect of a pink dress, in the richness of sunshine falling on a hillside, in the forms of a hill and figures, along with boldness, new expression, great harmony and homogeneous influence of* plein air *in the most modern sense.*[2]

Szinyei exhibited *Picnic in May* in Munich and in Vienna. In professional circles it achieved success, and he could have sold it, together with some of his earlier *plein air* paintings such as *Mother with Her Children* (1872). Instead, however, he offered the picture as a gift to the National Museum in Budapest.[3] It was not accepted. A nobleman with ample income from his properties, Szinyei withdrew to his estates in northern Hungary and hung *Picnic in May* on the wall of his room. He did not remove it until 1896, when he sent it to the Millennial Exhibition in Budapest. (*See Chapter 1.*)

NATURE AND SYMBOLISM: *PLEIN AIR* PAINTING IN NAGYBÁNYA An important school of *plein air* painting was established at Nagybánya (now Baia Mare, Romania) in 1896 by master artists who had returned from Munich, and by their Hungarian, Russian, Polish, Scottish, Armenian, American, and German students. The colony held a reverent view of nature. One of its most important masters was Károly Ferenczy (1862-1917), whose *Birdsong*, painted in 1893 in Munich, solved a problem similar to that of Szinyei in his *Picnic in May*: the subjective, lyrical, and clear handling of red and green. Along with the large decorative patches of color, lights and shadows are important elements of the composition.

The existence of the Nagybánya colony proved to be a turning point in the history of Hungarian art. (*See Chapter 2.*) On the one hand, it was the successor of Barbizon, the *plein air* painting school in France, where Hungarian landscape artists had worked from 1870 onward; on the other, its painters were drawn to the German naturalism and symbolism of Arnold Böcklin, Hans von Marées, and Fritz von Uhde. The Nagybánya artists also were in touch with contemporary naturalist and symbolist writers. The poet József Kiss, editor of the first modern literary periodical, *A Hét* [The Week], for example, asked some of them to provide illustrations for a volume of poems. Károly Ferenczy made lyrical charcoal drawings, while another master of the colony, Simon Hollósy, illustrated the ballads with grayish monochromatic paintings.

Fig. 3-2 KÁROLY FERENCZY, *An Evening in March*, 1902, Hungarian National Gallery, Budapest.

Mountains, forests, and gardens were the chief motifs of Hungarian painting of the period, often providing the background for mythological and religious scenes, as well as subjects of everyday life. Ferenczy portrayed life around him as monumental and solemn. Weighed down by the thought of the importance of the work on the canvas before her, the *Woman Painter* (1903) stands in her dark blue dress under the trees. In *An Evening in March* (1902), the hackney carriages and their horses cast violet shadows on the white wall behind them, and the dark blue of the March sky lends dignity to the scene (FIG. 3-2). Scenes from the Old and New Testaments are set in forests and fields and executed in dark tones that lend an air of mystery (*The Sacrifice of Abraham*, 1901; *The Three Magi*, 1898; *Joseph Sold by His Brothers*, 1900; *The Return of the Prodigal*, 1908). To Ferenczy, the region surrounding Nagybánya had a biblical monumentality, evident in his renderings of the mountains and rivers, and he admired the area with sincere devotion.

53. KÁROLY FERENCZY, Beech Woods, 1908

Ferenczy turned from the academic methods toward naturalism, and he retained the liveliness of naturalism even in his symbolist works. He also attempted impressionism (*Bathing Boys,* 1905), but in his view, the impressionists and post-impressionists (especially Gauguin) did not have sufficient respect for nature. Like Pál Szinyei Merse, Ferenczy was a painter *par excellence*. It is not surprising that when Szinyei Merse became the director of the academy of fine arts in Budapest, he invited Ferenczy to teach painting there. In his teaching he emphasized glowing colors, the harmony of expression, and classical compositional balance—a kind of academic naturalism. After 1906 Ferenczy spent only the summers at Nagybánya.

Simon Hollósy (1857-1918), another master of Nagybánya, left a smaller *oeuvre* behind. In some ways more conservative than Ferenczy, Hollósy was interested in historical compositions set in vivid open air settings. He experimented with naturalistic

52. KÁROLY FERENCZY, Woman Painter, 1903

123. VILMOS PERLROTT CSABA, Bathing Youths, c1910s

124. VILMOS PERLROTT CSABA, Deposition from the Cross, 1912

illustrations for literary works, and produced portraits that were academic and naturalistic at the same time. After 1900, however, when Hollósy left Nagybánya to paint near Lake Balaton and his native town of Técső in northeastern Hungary (now part of the Soviet Union), his landscapes began to reflect modern influences to a greater extent than those of Ferenczy. Hollósy must have known the haystacks and the cathedral series of Monet, as well as Gauguin's paintings from his Pont Aven period. Village landscapes of around 1912 with representations of thatched-roofed houses, carts standing in the yard, haystacks in green and violet, give ample evidence of his interests and talent.

The work of Vilmos Perlrott Csaba (1880-1955), also a Nagybánya artist, shows the influence of Cézanne's *Bathers*. A powerful example is his *Bathing Youths* (1910). In the summers, he left Nagybánya for Kecskemét, a colony devoted to art nouveau but tolerant of fauvist and cubist compositions. It was here in 1912 that he painted his exciting cubo-expressionist composition, *Deposition from the Cross*.

LÁSZLÓ MEDNYÁNSZKY: REALISM AND THE PHYSIOLOGY OF COLOR László Mednyánszky (1852-1919) approached his art with an attitude similar to that of Hollósy. Being less influenced by German academicism, however, Mednyánszky's realism was also less dependent on it. In his early years, László Mednyánszky, an artist of aristocratic origin, was taught landscape drawing and painting by the romantic painter Thomas Ender. In the 1870s he studied in Vienna, Munich, and Paris, and he became familiar with realism at Barbizon. László Paál (1846-1879), the master of Hungarian realist landscape painting, worked at Barbizon, and Mihály Munkácsy (1844-1900), the great Hungarian realist of genre and landscape painting, also made several visits there. Although Mednyánszky became acquainted with the impressionist approach to nature, in the 1880s his light and colorful landscapes followed romantic-realist traditions.

Mednyánszky wandered about the highlands and plains of Central Europe on foot. He met shepherds and peasants and was able to convey their attitudes in his works. But alongside the motifs of life in bloom, his canvases also convey a mood of decay. The diary he kept from the 1890s reveals Mednyánszky's fascination with the physiology of colors. The ensemble of green and violet, for example, created a lovely expression of suffering, as he writes:

There is a kind of brownish red which excites the nerves,...Rusty red, the color of dry or clotted blood, lights up the fermenting passions. This is the color of most beasts of prey.[4]

This rusty red of clotted blood is present in many of Mednyánszky's pictures, especially in the landscapes and in portraits of tramps with the expression of frightened animals.

Mednyánszky's paintings of factory workers and demonstrations were successful in Paris in the late 1890s, but he did not become a popular painter. He continued to work in solitude, and his friendship with simple people and his mystic relation to nature were more important to him than fame. In 1896, he wrote in his diary:

What form do the greatest innovations assume in painting? Do they go from old symbols to the simple realism of objective facts? From objective to subjective facts? From subjective facts toward a new symbolism?

Of these possibilities, the last was never an alterna-

Fig. 3-3 LÁSZLÓ MEDNYÁNSZKY, *War Prisoners*, 1916, Janus Pannonius Museum, Pécs.

Fig. 3-4 LÁSZLÓ MEDNYÁNSZKY, *Decay*, 1917, Katona József Museum, Kecskemét.

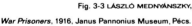

tive for Mednyánszky. Although he knew the French Rose-Croix *cathétique* and admired Edward Munch, Mednyánszky did not become a symbolist painter himself. His spiritual and deeply sensuous realism is most closely related to the works of the young painter whom he mentions in his diary with such enthusiasm: Van Gogh.

In Mednyánszky's huge *oeuvre*, comprising thousands of paintings and drawings, those that he made during World War I are perhaps the most significant. Of his own volition, he went to the front and became a war painter. He depicted the grinding ordeal of the war first hand, in its human perspective: soldiers on horse or spending their nights outdoors, the wounded, the march of the prisoners of war, the "spies" hanging on the gallows (FIGS. 3-3 AND 3-4). The tones of these war paintings are yellowish and brownish green and silverish grey, but sometimes the early morning sky or the sunset is depicted in magical pink. Under this sky, the greenish corpses lying on the yellowish brown ground, or the soldiers trying to hide under the earth, appear with a strange verisimilitude. The war paintings of Mednyánszky are the silent but monumental records of the Central European tragedy of the Great War.

JÓZSEF RIPPL-RÓNAI AND THE PARISIAN INFLUENCE The other independent Hungarian artist of the late 1800s, József Rippl-Rónai (1861-1927), took another path.[5] Neither tragic nor dramatic, his works are vital and decorative. He studied in Munich only for a short period, later moving to Paris in the 1880s. There he worked in the atelier of Mihály Munkácsy until 1889, when he left his aged master and formed a friendship with a group of French painters, the Nabis, whom he subsequently joined. He also admired the work of Gauguin and Cézanne, though he never became a direct follower of either. Rippl-Rónai exhibited in Paris at Gallery Bing, the center of art nouveau, in 1897 and took part in the exhibition of the Nabis group in 1899.

Rippl-Rónai developed a highly individual style. He began by working with only a few colors: the dominant chromatic elements of his early paintings, mostly portraits and genre scenes, are grey and black patches circumscribed by gentle contours, warm browns, and yellowish whites. In the spirit of contemporary photographs, the young Rippl-Rónai's pictures depict elderly ladies standing with a bunch of violets or sitting in a comfortable armchair, facing the spectator, in brown gowns, black gloves, and black bonnets. The psychological

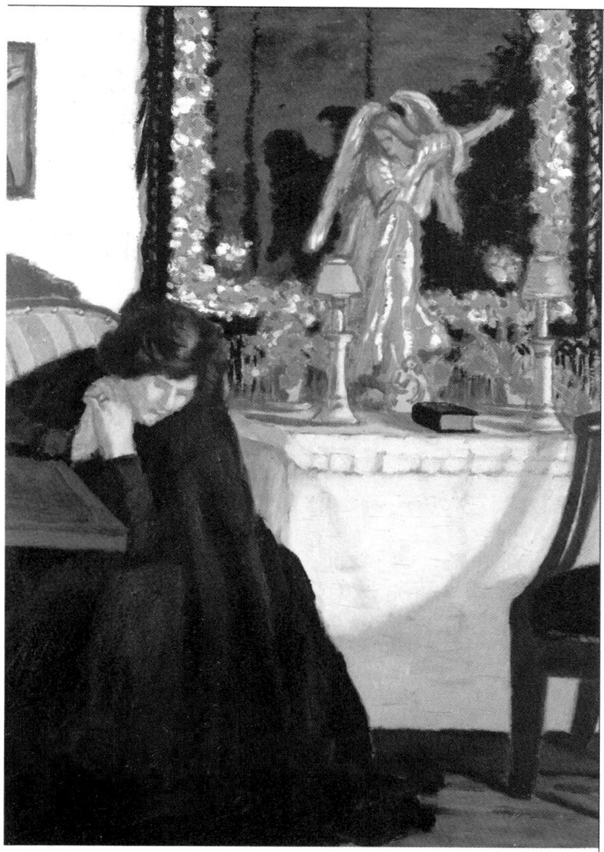

128. JÓZSEF RIPPL-RÓNAI, Sorrow, 1903

tension and the subdued colors and forms of these works were highly praised by contemporary French critics and artists. Picasso stood with astonishment in front of the painting entitled *Grandmother* (1894), while Crevalier wrote in *Le Soir* (April 29, 1894): *This powerful picture sings about the poetry of the infinite sadness of the old. Even Baudelaire's old ladies are not as sad and as attractive.*

Whistler's silver-grey-white impressionism, the planar compositions of the Nabis, the linearism of Toulouse-Lautrec, and the decorative style of art nouveau graphics and applied art all influenced Rippl-Rónai. Yet he depicted the skittle players on the square near his home in Neuilly, the graveyard of the Hungarian Plain, and his French friends Bonnard, Vuillard, and Maillol in an individual and lyrical way. *The Portrait of Aristide Maillol* (1899) was painted during a visit to Banyuls-sur-Mer, Maillol's favorite place of residence. It is a masterpiece. Rippl-Rónai presented it to the art patron Elek Petrovics, who offered it to the Louvre. Wearing his straw hat, the black-bearded Maillol faces the spectator. Behind him loom the houses of his town with their dark blue windows, blue walls, and red roofs. The sky is reddish blue and a tone of blue also appears on Maillol's tie. In the manner of Denis, the pictorial surface is composed of color planes and

127. JÓZSEF RIPPL-RÓNAI, Lady in a White Robe (Study), 1898

129. JÓZSEF RIPPL-RÓNAI, Sour Cherry Trees, 1909

patches, foreground and background serve the same function, the dynamism of color dominates, and the plasticity of forms nearly disappears.

Having left France in 1900, Rippl-Rónai also painted portraits in his native Hungary. After painting the members of his family, he turned to the depiction of the elegant ladies of his time with their bizarre hats, white-powdered faces, and dark red or light yellow dresses. Often these studies appeared in sketches for tapestries embroidered by Rippl-Rónai's French wife, Lazarine Boudrion. By this time Rippl-Rónai was not only a painter but a designer of everything from furniture, china, and glass to textiles. Now his works were imbued with more oily, sensual, material colors. He studied Monet and Gustave Klimt, but his impressionism bore only a loose resemblance to theirs. In his truly impressionist *Sour Cherry Tree in Bloom* (1903), a woman in dark violet dress leans against a violet trunk, merging with it and the white floating petals from the tree. But Rippl-Rónai never again achieved such light elegance in his work. In his later works, the dots of color are applied with much thicker paint, producing a powerfully contoured mosaic effect in an impressionist-pointillist style he himself described as "corn-like."

By the first decade of the twentieth century, Rippl-Rónai preferred the fauvist use of color to that of the Nabis, but the wildness of hues is softened by his taste for decorative and rounded forms. Though he was living in southern Hungary, in the typically provincial town of Kaposvár, Rippl-Rónai nevertheless enjoyed the stylized, theatrical way of life of the *belle époque*, with all its accessories: yellow walls, embroidered scarves on brown furniture, colorful cushions, and decorative dolls. Luscious color indeed is a basic element of Rippl-Rónai's "stage," and it goes hand in hand with the soft, wavy lines of art nouveau and harmonious gestures. His subjects are relatives, friends, collectors, artists, writers, architects, and actresses. He studied their character thoroughly and portrayed them with background patches of the colors suggested by his assessment.

Rippl-Rónai returned to France in the summer of 1914. At the outbreak of World War I, when the mobilization took place, he captured in his art the excitement and the ecstatic atmosphere, rendering the French soldiers in their blue uniforms and the colorful crowd saying goodby. Soon thereafter, however, he was arrested, charged with being a spy, and interned. It was six months before his friends and the Red Cross could effect his release and help him to return to Hungary. These experiences left Rippl-Rónai an enervated artist; his colors turned pale and weak, and his favorite technique changed from oil to pastel. In the private drawing school where he taught in Budapest, however, the snapshot clarity of his India ink and charcoal drawings had a profound influence on his pupils, among them János Máttis Teutsch, Sándor Bortnyik, and Gyula Derkovits.

Though Rippl-Rónai was well aware of the modern Hungarian art movements, he remained apart from contemporary radical tendencies and groups. He never had a clearly delineated artistic or social program, but as early as the 1880s he was the Hungarian representative of what was then called "Parisianism."[6] At the turn of the century, the dream of Hungarian writers and artists was to learn from Paris. Endre Ady, for example, moved to Paris to become a symbolist poet, while from the circles of literary and art reviews, the most influential of which was *Nyugat* [West], all looked to Paris for inspiration. But even earlier, Rippl-Rónai had loved the atmosphere of Paris, which he rendered imaginatively with the freshness of impressionism, the nostalgia of post-impressionism, the stylized and decorative elements of art nouveau, and a fauvist stentorian pursuit of reality.

131. JÓZSEF RIPPL-RÓNAI, Painter in the Park, 1910

TIVADAR CSONTVÁRY KOSZTKA: EXPERIMENT WITH LIGHT AND COLOR Early twentieth century Hungarian painting had its own solitary genius, who tamed tradition to his own needs: Tivadar Csontváry Kosztka (1853-1919). Following his death in 1919, Csontváry was praised as the forerunner of Hungarian post-impressionism, and later was compared with Seurat and Gauguin. More recently he has been regarded by Hungarians as the modern successor of romantic-historical landscape painting. He was indeed a late heroic landscapist, but he also was a modern painter who spent his entire life with painting in *plein air*.

Csontváry decided to become a painter in the 1880s in response to a "celestial voice." A pharmacist's assistant at the time, he decided to obtain an academic training, and visited the European art centers of Munich, Karlsruhe, Düsseldorf, Berlin, and Paris. He studied the art found in museums as well, and wished to surpass the Renaissance masters, especially Raphael. His favorite genre was the heroic-historic landscape, which he graced with themes from places he believed to be revered by his nation or the whole of mankind. In his paintings one can see, for example, the high Tátra mountains, the Greek theater of Taormina, Athens with the Acropolis, the ancient temples of Baalbek, and the Mount of Lebanon with its cedars.

25. TIVADAR CSONTVÁRY KOSZTKA, The Praying Saviour, 1903

Going beyond the representation of the emotionally charged landscapes of antiquity, Csontváry experimented with the picturesque and *plein air* methods of representation as well. The most important task he set for himself was the rendering of light and color in that hour of the day when the land was in its full majesty. Besides capturing the ephemeral quality of light and color, he also tried to reveal the essential character of a landscape, a group of buildings, or other works of man. Change and constancy, natural and symbolic motifs: these were Csontváry's major preoccupations. One of his masterpieces, *Pleasure Ride in Athens at the New Moon* (1904), appears to be a typical impressionist cityscape with its gliding carriages, but the shadow of the Acropolis falling over the scene, the pink evening sky, and the thin edge of the new moon turn the painting into a romantic vision redolent with the mystery of past millennia (FIG. 3-5).

Csontváry had personal reasons for visiting the Holy Land: in accord with the ideas of romantic Hungarian historians, he hoped to find the original Magyar homeland there. In *Pilgrimage to the Cedars of Lebanon* (1907), he depicted an ancient ritual under an enormous cedar,[7] the participants of which are two horses, one white and one black (perhaps the sacrificial animals of the ancient Magyar religion), girls in white robes dancing around the great tree, and riders, some watching the dancers and others looking out of the canvas, straight at the spectator (FIG. 3-6). Csontváry's highly sensitive handling of color and his penchant for the monumental are evident in the deep blue sky, the pink mountain range with the whites of snow, the greenish-blue foliage of the cedars, and the red glow on the boughs. The dignity of the painting is enhanced by the almost square form of the canvas coupled with the symmetry of the tree trunk and the crown. This painting is related to Böcklin's *Holiday in May* (1872 to the 1880s), Puvis de Chavannes's *Sacred Grove* (1884-1889), Ludwig von Hofmann's *Dancers* (1905), and Edward Burne-Jones's *The Gardens of the Hesperides* (c. 1880). With the motifs of the holy tree and the ritual dance, it also suggests a link with ancient Eurasian culture as well.

Pilgrimage was painted in 1907, after Csontváry's exhibition in Paris, when his work still awaited recognition. (Csontváry mentions a certain Pierre Weber, an American critic who considered

Fig. 3-5 TIVADAR CSONTVÁRY KOSZTKA, *Pleasure Drive in Athens at the New Moon*, 1904, Janus Pannonius Museum, Pécs.

Fig. 3-6 TIVADAR CSONTVÁRY KOSZTKA, *Pilgrimage to the Cedars of Lebanon*, 1907. Courtesy Hungarian Ministry of Culture, Budapest.

his paintings epoch-making, but Weber's newspaper review has never been found.[8]) In the summer of the same year, Csontváry went to the site in Lebanon of *Pilgrimage* and painted a companion picture, *The Solitary Cedar*. On this canvas, the tree with its slim trunk emerges from the mist and twilight clouds, and although its shape shows the merciless cruelty of storms, it is graceful and majestic. The lines of its boughs resemble art nouveau representations of trees by such contemporaries as Segantini and Jan Toorop, as well as the trees of Japanese woodcuts and drawings.

An independent painter, Csontváry also was familiar with impressionism, respected art nouveau, and knew about expressionism, cubism, and futurism. He was fascinated by Wilhelm Ostwald's researches into the physics of light and color, and like other notable European painters, he studied Japanese art. In the manner of his close friend Pál Szinyei Merse, he applied his colors on a bright white surface. He wished to find new ways of representing the movement of light and its effects on color.

Although Hungarian criticism has been dealing with Csontváry since the 1920s, his paintings are not yet included among works of European art. He stopped painting in 1910 but continued to make large charcoal sketches until his death in 1919. His legacy was sold at auction for use as canvas carriage covers; fortunately, most were acquired by Gedeon Gerlóczy, an enthusiastic young architect, and thus were preserved.

FROM ART NOUVEAU TO EXPRESSIVE REALISM

János Vaszary (1867-1939), perhaps one of the most fascinating of Csontváry's admirers, adapted himself with ease to the world of art nouveau and enjoyed great popularity early in his career. His *The Golden Age* (1898) was even selected for the Paris World Exhibition of 1900 (FIG. 2-3). In a mysterious yellowish-green garden, two figures embrace each other; in the foreground are sculptures of Venus

51. KÁROLY FERENCZY, Ruthenian Peasant Boy, 1898

and a muse, and suggested in the background is a faun in hiding. Foliage grows out of the picture and continues on the frame. Mystery and sensuality pervade the scene, and recall Golden Age representations of the Renaissance and mannerism.

Vaszary came from Kaposvár, as did Rippl-Rónai. In Budapest, he was the pupil of Bertalan Székely, a great master of academic historicism; later he studied in Munich and in Paris. His pictures reflect an eclectic style, which draws on the academic tradition, French art nouveau and its German counterpart Jugendstil, and the new picturesque qualities. Vaszary's brilliant painting, *Salome* (about 1919), portrays a familiar theme of the period enhanced with the forms of baroque composition: the biblical heroine looks provocative in the nude, and the head of John the Baptist lies at her feet as a red, black, and yellow patch of color. Vaszary often visited Italy, a favorite land of nineteenth century painters, where he painted *The Ancient Theater in Taormina* (about 1920) in powerful, bright colors. Like Csontváry, he sought to capture the momentary play of light over the ancient ruins.

The most astonishing pieces of Vaszary's *oeuvre* were executed during World War I. Initially, he drew the colorful crowds in large India ink pictures with some yellow, red and blue patches of watercolor. Later, at the front, he painted images of the burning houses, the flaming sky, and the refugess in both watercolor and oil.

Like Rippl-Rónai and other artists of art nouveau, Vaszary was not only a painter, but a designer of glass windows, as well as of embroideries, carpets, and tapestries, which he had made by the weaving workshop of the Hungarian Ruskin circle at the Gödöllő art colony. He also joined several groups of painters, including MIÉNK (Magyar Impresszionisták és Naturalisták Köre). He was respected by the Activists, and his drawings from World War I were published in *Ma*.

Most of the Hungarian artists did not follow the new European tendencies, but preferred a more provincial and heavy-handed art. This trend too had its masters, who deserve mention in a historical survey such as this. József Koszta (1861-1949), for example, represents nineteenth century realist tradition combined with heavy forms, deep, fiery colors, and a somewhat impressionistic handling of hue. He was born in Brassó (now Braşov,

Romania), and studied in Budapest and in Munich. He also worked at Nagybánya, but was not influenced by Ferenczy's elegant, bold style. Koszta's figures and spaces are sculptural. He had no predilection for the themes or forms of art nouveau, preferring to paint harvesters, haymakers, biblical scenes such as *The Adoration of the Magi* of 1906 (FIG. 3-7), the countryside, the ripening corn, and once a little peasant girl with a pot of red geraniums (1917), sitting in a chair as self-consciously as a Spanish *infanta*. His colors are wilder and more full of light than those of the nineteenth century realists, so he is often referred to as an "expressive realist." In 1925, the critic Ernő Kállai saw the importance of Koszta's work "in the glowing structure of the patches of his dark browns, violets and blues, whose hot impulsiveness melts and digests his forms."[9]

The paintings of István Nagy (1873-1937) are more stylized, "constructivist," and lyrical than those of Koszta. Like Koszta, Nagy came from Transylvania and studied in Munich. He also went to Paris but never abandoned the perspective of an Eastern European artist. Nagy wandered all over Hungary, painting landscapes and representing the people of the villages and farms with simple nobility in their everyday surroundings, as in *Peasant Girl with Milk Jug* of 1920 (FIG. 3-8).

During World War I, István Nagy was also at the front, where he made a series of soldiers' portraits in charcoal and pastel, remarkable for their plasticity of forms and soft colors. These portraits, although traditionally conceived, are fine examples of the independent handling of "constructive" realism.

GÖDÖLLŐ ART COLONY At the beginning of the twentieth century, most Hungarian painters only observed and described the world. But those who looked into the future wished to restructure life in its entirety. These were the first true modernists, and they also declared their program in written form. During its golden age (1903-20), Gödöllő had 16 members and engaged in activities similar to those of the English arts and crafts movement; the Pre-Raphaelite brotherhood; and the Swedish, Finnish, and Russian art colonies of the late 1800s. In the late romantic spirit of the unification of the arts, Gödöllő artists wove carpets; made paintings,

Fig. 3-7 JÓZSEF KOSZTA,
Adoration of the Magi, 1906–1907, Hungarian National Gallery, Budapest.

Fig. 3-8 ISTVÁN NAGY, *Peasant Girl with a Milk Jug*, c. 1920, Hungarian National Gallery, Budapest.

90. ALADÁR KÖRÖSFŐI KRIESCH, Ego sum via, veritas et vita, 1903

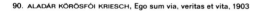

Fig. 3-9 ALADÁR KÖRÖSFŐI KRIESCH, *The Fountain of Art*, 1907, Budapest Music Academy.

sculptures, and prints; worked with leather; created embroidery; and so on.

The work and way of life of these artists were deeply influenced by the ideas and works of John Ruskin, William Morris, Leo Tolstoy, and Eugen Heinrich Schmidt. Through their art, Gödöllő members sought to express a new harmony in society. They found inspiration from the Middle Ages in Ruskin's *Stones of Venice*, published in several volumes in Budapest between 1896 and 1898.

The most important members of Gödöllő were Aladár Körösfői Kriesch and Sándor Nagy, both of whom, like their English predecessors, spent much time in Italy studying the work of medieval and Renaissance masters. In 1904 in Budapest, Körösfői Kriesch expounded (and later published) his ideas, denouncing "l'art pour l'art" and maintaining that a work of art should achieve organic harmony in its physical appearance, colors, lines and forms, and in so doing reveal the essence of the world.[1]

Although they hoped to foster social emancipation, the artists of Gödöllő cannot be called radical social reformers. They did not intend a radical break with nineteenth century culture, but rejected historicist-academic conventions. They were influenced by the impressionist and neo-impressionist handling of color, light, and form, but such pictorial considerations were never in the forefront of their interest.

The members of the Gödöllő art colony tried to realize this program in a variety of genres and means. Like their ideological predecessors they paid close attention to the selection of materials and techniques, they produced their own paints, and organized the life of their small community from the meals to literary readings, both considered forms of spiritual sustenance. Their relation to nature was close and humble. The ateliers and workshops were surrounded by gardens, which the artists cultivated with pleasure; and frequent subjects of their paintings and drawings are gardens of lush beauty, ethereal green lakes, nudes, and mythological and biblical figures.

Another favorite theme was the relationship of the artists themselves with their beloveds. Both Körösfői Kriesch and Sándor Nagy painted themselves several times with their wives, interpreting marriage as a mystical union. Nagy's painting *Holy Expectation* (1904), for example, represents the painter and his wife in their room, with the shape of the coming baby visible in a corner of heaven behind the window.

The painters of Gödöllő were also in close contact with Hungarian literary symbolism and the

Fig. 3-10 SÁNDOR NAGY, *Hungarian Folk Ballads*, 1913. Design for stained glass windows, Palace of Culture, Marosvásárhely (now Tirgu Mureş, Romania).

folk art of the countryside. They illustrated the volumes of the symbolist poets and, like their great contemporary Endre Ady, held a mythological interpretation of history. They painted the life of the ancient Magyar tribes and the medieval knightly past in a combination of historicist, Pre-Raphaelite, and art nouveau styles, which can be seen in such works as Korösfoi Kriesch's *Ego sum Via, Veritas, et Vita* of 1903. In the manner of composers Bartók and Kodály, Gödöllő artists regularly collected ballads and folk tales handed down by word of mouth in the countryside, preserving and elaborating on their canvases and in their sketchbooks the ancient forms of Hungarian folk art found in Transylvanian and Hungarian villages where tradition was still very much alive.

In 1909 the Gödöllő colony made its first major appearance in Budapest in a collective exhibition. By this time, the artists had gained a reputation for their decorative work on buildings. The Viennese-style secessionist building of the academy of music in Budapest, completed in 1907, has a beautiful fresco by Körösfői Kriesch, *The Fountain of Art* (1907), in the main lobby (FIG. 3-9). Körösfői Kriesch also designed the mosaic for the facade of the palace of culture in Marosvásárhely (now Tîrgu Mureş, Romania), finished in 1913, and Sándor Nagy designed one row of its large stained glass windows portraying Transylvanian folk ballads (FIG. 3-10).[11] This complex of public buildings is the major accomplishment of the Gödöllő colony. Later they worked on the permanent Hungarian pavilion of the Venice Biennale and accepted commissions from abroad; for instance, they shipped upholstery to the United States, and even wove a tapestry for the White House.[12]

LAJOS GULÁCSY, A HUNGARIAN SYMBOLIST An individual follower of the Pre-Raphaelites in Hungary at this time was Lajos Gulácsy (1882-1932), who had a talent for both literature and the fine arts. He studied in Budapest, spent several years in Italy from 1902 until the outbreak of World War I, and visited Paris in 1906.

In Italy, Gulácsy studied all the old masters such as Fra Filippo Lippi, Fra Angelico, Masaccio, and Botticelli; above all, he admired Leonardo da Vinci. In many drawings and paintings, Gulácsy represents the great heroes and heroines of the Italian past: *Dante and Beatrice* (1903-10) and *Paolo and Francesca*, the unhappy couple from the *Divine Comedy*. He copied one of Botticelli's figures for his painting *Prayer*. He also studied the art of Burne-Jones, Puvis de Chavannes, Böcklin, Monet, and Segantini. These deep intellectual studies were the first steps in developing his own style.

Gulácsy believed in the world harmony of the *fin-de-siècle*, but he also perceived the great dissonances. His pictures are stylized; the literary figures of his paintings and drawings seem to be on stage. He also worked in the theater, designing stage sets and painting scenery. Gulácsy's figures are in costume: they are monks, knights, ladies-in-waiting, and Don Juans. Some of his works depict scenes from a magic fairyland. And like Oscar Wilde or Hans Christian Andersen, Gulácsy wrote tales about his imagined realm. What he wrote about the works of one of his fictional heroes is also true for his own drawings and paintings:

Reminiscences, tunes, visions, memories, vibrations which are at times far removed from verisimilitude gain life through their purity, then are transformed into the most profound sensuality, floating freely in the abstract sphere of spacelessness only to be plunged into the voluptuous warmth of the senses, where a satiric scream and giggle from overfed lips come to meet it.[13]

Fig. 3-11 LAJOS GULÁCSY, *The Opium-Smoker's Dream*, 1913–1918, Janus Pannonius Museum, Pécs.

Fig. 3-12 LAJOS TIHANYI, *Gypsy Woman with her Child*, 1908, Janus Pannonius Museum, Pécs.

Gulácsy was in Italy at the outbreak of World War I. He suffered deeply from the tension of war and knew that an epoch had ended. He felt nervous anxiety, suffered from hallucinations, and spent months in a Venetian neurological clinic. When he was discharged, a confused and fragmented world appeared in his drawings and paintings. He cut one of his large canvases (*Rococo Concerto*, 1913-18) into pieces, one of which contains a lady listening to music. He set this figure in a damp reedy environment where poppies and toadstools grow side by side as symbols of a strange giddiness. At the lady's head, black men with white-powdered faces are blowing soap bubbles, a ship is sailing out over the sea in the background, and in the foreground, a freak emerges from the foam. In Gulácsy's painting, the motifs are layered on each other in the futurist manner, but they are less aggressive. The title of the painting, *The Opium-Smoker's Dream*, refers to a poem by Gulácsy's friend, the symbolist Gyula Juhász (FIG. 3-11).

Gulácsy was not an avant-garde artist, but he was in close contact with the Activists, then the most radical group of artists and writers in Hungary. He designed the title page for *The Lambs of God* (1916), a volume of plays by Lajos Kassák, and exhibited with the Activists in 1918. Around 1920, however, his mind lost its last hold on reality, and he spent his remaining years in a mental hospital.

Equilibrium of form and color: the eight

The programs and declarations of another group of artists, first known as The Seekers and later as The Eight, brought a new radicalism to Hungarian art. "The ways have parted!" declared the young György Lukács as he opened his lecture on The Eight in the democratic Galilei Circle in 1910. Instead of representing momentary sensations, ephemeral experiences, lights, colors, moods, Lukács observed, this group of artists analyzed the objective relationship between objects and space. "The new art is architectonic," stressed Lukács, and so opened a new way for painting:

...its colors, words, and lines are merely expressions of the essence, order and harmony of things, their emphasis and their equilibrium...and every line and every mark, as in architecture, is only beautiful and of value in so far as it expresses this: The equilibrium of stresses and forces that constitute everything in the simplest, clearest, most concentrated and most substantial way.[14]

This program assigned a well-defined aim for the artists, which they regarded as not only aesthetic but ethical as well. In the 1910s, Lukács and other philosophers, art historians, and aestheticians (Béla Fogarasi, Károly Mannheim, Lajos Fülep, Frigyes Antal, and Károly Tolnay) who formed the Sunday Circle ranged in their studies from Kant's theory of the categorical imperative to Fichte's theory of action. They were convinced that only those thinkers who immersed themselves in ethics could work out a viable historico-philosophical doctrine capable of reshaping the future. Although its members were not deeply involved with philosophy, The Eight revolted against social and cultural convention and created symbolic compositions for an imagined new, utopian society. For them this new society meant a republican, democratic Hungary and a Central Europe that had shed its feudal bonds and

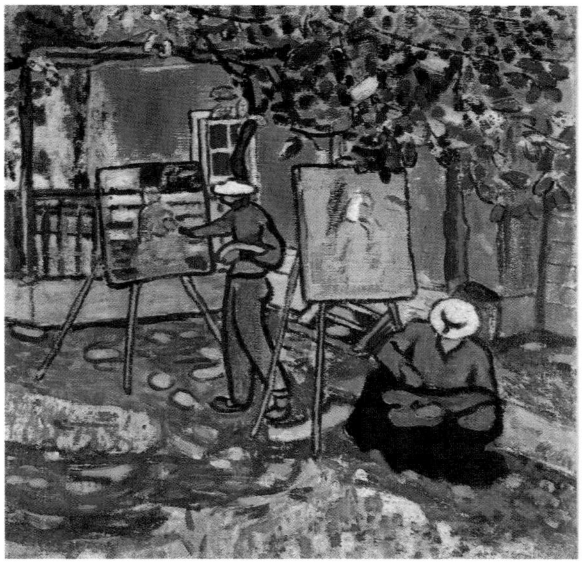

30. BÉLA CZÓBEL, Painter in the Open Air, 1906

resolved its national conflicts. (*See Chapter 2.*)

These concepts were extremely idealistic in the pre-war period, when conservative semi-feudal political powers still ruled in Hungary. Nevertheless, The Eight believed in the political mission of art. In 1912 Károly Kernstok (1873-1940), the leading artist of the group, writing in the sociological review *Huszadik Század* [Twentieth Century] noted that

...in the future, when the artist, through the creative power of his aesthetic values, will satisfy the needs of the spirit freed from burdens without any intermediary, he will be the priest of these aesthetics, which will replace dogmatic morals....[15]

This vision was related to the call of *Die Brücke*, written some time before in Dresden, by leading members of the German Expressionist movement. In drawing and painting, however, the style of The Eight lay closer to the fauves. The individual painters established this style earlier than the group itself. One of The Eight, Béla Czóbel (1883-1975), was a member of the fauves, while the others also looked to Paris more than to any other place for guidance. (After 1905, the young painters of the Nagybánya colony were also influenced by fauvism.) The Eight were followers of Gauguin, Cézanne, and Matisse, and had a special sense for rough form and wild color. Only two of them, Robert Berény (1887-1953) and Lajos Tihanyi (1885-1938), approached expressionism, and none became a cubist painter.

The most original artist among The Eight was Lajos Tihanyi, whose pictures show the fauvist influence, as well as an admiration for Picasso's Blue Period, especially in his choice of the poor as subjects and the use of vibrant deep blue tones. A fine example of such a work from 1908 is *Gypsy Woman with Her Child* (FIG. 3-12).

The movement of The Eight developed in Budapest, where the cultural role of the educated multinational (Hungarian, German, Jewish) middle class and that of the working class provided the

81. KÁROLY KERNSTOK, Portrait of Béla Czóbel, 1907

82. KÁROLY KERNSTOK, Rider at Dawn, 1911

Fig. 3-13 KÁROLY KERNSTOK, *Design for the Windows of Villa Schiffer*, 1911, Hungarian National Gallery, Budapest.

84. KÁROLY KERNSTOK, Storm, 1919

support and background for their activities. Budapest had been the intellectual center of the country since the middle of the nineteenth century (*see Chapter 1*). Though this role was shared with some other cities, in the capital different cultural trends coalesced and found an audience. The state supported academic art, but members of the upper class were already collecting modern art, both from home and abroad. In the National Salon and other exhibition halls, the latest trends were on display, and officials of the ministry of culture were open-eyed and receptive to contemporary art. The staff of the Budapest Museum of Fine Arts (Simon Meller, Edith Hoffmann, and others) bought the works of young artists and were present at auctions in Paris and elsewhere.[16] The paintings of The Eight were also exhibited in Berlin and in Vienna, and although the group did not own an independent periodical, its members—especially Károly Kernstok and Róbert Berény—wrote articles regularly for *Nyugat* [The West], *Huszadik Század* [Twentieth Century], and other journals.

At the turn of the century, Károly Kernstok painted his *Agitator* (1897), a factory worker in the canteen of a factory, in the academic style. Later he turned to *plein air* and symbolic realism coupled with religious subject matter and social consciousness. However, influenced by German and French art, especially the work of Hans von Marées and

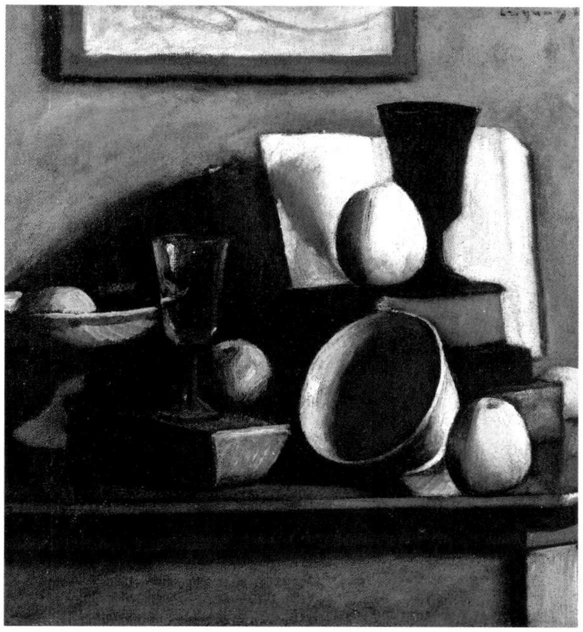

28. DEZSŐ CZIGÁNY, Still Life with Apples and Dishes, 1910

Henri Matisse, in 1908 he created what for him proved to be a new modernism: harsh rough forms, contrasts of color, and an unconventional, irreverent iconography. This style found an outlet in the designs for glass windows for the Villa Schiffer (FIG. 3-13). The most frequent theme of the age from Paris to Moscow was the nude figure in open air; another, in Central and Eastern Europe especially, was freely running horses. Between 1910 and 1922, Kernstok also produced a large number of ink drawings and gouaches with these themes. The canvas *Rider at Dawn* (1911) became the representative painting of the new modernism, and the theme is repeated in his 1919 painting, *Storm*.

All of The Eight achieved the most success with drawings and sketches in watercolor or gouache and were involved in the examination of plastic and stylized forms. In *Sermon on the Mount* (1911) and the allegorical composition *Longing for Pure Love* (1911), Bertalan Pór (1880-1964) realized his theme through ensembles of nude men and women (FIG. 2-4). Following the democratic and socialist revolutions of 1918, Pór designed a fresco for the new parliament; again, his symbolic work showed nude figures with horses on a shore. He also made a large poster with two nudes, *Workers of the World, Unite!* of 1919, the slogan of the international workers' movement.

Beside the nude compositions, primary thematic preoccupations of The Eight were the still life and the portrait. The more modest painters of the group composed still-life paintings in strict accord with the practices of Cézanne. Others, however, may have started out from life like Cézanne, and then tried to subordinate material and form to the principles of composition as in Dezső Czigány's *Still Life with Apples and a Plate* (1910).

The portrait paintings of The Eight are characterized by similar discipline of form. Those by Béla Czóbel, Róbert Berény, and Lajos Tihanyi are important examples of twentieth century Hungarian painting. The group's concept of portrait painting consists of intense emotion, rough characterization, and sometimes a touch of tart irony. Severity, a consciousness of vocation, resoluteness, inner conflict, and spiritual concentration are beautifully reflected by suggestive forms and vivid, dissonant colors.

118. DEZSŐ ORBÁN, Still Life

88. JÁNOS KMETTY, Woman with a Cup, 1916

132. JÁNOS SCHADL, Youth Reading, 1917

2. RÓBERT BERÉNY, Woman in Red Dress, 1908

146. LAJOS TIHANYI, Portrait of Lajos Kassák, 1918

Fig. 3-14 RÓBERT BERÉNY, *Portrait of Béla Bartók*, 1913, Collection of Péter Bartók.

Fig. 3-15 PÁL SZINYEI MERSE, color sketch for *Picnic in May*, 1872–1873, Hungarian National Gallery, Budapest.

Art critic Lajos Fülep, describing Tihanyi's 1915 portrait of him, declared: "I, the Platonic ideal of man in color and form!" and, along with the other great men of early twentieth century intellectual life, saw himself as a lovely Don Quixote.[17] Berény painted musician Leó Weiner (1911) as a veritable archaic statue, while the young Béla Bartók (1913), already famous for his study and collection of Hungarian folk songs and for his orchestral music, appears as a mythical hero, his face constructed of strips of light, his dark eyes gleaming (FIG. 3-14). This picture was included among the works of The Eight (Czóbel, Kernstok, Ödön Márffy) and other Hungarian painters (Vaszary, Béla Kádár) in 1913 at an international post-impressionist exhibition in Budapest where works of Franz Marc, Kandinsky, Robert Delaunay, and Picasso were also present.[18] This was a rare instance of coexistence between Hungarian modernism and the international avant-garde.

The Eight were introduced to international audiences in 1910, when Simon Meller arranged an exhibition of modern Hungarian painting in the halls of the Secession Building in Berlin. Works by Munkácsy, László Paál, Szinyei Merse, Ferenczy, Rippl-Rónai, members of the Gödöllő colony, and The Eight were all exhibited[19] and the exhibition was a great success. Paradoxically, it was not the works of The Eight that were considered the most modern in 1910, but Szinyei's sketches for *Picnic in May* (1872-73) (FIG. 3-15) and his *Atelier* (1873), which produced a great effect with their fauvist audacity. The German critics, even Julius Meier-Graefe, were astonished that these sketches were made back in the 1870s—and not in Paris but in Munich.[20] According to the German critics, the rest of Hungarian painting belonged to the trend of Parisianism, its development from László Paál to Bertalan Pór (of The Eight) paralleling that in French painting from the Barbizon to Cézanne. Hans Rosenhagen alone described the art of the young Hungarian masters (Czigány, Czóbel, Orbán) as being wild and primitive but concealing more thorough knowledge and skill than the works of the most modern German painters.[21] We can only guess that this hint refers to the members of Die Brücke, who held scandalous exhibitions at this time in Berlin and beside whom The Eight seemed classicist and academic.

MIHÁLY BIRÓ, MASTER OF HUNGARIAN POSTER DESIGN Mihály Biró (1886-1948), the greatest Hungarian poster designer, worked at the same time as The Eight, but never belonged to any group. Biró, who was born in Budapest, studied art in France, Belgium, and England. In London he won The Studio's poster competition. After his return to Budapest in 1910, he designed posters exclusively. From 1911 he was a member of the Social Democratic party, for which he created a number of

XLI. évfolyam. Budapest, 1913 január 1, szerda. 1. szám.
NÉPSZAVA
AZ ELŐFIZETÉS ÁRA:
EGYES SZÁM ÁRA 8 FILLÉR.
SZERKESZTŐSÉG: VIII., CONTI-UTCA 4.
(Telefon: József 3—29 és József 3—30.)
KIADÓHIVATAL: VIII., CONTI-UTCA 4. SZ.
(Telefon: József 3—31 és József 3—32.)
Itt az irás!
Seidner
Biró

8. MIHÁLY BIRÓ, The People's Voice, 1913

posters, the most famous being *Man with Hammer*, an enormous nude figure about to strike with his hammer. Another famous Biró poster represents the declaration of the Hungarian Soviet Republic at the Peace Conference of Paris in 1919: a big red fist strikes on the conference table where the repartitioning of Europe is being decided. This kind of dramatic style, a transition from art nouveau to expressionism, influenced many of Biró's contemporaries—from The Eight (Berény and Pór) to the most radical Hungarian avant-garde group, the Activists.

Hungarian Activism

EARLY YEARS: SYNTHESIS OF EXPRESSIONISM, FUTURISM, AND CUBISM In Hungary, the Activists were the first avant-garde group to follow, in part, the programs of the expressionists, cubists, and futurists. During World War I, influenced by the ideas of the Berlin periodicals *Der Sturm* and *Die Aktion*, the Activists took a stand against war and in support of internationalism and the potency of politics and art. They rejected the futurist cult of war, but accepted the trust in the accelerated world of machines and the concept of social dynamism. Activism was not a style: it was as much a literary, artistic, and political movement as the socialist, anarchist, and communist movements. (*See Chapter 2.*)

The Activists followed first of all expressionist methods; they worked with rough, provocative adjectives, infinitives, and superlatives on the one hand, and strong, lively colors and raw forms on the other. When some of the Activists decided to follow the cubist approach to spatial dimensions, they coupled it with expressive colors and futurist dynamism. The initial phase in their activity, between 1915 and 1919, may therefore be called cubo-expressionist or cubo-futurist.

60. SÁNDOR GALIMBERTI, Amsterdam, 1914

37. VALÉRIA DÉNES, The Street, 1913

VALÉRIA DÉNES AND SÁNDOR GALIMBERTI The true synthesis of these trends was best achieved in the works of Valéria Dénes (1877-1915) and Sándor Galimberti (1883-1915). Valéria Dénes had been a pupil of Henri Matisse, and both she and her husband had worked in Nagybánya. Valéria Dénes, who painted fauvist still lifes, cubist nudes, and townscapes, produced her masterpiece of cubist composition, *The Street*, in 1913. With its tondo forms it follows Picasso and Braque, but its greens and browns represent a special fauve-cubist interpretation of the landscape. Sándor Galimberti's masterpiece, *Amsterdam* (1914), depicts the town bursting with energy. It is most akin, perhaps, to Delaunay's painting of the Eiffel Tower and Léger's townscapes from the 1910s.

IMRE SZOBOTKA, ERVIN BOSSÁNYI, AND JÓZSEF CSÁKY The painters Imre Szobotka (1890-1961) and Ervin Bossányi and the sculptor József Csáky (1888-1971) were among the young artists who had spent time in Paris and worked together with the cubists. All three belonged to the circle of Albert Gleizes, Metzinger, La Fauconnier, and Robert Delaunay, and they were on friendly terms with the young Russian artists Udaltzova, Rosanova, and Popova, who were also in Paris at the time. When the war broke out, they did not return to Hungary; as a consequence they were interned by the French, marriage or the Foreign Legion offering the only means of escape. Bossányi joined the Foreign Legion, and Csáky married a French woman. Szobotka, however, remained in a workcamp in Britanny until the end of war: after his daily work at the camp was done, he painted and drew small cubistic pictures.

Szobotka was a rational, accurate composer and a sensible colorist. He painted portraits and still lifes in greenish, greyish, and brownish tones in accord with the principles of orthodox cubism, but the exquisite and sensual colors of the orphists—pink, light violet, purple—soon returned to his palette. His system of composition consists of colors delicately interwoven with light, and harmoniously arranged geometrical forms, as in the 1916 composition *Pipe Smokers*. Szobotka planned to join the Activist movement but by the time he returned from France its members had gone into exile.

86. JÁNOS KMETTY, View of Kecskemét, 1912

JÁNOS KMETTY The Activists did not have direct contact with cubism, which was known in Hungary mainly through written material and some short visits to Paris by artists just before the outbreak of World War I. A case in point is János Kmetty (1889-1975), who had exhibited with the group in 1918 and designed title pages for the Activist review *Ma* [Today]. Kmetty was a less eloquent cubist than Valéria Dénes, Sándor Galimberti, or Szobotka. After visiting Paris, however, he became an enthusiastic, if naive, convert to cubism. He often used a single hue in a composition: his dark blue self-portrait, the yellow cubist-orphist townscape, and *View of Kecskemét* (1912) are good examples. Kmetty followed cubism with an almost religious fervor; his *Self-Portrait* (1913), in which he drew himself with an apple in his hand, resembles a devotional picture.

141. IMRE SZOBOTKA, Pipe Smoker, c1914

87. JÁNOS KMETTY, Self Portrait, 1913

152. BÉLA UITZ, Seated Woman, 1918

BÉLA UITZ Béla Uitz (1887-1970) was the most provocative artist of early Activism. He was a pupil of Károly Ferenczy, but among his models were the great Renaissance masters (he saw Michelangelo's works in 1915 in Rome and Florence). His paintings in colored ink and charcoal drawings from the 1910s show classical influences and reflect the painter's nostalgia for the Renaissance; on the other hand, they are realistic in the spirit of Daumier. After these early works, Uitz turned to cubo-expressionism (*Seated Woman*, 1918; *Sewing Woman*, 1918; *Composition with Trees and Houses*, 1919).

Uitz represented the mourning mother with a combination of expressionist pathos, Renaissance symmetry, and baroque monumentality in *Lamentation* (1916). He painted working-class mothers (mostly modeled by his wife) after the hard, materialistic style of the portraits of Cézanne. He also painted gloomy suburban townscapes overcrowded with houses and trees with turbulent crowns. His vision was fundamentally dramatic, and the forms and figures of his paintings virtually explode with energy and dynamism. In 1919, Uitz became a devoted adherent of the Hungarian Soviet Repub-

151. BÉLA UITZ, Composition with Trees and Houses, 1918-19

153. BÉLA UITZ, Sewing Woman, 1918-19

lic, and like Mihály Biró, he designed several posters in which he subordinated expression to symmetry and balance. (*See also Chapter 2.*)

Uitz realized the cubist norms of Jacques Rivière in an individual way. Rivière, published in *Ma*, declared that the painter need not be concerned about "momentary impressions," and should arrange the shattered world of objects according to a "new hierarchy."[22] This hierarchy, however, was to be determined not by perspective but solely by the inner validity of things. This concept of inner validity resembles the expressionist idea of "inner necessity" or "inner construction." For Uitz this principle did not lead to an objectivization of the self but to the manifestation of collective consciousness.

Activism in Hungary was the art of the big towns, where life is rough and open, like the posters in the street—the signs of social conflict and political struggle. "This new painter is a moral individual, full of faith and desire for unity!" declared Lajos Kassák—poet, writer, editor, and artist—in his 1916 article "The Poster and the New Painting":

He is not much given to aesthetic musings, the nuances are never important, but only the essentials (in theme and execution), and these in the magnificence of their essence always create a lively and aggressive unity.... We desire with all our hearts that just as the poster is a magnificent complement to the modern town, the picture too should fill our room with a life outside us.[23]

JÓZSEF NEMES LAMPÉRTH A less politically minded Activist was József Nemes Lampérth (1891-1924), whose art betrayed an abiding expressive naturalism. He did not take part in the Ma group exhibitions, but he was often present on the pages of the periodical itself. He also was a pupil of Ferenczy in 1911-12. By 1913, when he lived in Paris, he had already painted his *Self-Portrait* (1911) and the monumental *Bier* (1912) of his dead father, which in their expressiveness and handling of color can be compared to the works of Schmidt-Rottluff or Nolde. His *Self-Portrait* is composed of dark blue, mauve, and white bands of paint, while in *Bier* the dead face and body and the candles are constructed of yellow, green, and violet bands.

In Paris, Nemes Lampérth was inspired by the rational spirit of the town's architecture, which further enhanced the expressive power of his works. He drew and painted the bridges of the

112. JÓZSEF NEMES LAMPÉRTH, Standing Nude (Front), 1916

113. JÓZSEF NEMES LAMPÉRTH, Turning Nude (Back), 1916

111. JÓZSEF NEMES LAMPÉRTH, Self-Portrait, 1911

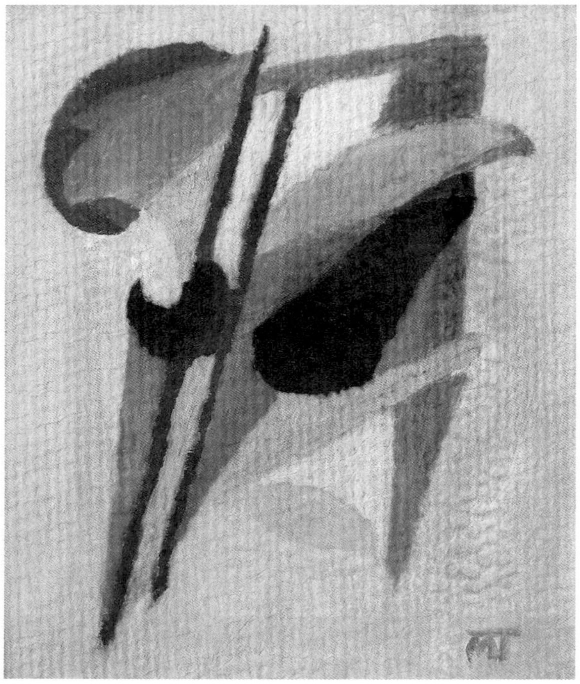

96. JÁNOS MÁTTIS TEUTSCH, Spiritual Flower, c1923

Seine in a way that the beautiful arched structures resemble human bodies, always of major importance to him. Lajos Kassák held Nemes Lampérth to be the most talented among the young artists, since his paintings were "ruled by the extreme intensity and contrast of colors."[24] Nemes Lampérth's work was devoted to the richness of the material world, and he never turned toward abstract painting.

JÁNOS MÁTTIS TEUTSCH The other great colorist of the Activist group, János Máttis Teutsch (1884-1960), could soar more easily in the direction of the abstract. He first studied sculpture at Munich early in the century, but among the Activists he was a painter *par excellence*. His favorite media were watercolor, pastel, and thinned oils on paper or canvas. He also made wood and linocuts, and carved statues of wood or made them of plaster,

95. JÁNOS MÁTTIS TEUTSCH, Dark Landscape with Trees, 1918

painting them with strong colors in the manner of Gauguin or the German Expressionists. Only by careful observation does one find the figural motifs in the texture of his pictures (*Lamenting Figure with Tree*, 1902; *Soldiers' Tombs at Lake Warte*, 1916): they represent the eternal cycles of the different forms of life, the birth or decline of the world of nature—of everything.

These early works display a measure of decoration suggestive of the art of József Rippl-Rónai, whose pupil Máttis Teutsch had been for a short time. German Expressionism and the works of Franz Marc and Kandinsky also influenced his aesthetics, however. The characteristic musical rhythm of his paintings is based on the repetition of organic forms and the sensitive use of color, as in *Dark Landscape with Trees* (1918). Earth and sky, nature and human beings suggest the inseparable unity of matter and spirit, or time and space, wherein man's task is to obey the will of the elements in compliance with a higher order.

A meditative artist by nature, follower of Eastern philosophy and religious thought, especially Buddhism, Máttis Teutsch nevertheless could feel and represent the free and dynamic attitude of the Activists, who sometimes saw themselves as the creators of a new universe. It took the perceptive Lajos Kassák to discover and exhibit the works of the reclusive Máttis Teutsch, who usually resided in his native Brassó (now Braşov, Romania). Yet he was one of the first in East-Central Europe to become a follower of Kandinsky's influential form of abstraction. In 1918, Máttis Teutsch became the first Activist to have his art published in *Der Sturm*, in whose exhibitions he participated from 1921.[25]

92. JÁNOS MÁTTIS TEUTSCH, Still Life, c1914

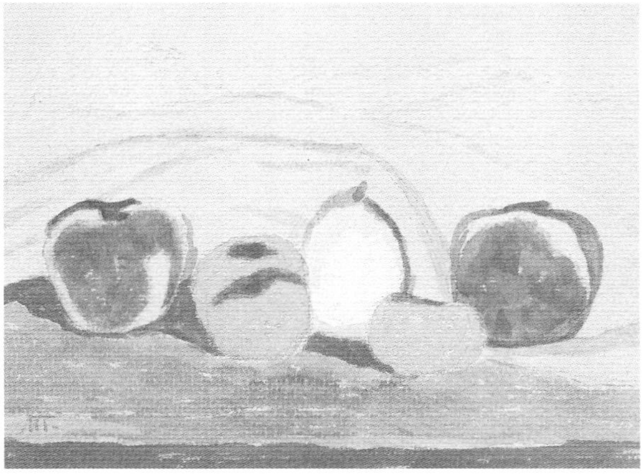

134. JÁNOS SCHADL, Village, n.d.

JÁNOS SCHADL A more dramatic expressionist among the Ma Activists was painter János Schadl (1892-1944). He also had been a pupil of Ferenczy, and studied music in conjunction with art. His drawings and canvases are full of ecstatic religious feeling; their dark blue, black, and gold colors are expressive of solemn meditation on the Gospels and the lives of heroic saints (*St. Sebastian*, 1920; *Carrying the Cross*, 1922; *Golgotha*, 1922). His townscapes,

133. JÁNOS SCHADL, Houses and Aurél Bernáth, 1919

such as *View of a Village* and *Houses and Aurél Bernáth*, display the influence of the Activists. In the 1920s, Schadl lived in Tata, a small town in western Hungary, where he continued to paint cosmic landscapes and symbolical pictures, which are similar to the works of Wilhelm Morgner, Moritz Melzer, Karl Schmidt-Rottluff, and other German Expressionists.

SÁNDOR BORTNYIK AND LÁSZLÓ MOHOLY-NAGY

The productive careers of both Bortnyik and Moholy-Nagy spanned the early development of Hungarian Activism and the innovations that came later. Both artists are considered at length in the section on Bildarchitektur and constructivism. The great contribution of Moholy-Nagy to Hungarian modernism lies in his dynamic constructive art, and by 1918, the contructivism of Bortnyik foreshadowed the challenges of the second phase of the Hungarian Activism, from 1920 to 1926, which took place largely in cities outside Hungary and concentrated on creating an international art.

21. SÁNDOR BORTNYIK, Still Life with Jug, 1923

Revolutions and Artists in Exile, 1918-1925

In 1918, at the end of a lost war, the Austro-Hungarian monarchy was dissolved, and Austria and Hungary were ravaged by revolution.[26] A democratic Hungarian republic existed for a few short euphoric months, followed by the establishment of the Hungarian Soviet Republic, one major achievement of which was in the arts. Private art collections were nationalized and shown to the public for the first time. Schools of fine arts were established for the lower classes with Activists Uitz and Nemes Lampérth among the faculty. Art was given a political, demonstrative function, which gave rise to a new genre: the poster as conceived by Biró, The Eight, and the Activists. (*See also Chapters 1 and 2.*)

Financial support for the artists was also organized: The starving Csontváry received aid, and the Budapest Museum of Fine Arts bought paintings and drawings from Lajos Gulácsy, Béla Uitz, Bertalan Pór, József Nemes Lampérth, and the young László Moholy-Nagy. At the same time, the government met resistance on the part of Activists who refused to be directly controlled by any political party. Nevertheless, the intelligentsia became deeply involved in government activities, and after the republic fell in August 1919, over three-quarters of the Hungarian intellectuals and artists emigrated.

The concepts of constructivism and internationalism were present at the very inception of the Activist movement. Constructivism was expressed in poems and in the modern typography on the pages of *Ma* and other publications, and internationalism prompted manifestoes and proposals for common actions with the European avant-garde. Despite their isolation during the war, the Activists believed in the common tasks of the different cultural and spiritual centers of Europe, in a modern international culture and the elimination of social conflict and conservative political thinking. The Activists followed the new poetry and art of Paris, Berlin, Moscow, London, and Rome; they knew and published the writings and art of neighboring countries, as well, especially Czech Cubism and Serbo-Croatian Expressionism (*see Chapter 5*). Furthermore, since they considered Walt Whitman an early prophet of their own aims, they also were open to the contributions of American art, life, and poetry.

143. JÁNOS TÁBOR, Red Soldiers, Forward!, 1919

89. JÁNOS KMETTY, Concert, 1918

50. JÓZSEF EGRY, Red Truth, 1919

38. GYULA DERKOVITS, Self-Portrait, 1921

Vienna and Berlin became centers of Hungarian emigration, with support from neighboring cultural centers with Hungarian populations: Kassa (now Košice, Czechoslovakia), Pozsony (Bratislava, Czechoslovakia), Kolozsvár (Cluj, Romania), Nagyvárad (Oradea, Romania), Arad (Romania), and Újvidék (Novi Sad, Yugoslavia). The artists and their public disregarded the national borders and offered new alternatives: the communist left wing fought for a world revolution and the anarchists for a spiritual revolution, while the center dreamed of a Danubian federation, a United States of Central Europe. Such programs were intimately connected to the progressive art tendencies of the 1920s and 1930s.

Transformation of the Expressionist Tradition

The intellectual horizons of Hungarian artists who remained in Hungary were more limited than those of the émigrés now living and working in the Weimar Republic, Austria, France, and elsewhere. They were isolated from the newest trends and were forced to organize exhibitions in small private galleries, away from the attention of officialdom. Some joined avant-garde theaters, but most led lives of seclusion. Yet expressionism survived until 1930, and some cubistic pictorial construction was evident in the paintings of former Activists and cubists who remained in Hungary such as Kmetty and Szobotka.

JÓZSEF EGRY The man perhaps most responsible for continuing the tradition of expressionism between the two world wars is József Egry (1883-1951), who came from a poor peasant family and was destined to be a worker. With the help of some art lovers, however, Egry was able to visit Paris and Belgium for a time, there to study the paintings in the museums and contemporary galleries. He admired Rembrandt, Van Gogh, Toulouse-Lautrec, Meunier, and above all, the Swiss graphic artist Théophile Steinlen. This influence is apparent in the greyish-brown drawings and paintings of laborers and the old furnishings of squalid rooms, which he executed in the 1910s.

While at a military hospital near Lake Balaton, where he was sent in 1916, Egry was profoundly affected by the trancendent meaning and pictorial qualities of light, new insights that are immediately reflected in his style. Formerly a symbolic element in his paintings, drawings, and watercolors, the richness of light now is depicted for its own sake. A good example of his symbolic use of light is his *Red Truth* (1919), where Christ appears as the new Messiah, an agitator standing among unconvinced peasants with his arms spread and the red sun behind him.

Egry presented many conflicts of the period, and like his *Cain and Abel*, which he painted three times between 1919 and 1926, they contrast sharply with the contemporary idyllic representations of socialist utopias. In the 1926 version, the theme is depicted on the shores of Lake Balaton where Egry built up a personal mythology. At the moment of the fratricide, a storm uproots a tree, threatening clouds fill the sky, and furious waves rise from the surface of the lake.

Expressionist impulsiveness and post-impressionist dynamics of light and color are hallmarks of Egry's painting. His religious peasant upbringing and pantheistic adoration of nature ensured his early artistic affinity with Franz Marc, Eric Heckel, and Lyonel Feininger. In the 1930s and 1940s, however, his subtle, almost white paintings — such as *St. John the Baptist* (1930) with its finely conceived structure and transcendental light — were among the best and most individualistic examples of post-Cézanne figural "constructive" painting in Central Europe.

GYULA DERKOVITS The other great solitary figure of interwar expressionism was Gyula Derkovits (1894-1934). Although he visited the editorial offices of *Ma*, he never joined the Activists. He studied drawing in a school in Budapest, where Kernstok and József Rippl-Rónai improved his work. At first he painted watercolors and oils with symbolic nude compositions. He was interested in cubism, which he learned from Kmetty and Szobotka, and became an expressionist. For a proletarian artist deeply involved with the philosophy of Marxism, expressionism seemed to be the most appropriate idiom for conveying the tragedies of the postwar, post-revolution era.

In 1923, Derkovits moved to Vienna, where he lived for three years. There he could be near Uitz, who was his true predecessor. At this time, his depictions of everyday life were always symbolic

44. GYULA DERKOVITS, Clash of Armies [VI]

45. GYULA DERKOVITS, Verböczy! Verböczy! [X]

42. GYULA DERKOVITS, Encounter - The Itinerant Fire-Eater, 1927

40. GYULA DERKOVITS, Last Supper, 1922

and often ironic. For instance, he painted his tubercular brother and vigorous sister-in-law together under a big tree in a suburban yard, and titled the picture *Life and Death* (1923). In *Encounter* (1927), he depicted traveling fire-eaters begging in a courtyard.

After returning home in 1927, Derkovits painted the working class figures and surroundings of Budapest in pious silvery, gold, and lyric pinkish-red tones, and the members of the ruling classes with unveiled satire. In one of these political still lifes (*Winter Window*, 1929), bayonets appear beyond a frosty window pane, while on the windowsill a piece of bread peeps out from its paper wrapping, the food of the lodger of the cold and bare room. This work, painted in the year of the Great Depression, resembles the grotesque lyricism of George Grosz and Otto Dix.

From 1929 until his early death in 1934, Derkovits was a master of social expressionism. He was not influenced by the false pathos and pseudo-monumentality of proletarian romanticism that characterized Soviet-Russian "official" painting. His paintings nevertheless evoke the warmth of Käthe Kollwitz's graphic works. An outstanding example of his graphic activity, the woodcut series *1514* depicts the Hungarian peasant uprising of that year with an eye on the white terror of 1920. The artist thus raised the struggles, suppression, and sufferings of sixteenth century Hungarian peasants into the realm of apocalyptic visions. These woodcuts are the best Hungarian equivalents of the German Expressionist graphic style created by Kollwitz and the Die Brücke artists. Yet Derkovits had never been to Germany. He did have two exhibitions in Vienna—at the Hagenbund in 1924 and at the

Weihburg gallery in 1925. In spite of the high regard of contemporary Austrian and Hungarian emigrant critics, he never attained a following outside Hungary.

HUGÓ SCHEIBER In the 1920s, the painters Hugó Scheiber (1873-1950) and Béla Kádár, who like Derkovits lived mostly in Budapest, joined the circle of Der Sturm. Both came from the periphery of society. Scheiber's father was a signboard painter in Vienna's Prater city park, and Scheiber worked with him from early childhood. After his father's death, Scheiber became the supporter of a large family of his own in Budapest. He attended an industrial drawing school in Budapest, but soon came under the influence of cubism and expressionism. In 1919 he had his first joint exhibition with Béla Kádár in Ludwig Hevesy's gallery in Vienna, and the Budapest Museum of Fine Arts subsequently bought some of their works.

In 1921, Scheiber met Herwarth Walden, editor of *Der Sturm*, who liked the artist's highly individual cubo-expressionist-futurist manner. A favorite theme of Scheiber's was the people—suburban proletariat rushing off to the factories, prostitutes, musicians, bar dancers, circus carousels, and acrobats. He drew and painted his subjects in cool India ink, gouache, oil, and pastel, and sometimes in gold and silver. He also depicted the cruelty of interwar Europe. Social conflicts and political excesses were increasing everywhere, and behind the jarring exoticism of the Jazz Years and the laughter of the cabarets and circuses loomed the forbidding shadow of the next world war.

Scheiber was also a notable portrait painter blessed with comic insight, as can be seen in his portrait of Lajos Kassák in which he renders the avant-garde impresario in the dynamic styles which Kassák himself advocated. His work appeared in many exhibitions, including several at Der Sturm in Berlin, and others in London, New York (at the exhibition of the Société Anonyme in 1927), and Rome. In 1933, at the invitation of Marinetti, Scheiber went to Rome to participate in a futurist meeting, but there he found an already degenerate movement and he soon returned to Hungary. In the 1930s and 1940s, he sank into poverty, selling his works for next to nothing. He was greatly depressed, first by fascist expansion, and after World War II by the incursion of Stalinism into Hungary. He died in Budapest in 1950.

136. HUGÓ SCHEIBER, Portrait of Lajos Kassák, c1930

138. HUGÓ SCHEIBER, Theater Interior, c1930

68. BÉLA KÁDÁR, Constructivist Composition (Theater Piece), c1928

BÉLA KÁDÁR The expressionism of Béla Kádár (1877-1956) was much less incisive than Scheiber's. In the late 1910s he painted neo-impressionist nude and horse compositions similar to those of Károly Kernstok and Bertalan Pór. In his later association with the Der Sturm circle, however, his colors turned clear and translucent, and he created lyrical narratives like those of Campendonk or Maria Uhden. In fact, Kádár was Herwarth Walden's favorite artist. In Kádár's watercolors and oil paintings, the wooden horses, peasant carts, peasant madonnas, dogs with almost human souls, cows tramping around in the world, flowers blooming in cheap jars, low-roofed houses, and village churches are all represented in a unique blend of the naive and the expressionist. A fine example is *Village Departure* (about 1925). His favorite colors at this time were pink, yellow, and light blue.

Kádár also moved the world of his canvases onto the stage. In the 1920s he designed sets for operas in Berlin, and for avant-garde recitals and

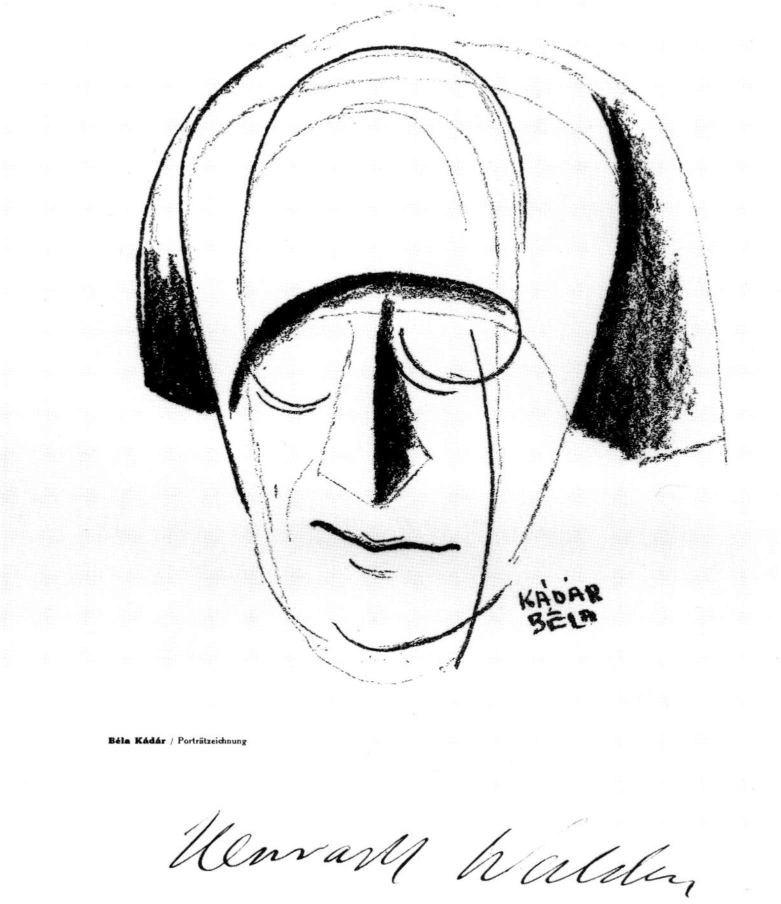

65. BÉLA KÁDÁR, Portrait of Herwarth Walden, 1924

66. BÉLA KÁDÁR, Village Departure, c1925

6. AURÉL BERNÁTH, Villages, 1920

eurhythmic performances in Budapest. Unfortunately, records of these works have survived only in sketches. In the late 1920s and 1930s, Kádár turned to art deco, a style that was born in Paris but became known and followed all over Western and Central Europe as the typical moderate modernism.

AURÉL BERNÁTH Like the young János Schadl and József Egry, Aurél Bernáth (1895-1982) was a true expressionist in his early work. His black and gold graphic series, painted and printed with patterns (1920), featured onion-domed churches, imaginary horsemen and peasants on foot, crucifixes, and crossroads cutting across vast wastelands. Elegant, mysterious, and poetic, these prints were near relatives of the paintings and graphic works of Vassily Kandinsky.

In the early 1920s, a powerful blue appeared on Bernáth's palette and dominated his paintings until 1927. In its symbolic character it was akin to the blue mysticism of *Der Blaue Reiter* [the Blue Riders] (the unofficial but closely knit group of painters that had rallied around Kandinsky in Berlin), to Vrubel's demons, and to the Russian Blue

7. AURÉL BERNÁTH, Tumble and Cry, 1922

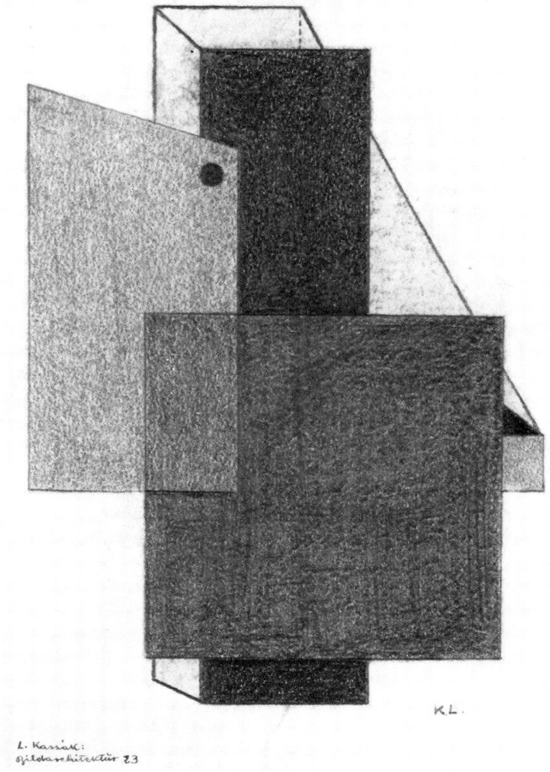

73. LAJOS KASSÁK, Bildarchitektur, 1923

Rose group, founded in Moscow in 1905. This blue appears as the shades of the lake and sky in Bernáth's *Lake Starnberg* (1924) and other landscapes such as *The Charles Bridge in Prague* (1925), *Genoa Harbor* (1926), and *Riviera* (1926-27), imbuing each scene with metaphysical implications. His lost masterpiece *Living Space* (1924), which represented a rocky, moonlike landscape, probably also was composed in shades of dark blue. Its crystalline structure is wonderful even in the available black-and-white reproduction.[27] After 1929, Bernáth consciously broke with the avant-garde, whose importance he had begun to question; for decades, he was a talented but enervated master of post-impressionism.

Bildarchitektur and Constructivism

The Hungarian Activists who lived and worked in Vienna, Berlin, Weimar, Dessau, and even Moscow had a greater opportunity to cultivate avant-garde ideas and art forms than did the artists who remained in Hungary. The anthology *Buch neuer Künstler* [Book of New Artists], compiled and published by Lajos Kassák and László Moholy-Nagy in 1922, included expressionism (Kandinsky, Chagall, and Aurél Bernáth). However, the editors made clear their view that the most important modern development was that leading from cubism to constructivism. In Vienna between 1920 and 1926, Kassák published in *Ma* the mechanistic and organic branches of dada (Kurt Schwitters, Francis Picabia, and Hans Arp), as well as the masters of international constructivism (for example, Tatlin, Gabo, Mondrian, and Moholy-Nagy). In 1921, Béla Uitz, who had been visiting Moscow, published the manifestoes of the constructivists and productivists in Vienna in his new magazine, *Egység* [Unity]. Uitz also published articles on Russian suprematism, urged the organization of Hungarian prolétkult groups, and espoused orthodox Marxism[28] (*see also Chapters 2 and 4*).

In 1923, *Egység* published a manifesto of the Hungarian constructivists, which was signed by the theorist critics Ernő Kállai and Alfréd Kemény, and by László Moholy-Nagy and László Péri.[29] Prior to this declaration, Kállai had written several essays concerning constructivism for *Ma* and other papers, and Moholy-Nagy and Kemény had published their "Dynamic-Constructive Force System" in *Der Sturm* in 1922.[30] All the declarations stressed the social

69. LAJOS KASSÁK, Noise, 1920

71. LAJOS KASSÁK, Bildarchitektur, 1922

and ideological role of constructivism: to create architectonic order and unity as a model for collective life in general.

LAJOS KASSÁK The Hungarian Activists were perhaps the first artists in Central Europe to understand and implement the theories of the most radical branch of the Russian avant-garde (*see Chapter 4*). Because of their enthusiasm, Ilya Ehrenburg referred to the Hungarian artists as the "romantics of constructivism."[31] The utopian perspectives of the Russian avant-garde were represented among the Activists by Lajos Kassák (1887-1967), who cited suprematism and constructivism as the art of the present and the future in his review on the First Russian Exhibition (Berlin 1922). By that time, Kassák had cut himself off from direct political involvement and stressed the importance of art in elaborating the visual patterns and spatial dimensions of a new utopian world (*see Chapter 2*).

In 1921 Kassák confessed his belief in the social task of art in his manifesto *Bildarchitektur* (architecture of the picture) in these terms:

Only the artist can be the one who particularizes and revolutionizes our emotions. The artist is one who does not command us to do anything but who makes us able to do the greatest things. Art transforms us, and we become capable of transforming our surroundings.... Bildarchitektur does not resemble anything, tells no story, has no beginning and no end anywhere.... It is like unwalled cities, an ocean that can be traversed by ships, a rambling wood or the creation that is closest to it—the Bible.[32]

In his theory of Bildarchitektur, Kassák thus broke with the tradition of mimetic art, and he even renounced the use of color in his 1921 manifesto, illustrating his text with black and white ink drawings and woodcuts. Six months later, however, he returned to the use of color, especially red, yellow, blue, gold, and silver, and his paintings and collages soon became as playfully colorful as the works of Sándor Bortnyik.

Kassák's reference to the art of Bortnyik as "Bildarchitektur" was the first use of that term in the history of the movement. At this time, Hungarian constructivism was moving toward the worlds of architecture, industrial design, and the theater. The works of Kassák, Bortnyik, and the Hungarian members of the Bauhaus illustrate this tendency well. Of these artists, Kassák was perhaps the most reserved and puritanical. His Bildarchitektur is radically laconic and highly aware of its mission.

SÁNDOR BORTNYIK The purest synthetist among the Activists group, Sándor Bortnyik (1893-1976) approached most closely the ideals of the first ideologists of the Hungarian movement (Lajos Kassák, Iván Hevesy, and Alfréd Kemény). For a time Bortnyik studied under Rippl-Rónai and Kernstok, but instead of following in their footsteps he turned for inspiration to the cubo-expressionist painters and graphic artists of Paris and Berlin. Beginning about 1918, Bortnyik's compositions are characterized by a simple, rational addition of geometrical forms, with the contrast of cold and warm colors playing a central role in his paintings. Color is often an important element of his titles as well: *Yellow-Green Landscape* (1919), *Red Factory* (1919), and *Red Locomotive* (1918). (In the case of the last two, the symbolic use of red is also significant.) He first made sketches in ink or watercolor, and sometimes prepared linocuts from his ink drawings.

Influenced by futurism, Bortnyik also drew and painted moving vehicles and figures in motion. But whatever the subject or technique, of all the Activists, Bortnyik's achieved most closely Kassák's ideal of poster-like painting, and his works illustrated the aims of the Activists perfectly. Bortnyik's geometrical compositions are more decorative and less emblematic than Kassák's. In some of his paintings, human figures resemble mechanical constructions in the manner of Oskar Schlemmer, Andor Weininger, and Farkas Molnár, with whom he associated at Weimar in 1923-24.

14. SÁNDOR BORTNYIK, Red Factory, 1919

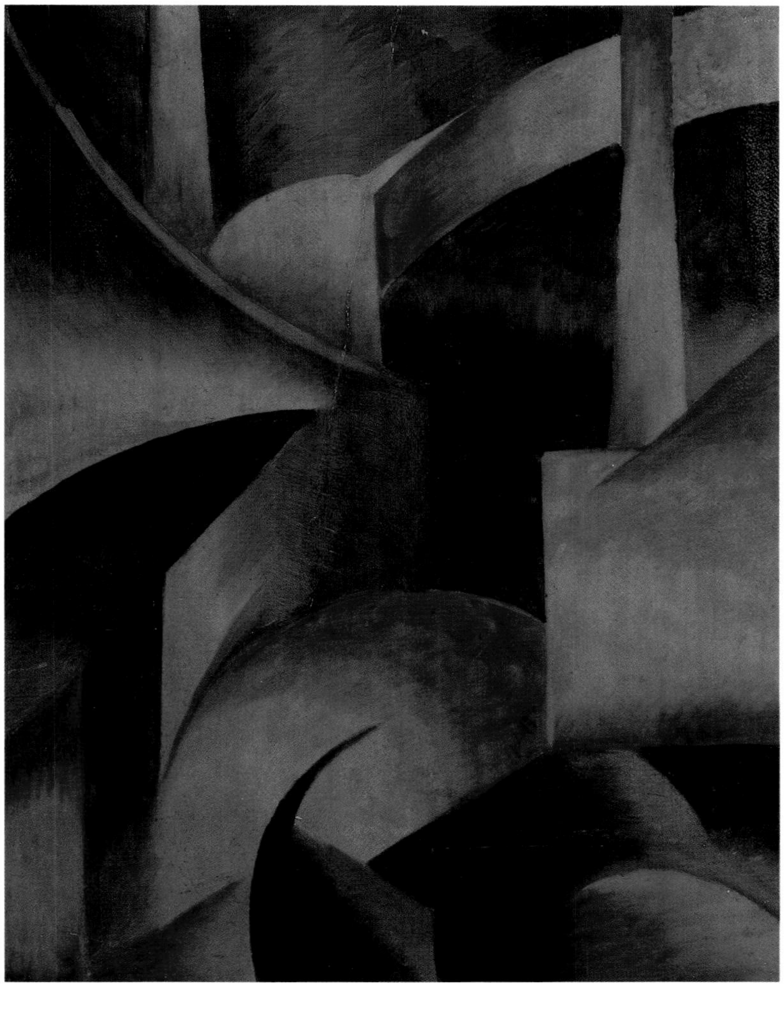

16. SÁNDOR BORTNYIK, Bildarchitektur (I), 1921

17. SÁNDOR BORTNYIK, Bildarchitektur (II), 1921

18. SÁNDOR BORTNYIK, Bildarchitektur (III), 1921

99. LÁSZLÓ MOHOLY-NAGY, Landscape - Tabán, 1919

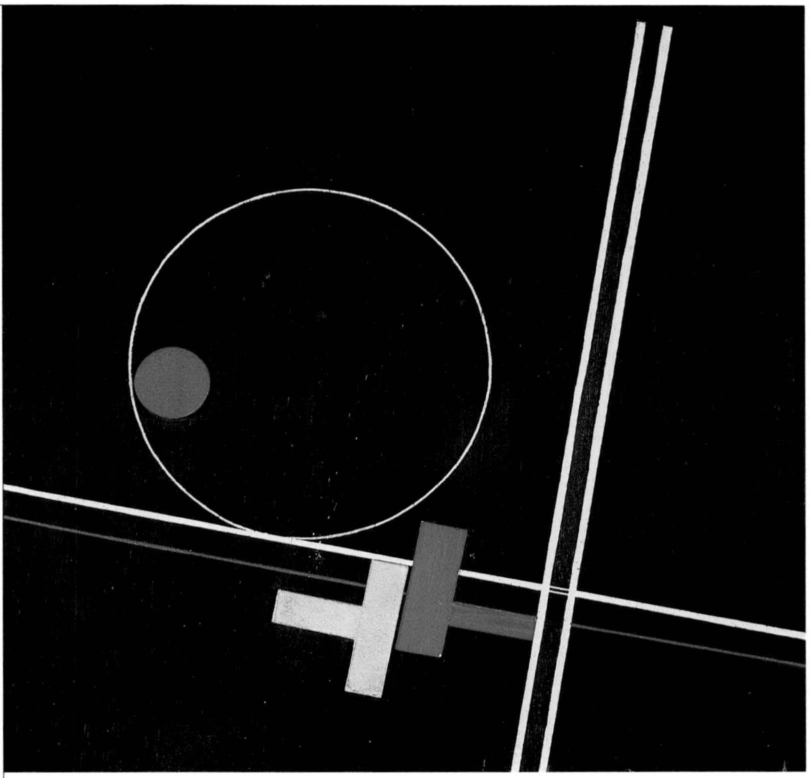

100. LÁSZLÓ MOHOLY-NAGY, Untitled Construction, 1922

LÁSZLÓ MOHOLY-NAGY László Moholy-Nagy (1895-1946) was an expressionist artist and became a member of the Activists around 1918. His early drawings and paintings show the influence of Berény, Tihanyi, and Bortnyik. His landscapes, portraits, and self-portraits show a tentative stylization and abstraction; his use of space, especially in the townscapes, is at times cubistic, in the manner of Sándor Bortnyik.

With their pure forms, clear color planes, and architectural constructions, Bortnyik and Kassák's works were the first representatives of the new visual culture. The works of László Moholy-Nagy enriched this new culture with even more devices, techniques, and dimensions. Because Moholy-Nagy lived and worked in Berlin, Weimar, and Dessau, and (after the rise of Nazism) in Amsterdam, London, and the United States, he is present in Hungarian art between the two world wars merely as a talented guest. In 1930, however, his works were exhibited with those of Bortnyik and Kassák at the International Exhibition of Poster and Book Design at the Museum of Applied Arts, Budapest. Sometimes he lectured on modern art, light, and photography at the Hungarian Music Academy, where lectures and performances of the Kassák circle were held after 1926.

The essays of Moholy-Nagy, mostly from his Bauhaus period, were published in the periodical *Korunk* [Our Era] in Kolozsvár (now Cluj, Romania), and he taught one semester at the School of Applied Arts in Pozsony (now Bratislava, Czechoslovakia). His activities were appreciated from the very first by Hungarian critics, especially Lajos Kassák and Ernő Kállai. The most important writing on the young Moholy-Nagy appeared in *Ma* in 1921 and in Kállai's book *Neue Malerei in Ungarn* [New Painting in Hungary], perhaps to this day the best survey of twentieth century Hungarian art.

In 1920-21, László Moholy-Nagy drew and painted expressionist portraits and landscapes. In some of his other works originating in these years, however, he was already breaking with all European and Hungarian traditions of art. It was in 1920 that he first transformed the shapes of semaphores, railways, and industrial architecture into highly abstract blue, yellow, and red constructions (*Great Railway Picture*, 1920-21; *Bridges*, 1921). Later he was influenced by Russian Constructivism (El Lissitzky, the 1922 Russian exhibition in Berlin), and to a lesser extent Dutch Neoplasticism (Mondrian and van Doesburg). He removed all naturalistic ele-

107. FARKAS MOLNÁR, Title Page - Italia Portfolio, 1921

ments from his pictures, and on white or light grey backgrounds he painted lines and simple geometric forms that became known as "glass architecture" (1921-22) because of their transparency. These works represented the most radical modern painting in Hungary and Central Europe at the time. In them one recognizes the youthful enthusiasm for intellectual forms. As Kállai writes:

Moholy-Nagy does not only summarize his impressions of technology and intellectual civilization, but is also its naive admirer with the barbarous, enthusiastic joy of a primitive child...and the real key to Moholy-Nagy's constructive painting is this joy of life, this always renewing, soaring activity.... That is why his forms are floating and are so finely articulated; that is the reason for the perfect transparent clearness of his colors and of his intention to make the structure of the picture less materialistic and more weightless.... Their perfectly stressed order seems to be a momentary equilibrium of parts, to be broken up any moment.... His use of ethereal lines and thinly painted colors increases the illusion of immaterial energies.[33]

There is no better description of Moholy-Nagy's "colorful" constructivism, which El Lissitzky and Arp called "abstractivism" in their *Kunstismen* [The Isms, Les Ismes], published in Zurich in 1925. His art is transparent and immaterial without Mondrian's puritanical ascetism, Malevich's transcendent non-objectivity, or Lissitzky's cosmic allusions; yet it shares their thoughts and deeds in creating a new visual world stamped by the artist's intellect and personality.

Repression and Rediscovery

Kassák and Bortnyik in Vienna, and Moholy-Nagy and other Hungarian artists working in the Bauhaus (including Farkas Molnár, Marcel Breuer, Andor Weininger, and Alfréd Forbát) broke with the traditions of mimetic art and also with the ideals of national art even more radically than did the moderns of the *fin-de-siècle* or The Eight and the first Activists. Internationalism was expressed in their paintings, graphic works, architectural plans, and designs. It was expressed in terms of clear geometrical structures free of cultural or geographical traditions, even if occasionally their compositions betray their native roots.

The problem of color was shared by all painters, whether tending toward the mimetic or the abstract, the decorative or the symbolic, from

Szinyei to Ferenczy, from Rippl-Rónai to Máttis Teutsch, from Csontváry to Egry, from Bortnyik to Moholy-Nagy. In the paintings of Mednyánszky or Gulácsy the colors are warm and sensitive; in the works of Nemes Lampérth and Uitz, they are harsh and aggressive, and in the lyrical paintings of Máttis Teutsch they are like a musical composition. Even Kassák, Bortnyik, and Moholy-Nagy used cold-warm color oppositions in their pure constructivist paintings. Red circles, yellow and red and blue squares, black lines, sometimes violet, pink, and even green, gold, and silver geometrical forms are found in the chief works of the Hungarian constructivists. Their colors are vivid and joyful, yet used in a most purposeful manner in paintings that, in spite of their small size and simple technique, compare favorably with those of the great pioneers of modern painting.

After 1932-33, several European states including Germany, the Soviet Union, and Romania, turned against the avant-garde movements. In Central and Eastern Europe, the expressionists, surrealists, and constructivists entered into opposition, unwilling to sublimate their art to the dictates of the state, as happened with futurism in Mussolini's Italy. Liberalism was supplanted by conservatism and tolerance was not a characteristic of the cultural policymakers. The activity of the avant-garde artists during the 1930s became a kind of inner emigration.

Kassák returned from Vienna and published the periodicals *Dokumentum* [Document] and *Munka* [Work] between 1926 and 1938. He consciously nurtured his wider international horizons and educated a new generation for what he called "reserve Activism." The chief painters of his new circle (Hegedűs, Trauner, Kepes, Korniss, and Vajda) experimented with the synthesis of constructivism and surrealism. Their main interest was to make linear compositions or collages, for which they turned to popular art and the art forms of past cultures for inspiration. From 1929 Kassák's interest turned to photography and in this medium too he was followed by his circle, who worked on social photography and photocollage as well.[34] Sándor Bortnyik opened a school for graphic design, where both Viktor Vásárhelyi and György Kepes studied.

Many good painters (Egry, Derkovits, Vaszary, Bernáth, Koszta, István Nagy) lived and worked in solitude or for exclusive intellectual circles. Only theater performances (Kassák circle, Róna-Madzsar-Palasovszky circle),[35] kept alive the tradition of incisive dada evenings, of expressionist and surrealist poetry, and providing a collective experience for the avant-garde and its supporters: intellectuals, emancipated workers, the petty bourgeoisie, and students. These theater experiments, preserved in photos, posters, and literary sources,[36] continued in Budapest until 1932-33, when they were banned.

Tristan Tzara, Mayakovsky, Ernst Toller, Ivan Goll, Cocteau, and their Hungarian counterparts Ödön Palasovszky and Sándor Bortnyik, were considered dangerous by the state because of their internationalism: their belief in a common European culture, spiritual revolution, and the political power

149. LAJOS TIHANYI, Portrait of Tristan Tzara, 1926

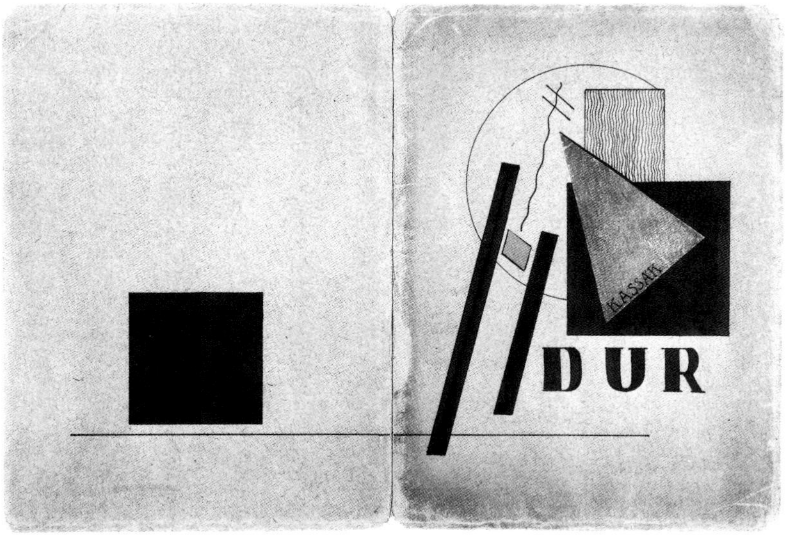

75. LAJOS KASSÁK, DUR Cover, 1924

of laughter and art. The administration launched a campaign against modern art. Teachers with a modern spirit (such as János Vaszary, who was the teacher of Korniss, Vajda, and their companions) were removed from their jobs at the art academy, and judicial proceedings were initiated against periodicals, especially Kassák's *Munka*.

The repetition of the conservative measures of the 1930s in the years of the Stalinist dictatorship (1949-56) was not inconsequential if one is familiar with the persecution of modern art in the Soviet Union from 1932 onward. In Hungary, the avant-garde and modernism lived a hidden existence during these years. Nevertheless, constructive surrealism had become the ruling tendency and was followed by the artists who in 1946 created the "European School," which continued the international aspirations of twentieth century Hungarian art.

Finally, in the 1960s, constructivism was reborn: Kassák and his group were rediscovered, and their works began to be exhibited at home and abroad,[37] in Paris, London, Rome, Helsinki, Kassel, Bochum, and other art centers. Deservedly, they have been accepted at last as a valuable part of the treasure trove of modern European art.

Acknowledgments

The author thanks Ms. Zsuzsanna Marosi, for the English translation of this essay and Ms. Judith Szöllősy, senior editor, Corvina Press, Budapest, for the supervision of the translation and for the final formulation of the English text.

Notes

Frequently cited works are identified by author, editor, or sponsoring organization an abbreviated title; journal articles, essays, and chapters in larger works are enclosed quotation marks, and book titles are set in italics. Interested readers are referred to comprehensive Select Bibliography at the end of this volume for full details of publication.

1. See Sándor Jeszenszky, "Le dejeuner sur l'herbe de Szinyei," *Bulletin de la Galerie Nationale Hongroise* 2 (Budapest, 1960), pp. 5-78, 129-59.

2. From Lajos Fülep, "Szinyei Merse Pál," in Árpád Tímár, ed., *Egybegyűjtött írások* [Collected Writings] (Budapest: Research Institute of Art History, 1988), pp. 87-93. Originally published in *Hazànk* (Budapest, Jan. 13, 1905).

3. See Anna Szinyei Merse, "Bildgattungen und Themen im Jugendwerk von Pál Szinyei Merse" [Motifs and Themes in the Early Works of Pál Szinyei Merse], *Acta Historiae Artium* 27, no. 3-4 (1981), pp. 287-361. For additional information about Szinyei Merse, see the recent monograph by the same author, *Szinyei Merse Pál és művészete* [The Life and Art of Pál Szinyei Merse] (Budapest: Hungarian National Gallery and Széchenyi-Corvina Press, 1990).

4. From László Mednyánszky, *Napló: Szemelvények* [Diary: Selections], Ilona Brestyánszky, ed. (Budapest, 1960); in Hungarian.

5. Cf. François F. Gachot, *József Rippl-Rónai* (Budapest, 1944) [in French]; Agnes Humbert, *Les Nabis et leur époque* (Geneva, 1954). Mária Bernáth, "Rippl-Rónai et l'art nouveau," *Acta Historiae Artium* 26, no. 3-4 (1980), pp. 285-316; and Patricia Eckert-Boyer, *The Nabis and the Parisian Avant-garde* (New Brunswick and London: Rutgers University Press, 1988).

6. The term *Parisianism* first occurs in Zsigmond Justh, "Parisianizmus," *Magyar Szalon* (Budapest, 1886), p. 646.

7. See Lajos Németh, *Csontváry* (Budapest, 1964); [also available in English (Budapest: Corvina, 1971)]; Júlia Szabó, "'Cedrus aeternitatis hieroglyphicum': Iconology of a Natural Motif," *Acta Historiae Artium* 27, no. 1-2, pp. 1-127.

8. Tivadar Csontváry, "A Tekintély" [Honor] in Gedeon Gerlóczy and Lajos Németh, *Csontváry emlékkönyv* [Csontváry Memorial Book] (Budapest: Corvina, 1976), p. 92.

9. Ernő Kállai, *Neue Malerei in Ungarn* [New Painting in Hungary] (Leipzig, 1925).

10. Aladár Körösfői Kriesch, *Ruskinról és az angol praeraffaelitákról* [About Ruskin and the English Pre-Raphaelites] (Budapest: Műbarátok Köre, 1904).

11. The academy of music in Budapest was built by Kálmán Giergl and Flóris Korb in 1904-1907. The palace of culture in Marosvásárhely was designed by Marcell Komor and Dezső Jakab, and decorated by Körösfői Kriesch, Sándor Nagy, and Ede Thorockai-Wigand.

12. *Magyar Iparművészet* 24, no. 4-6 (1921), p. 67, reports that a wall carpet designed by Sándor Nagy was sent to President Harding. The carpet, which was 3 meters long, depicted the American eagle and the 48 stars; on the lower part was the Hungarian national emblem.

13. Lajos Gulácsy, "Művészetről" [About Art], in Béla Szij, *Lajos Gulácsy* (Budapest, 1979); the original Gulácsy manuscript is in the National Széchényi Library, Budapest.

14. György Lukács, "Az utak elváltak" [The ways have parted], *Nyugat* 1 (Feb. 1910), pp. 190-93; in Arts Council, English trans. by George Cushing.

15. Károly Kernstok, "A művész társadalmi szerepe" [The Social Role of the Artist], *Huszadik Század* 1 (1912), pp. 377-80.

16. Ernő Marosi, ed., *Die Ungarische Kunstgeschichte und die Wiener Schule, 1846-1930* [Hungarian Art History and the School of Vienna] (Budapest: Research Institute of Art History, 1983), exhibition catalogue.

17. Lajos Fülep, "Az arckép festőjéról" [The Portrait on His Painter], *Nyugat* 2 (1918), pp. 109-11; in Arts Council, English trans. by George Cushing.

18. *A Művészház nemzetközi poszt-impresszionista kiállítása* [The International Post-Impressionist Exhibition of the Művészház] (Budapest, 1913); exhibition catalogue introduced by Károly Kernstok, János Vaszary, and others.

19. *Katalog der Ausstellung ungarischer Maler im Ausstellungsgebäude Kurfürstendamm* [Catalogue of Hungarian Painters in the Exhibition Building on the Kurfürstendamm] (Berlin, February 5 - March 3, 1910), n. 208-209.

20. For a summary of German criticism of the exhibition see Elek Petrovics, "Magyar festők a berlini Secessióban" [Hungarian painters in the Secession Palace of Berlin], *Művészet* 9, no. 4. (1910), pp. 218-22.

21. Rosenhagen and other German critics are cited by Géza Lengyel in "A berlini kiállítás mérlege" [An Account of the Berlin Exhibition], *Nyugat* 3 (April 1, 1910) pp. 440-44.

22. Jacques Rivière, "A festészet mai követelményei" [Today's Requirements of Painting], *Ma* 2 no. 6-7 (1917); originally published in *Revue d'Europe et d'Amerique* (Paris, March 1, 1912).

23. Lajos Kassák, "A plakát és az új festészet" [The Poster and the New Painting], *Ma* 1, no. 1 (Nov. 1916), pp. 112-13; in Arts Council, English trans. by George Cushing.

24. Lajos Kassák, "Nemes Lampérth Józsefről" [On József Nemes Lampérth] and "Fiatalok csoportkiállítása" [Exhibition of the Group of Young Artists], *Ma* 2, no. 9 (1917), pp. 146-47.

25. "János Máttis Teutsch und Paul Klee Gesamtschau" [Collective Exhibition], *Der Sturm* 12, no. 9 (1921).

26. For further reading on this period, see Stephen Borsody, "The Break-Up of Austria Hungary, Fifty Years After" (Comparative Communism Program, University of Pittsburgh), *The Central European Federalist* 16, no. 2 (December 1968); and S.A. Mansbach, "Revolutionary Events."

27. The painting is reproduced in Gassner, ed., *Wechselwirkungen*, Figure 146, p. 113.

28. *Egység* (Vienna-Berlin, 1922-24), Aladár Komját and Béla Uitz, eds.; German trans. in Gassner, ed., pp. 232-34.

29. Ernő Kállai, Alfréd Kemény, László Moholy-Nagy, and László Péri, "Nyilatkozat" [Manifesto], *Egység* (1923); in Arts Council, English trans. by George Cushing.

30. László Moholy-Nagy and Alfréd Kemény, "Dynamisch-konstrucktivistisches Kraftsystem" [Dynamic-Constructivist Force System], *Der Sturm* 13, no. 12 (December 1922), p. 186.

31. See the trilingual (Russian, German, and French) review by El Lissitzky and Ilya Ehrenburg in *Vesch'/Gegenstand/Objêt*, no. 1-2, published in Berlin, 1922-23.

32. Kassák's manifesto, *Képarchitektúra* [Bildarchitektur] was published in Vienna; Arts Council, pp. 114-17, English trans. by George Cushing.

33. Ernő Kállai: *Neue Malerei in Ungarn* (Leipzig, 1925).

34. See Ferenc Csaplár, *Munka és Dokumentum: Avantgárd és Proletkult.* [*Munka* and *Dokumentum*: Avant-garde and Proletcult] (Budapest: Lajos Kassák Memorial Museum, 1988); bilingual Hungarian-German exhibition catalogue.

35. See Ödön Palasovszky, *A lényegretörő színház* [The Theater of Essence] (Budapest, 1980); some details in German are provided in Gassner, ed., pp. 96-98.

36. The Palasovszky documents and photos are preserved in the Research Institute of Art History, Hungarian Academy of Sciences, Budapest.

37. See notes 14 and 27 and the following publications: *Ungarische Avantgarde, 1909-1930*; *Hungarian Art: The Twentieth Century Avant-Garde*; *Kunst in Ungarn, 1900-1950*; *Ungarische Avantgarde* (Basel: Galerie Bartha); Éva Bajkay-Rosch, ed., *Klassiker der Avantgarde: Die ungarischen Konstruktivisten*. Arts Council provides French, Italian, Finnish, and Serbo-Croatian versions.

155. BÉLA UITZ, Iconanalysis with the Holy Trinity, 1922

JOHN E. BOWLT

hungarian activism and the RUSSIAN AVANT-GARDE

A primary force in the derivation and development of Hungarian Activism was the art of El Lissitzky, Kazimir Malevich, Aleksandr Rodchenko, Vladimir Tatlin, and other members of the Russian avant-garde.[1] This connection demonstrates one of the salient characteristics of nineteenth and twentieth century Hungarian culture as a whole: the ability to borrow, blend, and reprocess foreign ideas so as to produce political and artistic syntheses of great power and vibrancy. The proximity of Hungary to Germany, Austria, Czecholosvakia, and Russia, and the constant mobility of her creative intelligentsia during the late 1800s and early 1900s thus contributed a great deal to the composition of modern Hungarian literature and art. (See also Chapter 1.)

These interactions benefited not only the Hungarians. The history of the Bauhaus, American constructive art and design, and, less obviously, Soviet socialist realism is replete with evidence that Hungarian artists and critics were just as capable of exporting intellectual commodities as they were of importing them. The ease with which certain members of the avant-garde such as László Moholy-Nagy, László Péri, and Béla Uitz exchanged their nationality for German, American, English, or Russian identities is one indication of their truly internationalist spirit. Many of the Activists not only changed geographical residences but also represented different nations at different exhibitions. For example, László Péri, one of several Activists who exhibited at the First Universal German Exhibition in Moscow in 1924, turned up eleven years later as an Englishman at the English Revolutionary Artists show in Moscow.

That artists of the Hungarian avant-garde felt an allegiance to the Soviet Union from the late 1910s onward, many becoming temporary or permanent exiles there, is a fact of considerable significance. This particular orientation affected such key representatives of Hungarian Activism as Alfréd Kemény (1895-1945, pseudonym Durus), Béla Uitz (1887-1972, pseudonym Martel), and János Mácza (1893-1974), who adopted the Russian Ivan Leopol'dovich Matsa after emigrating to Moscow in 1923.

From Symbolism to Futurism

There are several reasons that progressive Hungarian artists and critics were drawn to Russia in the 1910s and 1920s. First, there was the traditional cross-fertilization between the two countries. For example, a number of Hungary's leading nineteenth century artists studied and worked in Russia, including painters Miklós Barabás, János Rombauer, and Mihály Zichy.[2] At his private school in Munich, Simon Hollósy instructed an impressive number of Russian artists at the turn of the century, including Mstislav Dobuzhinsky, Vladimir Favorsky, Konstantin Istomin, and Kuz'ma Petrov-Vodkin, and made a vital contribution to the formation of the Russian *style moderne*.[3] Hollósy's student, Egon Kiss, also opened a studio in Moscow in the early 1900s, and attracted several important artists, including Vera Pestel and Konstantin Yuon.

Of greater significance than these irregular artistic encounters were the many parallels in the

JOHN E. BOWLT received his Ph.D. from the University of St. Andrews, Scotland, after extended graduate work at Moscow University. Dr Bowlt is a professor, Department of Slavic Languages, University of Southern California, Los Angeles; and director, Institute of Modern Russian Culture, Los Angeles. A specialist in the history of modern Russian art, he has published many books and articles on Russian symbolism, the avant-garde, and socialist realism. Recent publications include a monograph on Pavel Filonov (coauthor, Nicoletta Misler), a new edition of *Russian Avant-garde Theory and Criticism 1902-1934*, and essays on Natalia Goncharova and Kazimir Malevich. In progress are major writing projects for Princeton University Press and Iskusstvo Publishers, Moscow.

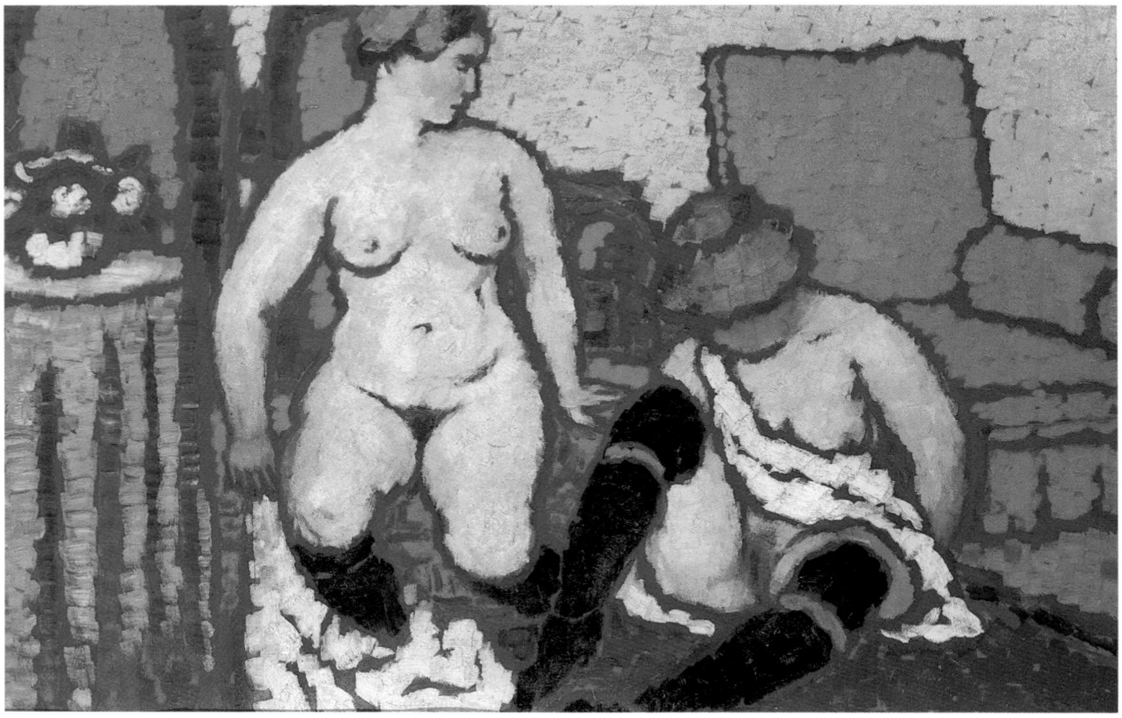

130. JÓZSEF RIPPL-RÓNAI, Models, 1910

social and political development of the Hungarian and Russian empires. Before their respective revolutions of October 1917 and March 1919, both nations were moving rapidly from an essentially feudal and agricultural society toward a capitalist, bourgeois one in which, to paraphrase Béla Uitz's ideological schemes, the "pure geometric forms" of the "pharaonic structure" were rapidly being destroyed.[4] Toward the end of the nineteenth century, Russia, like Hungary in the 1910s, suddenly experienced a sharp cultural acceleration and, while still looking to Paris and Munich for inspiration, rapidly established a self-assuredness and fresh identity.

To a large extent, both nations arrived at their artistic renaissance by way of international symbolism, and their belated but distinctive interpretations of this phenomenon did much to "liberate them from exteriorities"[5] and to bring them into the mainstream of modernism. In 1902, just as the Russian symbolists influenced by Maurice Denis were gaining momentum, József Rippl-Rónai returned to Budapest after working with the Nabis in Paris; in 1906, just as Aleksandr Blok was entering his darkest moment of urban decadence, Endre Ady published his first cycles of symbolist poetry; and both of the leading cultural reviews of that period, *Zolotoe runo* [Golden Fleece] in Moscow and *Nyugat* [West] in Budapest, paid homage to Baudelaire and Nietzsche. Hungarian Activist Sándor Bortnyik later illustrated Blok's famous poem *The Twelve* in 1923-24.[6]

That both Russia and Hungary approached their avant-garde movements via symbolism or post-impressionism is important. Inevitably, this background left a permanent imprint on their particular formulations of futurism, expressionism, and constructivism. For example, the concept of the "new man," streamlined, immortal and "watching eternity,"[7] interpreted by El Lissitzky and Malevich, Kassák and Uitz, was derived from symbolist interpretations and transcriptions of Nietzsche.

The Russian symbolists in particular regarded Nietzsche and his idea of the Superman as an immediate response to the moral and social fragmentation caused by industrial, bourgeois society. They argued that a cultural renovation would come about only when the prodigal individual re-entered the collective, when the individual became the Superman, and when external knowledge (science) was replaced by internal awareness (cognition). Viacheslav Ivanov, one of the primary thinkers of the symbolist movement, even affirmed that the new, perfect order would draw on the ideals of the ancient Greeks, whose society had been cohesive and harmonious, built upon the "deep, dark foundations of a truly popular religious feeling," which fused the individual with the collective and produced the "circumscribing form" that quelled the "ecstatic turbulence of musical intoxication."[8]

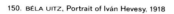

150. BÉLA UITZ, Portrait of Iván Hevesy, 1918

These ideas of the Greek collective, the Superman, and artistic synthesis were also repeated in many contexts of the Hungarian avant-garde, not least on the pages of *Ma* [Today] in 1919. Writing on the question of proletarian culture in the wake of the Hungarian revolution, Iván Hevesy declared:

That we should be thinking of the possibility of forming a mass culture and how to do this is confirmed by many examples in the history of culture. One is Greek art of the era of Pericles and another is the Christian art of the Middle Ages. Both testify to the fact that, once upon a time, individual art and social art were fused into one and that it was impossible to speak of differences in value or level.[9]

György Lukács echoed this sentiment a few weeks later in his analysis of the differences between culture and civilization, arguing that the former, an "expression of organic community," was identifiable with the Greeks, whereas the latter was the direct consequence of capitalist production.[10]

In this symbolist debate the Russians and the Hungarians also shared an exaggerated attention to the word and the message rather than to the abstract image. Both tended to regard the creative process as a messianic and eschatological force that could transform everyday life. Accordingly, both the Russian cubo-futurists and the Hungarian Activists stressed the importance of the manifesto, the declaration of intent, and the theoretical premise. (Not accidentally, the Hungarian journals *A Tett* [The Deed] and *Ma* both were primarily vehicles of literary or proclamatory expression.) Consequently, striking parallels exist between the various statements issued by the two groups. "Only we are the face of our time," wrote the Russians in 1912. "In

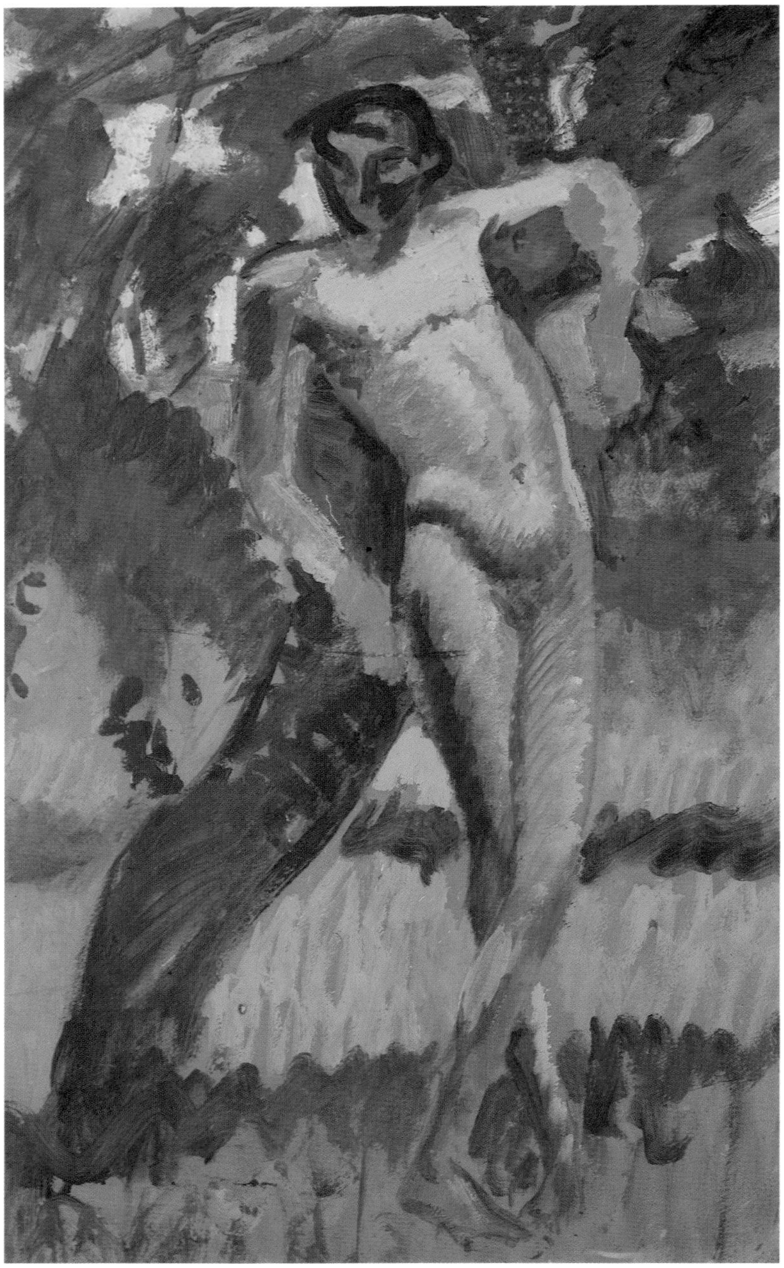

83. KÁROLY KERNSTOK, Nude Boy Leaning Against a Tree, 1911

122. VILMOS PERLROTT CSABA, Self-Portrait with Model, c1910-1912

31. BÉLA CZÓBEL, Garden at Nyergesújfalu, c1906

the art of the word the horn of time resounds through us."[11] "Art and literature," rejoined Kassák four years later, "must express the totality of the cosmos."[12] With their cultivation of the transcendental power of art, their fascination with the "new man," and their search for communality, it is not surprising that the two recurrent images among the Hungarian writers and artists of this time were the "male nude and the cosmic dancer."[13]

In retrospect, then, certain aesthetic connections can be detected between symbolism and the avant-garde in both Russia and Hungary. However, the apparent similarities should not be overemphasized. In fact, unlike the Russians, who rejected symbolism as "filthy saliva"[14] the Hungarian Activists welcomed the symbolists into their ranks.[15] The eclectic painting of The Eight, the new romanticism of Ady and Dezső Kosztolányi, and the early music of Béla Bartók and Zoltán Kodály therefore were distributed liberally among the arsenal of weapons with which to build the new order. Thus, although Kassák declared "Enough of 'Beauty'!" in 1915,[16] he still included the beauty of Mikhail Artsybashev, Paul Fort, Vasily Kandinsky, George Bernard Shaw, and Emil Verhaeren the following year in a special issue of *A Tett* (August 1, 1916) dedicated to foreign artists and writers.[17] With due respect to Kassák, by 1916 his Russian counterpart, Vladimir Maiakovsky, would have long considered these individuals to be hopelessly passé and would have thrown them "overboard from the Steamship of Modernity."[18]

Paradoxically, Kassák's curious cocktail of artists and writers, unified by neither symbolism nor futurism, also enjoyed a remarkable vogue among the "radical chic" of St. Petersburg's socialite salons in the early 1910s. Artsybashev was still benefiting from the notoriety of his erotic novel *Sanin* (1907); Paul Fort, crowned the "King of Poets" in 1912, was wined and dined in the Stray Dog cabaret in 1914; and Kandinsky had been accepted by the academic establishment in 1911.[19] No doubt, Kassák's famous poetical declaration *Mesteremberek* [Craftsmen] of 1915, with its belated evocations of Walt Whitman and Konstantin Bal'mont, would have appealed precisely to that tame bohemia.[20] Certainly, it lagged well behind Aleksei Kruchenykh and Velemir Khlebnikov's *zaum*, Malevich's suprematist painting, and Tatlin's reliefs, and, for that matter, Marinetti's *Parole in libertà*.

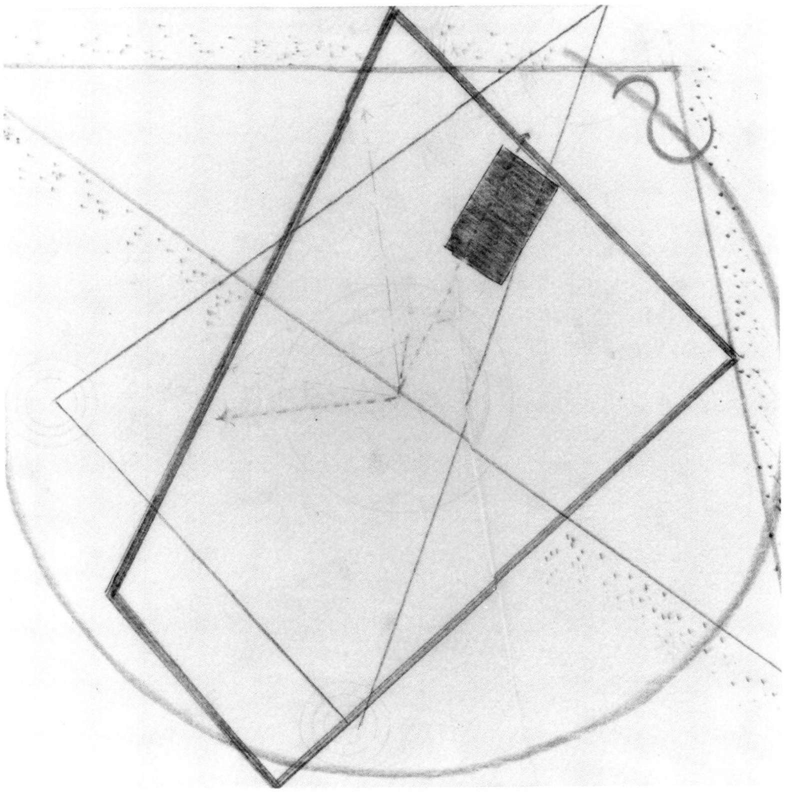

158. BÉLA UITZ, Compositional Analysis for Nedd Ludd, c1923

An Art of Social Change

In the 1910s the Hungarian attitude toward futurism and the extreme manifestations of the international avant-garde was, to say the least, ambivalent.[21] While sharing an uneasy attitude toward Italian futurism (and French cubism), the Russians and the Hungarians supported different views regarding the imminent development of the new art. The Russians enjoyed, as Livshits put it, an "inner proximity to the material, an exceptional sensation of it,"[22] and wished to explore the intrinsic ingredients of the work of art—texture, rhythm, composition, and dynamics—an orientation that prompted such bold investigations as Mikhail Larionov's rayonism and Malevich's suprematism. Perhaps these excursions were momentary lapses from the narrative and tendentious tradition of Russian art, symbolized as much by Il'ia Repin's realist painting as by Kandinsky's apocalyptic imagery. For better or worse, however, such minimal gestures were to become the identifying characteristic of modern Russian art.

The Hungarians, on the other hand, were rarely satisfied with mere formal combinations, but aspired to a utilitarian functional aesthetic. Moholy-Nagy's design experiments, Kassák's polygraphical projects, Uitz's social commentaries, Bortnyik's establishment of Műhely in 1928, Kemény's socialist realist criticism, and Mácza's sociology thus can be seen as extensions of this extrinsic orientation of the Hungarian avant-garde artists and of their constant desire to change sociopolitical structures by artistic devices. (*See also Chapter 2.*)

The same attitude was conveyed in the titles of their radical magazines *A Tett*, *Ma*, and *Egység* [Unity], and in their enthusiasm for German Expressionism. After all, Kassák's *A Tett*, with its call for "action against action,"[23] was a clear echo of the Berlin *Die Aktion* with its strong expressionist demand for an engaged art. Furthermore, it was from the expressionist tradition that much Hungarian agitational art of the late 1910s and early 1920s took its strength (unlike Russian agit art, which drew mainly on the indigenous tradition of the *lubok* and on cubo-futurism and suprematism).

These circumstances help explain the Activists' cult of particular historical figures such as the anarchist Mikhail Bakunin and the Marxist Ervin Szabó, and their unabashed call for the reintegration of art into the service of politics even before the

159. BÉLA UITZ, Nedd Ludd (I)

proclamation of the Hungarian Soviet Republic in March 1919. For example, in his November 1918 "Declaration for Art," Kassák asserted that:

We [artists, poets, anarchists] do not wish to be the toy of a dominant class or the parasites of somnolent strata, but, side by side with the exploited workers, we are the fanatical bearers of the banner of a new and free human community.[24]

Árpád Szélpál developed this idea of the marriage of the artist and the worker:

The man of Communism [is] not a proletarian exile transformed (degraded) into a robot, but is an individual who can realize himself. His form of life is not work, but art...Art as intuition must of necessity precede science...Consequently, next to Communism...art can serve and guide the new man now liberated by art.[25]

In these statements, neither spokesman is equating avant-garde art with a specific political party or assuming that art would be used by a party mechanism to further party aims. Ultimately, this subtle hiatus contributed to the rift between the Hungarian avant-garde and Béla Kun's revolutionary government in June 1919. (*See also Chapter 2.*)

Of course, the central event that focused Hungarian attention on Russia was the October revolution of 1917. Like some of the Russian avant-garde, the Activists identified the "activism of their drawings with the activism of the political and social mass movement of the Revolution,"[26] and assumed that the communists' ascendancy would guarantee the free practice of their radical art. By and large, however, the Hungarian artists and critics such as Ernő Kállai, Kemény, Mácza, and Uitz seemed to be more politically motivated than their Russian colleagues. Indeed, Moscow and Petrograd (formerly St. Petersburg) never experienced the equivalents of the Budapest Galileo and Sunday circles at which radical artists and radical politicans exchanged ideas over the political destiny of the new art.

Even so, for the Hungarians the appeal of Russia was primarily as a political matrix, an experimental laboratory in which socialism and communism were being researched for a subsequent international application. Indeed, Hungarian political thinkers, including Béla Kun, learned a good deal about Marxism during their military incarceration in Russia during World War I.[27] Moholy-Nagy may have listened to Marxist discourse while he was a prisoner of war in Odessa. Even Kassák, not a perceptive political being in spite of his radicalism, looked to the ideas of Bakunin and Lenin for cultural elucidation before the Hungarian communist revolution, and included references to their writings in the early issues of *Ma*.[28]

It is not surprising that the revolutionary regimes in Russia and Hungary behaved in similar ways in the context of cultural policy, and there are many evident artistic and political parallels. Both governments, for example, established bureaucratic mechanisms for organizing and controlling art education, censorship, exhibitions, museums, and the nationalization of private collections: the people's commissariat for enlightenment (NKP) in Moscow, directed by Anatoly Lunacharsky, and the people's commissariat for culture and public education in Budapest, directed by György Lukács.

Initially, both organizations tolerated a wide spectrum of artistic styles and procedures, although the avant-garde artists and critics—the Russians Natan Al'tman, Malevich, Nikolai Punin, and Tatlin, and the Hungarians Béni and Noémi Ferenczy, Kassák, Jolán Szilágyi, and Uitz—played a crucial role in the administration and reformation of the visual arts. Both the commissariat and the ministry, for example, sanctioned and encouraged programs of monumental propaganda in Moscow and Budapest for which artists were invited to "make the streets their brushes and the squares their palette."[29] (*See Chapter 2.*) Immediately, the poster emerged as a primary vehicle for distributing both propaganda and information, and many of the Russian and Hungarian radicals, including Maiakovsky, Dmitri Moor, Klucis, El Lissitzky, Malevich, Róbert Berény, Mihály Biró, Bortnyik, Uitz,and Marcell Vértes, designed images that drew on common themes of proletarian solidarity: the Red Army, brotherhood, and the like.

BOTH PROGRESSIVE AND CONSERVATIVE ARTISTS RESPONDED TO THE CALL to transform the visual aspect of the cities by concealing the architectural symbols of the old order with panels, banners, flags, and slogans that often incorporated suprematist or expressionist motifs. Mácza described the May Day celebration in Budapest in 1919:

Artists...attempted to dress up the city for the free May Day festivities...grandiose decorations in the center of Budapest that stretched from the square in front of the

120. JENÓ PAIZS GOEBEL, Lajos Kossuth's Message: Long Live the Republic!, 1918

9. MIHÁLY BIRÓ, We Want a Republic!, 1918

Parliament as far as the Millenium Monument...the sculpture of Marx by György Zala, the enormous panels by Béla Uitz, the rich ornament of the streets where the brilliant crimson of the flame of revolution was fluttering.[30]

Later on, while in temporary exile in Czechoslovakia, Mácza recalled the monumental propaganda campaign in Budapest, extending it to a "mass action" or historical theatricalization that he directed in Košice where "a choir of two hundred workers recited one of my pieces."[31]

Like Lenin and Lunacharsky, Kun and Lukács understood the need to select and reprocess the most expedient parts of the literary and artistic heritage to create a new proletarian culture. They also realized that the establishment and consolidation of such a culture could not be achieved immediately and that it would evolve as a natural consequence of the move toward the communist state. It is improbable, however, that Lenin or Kun understood what a new visual art could mean or that their artistic taste could ever have advanced beyond their personal preferences for Tolstoy, Michelangelo, and Beethoven—one reason why, in postrevolutionary Moscow and Budapest, the "revolutionary" fare being offered the masses consisted of "Strauss, Verdi, Puccini, and Wagner."[32]

From the first days of both revolutions, it was clear that the cultural tastes of the politicians did not coincide with that of the radical artists. It was equally clear that this communication gap would lead to a divorce between the two camps. As Kassák and Uitz continued to call for "permanent revolution,"[33] the members of Kun's government reacted ever more sharply against the political independence and the aesthetic experimentalism of the avant-garde artists. In an *Az Ember* [Mankind] article (April 1919) titled "Mácza," Pál Kéri affirmed that it was more valuable for the masses to enjoy bourgeois culture, now deprived of its original meaning, than to be estranged by the snobbism of the avant-garde.[34] György Lukács added that, in any case, the avant-garde did not represent the cultural policy of the Hungarian Communist party and that it had become a mere fashion.[35] Kun himself entered the polemic in June 1919 with his notorious dismissal of the avant-garde as an "excrescence of bourgeois decadence."[36] Kassák's acerbic response,[37] together with Árpád Szélpál's ironic comment that if the Activists were decadent then so were the socialists since both were the consequence of the capitalist system,[38] led to the banning of *Ma* in Budapest (*see also Chapter 2, note 39*).

These acrid exchanges between ideologues and unorthodox artists bring to mind a similar series of aspersions cast by Lenin and Lunacharsky at the Proletkult [proletarian culture] and Komfut [communist futurism] movements in Soviet Russia. After all, Proletkult too called for the total rejection of the past and for the establishment of truly proletarian art and literature. Its ideological and artistic leaders, among them Al'tman, Aleksandr Bogdanov, Osip Brik, Boris Kushner, Maiakovsky, and David Shterenberg, maintained a safe distance from the Communist party; they would not tolerate political or artistic compromise and were hostile toward Lunacharsky's wide dissemination of the classical repertoires. As they declared in 1919:

It is essential to wage merciless war against all the false ideologies of the bourgeois past.... It is essential to subordinate the Soviet cultural-educational organs to the guidance of a new cultural communist ideology.[39]

By 1919, Proletkult had a substantial sphere of influence, operating its own studios in the major urban areas, and its emphasis on industry allied it immediately with the emergent constructivist groups. Its formal annexation to the people's commissariat for enlightenment in 1922 and the automatic restriction of its activities presaged the increasing government interference in art affairs during the mid- and late 1920s. Finally, Proletkult was liquidated by the state for "high treason."

Constructivism

With the resignation of Kun and the collapse of the Hungarian Republic of Soviets on August 1, 1919, and the establishment of the Horthy regime, many radical artists and writers emigrated to Berlin, Prague, Paris, and especially Vienna, where Kassák, with contributions from Moholy-Nagy and Kállai in Berlin, reestablished *Ma* the following year. (*See Chapters 1 and 2.*) The Vienna group, which also included Sándor Bortnyik, still regarded Budapest as their national, spiritual home, and their artistic and publicist activities were still bolstered by the utopian vision of a successful Hungarian revolution. *Ma* continued in Vienna until 1926. While maintaining its interest in literature and politics, the journal now gave much more attention to the new painting, graphics, and sculpture. As several critics have pointed out, the decisive, unifying visual element during this period was the influence of the Russian avant-garde, specifically, the geometric experiments of Naum Gabo, Gustav Klucis, El Lissitzky, Malevich, Rodchenko, Tatlin, and the group called OBMOKhU [Society of Young Artists].

On November 13, 1920, Konstantin Umansky, who published his *Neue Kunst in Russland, 1914-1919,* the same year, organized a "Russian Evening" at the *Ma* premises with an illustrated lecture on the work of Kandinsky, Malevich, Rodchenko, Varvara Stepanova, Tatlin, Nadezhda Udal'tsova, and others.[40] (*See Chapter 2, note 51.*) In the spring of 1921, just a few months after the constructivist exhibition organized by Grigorii and Vladimir Stenberg and Konstantin Medunetsky in Moscow, *Ma* published its

22. SÁNDOR BORTNYIK, The First of May in Hungary, 1923

first constructivist manifesto and continued to inform its readers of the new Russian art until its closure in 1926. In 1922, members of the Ma group, including Kassák and Kemény, traveled to Berlin to see the Erste Russische Kunstausstellung [First Russian Art Exhibition] at the Galerie van Diemen.[41] Also in 1922 the journal *Egység*, edited by Aladár Komját and Béla Uitz in Vienna, published Naum Gabo and Anton Pevsner's *Realist Manifesto*, the so-called Program of the First Working Group of Constructivists, and a text by Uitz on suprematism.[42]

By 1922-23, the movement of international constructivism was unthinkable without the Hungarian contribution, as was demonstrated by the strong Hungarian contingent at the "Grosse Berliner Kunstausstellung" of 1923 (Vilmos Huszár, Moholy-Nagy, Péri) and in the El Lissitzky/Hans Arp survey *Die Kunstismen*, published two years later. Furthermore, like their Russian, German, Polish, and Czech colleagues, the Hungarian constructivists gave particular attention to architecture and design as the most potent vehicles of constructivist ideas, especially temporary and mobile architecture (kiosks, display stands, interiors, furniture). Marcel Breuer, Kassák, Farkas Molnár, Moholy-Nagy, Péri, and many other Hungarians achieved substantial reputations as designers in the 1920s. Although some of them distanced themselves from the original formulae of Russian constructivism, the impact of El Lissitzky, the OBMOKhU, Rodchenko, and Tatlin on their work is undeniable. "The new form is architecture," wrote Kassák in 1922.[43] Five years later he published El Lissitzky's essay on the new Russian architecture in his Budapest-based *Dokumentum*.[44]

During the early 1920s, there were several direct parallels between individual Hungarian and Russian artists: Bortnyik and Malevich, Kassák and Rodchenko, Moholy-Nagy and Lissitzky, Uitz and Rodchenko, etc. Some of these interconnections can be explained by the wide dissemination of illustrated articles and reviews dealing with suprematism and constructivism that appeared in *Ma*, *Egység*, and Sándor Barta's Vienna journals *Akasztott Ember* [Hanged Man] (1922) and *Ék* [Wedge] (1923-25). But more often than not, these coincidences in artistic thinking came about through personal encounters in Berlin. As Moholy-Nagy recalled much later:

In 1922 the Russian artists El Lissitzky, Ilya Ehrenburg, and later Gabo, came to Berlin. They brought news of Malevich, Rodchenko and the movement called Suprematism. The Dutch painter, Theo van Doesburg, told about Mondrian and neoplasticism; Matthew Josephson and Harold Loeb, the editors of Broom, *and the painter Lozowick, about the USA.... Out of these discoveries developed the Constructivist Congress of 1922 in Weimar, manifestoes of the Hungarian review* Ma, *of which I was then the Berlin representative, and exhibitions, all of which gave us greater assurance in regard to our work and future artistic prospects....*[45]

One of the favorite points of rendezvous was Gert Kaden's studio where Gabo, Kemény, El Lissitzky, Moholy-Nagy, Péri, and Hans Richter often met.[46] All also were involved in the various activities of Der Sturm gallery and journal.[47] Hungarian and Russian artists formed a major component of Herwarth Walden's repertoire. He often showed them singly or in groups, and the journal, with contributions by Moholy-Nagy, Kemény, and many others, was an important vehicle for Russo-Hungarian artistic propagation and critical commentary.

109. FARKAS MOLNÁR, Gropius Memorial - Study, 1923

As a result of this sudden, increased availability of the ideas and images of the Russian avant-garde, many direct and indirect borrowings, plagiarisms, and interpretations ensued that generated a good deal of discussion, which continues today. That Lissitzky's abstract system of Prouns [Projects for the Affirmation of the New], with their axonometric planes defying gravity, left a deep impression on Moholy-Nagy, for example, is evident from a simple comparison of the two lithograph albums published by the Kestner Gesellschaft in Hannover in 1923: Moholy-Nagy's *Kestnermappe* and El Lissitzky's *Die plastische Gestaltung der Elektromechanischen Schau "Sieg über die Sonne"* [The visual design of the electromechanical show "Victory over the Sun"]. Also, Moholy-Nagy's incorporation of the human hand into his presumed self-portrait of around 1925[48] brings to mind El Lissitzky's use of the same motif in his photograph *The Constructor* (1924).

The relationship between Moholy-Nagy's nickel sculpture of 1921 and Tatlin's model for *Monument to the Third International* (1919-20) has been discussed at some length by others.[49] However, Moholy-Nagy's anticipation of Ivan Leonidov's project for the Lenin Institute of 1927 in his *Two Constructional Systems Linked* (1921-22) seems to have

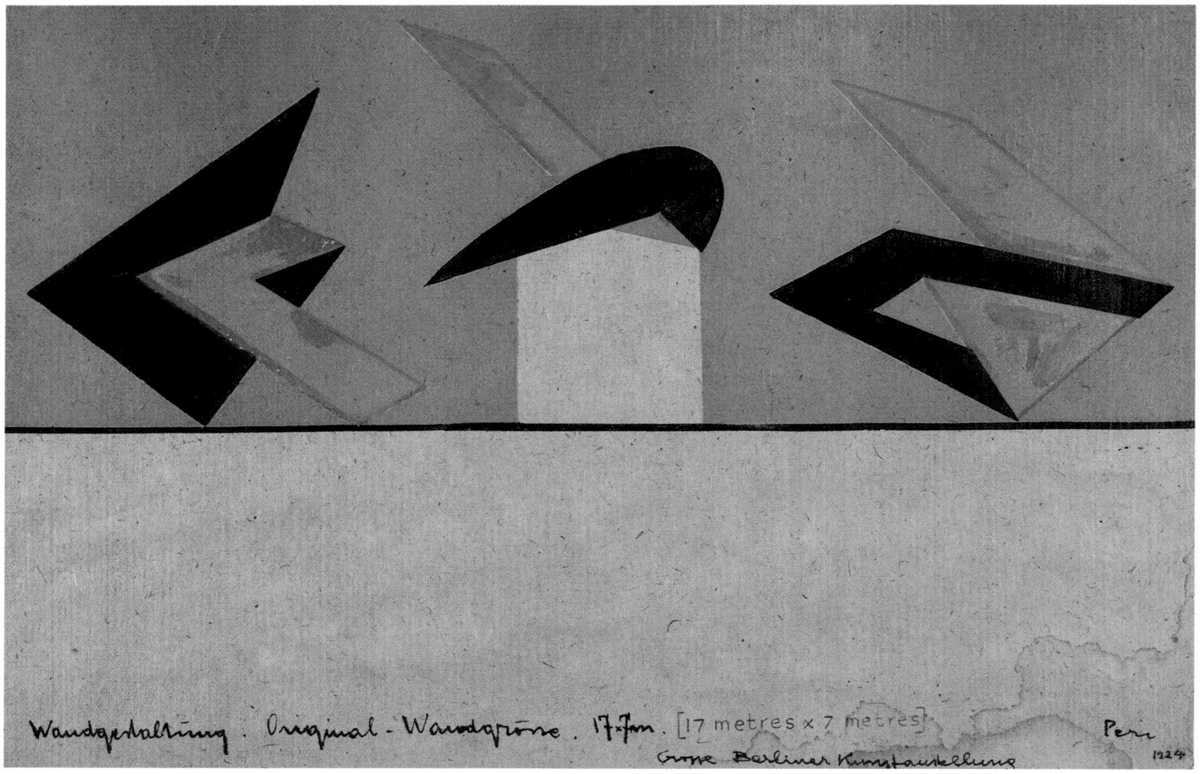

121. LÁSZLÓ PÉRI, Berlin Mural Design, c1923

been overlooked. Moreover, Moholy-Nagy's experimental photographs from (and of) balconies seem to have been recaptured by Rodchenko, an apparent borrowing that led to a bitter polemic on the pages of *Novyi lef* in 1927-28.[50] In turn, the 1920s photomontages and photocollages of Rodchenko, Klucis, El Lissitzky, and Solomon Telingater seem to have been appreciated and applied by the Hungarians in both their abstract compositions (for example, Kassák) and their agit designs (for example, György Kepes). There are striking parallels between Kepes's photomontages for the propaganda magazine *Das neue Russland* [The New Russia] in 1931-32 and those by Rodchenko, Stepanova, and, Kepes's fellow countryman János Reismann for the Moscow journal of the same period, *SSSR na stroike* [USSR in Construction].

The Move to Moscow

The intense cross-fertilization of visual images between Hungarian and Russian artists, strengthened by the political rapprochement between the Hungarian diaspora and the Soviet Union, was encouraged further by the presence of many Hungarians in Moscow, which, beginning in 1919, became the temporary or permanent home for many artists, writers, and politicians in exile. For Activists still fired by the communist spirit, Moscow was the Mecca to which they turned, and the Third International Congress held in Moscow in June-July 1921 attracted several of them, including Sándor Ék, Lukács, Uitz, and Jolán Szilágyi (the widow of Tibor Szamuely, cofounder of the Hungarian Communist party). While in Moscow, Ék, Szilágyi, and Uitz also visited VKhUTEMAS (Higher State Art-Technical Studios), where they became acquainted with El Lissitzky, Rodchenko, and other constructivists. Ék's memoirs suggest that his encounter did not draw him any closer to the avant-garde.[51] Kemény visited Moscow in December 1921 to lecture at the Institute of Artistic Culture (INKhUK), and Uitz to initiate his series of so-called analyses, a sequence of abstract analytical compositions, sometimes interpretations of other works of art. Mácza emigrated to Moscow in 1923; Uitz moved there in 1926 and invited his protégé László Dallos (known as Vladislav Griffel) to join him the following year. Kemény emigrated permanently in 1933.

In the early 1930s, the Hungarian emigration to the Soviet Union accelerated dramatically as both Hungary and Germany consolidated their fascist power. The poster artist Ilma Bernáth lived in Moscow from 1933 through 1946; Ék from 1932 to 1945 when he returned to Budapest; sculptor/medalist Béni Ferenczy from 1932 to 1935[52]; architect Fréd Forbát, working with Ernst May, in 1932-33; and Dallos-Griffel from 1926 through the mid-1930s.[53] Sculptor László Mészáros emigrated to Moscow in 1935; poster artist and muralist Bertalan Pór spent six months there in 1936; photographer and designer János Reismann contributed to propaganda magazines in the city from 1931 through 1938; the architect István Sebők worked with Moisei Ginzburg and El Lissitzky from 1930 until at least 1936; Szilágyi enrolled at the Repin Institute in Leningrad in 1933, returning to Budapest in 1948; and architect Tibor Weiner participated in Hannes Meyer's group in Moscow from 1931 through 1933. By the mid-1920s there were so many Hungarian émigrés living in Moscow that they established the Union of Hungarian Revolutionary Writers and Artists and even published their own journals: *Sarló és kalapács* [Hammer and Sickle] and *Új Hang* [New Voice].[54]

During the 1920s and 1930s, these direct contacts between Hungarian artists and the Soviet Union were reinforced by the strong Hungarian presence at international exhibitions in Moscow, Leningrad, and other cities. For example, the First Universal German Exhibition in Moscow, Saratov, and Leningrad in 1924 included works by members of the Hungarian avant-garde who were then living in Germany, including Aurél Bernáth, Bortnyik, Béla Czóbel, Hanna Dalos, Dallos-Griffel, Béla Kádár, Moholy-Nagy, and Péri. Péri even contributed an "extraordinary, but architecturally convincing, attempt to present a hammer and sickle as a monument crowned with the burning letters LENIN."[55]

Two years later, the state academy of artistic sciences (GAKhN) organized the exhibition Revolutionary Art of the West, which also contained works by Ilma Bernáth, Mihály Biró, Sándor Bortnyik, Tibor Gergely, János Máttis Teutsch, László Péri, Bela Uitz, and Gyula Zilzer. Over the next decade, at least five other Moscow exhibitions[56] displayed works by Hungarian artists, primarily posters, caricatures, and book designs by Ék, Dallos-Griffel, and Uitz. In any case, by the mid-1930s, with the increasing political presure for art to conform to a more accessible nineteenth-century style, the words *activist* and *avant-garde* had become terms of condemnation and abuse.

Among the many Hungarian artists and critics who felt a strong sympathy for the Soviet Union in the early years were Alfréd Kemény, Béla Uitz, and János Mácza.[57] They deserve particular attention since their direct exposure to Soviet life and culture affected their personal and intellectual lives profoundly, and, for better or for worse, their emigration to Moscow symbolized an end to the brief but intense interchange between the two avant-garde movements.

ALFRED KEMÉNY When Kemény first visited the Soviet Union in December 1921 as a guest lecturer, INKhUK was the principal center for the propagation of constructivism. Kandinsky had been its first director the year before, but his psychological approach to art had led to sharp disagreements with colleagues who were more inclined to regard art as a material object devoid of subjective, intuitive connotations. By the time Kemény arrived, Kandinsky was just leaving Moscow for the Bauhaus. The INKhUK administration had passed into the hands of a group of constructivists, including Rodchenko and Stepanova, who had already moved from their pure "culture of materials" toward a utilitarian esthetic that advocated the priority of industrial and applied art. By December 1921, with the addition of the constructivist theorists Boris Arvatov, Osip Brik, Kushner, and Nikolai Tarabukin, INKhUK was closely identifiable with production art, or the so-called productivist movement.

In the spirit of international communism and constructivism, INKhUK was eager to establish new affiliations both within the Soviet Union (Petrograd, Vitebsk, and other cities) and abroad. To this end, early in 1922 the Institute announced its links with various avant-garde groups:

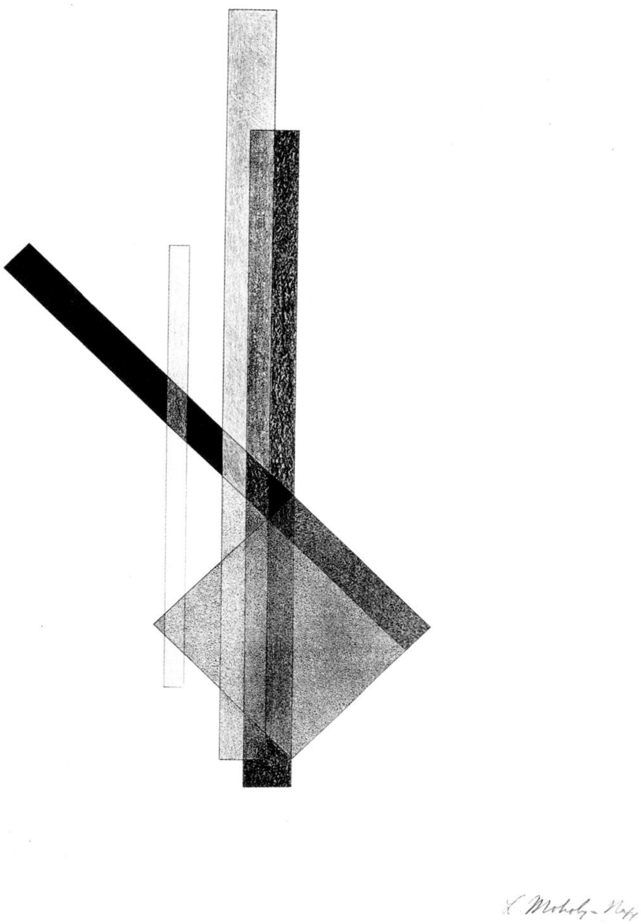

101. LÁSZLÓ MOHOLY-NAGY, Construction (1) (Kestner Portfolio), 1923

Gradually INKhUK is establishing links with foreign countries: a) Consequently, the Arts Section of the German Komsomol has made official and practical contact with the Institute via its member, the German art critic Kemény, who came to Moscow to deliver a number of lectures at INKhUK; b) Contact with Holland has been established through the artist Petrus Alma; c) INKhUK has a link with Berlin via its member Lissitzky, editor of Veshch' *[Object]...; d) INKhUK is also in touch with the Paris journal* L'Esprit nouveau *[The New Spirit] via Lissitzky; e) In Tokyo (Japan) our corresponding member is Bubnova;... g) Contact has been made with Hungary via the artist Béla Uitz, editor of* Egység *(Vienna);...*[58]

As an ardent communist and firm supporter of the new art, Kemény was a welcome guest at INKhUK. He gave two lectures during December 1921: "New Trends in German and Russian Contemporary Art" and "On the Constructive Works of OBMOKhU."[59] Both presentations were attended by the leaders of the artistic and architectural avant-garde in Moscow, including Arvatov, Aleksei Babichev, Karel Ioganson, Gustav Klucis, and Kushner (second session only); Nikolai Ladovsky, Pavel Mansurov, and Medunetsky, Popova, the Stenberg brothers, and Tarabukin (first session only); and Tatlin.

Before his arrival in Moscow, Kemény, like Kállai and other Hungarian colleagues, was well aware of the more famous members of the Russian avant-garde, above all, Malevich and Tatlin. However, he had little knowledge of the younger generation such as Ioganson, Medunetsky, and the Stenberg brothers (the leaders of OBMOKhU); clearly, he was deeply impressed by what he saw of their activities at INKhUK.[60] Founded in 1919 under the influence of Rodchenko and Tatlin, OBMOKhU emphasized abstract, free-standing constructions before its artists became the primary supporters of utilitarian constructivism, applying their geometric configurations to banners, movie posters, stencils, theater sets, among other things.

In his first lecture, Kemény contrasted this new constructivism ("art into life") with German expressionism ("the individual expression of the artist's subjective feelings"), implying, of course, that the former was superior to the latter. In the same context, Kemény also asserted that Malevich had little to do with this "material constructive tendency in Russian art," whereas Tatlin was the "father of Russian material constructivism," and the OBMOKhU works were "material constructions in the truest sense of the word....[because] they pass from surface to concrete space." Kemény returned to the same considerations in his second lecture, again emphasizing that Malevich, like Kandinsky, was an "expressionist" because "his forms are only illustrations of a certain ideal." This time, however, Kemény also insinuated that even Rodchenko's and Tatlin's constructions left something to be desired because they manifested "naturalist tendencies," and Rodchenko's wooden installations were "the schematic transmission of technological constructions that already exist."[61]

Kemény's enthusiasm for the latest phase of Russian constructivism soon waned; just a few months later, in a joint statement with Kállai, Péri, and Moholy-Nagy, he even described it as "bourgeois."[62] In his review of the Erste Russische Kunstausstellung in Berlin, Kemény repeated his criticism, arguing that the Russian constructivists had compromised and had not realized their potential: they had placed their constructions within a physical space, but they had not yet defined that space, whereas (so he implied) the Hungarian constructivists would provide the answer to this dilemma.[63] Kállai too had expressed disappointment in the Erste Russische Kunstaustellung, regarding it not only as an exercise in artistic compromise for the sake of diplomatic and financial advantages (Soviet Russia's economic overture to Germany), but also as a total failure to formulate a truly proletarian art.[64]

Kemény emigrated from Hitler's Germany to Stalin's Russia in 1933, but by then his artistic, if not his political, views had changed considerably. He was still a fervent Marxist, as his editorship of *Die Rote Fahne* [The Red Banner] in Berlin had demonstrated, and he still professed an interest in questions of constructivism and formal analysis (reflected in his last publications on Péri and Dziga Vertov).[65] Now, however, he supported (or acquiesced in) the reportorial narrative style of socialist realism. Under the pseudonym of Durus, Kemény published many articles in the monthly journals *Iskusstvo* [Art] and *Tvorchestvo* [Creativity] on the tendentious art of Ék, Helios Gomez, Jacob Burcke, and other artists of the international "committed" left.[66] His ideas and turns of phrase became stereotypical and lacked the incisive analysis of his earlier articles on the Russian, German, and Hungarian avant-gardes. Except for a few comments on Ék and Mészáros in 1935 and 1936, Kemény almost completely ignored his old Hungarian milieu.[67] In the mid-1930s he was appointed secretary of the International Bureau of Revolutionary Artists (IBRA) and a member of the foreign commission within the Moscow Union of Soviet Artists. He died in Budapest in 1945 while on active service as a Soviet officer.

BÉLA UITZ Like Kemény, Béla Uitz (in the Russian form, Bela Fridrikhovich Uits) was inclined politically to emigrate to the Soviet Union, which he did in 1926. Since his visit to the Third International Congress in Moscow in 1921 and his coeditorship of *Egység* in Vienna and Berlin (1922-24), Uitz showed an increasing sympathy for the Soviet Union, and seems to have been drawn there both by ideological optimism and by artistic conviction. Before and after the revolutions, Uitz was a figurative artist, and his series of analyses (1921-22) is a temporary deviation from his basic concept of art as a didactic, expository medium for the advancement of political ideals. Even during his 1921 sojourn in Moscow when he was close to Lissitzky and Rodchenko, Uitz created simple compositional schemes of icons and scenes of Moscow churches in which there was "still a good deal of aestheticism."[68] He did not venture into the realm of suprematist painting or three-dimensional reliefs, and one suspects that a principal reason for his break with Kassák in 1922 (they had coedited *A Tett* and then *Ma*) was Kassák's increasing concentration on abstract art and aesthetic play (*see Chapter 2*).

The Soviet cultural establishment afforded Uitz a particularly warm welcome when he arrived in Moscow in the summer of 1926. In the fall of that year, on Lunacharsky's recommendation, he was appointed professor of composition and dean of painting at VKhUTEIN (High State Art-Technical Institute). Immediately, he assumed partial responsibility for the reform of the painting department there, insisting that students should devote more time and energy to "Uninterrupted Industrial Practice" and less to enclosed studio work.[69] Perhaps because of this dubious innovation, whereby students were expected to work on location at factories and farms, or because of his brief tenure, Uitz does not seem to have enjoyed an especially fruitful rapport with students at VKhUTEIN. None of those who graduated in the mid-1920s seems to remember him as a charismatic teacher or brilliant administrator.

In December 1926 GAKhN organized a one-man show for Uitz at the state Museum of New Western Art. The exhibition, consisting of 116 drawings, watercolors, and prints, received wide critical attention for its "vivid and passionate advocacy of the triumph of the proletarian idea."[70] Uitz's works

108. FARKAS MOLNÁR, Fiorentina, 1921

156. BÉLA UITZ, Analysis (XXVI), 1922

157. BÉLA UITZ, Analysis (XXVIII), 1922

were reproduced widely in leading journals of the late 1920s and early 1930s such as *Prozhektor* [Projector], *Vestnik inostrannoi literatury* [Herald of Foreign Literature], and *Za proletarskoe iskusstvo* [For Proletarian Art], and he continued to exhibit regularly until the mid-1930s.

Perhaps unexpectedly, Uitz also played an active role in the October group, founded in 1928, one of the last strongholds of the constructivist cause. As a colleague, therefore, of Sergei Eisenstein, Ginzburg, Klucis, El Lissitzky, Mácza, Viktor Tóth, Diego Rivera (in Moscow 1927-28), Telingater, and others, Uitz advocated the value of the applied arts, photography, and monumental art, and he cosigned the association's *Declaration:*

...[T]he spatial arts must serve the proletariat and the working masses in two interconnected fields: in the field of ideological propaganda (by means of paintings, frescoes, prints, sculpture, photography, cinematography, etc.); in the field of production and direct organization of the collective way of life (by means of architecture, the industrial arts, the designing of mass festivals, etc.).:[71]

The activity that appealed perhaps the most to Uitz's radical internationalism was the founding of the IBRA in Khar'kov in 1930. The IBRA was organized in the wake of the second plenum of the International Bureau of Revolutionary Literature that took place in Khar'kov in November 1930. At that time Khar'kov was the last stronghold of the avant-garde in the Soviet bloc: that was where the Ukrainian modernists such as Vasily Ermilov and Mariia Siniakova were still active, where Malevich was publishing his last articles in the journal *Novaia generatsiia* [New Generation], and where the design competition for the construction of the city theater had drawn entries from all over the world, including one from Marcel Breuer.[72]

The meeting of the International Bureau of Revolutionary Literature at Khar'kov also had attracted delegates from 23 countries. Although the consensus was that literature and art should serve the cause of the international proletariat, there was no firm agreement regarding the aesthetic form or style that this movement should assume.[73] The IBRA supported a limited variety of trends, although Uitz, as secretary, issued a clear mandate for an art that would expose the ills of the capitalist West and extol the virtues of the Soviet Union. Perhaps remembering his demand in April 1919 for an artistic dictatorship that would protect the purity of the revolutionary cause,[74] Uitz and his colleagues — Fred Ellis and William Gropper representing the United States, Jules Félix Grandjouan (France), Dallos-Griffel (Hungary), Max Keilson and Alfred Kurella (Germany), Krun Kiuliakov (Bulgaria), and Anton Komashko (the Ukraine) — issued the following appeal to all revolutionary artists:

1. The unification of all revolutionary artists in all countries must be our tactic.
2. We should not be a sect, but an open organization uniting the broad masses.
3. We must wage our struggle on political ground and not enclose ourselves in a circle of purely artistic problems....A political problem is not solved by an artistic one, but by a synthesis of political content and artistic form.[75]

Under the supervision of Uitz (and later Ék and Kemény), the IBRA established contact with many radical organizations in Europe, Japan, and the United States (including the John Reed Club) and arranged or encouraged important exhibitions in Moscow, including the Anti-Imperialist Exhibition (1931), the John Reed Club Exhibition (1932), Revolutionary Art in the Countries of Capitalism (1932-33), and Gomez's one-man show at the state Museum of New Western Art in 1933.

Apart from his administrative duties, Uitz continued to draw and paint, although the works that survive from the period of the 1930s-60s such as *Chapaev*, *Red Army on the Alert*, and *Young Girls Singing* are more primitive and simplistic than his expressionist graphics of the 1910s-20s. That these later works seem to be preliminary studies for murals rather than finished works of art is not accidental, since Uitz continued to be attracted to monumental art as an appropriate reflection of the workers' movement. After all, that is how he had first communicated his ideas of class struggle and social equality in his revolutionary decorations for Budapest in 1919.[76] During the 1930s, for example, he worked on murals for the projected Palace of Soviets in Moscow and with Mészáros (in 1936-38) on decorations for the government building in Frunze where he had relocated in 1935. Frunze marked the end of Uitz's public career; he was arrested there and imprisoned in 1938. Some of his later works were exhibited in a one-man show in Budapest in 1968, and he returned to Hungary in 1970.

163. BÉLA UITZ, Prolétaires de tous les pays, unissez-vous!, 1925-26

140. ARMAND SCHÖNBERGER, At the Well, c1928

Although much of Uitz's work of the Soviet period was lost, it is clear from the examples available that he was deeply interested in the problem of composition, and his drawings, early and late, often contain the traces of his careful structural annotations, whether in the icon analyses of 1921-22, the Kirghizian sketches of the 1930s, or the portraits of Lenin, Nadezhda Krupskaia, and Maksim Gor'ky of the 1950s. That Uitz gave particular attention to the theory of composition is evident not only from his own geometrical diagrams illustrating his theory of social progress, but also from comments by distinguished artists who saw his work. In a letter to Uitz dated June 6, 1934, for example, Paul Signac wrote:

First and foremost, it is your knowledge of composition that is clear. Everything is built on rhythms, at once Classical and new, that guarantee a total balance of composition. At the same time, you really know how to play with the lines and values that supplement the elements of composition.[77]

Strangely enough, it was this expertise that attracted János Mácza, almost in spite of himself, to Uitz's art in the 1920s.[78]

In general, Mácza had chosen to maintain a safe distance from his Hungarian colleagues during his Moscow exile (except for Ferenczy and art historian Frigyes Antal); he also had become one of the Soviet Union's fiercest opponents of abstract art and formal analysis. As late as the 1970s, he wrote *Breaking up lines, mixing up colors, sounds, and words, and putting out all this mixture saying that it's some new method is simply being irresponsible.*[79]

JÁNOS MÁCZA János Mácza was among the first of the Hungarian radicals to emigrate to the Soviet Union, arriving in Moscow in June 1923, with the help of the International Association for Aiding Workers. In 1926, he published his first book in Russian, *Iskusstvo sovremennoi Evropy* [The Art of Contemporary Europe], after which Lunacharsky invited him to work at the Section for the Spatial Arts at the Communist Academy and at the Russian Association of Scientific Research Institutes in the Social Sciences (RANION). In 1928 he became a professor of art history at Moscow State University, joined the October group, and continued to publish and edit a wide variety of books on art history, art groups, architecture, and aesthetics, until his death in 1974.

As in the case of Kemény and Uitz, Mácza's emigration to the Soviet Union coincided with a noticeable change in his aesthetic and critical orientation. Like them, Mácza never wavered in his socialist and Marxist views, and his early contributions to *A Tett* and *Ma*, his supervision of the *Ma* theater studio in Budapest in 1917, and his production of the mass oratorio in Košice in 1922 all demanded an attention to leftist form and content.[80] While he always believed in the direct connection between art and politics, in the early years he was ready to accept a plurality of artistic expression (futurism, suprematism, expressionism, constructivism). By 1926 in his *Iskusstvo sovremennoi Evropy*, however, he demonstrates a sharp intolerance of most forms of modern art.[81] Now, in Mácza's view, the Activists in general "had been fighting for a dead cause" (p. 36), and Kassák and *A Tett* symbolized a "petit bourgeois mutiny" (p. 47).

The principal exception to Mácza's sociological tirade against modern art was Uitz, to whom he devoted a substantial part of his 1926 book. Curiously enough, Mácza did not concentrate on Uitz's heroic realism and didactic graphics such as the Luddite cycle, but rather on the artist's intriguing geometric renderings of social epochs. According to Mácza's description of Uitz's theory, there are two kinds of social structure: centralist (as in ancient Egypt and feudal times) and anarchical (as in ancient Greek and modern bourgeois democracies). The graphic symbol of the former is a hieratic triangle where the slaves are at the base and the pharaoh at the apex; since those classes were ignorant of the concept of "upward mobility," the triangle remained equilateral and static like a pyramid. In feudal times the distribution of power persisted, but the social forces now aspired upward, thereby undermining the equilibrium of the triangle and culminating in the irregularities of the gothic style. In Greek and capitalist democracies the social ferment intensified, and even though the outward social structure returned to an equilateral triangle, the upward and lateral movements created an intrasocial migration that prepared the way for the classless democracy of communism. The result was that (p. 89):

The forces here strive to ascend, but not toward a "hierarchical" center on top, but toward an extended summit — *toward a communist society in which there are no longer classes.*

Such "vulgar sociology" as it later came to be called, appealed to Mácza, and he repeated the same theme in subsequent publications. However, the redeeming feature in this particular context is the visual beauty of Uitz's diagrams, especially the extraordinary compass and ruler composition, which illustrates the "greatest possible wealth of formal possibilities" (p. 90) and deserves comparison with any graphic design by Moholy-Nagy or Rodchenko. Uitz's scheme inspired Mácza to illustrate his text with a number of simple formal analyses of works by Bellini, Velasquez, and other masters, in addition to four of his own socio-artistic tables.

Mácza's Soviet publications fall into two main categories: those that repeat and amplify the sociological and esthetic denominations mentioned above, and those that document the evolution of modern art without critical interpretation.[82] Publications in the first group ignore Kassák, dismiss Moholy-Nagy as a "repetition of Léger,"[83] and describe Kandinsky as the "anarchic world of a symbology of individual sensations evoked by subjective moods." On the other hand, Rivera and Uitz he notes, "have arrived at a rich, emotional imagery in which they have set themselves the aim of reflecting synthetically the class struggle of the proletariat."[84]

The second and more felicitous type of research undertaken by Mácza in the late 1920s and early 1930s includes his documentary collections, especially the *Ezhegodnik literatury i iskusstva na 1929* [Annual for Literature and Art for 1929] and the famous *Sovetskoe iskusstvo za 15 let* [Soviet Art during the Last 15 Years) of 1933.[85] Paradoxically, it is for these objective and accurate compilations and not for his Marxist interpretations that Mácza is now remembered, since *Sovetskoe iskusstvo za 15 let* has become an indispensable guide to the groups and exhibitions that determined the course of the Soviet avant-garde. Until very recently, for example, this work was the principal published source of information on INKhUK, for it both reprinted Kandinsky's research program and listed its international connections.

Mácza's dispassionate presentation of these materials contrasted with the predictable ideological formulae which he often used in his discussions of artists and exhibitions: "solidarity of the revolutionary detachments of the world proletariat," "militant unity of the international proletariat," and "truth about reality sharpened by the Party"[86] were part of a pre-ordained jargon that earned him a doctorate in art history in 1935. In all, Mácza's contribution to the development of Soviet art criticism and history is considerable, and the Marxist sociological approach practiced in the late 1920s-50s, however vulgar, owes much to his categories and conclusions.

IN 1915, KASSÁK CALLED FOR THE CREATION OF A NEW ARTISTIC CULTURE that would be enjoyed in "Rome, Paris, Moscow, Berlin, London, and Budapest."[87] Kassák never really determined what the new esthetic would be, but obviously he hoped for a radical and revolutionary one. On one level, his hopes were justified, because in the 1920s the Hungarian and Russian diasporas contributed much to the international style in Soviet Russia, Europe, and the United States. In this respect, the real strength of the new Hungarian artists lay precisely in their anonymity and ability to merge with forces already present, an aesthetic sophistication that achieved its brightest manifestation at the Bauhaus on both sides of the Atlantic. On the other hand, as Kassák again emphasized, the Hungarian avant-garde "unified all new schools within itself"[88] and, therefore, defied definition. Certainly, the Russian connection was of great importance to Hungarian Activism, but it was only one of many ingredients. For us to appreciate the rich diversity of its aesthetic and ideological composition, we must also take account of the concurrent influences from France and Germany. The result is a mosaic of magical effects that once again testifies to the extraordinary malleability and cosmopolitan nature of modern Hungarian culture.

Notes

Frequently cited works, except for those in Russian, are identified by author, editor, or sponsoring organization and abbreviated titles; journal articles, essays, and chapters in larger works are enclosed in quotation marks, and book titles are set in italics. See the comprehensive Select Bibliography at the end of this volume for full details of publication. Works in Russian are fully documented.

1. A detailed monographic study of the intricate inter-relationships of the Hungarian and Russian avant-gardes has yet to be published, but some information is provided in the following sources. Ernő Kállai, *Neue Malerei in Ungarn* [New Art in Hungary]; Krisztina Passuth, *Magyar művészek az európai avantgarde-ban* [Hungarian Artists in the European Avant-garde] *1919-1925*; D. Bizo, O. Shvidkovsky, et al., eds., *Sovetsko-vengerskie sviazi v khudozhestvennoi kul'ture* [Soviet-Hungarian Relations in Artistic Culture] (Moscow: Nauka, 1975); Tania Frank, ed., *Ernst Kállai: Vision und Formgesetz* [Vision and Form Discipline]; L. Aleshina and N. Yavorskaia, eds., *Iz istorii khudozhestvennoi zhizni SSSR: Internatsional'nye sviazi v oblasti izobrazitel'nogo iskusstva* [From the Art History of the USSR: International Relations in the Field of Visual Art], *1917-1940* (Moscow: Iskusstvo, 1987); and Hubertus Gassner, ed., *Wechselwirkungen: Ungarische Avantgarde in der Weimarer Republik* [Interactions: The Hungarian Avant-garde in the Weimar Republic]. The author acknowledges the generosity of Professor G. Cavaglià for allowing the use of his texts, especially *Le avanguardie artistiche e la Reppublica ungherese dei Consigli* [The Artistic Avant-garde and the Hungarian Republic of Councils], ca. 1980; this unpublished manuscript contains valuable material on the development of Hungarian Activism together with extracts from the theoretical and ideological writings of the time (in Italian translation).

2. For information on these nineteenth century connections see L. Aleshina, "Vengerskaia zhivopis' v muzeiakh SSSR," [Hungarian Painting in the Museums of the USSR], in Bizo et al., eds., pp. 169-78.

3. On Hollósy and his Russian students, see A. Tikhomirov, "Shimon Kholloshi i ego russkie ucheniki," [Shimon Kholloshi and his Russian students] *Iskusstvo*, no. 8 (1957); M. V. Dobuzhinsky, *Vospominaniia*, edited by G. Chugunov (Moscow: Nauka, 1987), pp. 157-62.

4. On Uitz's social diagrams see J. Mácza (I. L. Matsa) *Iskusstvo sovremennoi Evropy* [The Art of Contemporary Europe] (Moscow-Leningrad: Gosudarstvennoe izdatel'stvo, 1926), pp. 87-90; preface by Vladimir Friche.

5. Éva Körner, untitled essay, in *Avanguardia ungherese* (Milan: Galleria del Levante, 1973), exhibition catalogue; German trans. in *Kunst in Ungarn, 1900-1950*.

6. On the relationship of symbolism to activism, see M. d'Alessandro, "Dal futurismo all'avanguardia ungherese." [From Futurism to the Hungarian Avant-garde].

7. Lajos Kassák, Programm, *A Tett*, no. 10 (March 20, 1916), p. 155; trans. in Cavaglià, p. 5.

8. Viacheslav Ivanov, "Ellinskaia religiia stradaiushchego boga" (1905), in J. West, *Russian Symbolism* (London: Methuen, 1970), pp. 76, 80.

9. Iván Hevesy, "Tömegkultúra—Tömegmuvészet" [Mass Culture, Mass Art], in *Ma*, no. 3 (April 1, 1919), pp. 70-71; trans. in Cavaglià, p. 38.

10. György Lukács, "Régi kultúra, új kultúra," [Old Culture, New Culture] *Internationale* (June 15, 1919); trans. in Cavaglià, p. 26.

11. D. Burliuk, A. Kruchenykh, V. Khlebnikov, B. Livshits, *Poshchechina obshchestvennomu vkusu* [Yielding to Public Taste] (Moscow: Dolinsky-Kuzmin, 1912).

12. Kassák, Programm.

13. d'Alessandro, p. 285.

14. Ibid., especially pp. 289-90.

15. Burliuk, et al.

16. Kassák, Programm.

17. d'Alessandro, p. 277.

18. From Burliuk, et al. The full line is: "Throw Pushkin, Dostoevsky, Tolstoi, . . . overboard from the Steamship of Modernity."

19. Kandinsky's high standing within the Russian artistic establishment is indicated by the presentation of his essay "On the Spiritual in Art" at the prestigious and scholarly All-Russian Congress of Artists in St. Petersburg in December 1911. His text was read by the physician and painter Nikolai Kul'bin to whom Kassák later referred in his foreign issue of *A Tett* (August 1, 1916). For information on the Kandinsky lecture, see J. Bowlt and R. C. Washton Long, *The Life of Vasili Kandinsky in Russian Art* (Newtonville: Oriental Research Partners, 1980).

20. Kassák's *Mesteremberek* [Craftsmen] was first published in *A Tett*, no. 2 (1915). There is a Russian translation in Mácza, pp. 46-47, and a partial French translation in Júlia Szabó, *A Magyar aktivizmus története*, [The History of Hungarian Activism] p. 85; reprinted in *Kunst in Ungarn, 1990-1950*.

21. For example, reviewing Marinetti's poetry in 1910, Mihály Babits could find little of value in it (*Nyugat*, 1910; see Cavaglià, p. 1), whereas two years later Béla Balázs (Futuristák, *Nyugat*, no. 7, April 1912, pp. 645-47) praised the basic principle of the futurists:
The objects that we see, deprived of motion, are empty abstractions. They do not correspond to our states of soul either. Inside and outside of us there is only movement. It is not what we see that is important as much as the links between things, because these are our true interior experiences.
However, in his anthology of new poetry in 1914, Kosztolányi emphasized the "politically reactionary" nature of futurism, just as Kassák was beginning to assume the outward trappings of a Hungarian Marinetti. See D. Kosztolányi, *Modern Költők* [Modern Poets] (Budapest, 1914), p. 426; information from Cavaglià, p. 2. D'Alessandro (p. 280) discusses Kassák as the Hungarian Marinetti.
The Hungarians' zig-zag appreciation of Italian Futurism reminds us of the Russians' apprehension, although the latter had a much clearer idea of its theory and practice through the extensive translations of manifestoes, joint exhibitions, and Marinetti's visit to St. Petersburg in 1914. While understanding the pioneering work of Boccioni, Carrà, Severini, and Marinetti, the Russian Avant-garde concluded that Italian Futurism was artistically superficial, narrowly nationalistic, and dangerously militaristic. This became clear during the public discourse in 1914 between the Russian futurist poet Benedikt Livshits and Marinetti in St. Petersburg:
B.L.: We emphasize the continuity of the verbal mass—its elemental, cosmic essence. The only substance a poet can possess is the material of his art. He possesses this substance by immersing himself in the elements of the word. That is not being archaic. It is the practice of cosmology and that admits no temporal measurement.
F.T.M.: That's metaphysics...metaphysics of the most loathsome kind, claiming exclusive exploitation of all "otherworldly" values! What's that got to do with futurism?
B.L.: And why should futurism be the prisoner of Tripolitania?
Quoted in Benedikt Livshits, *The One-and-a-Half-eyed Archer*, trans. J. Bowlt (Newtonville: Oriental Research Partners, 1977), pp. 193-94.

22. Ibid., p. 208.

23. L. Kassák: "Kiáltvány a művészetért," [A Manifesto for Art] *Ma* (1918), first special number (November); quoted in Cavaglià, p. 13.

24. Cavaglià, p. 14.

25. Árpád Szélpál: "Művészet és kommunizmus," *Ma*, no. 3 (December 20, 1918); trans. in Cavaglià, pp. 45-46.

26. From Kállai.

27. On Kun's experiences as a prisoner-of-war in Russia, see R. Tőkés, *Béla Kun and the Hungarian Soviet Republic* (New York: Praeger, 1967), pp. 49-57.

28. An extract from Lenin's *State and Revolution* was published in *Ma*, 1919.

29. A paraphrase of Maiakovsky's 1918 poem *Prikaz armii iskusstva*.

30. Mácza, "Vospominaniia," [Memories] in Bizo et al., eds., p. 100.

31. Ibid., p. 98.

32. See Cavaglià, p. 19.

33. Lajos Kassák, "Aktivizmus," *Ma* (April 15, 1919), pp. 46-51.

34. Pal Kéri, "Mácza," *Az ember* (April 15, 1919); quoted in Cavaglià, p. 22.

35. György Lukács: "Felvilágosításul," [For Enlightment], *Vörös Újság* (April 18, 1919); quoted in Cavaglià, p. 23.

36. Béla Kun, "Részlet Kun Béla válaszából az országos pártgyűlés második napján," *Vörös Újság* [Excerpt from Béla Kun's answer on the second day of the national party congress] (June 14, 1919); quoted in Cavaglià, p. 27.

37. L. Kassák: "Levél Kun Bélához a művészet nevében," [Letter to Béla Kun in the Name of Art], *Ma*, no. 7 (June 15, 1919), pp. 146-48; quoted in Cavaglià, pp. 27-28.

38. Árpád Szélpál: "Kun Béla," *Ma*, no. 7 (June 15, 1919), trans. in Cavaglià, p. 3.

39. Komfut, "Programmnaia deklaratsiia," *Iskusstvo kommuny*, no. 8 (January 26, 1919), p. 3; English trans. in J. Bowlt, ed.: *Russian Art of the Avant-Garde: Theory and Criticism* (London: Thames and Hudson, 1988), p. 166.

40. Béla Uitz commented on the "Russian Evening" in a note in *Ma* (January 1921). See also C. Lodder, *Russian Constructivism* (New Haven: Yale University, 1983), pp. 235-36.

41. Kállai, Kassák, and Kemény wrote reviews of the exhibition. Ernő Kállai, "A berlini orosz kiállítás," *Akasztott Ember*, (February 15, 1923), German trans. in Frank, ed., pp. 26-29; Lajos Kassák: A berlini orosz kiállítás, *Ma* (December 1922); Alfred Kemény: Jegyzétek az orosz művészet berlini kiállításához, *Egység* (February 4, 1923), German trans. in Gassner, ed., pp. 232-33.

42. The *Realist Manifesto* was published in Hungarian translation in *Egység* no. 2 (1922), pp. 3-4. See Chapter 2 of this volume.

43. Lajos Kassák, introduction to Lajos Kassák and László Moholy-Nagy, *Buch neuer Künstler* (Vienna: *Ma* edition, 1922), n.p. For information on Hungarian architecture of this period, see F. Merényi, *1867-1967, Cento anni architettura ungherese* [One Hundred Years of Hungarian Architecture] (Rome: Accademia d'Ungheria, 1965).

44. "A mai orosz építészet," [Russian Architecture Today], in *Dokumentum* (March 1927), pp. 17-20.

45. László Moholy-Nagy, "Abstract of an Artist" (1944) in Krisztina Passuth, *Moholy-Nagy*, p. 381; see also pp. 24-25 and 28-29 for Passuth's discussion of Moholy-Nagy and Malevich, Gabo, and Pevsner. Most sources give 1922 as the year in which Moholy-Nagy met El Lissitzky in Berlin. However, Gassner, ed., gives 1921 (p. 578).

46. U. Kukhirt et al., eds., *Vzaimosviazi russkoi i nemetskoi khudozhestvennoi kul'tury* [Interactions of Russian and German Art Culture] (Moscow: Nauka, 1980), p. 171. Mácza reproduced one of Kaden's constructions in his *Iskusstvo sovremennoi Evropy*, p. 81.

47. See, for example, László Moholy-Nagy and Alfréd Kemény, "Dynamisch-konstruktives Kraftsystem," *Der Sturm*, no. 12 (1922) p. 186; Alfréd Kemény: "Das dynamische Prinzip der Weltkonstruktion," [The Dynamic Principle of World Construction], *Der Sturm*, no. 14 (1924) pp. 62-64; A. Gáspár, "Die Bewegung der ungarischen Aktivisten," [The Movement of the Hungarian Activists], *Der Sturm* no. 15 (1924) pp. 163-67. The relations of the Activists to *Der Sturm* have been covered well by Krisztina Passuth, "'Der Sturm' der Ungarn," and Ildikó Hajnal-Neukäter, "Herwarth Walden und Lajos Kassák—ein Porträt," in Gassner, ed., pp. 56-60, 61-67.

48. This work is reproduced in Gassner, ed., p. 578. El Lissitzky used the motif of the human hand on a number of occasions. In addition to *The Constructor* (1924), he incorporated it into his illustration called *Boat Ticket* for Ilya Ehrenburg's *Shest' povestei o legkikh kontsakh* (Berlin: Helikon, 1922) and his cover for the *Vkhutemas* program (Moscow: Vkhutemas, 1927).

49. For a discussion of Moholy-Nagy's nickel sculpture and Tatlin's Monument, see H. Gassner: "'Ersehnte Einheit' oder 'erpresste Versöhnung'," in Gassner, ed., op. cit., especially pp. 218-19.

50. Moholy-Nagy's *Two Constructional Systems Linked* (also called *Metal Sculpture*) of 1921-22 (now lost), is reproduced as no. 67 in Passuth, *Moholy-Nagy*. Ivan Leonidov's project for the Lenin Institute is reproduced in A. Gozak and A. Leonidov, *Ivan Leonidov* (London: Academy Editions, 1988), pp. 41-49. For information on the polemic, see "Illiustrirovannoe pis'mo redaktoru," *Sovetskoe foto*, no. 4 (1928) and A. Rodchenko, "Krupnaia bezgramotnost' ili melkaia gadost'?," *Novyi lef*, no. 6 (1928), pp. 42-44.

51. See Sándor Ék, *Vchera i segodnia* [Yesterday and Today] (Moscow: Progress, 1972), pp. 157-58.

52. During his Moscow sojourn (1932-35), Ferenczy lived with other Hungarian émigrés, including Béla Balázs, László Dallos-Griffel, and Andor Gábor, working as a sculptor and medalist. He received some prestigious commissions, including a bust of Marx for the Institute of Marx and Engels (then directed by the Hungarian Ernő Czóbel). For information on Ferenczy in this period, see A. Kosarev, "Moskovskii tsikl medalei Beni Ferentsii," in Bizo et al., eds., pp. 111-14.

53. During his Soviet emigration Dallos-Griffel was especially close to Uitz, and in the early 1930s he lived with Béni Ferenczy. In 1934 he published an article, "Konkretnoe predlozhenie," in the Moscow journal *Tvorchestvo*, no. 6, on his artistic world view.

54. On the Union of Hungarian Revolutionary Writers and Artists, see Aleshina and Yavorskaia, eds., p. 39.

55. A. Sidorov in *Biulleten GAKhN*, no. 1 (1925); quoted in Aleshina and Yavorskala, eds., p. 111.

56. Among the more important exhibitions to which Hungarian nationals contributed were the Exhibition of the Political Poster (Moscow, 1932); 15 Years of the Red Army (Moscow, Leningrad, Kiev, Khar'kov, 1933-35); and the Exhibition of Paintings and Graphics by the Brigade of Foreign Revolutionary Artists (Moscow, 1934).

57. For information on Kemény see Gassner, ed., pp. 575; this source also contains German translations of some of Kemény's essays (pp. 40-41, 111, 209-10, 219, 222-50, 456-66). On Uitz, see Gassner, ed., p. 587; Kállai, *Neue Malerei in Ungarn*, passim; and the catalogue of Uitz's one-man show, *Uitz Béla kiállítása*. On Mácza, see his memoirs in Bizo et al., pp. 98-106, 274; also his *Eszmeiség, avantgarde, művészet* [Ideas, Avant-Garde, Art] (Budapest: Petőfi Irodalmi Múzeum, 1982).

58. János Mácza et al., eds.: *Sovetskoe iskusstvo za 15 let* [Soviet Art after 15 Years] (Moscow-Leningrad: Ogiz, 1933), p. 201. The Berlin journal *Veshch'* was a trilingual monthly (Vesch'/Gegenstand/Objêt, or Object) edited by El Lissitzky and Ilya Ehrenburg in 1922-23.

59. Kemény's INKhUK lectures are quoted, paraphrased, and discussed in S. Khan-Magomedov: "Molodoe i staroe pokolenie khudozhnikov-proizvodstvennikov na etape 'ot izobrazheniia k konstruktsii'" in *Trudy VNIITE* (Moscow, 1979), no. 21, pp. 63-109, especially pp. 81-92. German trans. in Gassner, ed., op. cit., pp. 226-30.

60. After his Moscow visit Kemény no doubt discussed Rodchenko, Tatlin, and the OBMOKhU group with Kassák, who then included references to their work in his *Buch neuer Künstler*.

61. Quotations from Kemény's lectures appear in Khan-Magomedov, pp. 81-84.

62. E. Kállai, A. Kemény, L. Moholy-Nagy, and L. Péri, "Nyilatkozat" [Declaration], *Egység*, no. 4 (1923) p. 5; German trans. in Gassner, ed., pp. 233-34.

63. Kemény, Jeqyzétek az orosz művészet berlini kiállításához.

64. Kállai, "A berlini orosz kiállítás."

65. See Durus [A. Kemény], "Dziga Wertow: Der Mann mit der Kamera," *Die Rote Fahne* (July 5, 1929); "Eine Sinfonie des Donbass 'Enthusiasmus'," *Die Rote Fahne* (August 26, 1931). Trans. in Gassner, ed., pp. 465-66; for details on Kemény's article on Péri, see note 47.

66. For references to Kemény's articles written in the Soviet Union during the 1930s, see Aleshina and Yavorskaia, eds., pp. 206-26.

67. For example, Kemény wrote the introduction to the catalogue for Ék's one-man exhibition in Moscow and Leningrad in 1936, and he published an article on Mészáros, "Vengerskii revoliutsionnyi skul'ptor Laslo Mesarosh," [The Hungarian Revolutionary Sculptor Mészáros], *Iskusstvo*, no. 6 (1935). For information on Mészáros's Soviet residence see Sándor Kontha, "Laslo Mesarosh v Sovetskom Soiuze," in Bizo et al., pp. 107-10.

68. János Mácza (I. L. Matsa), *Iskusstvo epokhi zrelogo kapitalizma na Zapade* [Art of the Epoch of Mature Capitalism in the West] (Moscow: Komakademiia, 1929), p. 235.

69. V. Kostin, *Sredi khudozhnikov* (Moscow: Sovetskii khudozhnik, 1986), p. 113. According to this source, another artist of Hungarian extraction, Viktor Tóth, was also a part of the reform commission at VKhUTEIN in 1926. Tóth, like Mácza and Uitz, became a member of the constructivist group formed in 1928.

70. I. Khvoinik, " Proletarskii khudozhnik Bela Uits," *Sovetskoe iskusstvo*, no. 1 (1927) p. 34.

71. A. Alekseev, et al., "Oktiabr. Ob'edinenie khudozhestvennogo truda. Deklaratsiia," *Sovremennaia arkhitecktura*, (Moscow, 1928), pp. 73; trans. in Bowlt, ed., pp. 275-76.

72. For information on the Ukrainian avant-garde and its activities in Khar'kov, see M. Mudrak, *The New Generation and the Ukrainian Avant-Garde* (Ann Arbor: UMI, 1986).

73. That question was resolved two years later by the advocacy of socialist realism at the First Congress of Soviet Writers in Moscow at which, incidentally, the Hungarians Gyula Illyés and László Mészáros were also present. See Kontha, in Bizo et al., p. 107.

74. Béla Uitz: "Diktatura kell!," [There must be a Dictatorship!], *Vörös Újság* (April 10, 1919).

75. Béla Uitz: *Tezisy* [Theses]. Archive of the International Bureau of Revolutionary Artists, Central State Archive of Literature and Art (Moscow), fund 2707, opus 1, item 11, pp. 9-11. Quoted in Aleshina and Yavorskaia, eds., p. 20.

76. One example of Uitz's early monumental work is his wall painting *Humanity* that he created for the Palace of Labor, Budapest, in 1919. A sketch for this work is reproduced in Gassner, ed., p. 41; the finished work is reproduced in Mácza, *Iskusstvo sovremennoi Evropy*, p. 69.

77. Archive of Boris Ternovets, State Pushkin Museum of Fine Arts, Moscow, fund 55; quoted in Aleshina and Yavorskaia, eds., p. 284. Kállai was also struck more by the formal elements of Uitz's art than by its didactic content, as he indicated in his appraisal of Uitz in *Neue Malerei in Ungarn*.

78. Uitz wrote about his "social geometries" in "Kísérlet az ideológiai formáról," [Experiment with the Ideological Form], *Ék* (1923). Mácza then quoted and discussed the results in *Iskusstvo sovremmenoi Evropy*, pp. 87-90.

79. Mácza, "Vospominaniia," p. 99.

80. Mácza was especially interested in the notion of total theater and published a book on the subject, *A teljes színpad* (Vienna, 1922); see also his comment on theater in *A Tett*, no. 13 (1916). For a reproduction of one of his stage designs see Gassner, ed., p. 213.

81. Mácza (1926) op. cit., pp. 36, 47, 87-90.

82. Mácza's (Matsa's) principal art historical and critical books of the late 1920s and early 1930s are: *Iskusstvo epokhi zrelogo kapitalizma na Zapade* [Art of the Epoch of Mature Capitalism in the West] (Moscow: Komakademiia, 1929); *Literatura i proletariat na Zapade* [Literature and the Proletariat in the West] (Moscow: Komakdemiia, 1929); *Ocherki po teoreticheskomu iskusstvoznaniiu* [The Theoretical Knowledge of Art] (Moscow: Komakademiia, 1930); *Tvorcheskie voprosy sovetskogo iskusstva* [The Creative Questions of Soviet Art] (Moscow: Komakademiia, 1933); *Besedy ob arkhitekture* [Talks on Architecture] (Moscow: Ogiz-Izogiz, 1935).

83. Matsa, *Iskusstvo epokhi*, p. 158. However, just as Mácza (Matsa) wrote this negative appraisal, Moholy-Nagy's *Malerei Fotografie Film* was published in Russian translation: *Zhivopis' ili fotografiia* (Moscow: Ogonek, 1929); preface by A. Fedorov-Davydov.

84. Mácza, *Iskusstvo epokhi*, pp. 179, 234.

85. János Mácza (Matsa), ed.: *Ezhegodnik literatury i iskusstva na 1929* [Survey of Literature and Art in the Year 1929] (Moscow: Komakademiia, 1929; I. Matsa, et al., *Reingardt Sovetskoe iskusstvo za 15 let*.

86. From Mácza's review of the non-Russian contributors to the exhibition 15 Years of the Red Army, "Inostrannye khudozhniki na vystavke" [Foreign Artists on the Exhibition], *Izvestiia* (Moscow, July 24, 1933), no. 183, p. 3.

87. Last line of Kassák's poem *Mesterem-berek* [Artisans] (1915). From the Russian translation in Mácza, *Iskusstvo sovremennoi Evropy*, p. 47.

88. L. Kassák: "Szintétikus irodalom," [Synthetic Literature], in *Ma*, no. 2 (January 1916), p. 18. Quoted in d'Alessandro, p. 287.

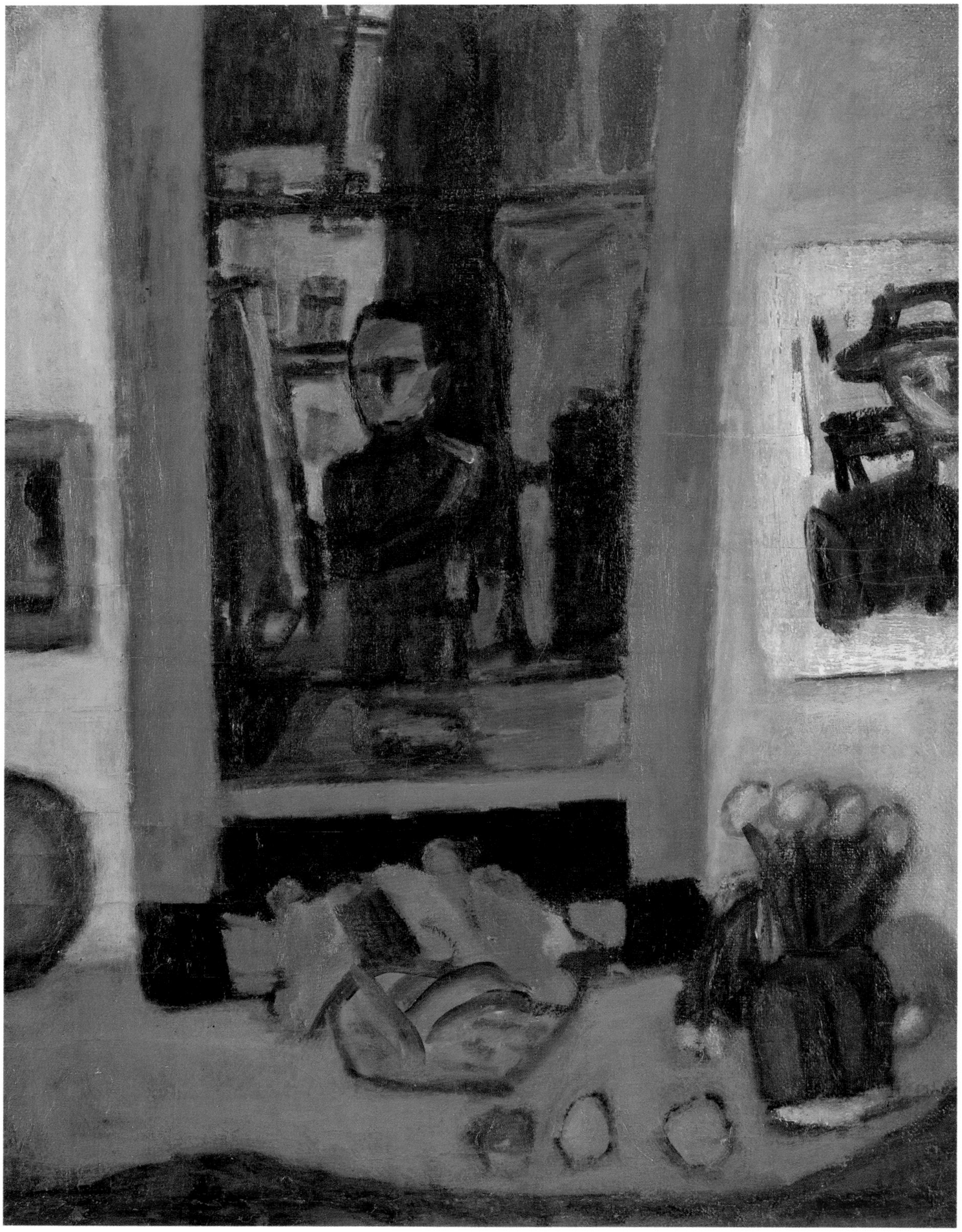

34. BÉLA CZÓBEL, In the Studio, 1922

KRISZTINA PASSUTH

THE AVANT-GARDE in HUNGARY and EASTERN EUROPE

Only in the past decade has the existence of the Hungarian avant-garde as an equal partner with the other major European movements of its time become a topic of scholarly discussion, and then primarily among Hungarian art historians. Recent Western European studies do refer to the Hungarian avant-garde, but without an appreciation of the number of artists involved or an understanding of the interaction of the Hungarian movement with others in Eastern Europe. Current scholarship regarding the Czech, Serbian, Croatian, Slovenian, Romanian, and Polish artistic movements is similarly isolationist in nature and lacks integration into a comprehensive pan-European conceptual framework. The exception is the Russian avant-garde, the first to attract attention throughout the region (See Chapter 4).

Most Hungarian artists and critics of the early 1900s wanted to be associated with the West. As a result of the cultural isolation attending the political and social developments of the 1800s (*see Chapter 1*), they either denied the authentic and historical psychological values of their native cultures or refused to acknowledge those that did not conform to preconceived concepts of artistic expression. Hungarian critics of the avant-garde period did not consider their own national art equal to that of Western countries, and they thought even less of the art of other East-Central European countries, often denying that it existed at all. By the 1950s, official Hungarian art criticism (actually a product of the 1930s, with antecedents in the last half of the nineteenth century) considered all urban and Western avant-garde experiments as "cosmopolitan," and corrupt, and foreign to the goals of the Hungarian nation. Thereby excluded, without hesitation, were the most dynamic and forceful aspirations of the avant-garde period.

The avant-garde movements and their ambitious personalities and works were rediscovered only in the 1960s, beginning with examinations of events and developments during the period. Focusing their interest first on interactions with Western European artists and cultural centers, only recently have scholars turned to Hungary's contributions to artistic developments in East-Central European and the international community.

The first phase of the Hungarian avant-garde movement (1909-14) bears the stamp of *Nyolcak* [The Eight], the second is marked by the work of the Activists (1915-19), and the third is dominated by the activities centering on the journal *Ma* [Today] in Vienna (1920-25). After 1925, avant-garde development continued, but as a less cohesive movement, in such centers as the Dessau Bauhaus, Berlin, and Budapest. Although the earliest and final stages of the Hungarian avant-garde are tied to Hungary itself, the richest, most dynamic period (1920-25) is associated with the West — with Vienna and Berlin (*see Chapter 2*). During this period similarities in styles and interests emerged between Hungarian and other East-Central European avant-garde movements, leading frequently to active cooperation and collaboration. This chapter focuses on shared and divergent characteristics of, and interactions between, the East-Central European movements and the Hungarian avant-garde.

Art historian Krisztina Passuth, born in Budapest, attended Lóránd Eötvös University, where her thesis was devoted to The Eight. Formerly on the staff of the Hungarian National Gallery (1962-66), she served as curator of nineteenth and twentieth century collections at the Museum of Fine Arts (1966-77), where she organized some of the twentieth century art exhibitions. In Paris since 1977, she collaborated in the Paris-Berlin and Paris-Moscow exhibitions; organized the Hungarian avant-garde (1980) and the František Kupka (1989) exhibitions at the Musée d'Art Moderne de la Ville de Paris, where she is on the staff; and earned her Doctorat d'Etat at the Sorbonne (1987). Passuth has published extensively on the Hungarian and international avant-garde; many of her publications are listed in the comprehensive bibliography at the end of this volume.

The East-Central European Context

The modern historical development of the East-Central European countries (Czechoslovakia, Hungary, Poland, Yugoslavia, and Romania) consists of two major periods: the era of the Habsburg monarchy up to 1918, and the postwar era after 1918. The two periods are marked by significant political, demographic, and geographical changes, as well as by related cultural transformations that affected both the development and the fate of numerous artistic movements in the region.

The earliest avant-garde associations were formed prior to 1914 in Hungary and in the Bohemian region of what is now Czechoslovakia: The Hungarian *Nyolcak* [The Eight], an offshoot of MIÉNK (Magyar Impresszionisták és Naturalisták Köre) [The Hungarian Impressionist and Naturalist Circle], and its Czech counterpart *Osma* [The Eight]. In both countries, radical wings gradually emerged and separated from the original groups. Of the two analogous Eight movements, the Czech Osma was the earlier one, having had its first major exhibition in Prague in 1907.

A notable group that formed (in 1911) from Osma was *Skupina výtvarnýeh umělcu* [Group of Fine Artists]. Skupina developed a forceful painting style that was a unique blend of cubism and expressionism. The two outstanding Skupina personalities were the painter Bohumil Kubišta and the sculptor Otto Gutfreund. The Hungarian Eight followed in 1909 with a less daring style; its leading talent was Lajos Tihanyi, who created his major works well after the formation of Skupina. Although Osma exhibited at the Hungarian National Salon in Budapest in 1913, the two Eight groups did not acknowledge each other's existence.[1] This mutual disregard seems surprising: Both groups were radically new and represented urban, quite Western views. It may have been this very preoccupation with the assimilation of Western themes that impeded productive interaction between the two neighboring movements.

Between 1915 and 1919, Hungarian artistic development proceeded in quantum leaps. In Budapest, *A Tett* [The Deed] in 1915 and *Ma* [Today] from 1916 attracted young proletarian artists who formed the "Activists" led by Lajos Kassák. In their artistic and social ambitions, the Hungarian Activists were unsurpassed among artists in East-Central Europe at this time (*see Chapter 2*). The Osma and Skupina disbanded and were replaced by the less significant *Tvrdošíjní*, [Stubborn Ones]. Certain expressionist-oriented movements formed in Slovenia (*Proljétni Salon* [Spring salon]), Poland (*Formici* [Formists]), and Romania, but after 1920 their development ceased and their artistic styles were abandoned by contemporary painters. The Hungarian Activists, on the other hand, continued to flourish, developing their own unique styles from 1915 well into the 1920s.

Kassák and the Activists

The leader and dominating personality of the Hungarian Activists was Lajos Kassák, himself of Slovakian extraction. Kassák's background is one likely reason for the frequent appearance of Czech art in *Ma*. Although the first issue of *Ma* in 1916 featured a linoleum cut on the cover by the outstanding Czech painter Vincenc Beneš and illustrations by Emil Filla, also Czech, evidence indicates that Kassák had no direct contact, not even by way of correspondence, with Czech artists, but rather became informed of them through *Der Sturm* illustrations and insert postcards from Berlin. That Kassák probably had no opportunity to become acquainted with these artists during World War I is understandable. What is surprising, however, is that later, in 1921, when he could have established contact, he chose instead to include them in his *Új művészek könyve* [Book of New Artists] without ever becoming personally familiar with them.[2]

In relying on *Der Sturm* for information about the artistic trends of the surrounding countries in 1916, Kassák employed methods for information gathering that he was to continue in later years.

During this early period in Budapest, some of Kassák's colleagues were from Transylvania (such as Béla Uitz and János Máttis Teutsch), Slovakia (János Mácza, Lajos Kudlák, and Ödön Mihályi, and Serbia (Vera Biller, and others). The intervention of World War I limited their activities and prevented communication with neighboring countries (in which several of these artists were posted as soldiers). Despite the apparent lack of direct contacts among members of the East-Central European artistic community, numerous artistic groups emerged with surprisingly similar world views and cultural objectives.[3] Cubism, for example, had

139. ARMAND SCHÖNBERGER, Café Scene, 1924

32. BÉLA CZÓBEL, Working Boy, 1917

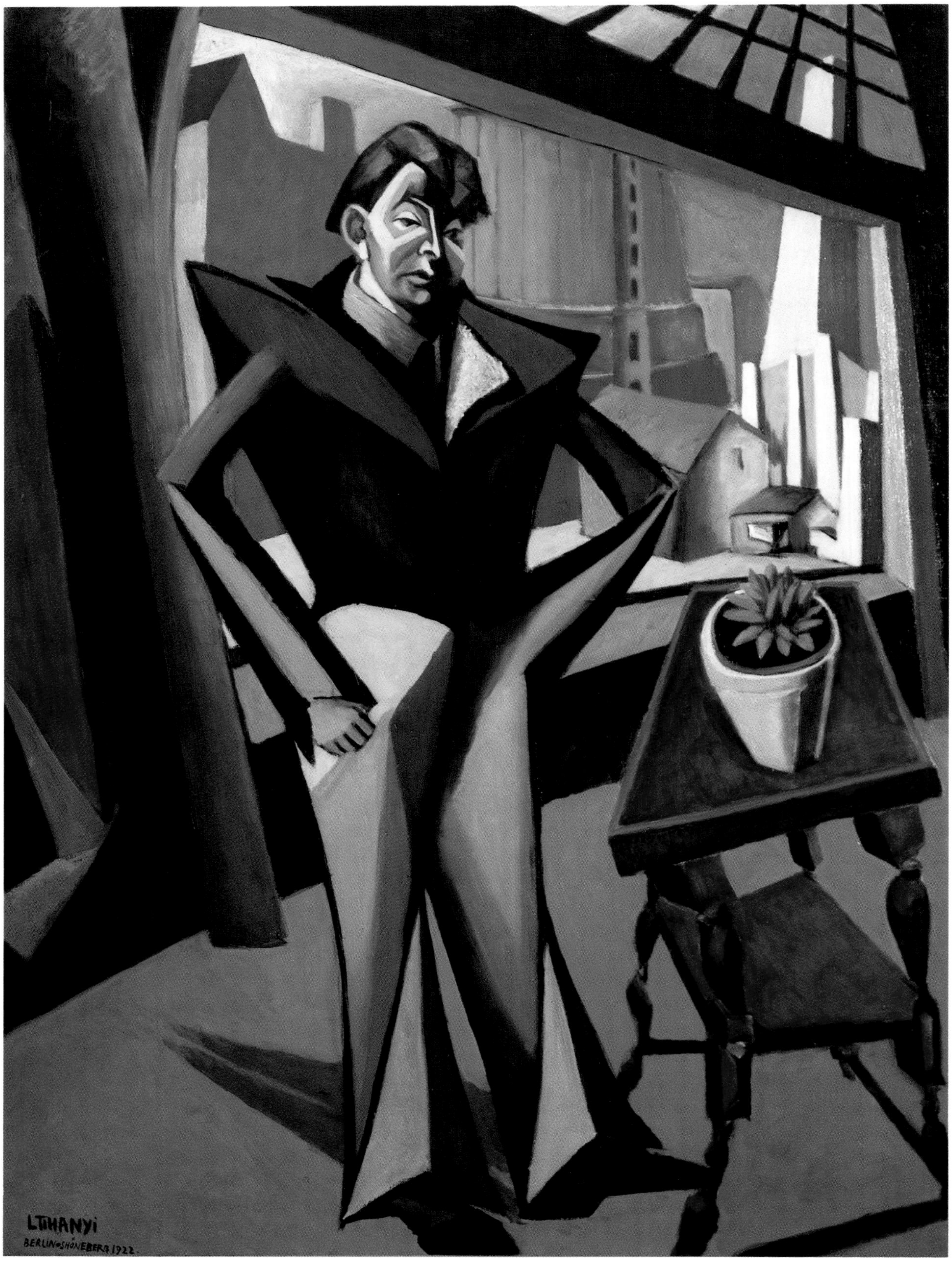

148. LAJOS TIHANYI, Man at a Window, 1922

taken on a national character in the works of Czech sculptors and painters even before 1914, as demonstrated in the sculpture of Gutfreund and canvases of Kubišta. Works of Czech cubist and cubo-expressionist artists were created in Prague (with some foreign influence), while Hungarian cubist-inspired works were completed almost exclusively in Paris, where Hungarian artists Imre Szobotka, Valéria Dénes, Sándor Galimberti, and others worked independently, never having established an active group there. The only Hungarian cubist sculptor, József Csáky, left Hungary permanently in 1905 and joined the French movement; Czech sculptor Gutfreund on the other hand, although he studied with Antoine Bourdelle and served in the French army, became one of the most forceful representatives of the Czech avant-garde movement.

While Hungarian cubist attempts were restricted primarily to isolated experiments in Paris, from 1915 to 1919 Hungarian Activism was forged into an autonomous and unified movement. There are certain spiritual and stylistic similarities, especially in the use of expressionism (rather than cubism), between the works of the Hungarian activist painters and the Czech Osma, even if one cannot identify any specific influence or transfer of technique. The portraits of the Czech Kubišta and the Hungarian Lajos Tihanyi attest to a common emotional source, and their models are endowed with a similar restless energy. The same can be said about the still life works of Kubišta and, later, of József Nemes Lampérth.[4]

These similarities developed in the absence of a common value structure or comprehensive system of contacts prior to 1920. Each national avant-garde movement had been driven by the desire to attain autonomy first, preserving this hard-fought independence against all conservative political and artistic trends. The primary shared experience of European countries East and West was World War I itself. While Hungarian Activism emerged as a cohesive force prior to 1920, the other East-Central European movements for the most part derived from the Versailles Treaty, which dismembered the Austro-Hungarian empire and established the successor states of Yugoslavia and Czechoslovakia, among others (*see Chapter 1*). Nevertheless, from 1920 on, all avant-garde movements, including the Hungarian, strove for internationalism. Some of

115. JÓZSEF NEMES LAMPÉRTH, Still Life with Lamp, 1916

Kassák's circle moved to the newly formed states after 1920: Vera Biller and Péter Dobrovics (Petar Dobrovič) to Yugoslavia; Máttis Teutsch to Romania in 1922; and János Mácza to Czechoslovakia at about the same time (*see Chapter 4*). Biller and Dobrovics apparently left Ma entirely, while Máttis Teutsch and Mácza respectively played mediating roles between the Hungarian group and those in Romania and Czechoslovakia.

Much as Hungarian writers and artists suffered from the cultural politics of the Hungarian Soviet Republic and the subsequent white terror, which forced them into exile (*see Chapters 1 and 2*), they also gained intellectually from their experiences abroad. The international aspect, previously ignored, all of a sudden opened up to them. And this "international horizon" included more than just the West: paradoxically, as a direct result of their stay in Western Europe, the Activists began to pay more attention to their East-Central European colleagues. At about the same time, their neighbors began to develop their own styles within their respective rapidly proliferating avant-garde movements.

Lajos Kassák was influenced by many factors in shaping a system of East-Central European relations between 1920 and 1925. The first years of *Ma* in Viennese exile focused on relations with smaller

Hungarian circles in the successor states. It is possible that Kassák did not immediately discover or understand the extreme importance of newly developing large-scale national movements such as Devětsil in Prague. However, in 1921-22 he did begin to expand *Ma*'s coverage of the independent national groups, which had reached a truly dynamic stage of development. By this time *Ma*'s correspondents, having had a few years of local experience, also were better able to understand and evaluate the artistic programs of Hungary's neighbors. Initially, most contacts were made with Slovak and Czech artists, and Czechoslovakia was perhaps the only country with which Hungary developed unbroken and permanent relations. In contrast, cooperation with Serbia materialized first in 1921 (and later, in 1924), and Romanian ties were formed in 1922; relations with Poland, realized only after 1924, were quite sporadic. Nevertheless, the period 1921-25 saw the liveliest exchanges of ideas, articles, photographs and periodicals between *Ma* and the intellectual movements of East-Central Europe.

Ma contacts expanded into two types of East-Central European networks. The first consisted of the locally proliferating, smaller Hungarian-language movements in the successor states: for example, *Kassai Munkás* [Kassa Worker] in Slovakia, *Út* [The Way] in Novi Sad (Yugoslavia), and *Periszkóp* [Periscope] and *Korunk* [Our Age] in Transylvania. The second network comprised the autonomous East Central European publications—that is, the Czech *Devětsil*, the Serbian *Zenit* [Zenith], the Romanian *Contimporanul* [Contemporary], and to a smaller extent, the Polish *Blok* [Block].

The two networks were interconnected, and Hungarian language movements tended to initiate contact with the more important autonomous national intellectual journals and their circles. These relations were by no means abstract, taking the form of personal friendships, and at times personal disagreements. The first Hungarian ties to *Zenit* were established through Boško Tokin, who contributed simultaneously to *Zenit* and *Ma*. According to letters preserved in the Belgrade National Museum, when Tokin left *Zenit*, the resulting void was filled only partially by sporadic correspondence between the two editors, Ljubomir Micić of *Zenit* and Kassák of *Ma*. The intricate web of personal relationships is difficult to uncover, for there are few witnesses still alive to tell about it. Without such personal contacts and cooperation, even such similar movements as Ma and Blok largely ignored one another. By the time the avant-garde surfaced in Poland, (1923-24), *Ma* had already reached maturity, and the Polish movement went largely unnoticed by Kassák and his colleagues. Furthermore, Poland was the only remaining East-Central European state that had no Hungarian-language avant-garde periodicals or smaller Hungarian circles. Thus, she lacked the very platform from which to promote national exchanges and contacts in publishing, translations, publicity, and photography.

Kassák acknowledged the financial importance of relations with neighboring countries. Consequently, he had to design a publication that would cater to their local needs so that subscriptions would increase and the other Kassák-sponsored publications would gain in popularity as well. *Ma* could only survive through the voluntary contributions of a few patrons in Budapest. In Vienna, where *Ma* was reestablished by Kassák in 1920, it was a miracle that the journal was published at all. There were few subscribers to be found in Vienna; moreover, since *Ma*'s banishment from Hungary, only a limited number of copies could be smuggled into that country from Vienna and sold through unofficial channels (mostly organized by Kassák's wife, Jolán Simon). Since Kassák desperately needed subscribers from other East-Central European countries, he strengthened his contacts with Czechoslovakia, Yugoslavia, and Romania, as evidenced by the publication of subscription rates in the local currencies of those countries. Again, Poland was not targeted.

Ma's subscription rates indicate that Kassák's aim was to increase his magazine's circulation incrementally. Other than the Viennese and Budapest readership, the best potential base was the ethnic Hungarian population in Czechoslovakia. The first Vienna issue of *Ma* in 1920 included the rates in Czech crowns, and in January 1921 the rates appeared in Austrian currency. In the fourth issue (February 1921), around the time that Hungarian-Serbian relations were stabilized, the Yugoslav dinar rate was added. The inclusion of rates in Italian lira a month later and the Romanian currency price (as well as the U.S. dollar and the

German mark) in April 1921 attest to Kassák's continuing effort to broaden circulation. Subscription rates in these currencies were included in *Ma*'s last issue in June 1925, although by this time continued publication of the magazine was unlikely. As Ferenc Csaplár concludes:

After its banishment from Hungary and later, from Romania and Czechoslovakia, following the disintegration of Hungarian émigré circles in Vienna, Ma's *only hope was to win subscribers among ethnic Austrians.*[5]

This hopeless situation came about in 1925, when Kassák, after several futile attempts to save his magazine, finally had to give up the publication entirely (*see Chapter 2*).

Before its collapse, *Ma* had established certain strongholds in Berlin (with the help of László Moholy-Nagy) and in some East-Central European countries. Some of these regional centers were quite temporary and others more permanent. The nourishment for these regional centers came from ex-*Ma* associates who did not remain in Budapest or go to Vienna after the fall of the Hungarian Soviet Republic, settling instead in Kassa (Košice), Prague, Brassó (Braşov), and other cities. For example, János Mácza lived in Košice from 1920 to 1922 (until he was banned from there), Lajos Kudlák in Losonc (Lučenec) from June 1921, Ödön Mihályi in Košice, and Imre Forbáth in Prague from 1920 on. Relations presumably were established with Ferenc Gömöri in Pozsony (Bratislava) after 1920, as well as with Boško Tokin, who became the *Ma* representative in Zagreb in 1921.

Connections with Romania were sustained by Aladár Tamás starting in 1920, and the Újvidék [Novi Sad] region of Yugoslavia was covered by Zoltán Csuka and his Hungarian-language publication *Út*. These connections operated somewhat sporadically and accounted for only a portion of *Ma*'s international influence. That the successor states had to be viewed as more than mere sources of funding was correctly pointed out in Jenő Gömöri's 1921 Pozsony (Bratislava) publication *Tűz* [Fire]:

We live together—physically live together with the Czech and Slovak peoples. It is necessary that—in order to maintain peace and nurture mutually advantageous cultural ties, including global cultural progress—we get closer to each other spiritually. This spiritual rapprochement is what we would like to promote in our publication....[6]

Kassák is believed to have had a similar goal, although he never put it into a concrete form, in part because of his preoccupation with the struggle to keep *Ma* afloat.

Hungary and the Other National Movements

In a complicated system of influence and counterinfluence, it is necessary to examine trends in specific countries and the activities of individual groups to determine who was transmitting new concepts and who was adopting them. The Hungarian national movements, which developed early and forcefully, appear to have had the strongest influence on their neighbors. The closest, earliest, and strongest ties were with Czechoslovakia.

CZECHOSLOVAKIA Among the Eastern European avant-gardists, Czechs and the Slovaks provided the most durable cooperation, largely because of a multitude of personal relationships. Kassák's Slovakian background made it easier for *Ma* to build up a network of contacts in the region. Kassák could rely on sympathizers in Czechoslovakia who identified with the Activist agenda and published articles, written by *Ma*'s correspondents. The earliest contacts were formed in the ethnic Hungarian territories of Slovakia: in Pozsony (Bratislava), Lučenec (Losonc) and Košice (Kassa). One disseminator of *Ma*'s views was Lajos Kudlák—poet, graphic artist, and mechanical engineer—whose book *Gitár és Konflisló* [Guitar and Hackney Horse] was published by *Ma* in 1920. Kudlák became *Ma*'s representative in Lučenec in June 1921, and although not one of its greatest talents, he provided a useful service to the journal through his multifaceted activities. An even greater role was filled by the poet Ödön Mihályi at Košice. Mihályi, not only promoted *Ma* but prepared translations for Kassák and maintained contact with *Zenit* as well.

In *Ma*'s first years of exile, 1920-22, János Mácza, a theoretician of the theater and a promoter of avant-garde mass theater, played an important role (*see Chapter 4*). During his two-year stay in Slovakia, Mácza attempted to stage a mass theatrical production while keeping in touch with *Ma* and the new Soviet literature as well. More to the left than Kassák, he became editor of *Kassai Munkás*, [Kassa Worker] a Communist party publication. Despite his diverging views with Kassák, it likely

Fig. 5-1 LAJOS KASSÁK, *Bildarchitektur*, 1922, formerly Jilkovsky Collection, Prague.

15. SÁNDOR BORTNYIK, Bildarchitektur 31, 1921

was Mácza who introduced his *Ma* colleagues to the new Czech literary trends, which Kassák later featured in *Horizont* [Horizon].[7] *Kassai Munkás* also organized an exhibit of Sándor Bortnyik's works in 1924 at Košice, where *Bildarchitektur* [architecture of the picture, pictorial architecture] was introduced (*see Chapters 2 and 3*).

After 1924, Vojtech Tilkovsky was another active disseminator of *Ma*'s views. The deep friendship between Kassák and Tilkovsky is suggested in the gift to Tilkovsky of a watercolor made by Kassák during his exile in Vienna (FIG. 5-1). This watercolor is one of the few remaining works of Kassák's Bildarchitektur.[8] Tilkovsky recalls:

I left Vienna in 1924 and enrolled at the University of Bratislava. My relations with Kassák continued, however, and entered a new stage and acquired a new meaning. I had been automatically endowed with the task of expanding the Kassák circle's influence among the progressive, young Slovak intelligentsia. Our avant-garde periodical, DAV, *published many articles by Kassák.... our nightly poetry readings, at which Kassák personally appeared on many occasions, slowly incorporated the workers into its rank and file. And later, Kassák's influence spread from Bratislava to Brno.*[9]

The *Ma* platform consequently spread throughout the ethnic Hungarian territories, in Slovakia first, later permeating the Czech readership in Brno as well.

Although Kassák painstakingly developed Slovak and Czech contacts, he still managed to exclude the Devětsil group of Prague from his sphere of influence. Imre Bori notes that among Kassák's associates, the poet Imre Forbáth

with the consciousness of a great Hungarian poet and with a collection of expressionist poems, frequented the tables at Prague's avant-garde cafes as early as 1920, and became acquainted with E. E. [Egon Erwin] Kisch, St. K. [Stanislav Kostka] Neumann, and [Vítěslav] Nezval's circle.[10]

This Prague circle, together with Jaroslav Seifert, Karel Teige, and several other creative artists, constituted the nucleus of the Czech equivalent of *Ma*'s writer-artist group. During its ten-year existence (1920-30), this Czech movement consisted of 60 members.[11]

Despite Imre Forbáth's activity, the two parallel movements ignored each other and developed independently. Kassák did attempt to gain legitimacy and readership for *Ma* among this group during several visits to Czechoslovakia, apparently the only country he frequented with lecture tours. Banned completely from Hungary, Kassák either did not warrant tours there, did not have the financial organizational resources or lacked a strong enough following in the East-Central countries to make similar tours.

Kassak's visit to Czechoslovakia in March 1922 is remembered by Teige, a leader of the Czech avant-garde, in a peculiar way:

There was never much talk of dadaism in Czechoslovakia... Hungarian emigrants, members of the Ma *circle, participated at a few dadaist-communist gatherings in Prague and gave unorthodox lectures on the subject.*[12]

At first, it seems surprising that the revolutionary Activist Ma circle would wear the label of dadaism, especially for its Czech tour (*see Chapter 2*). It should be remembered, however, that dadaism was not well known in Prague at the time; the only information was circulated there by Dragan Aleksić, a Serbian poet, and through the visits of Raoul Hausmann and Kurt Schwitters in 1921.[13] Although the Czechs did not adopt dadaism in its entirety, they reacted with sensitivity to all dadaist-like initiatives. Kassák himself, somewhat earlier (1921), dispatched several letters to Ödön Mihályi in Košice requesting the translation of certain dadaist materials: "...an article by Tristan Tzara on dadaism, and secondly a poem by F. [Francis] Picabia..."[14]

Presumably after the Czech excursion and its critical reception, Kassák again wrote to Mihályi:

I can assure you that dadaists have nothing to do with Ma, *and unlike you, I see dadaists quite differently: since they are an already established* conservative *school, I am in no mood to be associated with them and I will not let* Ma *come under their influence....*[15]

Nevertheless, in light of the program of that evening in March 1922, Prague critics considered the entire Hungarian group dadaist, and with reason, especially since Jean (Hans) Arp, Richard Huelsenbeck, Kurt Schwitters, Lajos Kudlák, and the Hungarian dadaist writer Sándor Barta were among those featured at the meeting.[16]

In 1922, therefore, the dadaist label was quite appropriate insofar as *Ma* was concerned. In 1927, however, Teige was less accurate in characterizing Moholy-Nagy and Kassák as follows:

Those who made a transition from dadaism to constructivism, or at least approached that, could never outgrow their experiences in dadaist romanticism.[17]

After 1924, it was not so much Kassák as Moholy-Nagy who fostered cooperative Hungarian-Czech avant-garde relations. In April 1921, Moholy-Nagy became editor of *Ma*'s German branch and beginning in April 1923 he taught at the Bauhaus. His system of contacts largely derived from these two centers of activity. All the while, however, he maintained his own personal style of art, which developed forcefully in this period. Moholy-Nagy established international contacts more easily than Kassák. He not only courted the Slovaks, he made important contacts within the Czech avant-garde movement as well. His name was known and highly esteemed, his influence having spread quickly due to both his art and his writings. He was able to locate related trends more easily at the Weimar and Dessau Bauhaus than Kassák could from his peripheral base in Vienna.

By this time, Moholy-Nagy was not seeking merely to promote *Ma* and to attract subscribers when he cooperated with Karel Teige, Bedřich Václavek, Artuš Černik, František Kalivoda, and other outstanding representative writers and artists of the Czech avant-garde. His was a greater vision than Kassák's goal of East-Central European cooperation. Since he did not have to worry personally about *Ma*'s survival, he was able freely to express his artistic and editorial conceptions.

Surviving documentation indicates that Moholy-Nagy made his initial Czech connections in 1925, when *Ma* was on the verge of collapse. The Bauhaus was prospering, however, and there he was able actively to pursue editing, book design, teaching, and other matters, in addition to his painting. Unlike Kassák, Moholy-Nagy became directly involved in 1925 with Devětsil, the leading and most innovative of Czech avant-garde movements. According to František Šmejkal:

At the invitation of Devětsil and/or the Architects' Club, J.J.P. [Johannes Jacobus Pieter] Oud, Le Corbusier, [Amédée] Ozenfant, [Theo van] Doesburg, Moholy-Nagy and [Hans] Richter are among those to [participate in] a lecture series in Prague and Brno.[18]

Moholy-Nagy himself seems to have been more strongly connected with the Brno faction of Devětsil (that is, Černik and Václavek) than with the Prague circle. Devětsil's Brno periodical *Pásmo* published one of Moholy-Nagy's most important articles, "Richtlinien für eine synthetische Zeitschrift" [Guidelines for a Synthetical Journal],[19] as well as three chapters from his book *Malerei, Photographie, Film* [Painting, Photography, Film].[20] *Pásmo* was more interested in Moholy-Nagy's writings on typography, film theory, and film scenario, than in his artistic activities. The same was true of František Kalivoda, also in Brno, who published the first monograph on Moholy-Nagy in 1936.

Cooperation between the Czech avant-garde and its Bauhaus representative apparently was at its peak in 1927. The year before, at Christmas 1926, when Kassák returned to Hungary, Moholy-Nagy continued as the most significant international representative of Hungarian avant-garde. In 1927, as editor of the *Bauhausbücher,* Moholy-Nagy drafted the outline of a volume in which Ernő Kállai and Lajos Kassák were to cover Ma and Karel Teige the Czech avant-garde.[21] This intended volume, like Kassák's *Horizont* project, would have featured only the Czech and Hungarian movements, omitting completely those of other East-Central European countries.

In 1927 Moholy-Nagy also became a frequently published correspondent of *ReD* [*Revue Devětsilu* (Review of Devětsil)], a Prague periodical. Published by Teige, *ReD* featured several of Moholy-Nagy's "constructions" and photomontages,[22] again focusing on the artist's avant-garde photography, rather than on his paintings. Moholy-Nagy was associated with *ReD* during the period 1927-29, as well as with *Fronta* which published his important article "Ismus oder Kunst" [Ism or Art] in Czech translation.[23] Edited by František Halas, Bedřich Václavek, and others, *Fronta* featured Moholy-Nagy together with Tatlin, Kurt Schwitters, El Lissitzky, and Zdeněk Pešánek.[24] Moholy-Nagy's nickel-sculpture and photomontages were introduced in *Fronta*, again emphasizing his work as a constructivist and photographer rather than as a painter.

Moholy-Nagy's personal friendships with the editor of *Pásmo*, Bedřich Václavek, avant-garde critic and director of the Bratislava Academy of Applied Arts, and with the outstanding architect and theoretician František Kalivoda, may explain how his ideas, many not yet realized in his own work, influenced the art of Zdeněk Pešánek, one of the most innovative representatives of the Czech avant-garde. Just as there are certain similarities between Kassák's picture-poems and Teige's "poetisme," parallel tendencies are observable between the works of Moholy-Nagy and Pešánek. In both cases, however, there is no evidence of a personal acquaintance between the artists that would explain the similarities in their work. It seems certain that even without personal contacts a mutual influence was there, and an exchange of ideas apparently took place.

Moholy-Nagy started to work on the creation of the *Light-Space-Modulator* in 1922; several of his drawings survive. However, not until 1930 was he able to perfect a kinetic chrome steel modulator of light effects, with the help of Hungarian engineer István Sebők. In 1925 Pešánek created his famous colored light-effects organ in Prague, and in 1930 his Edison memorial, which relied on a technique (sculpture using electric current) similar to that of Moholy-Nagy.

YUGOSLAVIA In contrast to the Czech avant-garde the (mostly) Serbian artist-adherents of Zenit perceived *Ma* and its Activist circle to be closely aligned with Russian Constructivism, a style and revolutionary outlook they favored. Therefore, *Zenit* editors tried to publish as many Hungarian avant-garde works as possible. While Czech and Slovak cooperation was important for the Hungarians, *Ma* placed visibly less emphasis on Yugoslav connections.

After 1920, when Kassák forged relations with the newly established Serbian-Croatian-Slovenian kingdom and its avant-garde circles, he did not rely on his old colleagues of the Activist era, Vera Biller and Péter Dobrovics, who moved to Serbia after 1919. Instead, he searched for new contacts who were closely associated with the Zagreb Zenit movement, primarily Boško Tokin and Dragan Aleksić. Tokin, with Ljubomir Micić and Ivan Goll, was an author of the *Zenit Manifesto*, published in Zagreb in June 1921, which signaled the international consciousness of the Serbian avant-garde. Although Kassák's relationship with Tokin unfolded at around the time the *Manifesto* appeared, Kassák never published this important document. Instead, Tokin wrote in *Ma* a dry and impartial overview of

Zenit's activities in the field of literature, which to an extent reads like a manifesto:

Zenit *undoubtedly signals a new phase and new aspirations. Its goal is the creation of a unified, international movement. It believes and teaches that an all-encompassing philosophy and art can only be created by the global artistic and philosophical community: by the new artists and the new philosophers.*[25]

Two months later, in August 1921, Boško Tokin became the Zagreb correspondent of *Ma*, remaining in that position until March 1922. During the Summer of 1921, *Zenit* published lengthy accounts of *Ma*'s activist and constructivist tendencies, comparing "Zenitism closely to Hungarian activism."[26] It would have been in the spirit of this tight cooperation had Kassák's "A máglyák énekelnek" [The Bonfires Are Singing] been published in Serbian translation by Boško Tokin.[27] This was not to be the case, however, for Tokin left *Ma* in March 1922 and no longer represented Kassák's movement.

While Tokin furthered primarily literary relations, artistic connections were shaped by Virgil Poljanski and Micić. *Zenit* published a Kassák linocut (FIG. 5-2) and featured the works of other Hungarian artists not published by Kassák himself, for example, József Csáky, and a relatively large number of Moholy-Nagy creations (FIG. 5-3).

The Micić-led Zenit gallery collected international (including Hungarian) works of art from 1922 which, with works of Mikhail Larionov, Alexander Archipenko, Robert Delaunay, El Lissitzky, Vera Biller, Jo Klek (Josip Seissel), Mihailo S. Petrov, and others, served as the bulk of the 1924 Belgrade international exhibition. The exhibition also included works of Ladislas Medgyes and Moholy-Nagy (FIG. 5-4), but none by Kassák or Bortnyik (whose Bildarchitektur album was advertised in *Zenit*, no. 6). The reasons for these omissions are unclear, but they may have resulted from poor exhibition management or the estrangement of the two leading personalities of the two competing movements. It also is possible that Kassák may not have considered the exhibition worthy of the effort required for participation. Moholy-Nagy's presence was stressed, however, with four important drawings from 1921.

From the beginning, Kassák had ties with Micić and his movement. When *Út* was founded

Fig. 5-2 LAJOS KASSÁK, title page of review *Zenit*, Zagreb, June 1922, no. 15.

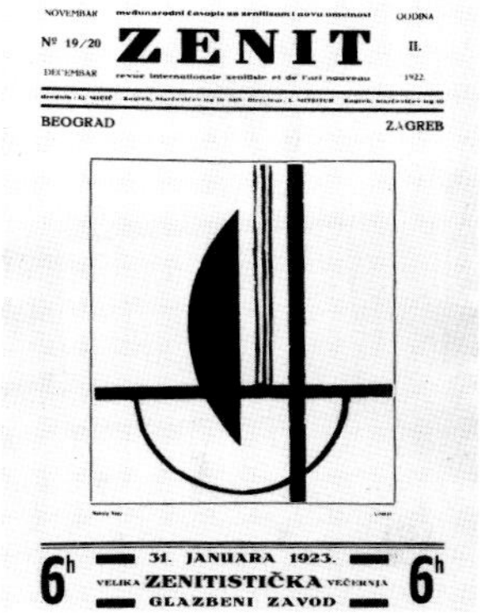

Fig. 5-3 LÁSZLÓ MOHOLY-NAGY, title page of review *Zenit*, November-December 1922, no. 19/20.

Fig. 5-4 LÁSZLÓ MOHOLY-NAGY, *The Big Emotion*, 1920–1921, National Museum of Belgrad. Shown in 1924 at the Belgrade *Zenit* exhibition and formerly in the Micić collection.

(1922) in Novi Sad, under Zoltán Csuka's editorship Kassák welcomed it as *Ma*'s sister publication (*Ma*, May 1922). As a Hungarian language publication in Yugoslav territory, *Út* played a certain mediating role between Serbian and Hungarian avant-garde groups although *Út*'s relations with the Serbian movement were controversial. *Út* published the *Zenit Manifesto* in April 1923, and Kassák was cited as an *Út* correspondent.

Zenit (no. 23) published the following poem (presumably by Kassák, but signed by János Mester):

...We threw our sorrows under the shadow of Lajos Kassák and Ljubomir Micić, our eye wrapped in one bunch with them
We are an infinite plus:
MA + ÚT + ZENIT =
WE ARE THE NEW ARTISTS!"

In 1923, however, Micić proclaimed in *Zenit* (no. 24) that he had "absolutely no connection with the young circles associated with *Út* published in Novi Sad."[28]

Two other Hungarian-language periodicals, *Akasztott Ember* [Hanged Man] in Vienna and *Magyar Írás* [Hungarian Writing] in Budapest, reacted in essentially different ways to the *Zenit* philosophy. *Akasztott Ember* (1922, no. 3-4), edited by Sándor Barta, reviewed *Zenit*'s German edition, commenting:

This means not only that the international clichés of dadaism have reached the Balkans, but also that the deterioration of civic culture and its smell of death crosses geographical and national boundaries.

The editor of *Magyar Írás*, Tivadar Raith, had other views on *Zenit*. In an introduction to the *Zenit* articles published in his periodical, he writes:

It is unquestionable that the rebirth of the European spirit will be decided not in Western, but in Eastern Europe.... This hope makes the new Serbian artistic movements attractive for us, which [movements] are based on a large-scale humanistic approach, while directly confronting Western European Isms and building a future that incorporates its own "barbarism and balkanism."[29]

Raith's article was published at the end of 1925 when *Akasztott Ember* and *Ma* no longer existed; hence there was no competition, and *Magyar Írás* attempted to carry on its tradition in a calmer, more objective manner. By this time, however, *Zenit* itself was nearing its end, and Raith's supportive comments came too late to the rescue.

One of the last revelations about the connection between the Hungarian and Serbian movements is János Mácza's article about Yugoslav Zenitism in his 1926 *A mai Európa művészete* [Art in Today's Europe]. At the time, Mácza lived in the Soviet Union and was somewhat removed from these movements.[30] In the name of universal proletarian revolution, he condemned emphatically the "pan-Balkanism" of Zenit.

Kassák made a final effort to revive the Hungarian avant-garde movement in 1927; now back in Budapest, he founded yet another periodical, *Dokumentum* (a successor to *Ma*). At the same time Micić was making a futile attempt to revive *Zenit* in Paris. Both of these movements (Hungarian and Serbian) had already surrendered their close affiliation with avant-garde tendencies at the time, and their views could not be legitimized, either jointly or separately.

ROMANIA The Romanian avant-garde gathered around the Bucharest publication *Contimporanul*, at least from 1922 to 1924. Like *Ma* (1916-25), *Contimporanul* survived for about 10 years (1922-32). *Contimporanul*'s soul and motivator was Ion Vinea. The emergence of the Romanian avant-garde emerged later than the Hungarian movement and continued longer, almost unnoticeably extending itself into the 1930s on a surrealist vision that conflicted with the essence of constructivism.

Although the publication *Contimporanul* was the exclusive initiator of the Romanian modernist movement in 1922, numerous other Romanian and Hungarian-language periodicals later shared in the development of the Romanian avant-garde. Almost in competition, they established different centers of various sizes in Bucharest and in Hungarian-populated Transylvania as well. *Ma* was in touch with both the Hungarian and Romanian centers, and apart from nationalistic differences a relatively fulfilling cooperation developed.

The first and perhaps most important link between the Hungarian and Romanian avant-garde was János Máttis Teutsch, whom Lajos Kassák had twice introduced as an Activist-expressionist painter at *Ma*'s local exhibits in 1917 and 1918, and whose linoleum block prints were featured on *Ma*'s pages. In 1917, Kassák also published an album of Máttis Teutsch's energetic expressionist linocuts.

94. JÁNOS MÁTTIS TEUTSCH, Landscape in Sunshine, 1916

93. JÁNOS MÁTTIS TEUTSCH, Landscape, 1915-1916

Fig. 5-5 JÁNOS MÁTTIS TEUTSCH, title page of review *Napkelet*, published in Kolozsvár (Cluj), May 1922.

Máttis Teutsch thus had a central role in *Ma*'s initial Budapest period, in contrast to Serbian Vera Biller and Péter Dobrovics, whose roles were secondary in both the Hungarian and in the Serbian movements.

AFTER THE FALL OF THE HUNGARIAN SOVIET REPUBLIC, Máttis Teutsch returned to Braşov, his birthplace in Transylvania, where several exhibitions of his paintings, sculptures, and graphics were mounted. He exhibited in Bucharest's Maison d'Art in 1919 and in Braşov in 1921, and presumably he participated in the organization of a November 1924 international exhibit arranged by *Contimporanul*. This exhibition paralleled the 1924 Belgrade international exhibition without any concrete evidence of connections between the two. It featured seven paintings and nine sculptures by Máttis Teutsch. Unlike the Belgrade exhibition, however, the Bucharest showing did not include any works by Moholy-Nagy, Tihanyi, or Ladislas Medgyes. Instead, Hungarians were represented exclusively by Lajos Kassák, whose privileged status can be attributed to Máttis Teutsch, the poet-editor Ion Vinea of *Contimporanul*, or perhaps the translator-writer Tamás Aladár.[31]

Prior to Kassák's participation at the Bucharest exhibition, *Ma* and *Contimporanul* engaged in some information exchange. In 1924 *Contimporanul* introduced the Hungarian avant-garde to its readers (no. 64), published Kassák's article about Hungarian art (no. 59), and featured illustrations in three separate issues. *Ma*'s July 1924 edition included Tamás Aladár's article about new Romanian artistic trends, a poem by Ion Vinea, and a print by Marcel Janco.[33]

By 1925, *Contimporanul* had lost its vitality and influence. Máttis Teutsch became involved with other Romanian periodicals, as an associate of *Punct* (1925) and as editor of *Integral* in Paris from 1925 to 1928. During the same period, when Romanian avant-garde diversified among many artistic centers, a few Hungarian-language publications, primarily literary and secondarily fine art, gained preeminence. One of these was *Periszkóp* [Periscope] in Arad (Oradea), whose editor, painter György Szántó, envisioned the journal as a bridge between East and West. *Periszkóp*, with its rich stock of illustrations, was the most important Hungarian-language periodical in the Romanian literary network. In Paris, *Periszkóp* was edited by long-time Hungarian Activist Lajos Tihanyi. *Napkelet* [Orient] from Kolozsvár (Cluj) (FIG. 5-5) and *Új Géniusz* [New Genius] from Arad also published avant-garde, mostly literary, reviews and short works. As József Meliusz concludes: "...the Ma movement's initiator, Kassák, was soon influenced by the Paris-clone Romanian avant-garde movements which produced [Tristan] Tzara, [Ilarie] Voronca, and [Benjamin] Fundoianu."[33]

It was not the Romanians but the Hungarian minority in Romania that sensed the importance of Kassák's movement. At this time, between the summer of 1925 and the winter of 1926, Kassák's *Ma* was enduring its most intense crises. Kassák lacked the financial means to publish in Vienna and elected to return to Hungary. There was an interval of a year and a half between *Ma*'s termination and the appearance of his new Budapest publication *Dokumentum* (December 1926). During this period, in February 1926, the most important Hungarian-language periodical of Romania was created, *Korunk* [Our Age], edited by László Dienes.[34]

Korunk inherited the trends initiated by *Új Géniusz*, *Napkelet*, and *Periszkóp* for a lasting publication that focused primarily on contemporary literature and poetry and only secondarily on the visual arts.[35] Although many of those associated with *Korunk* were the same people who had made *Ma* a viable publication—Iván Hevesy, Ernő Kállai,

Lajos Kassák, and László Moholy-Nagy, among others—this new publication was never able to achieve the international influence of *Ma*. By the time *Korunk* appeared, the avant-garde movements had lost their momentum, not only in Transylvania and Budapest but throughout Europe. Neither *Korunk* nor the Budapest-based *Dokumentum* could convey the vitality and conviction of earlier times, despite the appearance of numerous excellent articles by Moholy-Nagy and Kassák, including the latter's 1926 essay "Az új művészet él" [The New Art Lives On]. Gone from these writings was the utopian idealism based on the freedom of artistic creation; instead, the emphasis was on a need to return to order. At the same time, Romanian avant-gardists were moving toward more decorative styles while also testing the waters of surrealism. From this point, Hungarian and Romanian avant-garde tendencies were to diverge for a long time to come.

POLAND Hungarian avant-garde relations with Poland were not as productive as those with the Czech and Romanian movements. The Polish avant-garde truly got under way in 1924, only a year before the collapse of *Ma*. There was no Hungarian-language center or personal contact for *Ma* in Poland. As a result, the Polish Blok and Praesens [Present] circles were excluded from the conceptual understanding of Hungarian avant-garde artists and critics, even though there clearly were many areas of agreement between the Poles and Hungarians in the practice and theory of constructivism, and in a socially committed, rational avant-garde philosophy.

No special link developed between the two movements, which learned of one another's accomplishments through Der Sturm gallery and its periodical rather than by direct contact. In 1924, *Blok* (no. 6-7) printed Endre Gáspár's review of Hungarian Activist literature, presumably cited from *Der Sturm*, with illustrations by Moholy-Nagy. In its special anniversary edition the next year, *Ma* published a drama and two stage drawings by Günter Hirschel-Protsch, borrowed in all likelihood from a Viennese theatrical exhibition, without acknowledging the author or his Polish nationality. This same issue also presented, without comment, prints by the two leading artists of the Polish avant-garde, Henryk Štażewski and Teresa Žarnower.

Perhaps the most productive interaction between the Polish and Hungarian avant-garde movements was the authentic conceptual relationship that developed between two artists of equal status: Wladyslaw Strzemínski and Moholy-Nagy. As an artist and theorist, Strzemínski reviewed Moholy-Nagy's *Von Material zu Architektur* [From Material to Architecture] in 1928.[36] In his review, Strzemínski proposed to take Moholy-Nagy's ideas one step further: to organize space and the rhythmic relationship between space and time. By the time this critique was written, in 1930, avant-garde activity had already subsided. In the absence of association, movement, or common campaign, this was but a momentary conceptual union between two remarkable artists of geographically removed lands.

97. JÁNOS MÁTTIS TEUTSCH, Composition, 1925

The Hungarian Contribution

What Hungarians offered to the artists and movements of their East-Central European neighbors can be deduced from the published writings in each of these countries. What the Hungarians absorbed from surrounding movements can be inferred from review of the pages of *Ma*. Kassák introduced the best representatives of dadaism such as Kurt Schwitters, Hans Arp, and Raul Hausmann, through their writings and illustrations. He also featured some of the best works of Dutch De Stijl, Russian Constructivism and Suprematism, French Purism, and Italian Futurism while virtually ignoring the movements of other East-Central European countries. He did not publish any comprehensive review of Devětsil; in fact, he hardly even mentioned it. Similarly, Kassák did not present the programs or manifestoes of any of the other East-Central European leaders of the avant-garde, such as Karel Teige, Ljubomir Micić, or Mieczyslaw Szczuka.

In the preface of *Új művészek könyve* Kassák cites only four movements: futurism, expressionism, cubism, and dadaism. None of the East-Central European movements, not even constructivism, is mentioned. Among the many reproductions in the book are numerous Russian and Hungarian works, but of other East-Central Europeans Kassák cites only the Romanian-born Arthur Segal, by then a long-time resident of Berlin, and the Transylvanian Máttis Teutsch, who had his own exhibition with *Ma* and, to Kassák, represented Hungarian Activism, not the Romanian avant-garde.

Kassák's original draft for *Új művészek könyve* (spring 1921) reveals that for Kassák it was not all that important, at least during *Ma*'s golden years in Vienna, to form any kind of East-Central European artistic or cultural community.[37] Instead, he focused on the forerunners of the movement. Despite his ardent avant-garde spirit, he preferred the Germans, the French, the Dutch, and the Italians, whom he considered models and rivals at the same time.[38] All avant-garde movements were to be examined, but the East-Central European artistic and literary material in Kassák's draft amounted to less than five percent of the total.

Kassák had assembled his manuscript with obvious care, and it was not by chance, but in accord with his own intellectual perspective, that French dadaists and the Spanish avant-garde artists received preferential treatment over representatives of the neighboring movements. He discovered Russian avant-garde art relatively late, after 1920, at which time he was rapidly consumed by it to the extent that it overshadowed the later movements (*see Chapters 2 and 4*).

For Kassák, these movements were hardly autonomous entities, but rather mirror images, sometimes simply the tools or outposts, of his own movement: "*Út*, *Ma*'s sister publication is born!" proclaimed Kassák in the May 1922 issue. Presumably, Kassák believed that as an East-Central European group in Western exile, the Hungarian Activists had a role in bridging Eastern (Russian) and Western European art, and he apparently thought that the Czechs, the Serbians, and the Romanians had no business doing the same. Kassák's confidence (and occasionally conceit) was indispensable for the Ma movement's survival and progress. His chauvinism vis-à-vis competing publications and movements may have been the direct result of his survival instinct, but at least he recognized that a renewal of European culture depended on a heroic undertaking by leading figures of the East-Central European avant-gardes. That he was extremely proud of *Ma*'s achievements is evident in his "Válasz és sokféle álláspont" [Reply and Various Views], which states in part:

Ma *had a unique role in that it did not formally belong to any specific party or group....It functioned continuously and instead of a limited, narrow vision at home, without any assistance, it carved a role for itself between friends and enemies, rising to the occasion, growing from a restricted Hungarian enclave to a solid and important universal forum for the young artists of the world.*

Frequently cited works are identified by author, editor, or sponsoring organization and abbreviated title; journal articles, essays, and chapters in larger works are enclosed in quotation marks, and book titles are set in italics. Interested readers are referred to the comprehensive Select Bibliography at the end of this volume for full details of publication.

1. An exception was Róbert Berény's sharp criticism of the work of Kubišta in "A Nemzeti Szalon-beli képekröl" [On the Pictures at the National Salon], *Nyugat* 1 (1913), pp. 197-98.

2. See Ferenc Csaplár, *Kassák körei* [Kassák's Circles], pp. 9, 11. See also Lilla Szabó, "Kassák Lajos és a cseh avantgárd," in Ferenc Csaplár, ed. *Magam törvénye szerint*, [According to My Own Laws], pp. 73-81.

3. See Júlia Szabó, "Le rayonnement de l'avant-garde hongroise en Yugoslavia, en Transylvania et en Slovaquie entre les deux guerres mondiales," [The Impact of the Hungarian Avant-garde on the Yugoslavian, Transylvanian and Slovakian Avant-garde between the Two World Wars].

4. See Júlia Szabó: *A magyar aktivizmus művészete* [The Art of Hungarian Activism] p. 45.

5. Ferenc Csaplár, 23.

6. See Jaroslav Pasiaková, "Az emberi integralitás költője" [A Poet of Human Integrity], *Literary Review*, no. 3 (1969), p. 269.

7. See János Mácza, "Az új cseh irodalom" [The New Czech Literature] and "A jugoszláv Zenitizmos" [Zenitism in Yugoslavia]. Both are chapters in Mácza's *Iskusstvo sovremennoi Evropy* [The Art of Contemporary Europe] (Moscow-Leningrad, Gosudarstvennoe izdatel'stvo, 1926). See also Iva Mojzisová, "A Slovak Contribution" *Actes du Colloque international de l'histoire de l'art* (Budapest, Akadémial Kiadó, 1969).

8. Lajos Kassák, *Bildarchitektur 1922*, watercolor on paper, 20 x 26 cm, collection of Maria Tilkovsky, Prague. Reproduced in *Kassák Lajos 1887-1967*, no. 151.

9. Vojtêch Tilkovsky, "Az én Kassák Lajosom" [My Lajos Kassák]. In *Kortársak Kassák Lajosról* [Contemporaries about Lajos Kassák] (Budapest, Petőfi Museum of Literature, n.d.), 47.

10. Imre Bori: *A szecessziótól a dadáig* [From Secession to Dada], p. 235.

11. František Šmejkal, *Devětsil* (Prague, 1985).

12. Karel Teige: "O dadaistech" [About the Dadaists], *Tvorba* (1927), p. 168; cited by Lilla Szabó, p. 76. See also Karel Teige: *Svět, který se směje*, (1928); and Endre Bojtár, *A kelet-európai avantgard irodalom* [East European Avant-garde Literature], p. 40.

13. Concerning Dragan Aleksić, see Imre Bori, *A magyar, szerb és horvát avantgarde* [The Hungarian, Serbian, and Croatian Avant-garde] (Novi Sad: *A Híd*), pp. 259-60; Irina Subotić, *Az avantgarde Jugoszláviában. A Zenit Köre 1921-1926* [The Avant-garde in Yugoslavia: The Zenit Circle 1921-1926]. Concerning Kurt Schwitters, see František Šmejkal, "Schwitters und Prag" [Schwitters and Prague], in *Kurt Schwitters Almanach* (Hannover: Postskriptum Verlag, 1983), pp. 109-40.

14. Letter to Ödön Mihályi (from Vienna to Košice), 1921. (Budapest: Kassák Memorial Museum), 2293/no. 116.

15. Letter to Ödön Mihályi (from Vienna to Košice), 2293/no.113.

16. L. Szabó, p. 76.

17. *Ibid.*, 74.

18. Šmejkal, p. 11.

19. *Pásmo* 1 (1924-25), no. 7-8.

20. *Pásmo* 1 (1924-25) no. 11; and 1925-26, no. 1.

21. Lajos Kassák and Ernő Kállai (Hungary), *Die Ma-Gruppe* [The *Ma* Group], and Karel Teige (Prague), *Tschechische Kunst* [Czech Art]. The subscription form (1927) is at the Bauhaus Archives, Berlin.

22. Among Moholy-Nagy's featured works in *ReD*, are a photogram (issue no. 3, 1927), an illustration (no. 4, 1927), "Konstruktion 21" (no. 10, 1927) two photomontages (no. 8, 1928), and other photo montages (no. 3, 6, 10, 1929).

23. Moholy-Nagy, "Ismus nebo umění" [Ism or Art], *Fronta*, (1927), 128-31.

24. From the archives of the family of František Šmejkal (Prague).

25. *Ma*, no. 7 (June 1921), 100.

26. See Irina Subotić, "A Zenit és köre," in *Az avantgarde Jugoszláviában.*

27. Irina Subotić, [Zenitism and Avant-garde], p. 38.

28. Irina Subotić, "A Zenit és Köre."

29. Tivadar Raith, paper, Raith Tivadar: Az európai kulturválság dokumentumaihoz (on the documents of the European cultural chaos), *Magyar Irás* [Hungarian Writing] no. 10 (1925), p. 125.

30. János Mácza, *A mai Európa művészete* [Art in Today's Europe], *1962*. (Budapest: Petőfi Museum of Literature, 1978), pp. 79-82.

31. Regarding these exhibitions, see Irina Subotić, *Az avantgarde Jugoszláviában*. Also see Krisztina Passuth, *Les avant-gardes d'Europe Centrale* [The Avant-gardes of Central Europe], pp. 217-20.

32. See Marina Vanci, Les relations entre l'avant-garde hongroise et l'avant-garde roumaine [Relations between the Hungarian and Romanian Avant-gardes].

33. József Meliusz as quoted by Lajos Kántor in *Kép, világkép*, p. 8.

34. Kántor, pp. 38-39.

35. József Meliusz as quoted by Kántor p. 40.

36. See Wladyslaw Strzemínski's review of L. Moholy-Nagy's *Von Material zu Architektur* [From Material to Architecture] (Munich: Albert Langen Verlag, 1928) in *Europa*, no. 13 (Warsaw, 1930). An American edition of Moholy-Nagy's book was published in 1947 under the title *The New Vision*.

37. Csaplár, pp.7-12.

38. In *Ma*, no. 8 (August 1922), p. 53.

39. GYULA DERKOVITS, Old Cemetery in Buda, 1922

A COMPARATIVE CHRONOLOGY

OLIVER A. I. BOTAR

Hungarian and International Avant-Garde Art: 1905-1930

This chronology consists of three components. The first is a chronology of events concerned directly with Hungarian avant-garde artists and focused on those dimensions of avant-garde activity that took place mainly in a Hungarian context (within or outside Hungary), or that affected a Hungarian artist not established within the host artistic community while abroad. This is a fairly detailed chronology, with information ordered on a yearly, seasonal, or month by month basis, depending on the information available or the level of specificity considered necessary for an understanding of developments. Where deemed to be important, exact dates are provided.

The second component of the chronology, on the international avant-garde, contains information regarding European and North American avant-garde events that paralleled and informed the development of their Hungarian counterparts. Included here are events or achievements associated with Hungarian artists abroad that took place in a non-Hungarian context, or are associated with expatriate Hungarians who spent significant periods abroad. As this is an adjunct chronology, it is less detailed than the Hungarian section. Arranged on an annual basis, the information within each yearly entry is roughly ordered in geographic progression, from east to west, generally starting with Russia and ending with the United States. At the end of each annual entry is a list of major works of art, literature, and film deemed to be of outstanding importance. [Titles of works in the visual arts are enclosed in quotation marks to distinguish them from literary, musical, theater, film and dance works, which are italicized.]

Integrated into the international chronology is the third component, brief annual resumés of political events, both in Hungary and abroad, as well of the occasional scientific development of extraordinary import. Because of their importance to Hungarian artistic development, and their complexity, the political events of 1918, 1919, and 1920 are listed in greater detail, by month or date.

OLIVER A.I. BOTAR was born of Hungarian refugee parents in Toronto. He received an honors B.A. in urban geography, English, and philosophy from the University of Alberta in 1979, spending the following year on scholarship in Hungary. In Hungary during 1984-85, he researched his master's thesis (modernist elements of Hungarian urban planning between 1906 and 1938), and he is currently working on his Ph.D. dissertation (on international contructivism). Since 1981 Botar has published, organized exhibitions, scholarly meetings, and delivered papers on the Hungarian avant-garde, in both North America and Europe. Most recently he organized the exhibition and edited the catalogue *Tibor Pólya and the Group of Seven: Hungarian Art in Toronto Collections* (University of Toronto, Justina Barnicke Gallery).

62. BÉLA IVÁNYI GRÜNWALD, In the Valley, 1901

Hungarian Avant-Garde	International Avant-Garde
1905-06 The influence of post-impressionism and the fauves begins to be felt among some young Hungarian painters at the school of impressionist-symbolist painting in Nagybánya, Transylvania (now Baia Mare, Romania), where Károly Ferenczy is one of the important masters. Béla Czóbel, Lajos Tihanyi, Sándor Galimberti, Valéria Dénes, Vilmos Perlrott Csaba, Vilmos Huszár, Armand Schönberger, and Alfréd Réth, among others, are labeled "Neos" (for "Neo-Impressionists") by the older painters, who still promote in their own art the secessionist attitudes of the turn of the century. In 1905 Réth moves to Paris, and in the fall of 1906 Huszár moves to Holland. Both spend the remainder of their lives abroad. The Munich-trained Tivadar Csontváry Kosztka has his first exhibition in Budapest. His highly original works, with their free approach to color, cause excitement. A group of radical intellectuals and artists (including Béla Czóbel, Ödön Márffy, and Márk Vedres) forms around the painter Károly Kernstok at his home in Nyergesújfalu near Budapest.	Cézanne dies.
1906 Ödön Márffy returns from four years of study in Paris, and exhibits his fauve-influenced paintings at the Műcsarnok Exhibition Hall in Budapest. FEBRUARY A large exhibition of József Rippl-Rónai's works is held at the Kálmán Könyves Salon in Budapest. This is the first critical and financial success for post-impressionist art in Hungary.	
1907 Sándor Galimberti moves to Paris and begins studies at the Académie Julian. He exhibits at the *Salon d'automne* and *Salon des Indépendents* between 1908 and 1914. Under the leadership of Béla Iványi Grünwald (1867-1940), the Neos leave Nagybánya and establish a post-impressionist artists' colony at Kecskemét. Tivadar Csontváry Kosztka paints "Solitary Cedar" and "Pilgrimage to the Cedars of Lebanon." MAY Works by Cézanne, Gauguin, and Matisse are shown for the first time in Hungary, in a major exhibition of modern French art held at the National Salon in Budapest. OCTOBER The MIÉNK (Hungarian Impressionists and Naturalists) is established. An exhibition of the works of Ödön Márffy and Lajos Gulácsy opens at the Uránia bookshop in Budapest. It is supported in the press by Rippl-Rónai and Kernstok; the first customer is György Lukács.	Prague is the site for a major exhibition of post-impressionist painting and the first exhibition of the Czech *Osma (Eight)*. A commercial outlet of the Wiener Werkstätte opens in Vienna. The first traveling exhibition of "Die Brücke" is organized. A major retrospective exhibition of Cézanne's art is held in Paris. Alfred Stieglitz begins to mount exhibitions of modern European art at his The Little Galleries of the Photo-Secession in New York. Works: Picasso (Paris), "Les Demoiselles d'Avignon"; Matisse (Paris), "Le Luxe 1."
1908 The journal *Nyugat* [West], the first important forum for modern Hungarian literature, and *A Ház* [The House], the first journal of modern architecture and art in Hungary, appear in Budapest. József Csáky walks from Budapest to Paris where he settles. He stays at "La Ruche" with Léger, Archipenko, and (later) Chagall, Soutine, and Laurens. He befriends Picasso and Braque. The first exhibition of MIÉNK takes place in Budapest at the National Salon.	Osma's second exhibition is held in Prague. Kandinsky settles in Munich. Braque and Picasso begin to paint in a cubist manner. Stieglitz relocates his New York gallery, which becomes known as "291." Works: Adolf Loos (Vienna), *Ornament and Crime* and design for the "American Bar"; Brâncuşi (Paris), "The Kiss."

1909 Lajos Kassák walks from Budapest to Paris. He begins to write free verse and takes an interest in modern art.

SPRING The second exhibition of MIÉNK is held. Soon afterwards, the Neos break with the group. The group known as *Keresők* (The Seekers) is formed, consisting of painters who consciously reject the impressionist manner of painting. The early members (mostly former Neos) are: Róbert Berény, Béla Czóbel, Dezső Czigány, Károly Kernstok, Ödön Márffy, Dezső Orbán, Bertalan Pór, and Lajos Tihanyi.

JUNE-JULY The Neos organize a touring show of their work in the cities of Kolozsvár, Nagyvárad, and Arad (all now in Romania). Literary matinées are held in conjunction with the exhibitions.

DECEMBER The critic Miklós Rózsa and some artists establish the Művészház [Artists' House] in Budapest. This first independent exhibiting space for artists in Hungary becomes an important center of new art. The first exhibition of The Seekers opens at the Kálmán Könyves Salon in Budapest.

Klimt and others found the "Neukunstgruppe" in Vienna. Marsden Hartley's first one-man show opens at the 291 gallery in New York. Works: Klimt (Vienna), "Salome"; Nolde (Berlin), "The Last Supper"; Marinetti (Paris), *Futurist Manifesto*; Matisse (Paris), "La Danse"; Braque (Paris), "Piano and Mandolin."

1910 József Nemes Lampérth begins painting; the bold brushstrokes of his mature art are already in evidence. Sándor Bortnyik moves from his native Marosvásárhely (now in Romania) to Budapest. He works as an advertising and packaging designer. The poet Mihály Babits writes on futurism in *Nyugat*. Imre Szobotka finishes his studies at the Academy of Applied Arts in Budapest and moves to Paris, where his friend Csáky helps him enroll at l'Ecole libre la palette. Valéria Dénes moves to Paris where she studies with Matisse for two years. An exhibition of the work of occultist artist Dezső Mokry-Mészáros ("Life on Strange Planets") opens at the Artists' House.

JANUARY 9 Lectures are given by Károly Kernstok and György Lukács at the *Galilei Kör* (Galileo Circle), a Budapest group of young leftist intellectuals. Kernstok's lecture "Art as Exploration" amounts to an artistic program for The Seekers, while Lukács's supportive essay, "The Ways Have Parted," is the first important contribution to the theory of postimpressionism in Hungary.

FEBRUARY 5 - MARCH 3 On Baron Lajos Hatvany's initiative, a large government-supported exhibition of Hungarian painting, including that of The Seekers, is organized at the Berlin Secession, and is favorably received by the German-Hungarian critic Julius Meier-Graefe.

APRIL-MAY An exhibition at the Artists' House includes four cubist works by Picasso.

The Union of Youth is founded and has its first exhibition in St. Petersburg. Larionov organizes the first Jack of Diamonds exhibition in Moscow. An exhibition of Arnold Schönberg's paintings is held in Vienna. In Berlin, Herwarth Walden founds the journal *Der Sturm*, and the "Neue Sezession" is founded, with Max Pechstein as president. It attracts members of Die Brücke. Roger Fry organizes the First Post-Impressionist Exhibition in London. Kandinsky and Kupka turn to abstraction. In Paris, Boccioni, Carrà, Russolo, Balla, and Severini issue the *Technical Manifesto of Futurist Painting*. In New York, Arthur Dove's "Abstractions 1-6" are America's first non-representational paintings, and the first American exhibition of Cézanne is presented at 291. Works: Kokoschka (Vienna), "Portrait of Herwarth Walden"; Picasso (Paris), "Portrait of Ambroise Vollard"; Léger (Paris), "Nudes in the Forest"; Boccioni (Milan), "The City Rises."

59. SÁNDOR GALIMBERTI, Roofs, c1910

168. SÁNDOR ZIFFER, Ships on the River Seine, 1911

1911

The publication of Béla Bartók's "Allegro Barbaro" marks the beginning of modern Hungarian music. Bartók finishes work on his only opera, *Bluebeard's Castle*. József Csáky turns to cubism, one of the first sculptors to do so. János Kmetty goes to Paris, studies at the Académie Julian, and returns six months later, having adopted a cubist mode of painting.
FEBRUARY Bertalan Pór's exhibition at the Könyves Kálmán Salon becomes a *cause célèbre* when Prime Minister István Tisza attacks it in the press.
APRIL-MAY The Seekers rename themselves *Nyolcak* (The Eight). They hold their second exhibition at the National Salon. The sculptors Márk Vedres and Vilmos Fémes-Beck take part, as does the writer Anna Lesznai with her folk-art-inspired embroidery and book design. The exhibition causes a controversy. Members of The Eight sign a statement opposing Prime Minister Tisza's views on modern art.
NOVEMBER-DECEMBER Kernstok has a retrospective exhibition at the Artists' House. Lajos Fülep's journal of aesthetics, *Szellem* [Spirit], appears in Florence. György Lukács contributes.

The second Union of Youth exhibition is held in St. Petersburg. The cubist Artists' Group forms in Prague. Kandinsky and Marc found Der Blaue Reiter group in Munich and publish *Der Blaue Reiter Almanach*; August Macke, Campendonk, and Klee join. Franz Pfemfert begins publishing *Die Aktion* in Berlin. The Puteaux group of cubist artists forms in Paris. Max Weber's first exhibition, consisting of analytical cubist paintings, is held at 291 in New York. Works: Malevich (Moscow), "Taking in the Harvest"; Kandinsky (Munich), *Concerning the Spiritual in Art*. Chagall (Paris), "My Village and I"; Braque (Paris), "The Man with the Guitar"; Matisse (Paris), "The Red Studio No. 1"; Boccioni (Milan), "States of Mind"; Carrà (Milan), "Funeral of the Anarchist Galli."

1912

In Paris, Sándor Galimberti, Valéria Dénes, Alfréd Réth, and Imre Szobotka are influenced by analytical cubism. Kassák begins to take part in the life of the Budapest avant-garde. He publishes free verse, a novel, and a volume of novellas. János Máttis Teutsch moves to Budapest, remaining until 1919.
JANUARY The Neukunst Wien exhibition in Budapest includes works by Egon Schiele, Oskar Kokoschka, and Arnold Schoenberg.
MAY 25 - SEPTEMBER 30 Some members of The Eight (Kernstok, Márffy, Orbán, and Tihanyi) exhibit together in Cologne at the Sonderbund Internationaler Kunstausstellung Westdeutscher Kunstfreunde und Künstler [Special International Exhibition of West German Art Lovers and Artists].
NOVEMBER-DECEMBER The Eight have their third and final exhibition at the National Salon. The group is near disintegration.

In Moscow, the second Jack of Diamonds exhibition is held; the Donkey's Tail exhibition is organized by Larionov; and the Russian Futurist anthology, *A Slap in the Face of Public Taste*, is published. Herwarth Walden's Der Sturm gallery opens in Berlin with an exhibition of works by Der Blaue Reiter artists, Kokoschka, and other expressionists. In Holland, Theo van Doesburg begins to write art criticism. In Paris, Braque and Picasso make cubist collages; Picasso builds cubist reliefs; Mondrian enters his cubist period, and Delaunay paints his "Windows" series, establishing "orphism." An Italian Futurist exhibition is held at the Bernheim-Jeune gallery in Paris. In London, Roger Fry organizes the Second Post-Impressionist Exhibition, which includes works by Larionov and Goncharova. The Great Futurist Traveling Exhibition visits the capitals of Europe. Arthur Dove's abstract pastels are displayed at 291 and in Chicago. Works: Picasso (Paris), "Ma Jolie"; Duchamp (Paris), "Nude Descending a Staircase"; Picabia (Paris), "Procession at Seville"; de Chirico (Milan), "Melancholy"; Severini (Milan), "Bal Tabarin"; Balla (Milan), "Young Girl Running on a Balcony"; Marsden Hartley (Paris), "Intuitive Abstractions."

First Balkan War takes place during late fall. Creation of Kingdom of Albania. Woodrow Wilson elected President of the United States.

63. BÉLA IVÁNYI GRÜNWALD, Villa Schiffer Panel Design, c1911

1913 Nemes Lampérth travels to Paris, where he remains until war breaks out. Bortnyik enrolls at the Rippl-Rónai-Kernstok-Vaszary free school of art in Budapest. Mária Pásztor-Freund's "The Spatial Concerns of Cubism" appears in *Nyugat* 6. Alfréd Réth exhibits with Jean Metzinger at the Galerie Berthe Weill in Paris. In January, Réth has a major exhibition at the Der Sturm gallery in Berlin. Miklós Rózsa, arranging the display of the International Post-Impressionist Exhibition in Budapest, sees Réth's exhibition and includes it in the Hungarian showing.

JANUARY-FEBRUARY The large traveling exhibition of futurists and expressionists is displayed at the National Salon in Budapest, and includes works by Boccioni, Carrà, Jawlensky, Kandinsky, Kubišta, Kokoschka, Russolo, Segal, and Severini. Kassák and Uitz (by this time Kassák's brother-in-law) view the exhibition together, and are profoundly affected by it.

APRIL-MAY The International Post-Impressionist Exhibition, including work by members of The Eight, is held at the Artists' House in Budapest. The exhibition includes the 100 canvases shown by Réth in January.

FALL László Nagy (later adopting the name "Moholy") moves from Szeged, the city of his schooling, to Budapest, where he begins his study of law. *Nyugat* publishes Róbert Berény's "The Painter as Communicator."

In St. Petersburg, Russian avant-gardists produce the futurist opera *Victory Over the Sun*, with stage sets by Malevich that prefigure suprematism. In Moscow, Larionov organizes the Target exhibition, which includes rayonist paintings, and Tatlin produces his first relief. Czech Cubism is in full flower; the Artists' Group exhibits in Prague and Munich, as well as at Der Sturm in Berlin. The *Erster deutscher Herbstsalon* [First German Autumn salon] is on display at Der Sturm, including works by Picabia, Arp, Ernst, Klee, Chagall, and the futurists; Marinetti gives two lectures on the occasion. The Brücke group disbands. In Bonn, Macke produces geometrical-abstract paintings. Morgan Russel and Stanton Macdonald-Wright exhibit their "synchromist" works in Munich and Paris. The first issue of *Lacerba*, principal journal of Italian Futurism, appears in Florence. Wyndham Lewis founds the Rebel Art Centre in London. In New York, the International Exhibition of Modern Art (The Armory Show) introduces the new European avant-garde to America, and Picabia has an exhibition at the 291. Works: Larionov (Moscow), *Rayonist Manifesto*; Kirchner (Berlin), "Berlin Street Scene"; Léger (Paris), "Contrastes de formes"; Duchamp (Paris), "Bicycle Wheel"; Boccioni (Milan), "The Dynamism of a Soccer Player"; Epstein (London), "Rock Drill"; Marsden Hartley (United States), "Forms Abstracted."

SPRING Second Balkan War.

SUMMER Third Balkan War. Germany begins to expand its army.

1914 Béla Uitz travels to Italy and is enamored of the art of the Italian Renaissance. Lajos Gulácsy designs the cover for Kassák's collection of three dramas. Writing of the *Salon des indépendents* in *Nyugat*, the critic Tivadar Raith emphasizes that it is Picasso and Cézanne, not the impressionists, who dominate. He notes the quality and success of Csáky and Szobotka's art. Tihanyi's drawings are shown at an international exhibition of graphic art in Buffalo.

FEBRUARY Valéria Dénes and her husband, Sándor Galimberti, have a major showing of their cubist works at the National Salon, and enjoy success with the critics. Former members of The Eight include their works in a major exhibition in the Artists' House.

MARCH An exhibition is mounted of works by Berény, Pór, Tihanyi, and sculptor Vilmos Fémes Beck at the Galerie Brüko in Vienna.

FALL Szobotka and Réth are interned in France as enemy aliens. Csáky loses most of his pre-1914 production of sculpture and

Marinetti visits Russia. Kandinsky returns to Moscow. Klee and Macke travel to Tunisia and intensify their use of color. In London, Wyndham Lewis and others found the Vorticist group and publish the journal *Blast*; a one-man show of the work of David Bomberg is held. Margaret Anderson establishes *The Little Review* in Chicago. An exhibition of Negro art and the first Brâncuşi exhibition are held at 291. Works: Kokoschka (Vienna), "The Vortex"; Mondrian (Holland), "Pier and ocean" paintings; Raymond Duchamp-Villon (Paris), "Head of a Horse"; Picabia (Paris), "Edtaonisl"; de Chirico (Milan), "Gare Montparnasse"; Marsden Hartley (Berlin), "Portrait of a German Officer."

Archduke Ferdinand of Austria-Hungary and his wife assassinated at Sarajevo, Serbia, in June. By August the Great War breaks out; Austria-Hungary declares war on Serbia and allies herself with the German Empire; Germany inflicts defeats on Russia.

volunteers for the French army to avoid internment. Nemes Lampérth and the Galimbertis return to Hungary; Galimberti and Nemes Lampérth are conscripted. With the wartime severing of French and Italian connections, Germany and especially the journal *Der Sturm* become the major sources of influence on the Hungarian avant-garde. This German Expressionist and Activist influence is felt both in literature and art.

1915

Kassák publishes his first volume of poetry, *Eposz Wagner maszkjában* [An Epic in Wagner's Mask]. Nemes Lampérth is injured while serving in Galicia on the Russian front. The artist Ede Bohacsek dies; later, his work is championed by Kassák's Ma group. János Mácza comes to Budapest to sit for veterinary examinations. Béla Uitz wins the gold medal of the International Exhibition of Graphic Art at the San Francisco World Fair. Some members of The Eight exhibit there together for the last time. János Máttis Teutsch turns to an expressionist style of painting influenced by Franz Marc and Wassily Kandinsky. He becomes interested in esoteric doctrines.
JULY Valéria Dénes dies of pneumonia at Pécs. Her husband Sándor Galimberti commits suicide shortly after her funeral.
NOVEMBER 1 Lajos Kassák publishes the first journal of the twentieth century Hungarian avant-garde, *A Tett* [The Deed]. Before the journal is banned a year later, Kassák publishes works by Kandinsky, Picasso, Braque, Marc, Derain, and Boccioni.

At Ivan Puni's First Futurist Exhibition Tramway V in Petrograd, Tatlin exhibits "counter-reliefs" for the first time. At Puni's Last Futurist Exhibition 0.10 in Petrograd, Malevich exhibits his suprematist pictures for the first time, Tatlin exhibits his "counter-reliefs," and Rosanova presents her abstract compositions. Hugo Kersten and Emil Szittya publish *Der Mistral* in Zurich, a forerunner of dada. Van Doesburg and Mondrian meet in Holland. In London, the second issue of *Blast* appears, and a vorticist exhibition is held at the Doré Galleries. In New York, Duchamp begins work on "The Bride Stripped Bare by Her Bachelors, Even"; Picabia on "Paroxysme de la douleur"; Max Weber produces synthetic cubist paintings; Alfred Stieglitz publishes *291* (edited by Paul Haviland and Marius de Zayas); and Walter Arensberg and de Zayas open the Modern Gallery. In various European cities, Arp, Sophie Taueber, Muche, and Itten produce abstract paintings. Late in the year Malevich publishes *From Cubism to Suprematism: The New Painterly Realism*. Works: Picasso (Paris), "Harlequin"; Balla and Depero (Milan), *Futurist Reconstruction of the Universe*.

Poison gas introduced as weapon by German army. Italy joins war on side of Entente (France, Great Britain, and Italy), Bulgaria on side of Central Powers. Revival of the Ku Klux Klan in the United States.

1916

Máttis Teutsch introduces Bortnyik to Kassák. Mácza's *Modern Hungarian Drama* is published (Budapest). László Moholy-Nagy is conscripted.
APRIL The inaugural exhibition of the group *A Fiatalok* (The Young) takes place at the National Salon. Included are the artists who were to form the core of the Ma group: Péter Dobrovics (Petar Dobrovič), Gulácsy, Kmetty, Nemes Lampérth, and Uitz.
FALL In September Kassák produces an international issue of *A Tett*, which publishes work by citizens of enemy states. This turns out to be the last issue; on October 2, *A Tett* is banned by the authorities. On October 17 Kassák successfully applies for permission to publish a new journal, and by November 15 the inaugural issue of *Ma* [Today] appears in Budapest. The cover art by Czech cubist Vincenz Beneš and Kassák's article "The Poster and New Painting" set the tone for the visual arts in the journal by emphasizing the flatness of the picture plane and what Kassák saw as the non-mimetic nature of art.

Rodchenko exhibits geometrical drawings at Tatlin's The Store exhibition in Moscow. Supremus group forms around Malevich, including Popova, Udaltsova, Exter, Kliun, Rosanova, and others. Marc and Boccioni die in the war. Hugo Ball establishes the Cabaret Voltaire in Zurich; dada activity there is at its peak. Huszár and van Doesburg produce their first abstract paintings. In New York, Duchamp and Roché publish *The Blind Man*, and the first exhibition of works by Georgia O'Keeffe is held at 291. The Panama Pacific Exhibition is organized in San Francisco, and it includes a large selection of futurist works. Works: George Grosz (Berlin), "The City"; Arp (Zurich), constructed wood reliefs and "automatic drawings"; Man Ray (New York), "The Rope Dancer Accompanies Herself and her Shadows."

Severe food rationing in Germany. Emperor-King Francis Joseph of Austria-Hungary dies on November 21, after 68 years of rule; Charles IV becomes Emperor-King. Murder of Rasputin. Romania joins Entente and declares war on Austria-Hungary. Formation, in exile, of Czech national council. Publication of Einstein's *The Special and General Theory of Relativity* and of Carl Gustav Jung's *Psychology of the Unconscious*.

114. JÓZSEF NEMES LAMPÉRTH, Landscape at Tabán, 1916

145. LAJOS TIHANYI, Reclining Nude, 1917

1917 Farkas Molnár, a young man from Pécs, arrives in Budapest and enrolls at the Academy of Fine Arts. László Moholy-Nagy is injured on the front and returns to Budapest. He finishes his legal studies but never passes the final examinations.
MARCH 18 Károly Ferenczy dies in Budapest.
JUNE The second A Fiatalok exhibition takes place at the National Salon. Géza Csorba, Rudolf Diener-Dénes, Dobrovics, Andor Erős, Kmetty, Nemes Lampérth, and Armand Schönberger participate.
AUGUST János Mácza founds Ma's theater workshop in Budapest. The young László Péri becomes one of the principal participants.
OCTOBER The inaugural exhibition at the new Ma gallery in Budapest consists of János Máttis Teutsch's expressionist paintings, sculptures, and linocuts. Máttis Teutsch remains the most frequently promoted artist of the Ma group.

John Heartfield founds the Malik-Verlag in Berlin. Richard Huelsenbeck returns to Berlin from Zurich. In Zurich, *Dada 1* and *Dada 2* appear, and the Galerie Dada opens. In Holland Theo van Doesburg, Piet Mondrian, Vilmos Huszár, and others found *De Stijl*. The ballet *Parade* is produced in Paris. The journal *Noi* appears in Rome. Picabia founds his review *391* in Barcelona. A one-man show of Jacob Epstein's sculptures is held in London. In New York, Duchamp exhibits "ready-mades," including "Fountain" (a urinal) and a vorticist exhibition is held at the Penguin Club. After exhibitions of works by Severini and Macdonald-Wright, Stieglitz's 291 gallery and his journal *Camera Work* fold. November and after: with the Soviet revolution, many avant-garde artists assume positions of responsibility in the newly organized artistic life of Russia; Lunacharsky is appointed head of Narkompros; Proletkult is organized, and public spaces are decorated in Moscow and Petrograd by cubo-futurists. Works: Gabo (Russia), "Head of a Woman"; Van der Leck (Holland), geometrical abstractions; Vantongerloo (Holland), abstract sculptures; Lipschitz (Paris), "Seated Bather"; Carrà (Milan), "The Metaphysical Muse"; de Chirico (Milan), "The Great Metaphysicist."

Abdication of Czar Nicholas II of Russia; parliamentary government takes over, and by November Bolsheviks take power. Germany initiates submarine warfare. United States declares war on Central Powers. Treaty of Brest-Litovsk between Germany and Russia. Corfu Declaration sets out unified South Slav kingdom as goal.

98. LÁSZLÓ MOHOLY-NAGY, Wounded Soldier - Prisoner of War, 1917

NOVEMBER The critic Iván Hevesy begins publication of his journal *Jelenkor* [The Present Age]. László Moholy-Nagy, a university friend, participates in the journal's production. It survives until early the next year. The back page of *Ma* announces the availability of copies of material published by *Der Sturm* and *Die Aktion* (the radical Activist cultural journal edited by Franz Pfemfert in Berlin).
DECEMBER 9 The first literary matinée of the Ma group takes place at the Ferenc Liszt Academy of Music in Budapest.

1918

László Moholy-Nagy exhibits a few of his drawings at the Hungarian National Salon. Kassák meets a young art critic, Ernő Kállai, at a Ma exhibition. This is Kállai's first exposure to the avant-garde.
FEBRUARY The second exhibition at the Ma gallery displays works by the late Ede Bohacsek and by sculptor Pál Pátzay.
JUNE An issue of *Ma* features the work of Béla Uitz. Though *Der Sturm* had been publishing Hungarian literature in translation since its first year of publication in 1910, this issue publishes Hungarian art for the first time: a linocut by Máttis Teutsch.
JULY Moholy-Nagy visits Béla Uitz in his Budapest studio. Bortnyik and Hevesy join the Ma group. Máttis Teutsch has a one-man show at the Der Sturm gallery in Berlin. Bortnyik's and János Schadl's works appear in *Ma* for the first time. The influence of the works of artists reproduced in *Der Sturm* between 1916 and 1918 is evident.
AUGUST A woodcut by Máttis Teutsch appears on the cover of *Der Sturm*. The founder and editor of the journal, Herwarth Walden, continues to reproduce works by Máttis Teutsch regularly in his journal until 1925.
SEPTEMBER The Ma gallery's third exhibition presents the artists who at the time make up the Ma group: Bortnyik, Diener-Dénes, Sándor Gergely, Gulácsy, Kmetty, Máttis Teutsch, Nemes Lampérth, Pátzay, György Ruttkay, János Schadl, Ferenc Spangher, and Uitz, with the addition of works by the late Ede Bohacsek.
OCTOBER Lajos Tihanyi's first one-man show is mounted at the Ma gallery.
NOVEMBER An exhibition of Máttis Teutsch's paintings and linocuts and Gergely's sculptures takes place at the Ma gallery. Probably soon afterward, Máttis Teutsch begins painting his "Seelenblumen" [Soul Flowers] series of esoterically inspired abstract expressionist oil paintings. Károly Kernstok's leading role in the cultural apparatus of the social democratic government of the newly independent Hungary is the first such position held by a member of the Hungarian artistic avant-garde.
DECEMBER The retrospective exhibition of Sándor Galimberti and Valéria Dénes is announced in *Ma*. The cover of the issue reproduces one of Bortnyik's German Expressionist-inspired works. Iván Hevesy writes on art for the new journal *Vörös Lobogó* [Red Flag].

Tatlin, Rodchenko, and others decorate the Café Pittoresque in Moscow. In Petrograd Puni founds the journal *Isskustvo kommuny* [Communal Art]. Klimt, Schiele, Koloman Moser, and Otto Wagner die in Vienna. In Berlin, the Novembergruppe is founded; Huelsenbeck founds the left-wing Club Dada and later rejects Schwitters' application to join; and the first photomontages are made by Hausmann, Hannah Höch, and George Grosz. The first De Stijl manifesto is issued. In Paris, Ozenfant and Jeanneret (later Le Corbusier) found "purism" and publish *Après le cubisme*; Apollinaire dies. A memorial exhibition is held for Henri Gaudier-Brzeska in London. Duchamp paints "Tu m'," his last painting, for Katherine Dreier in New York. The first museum of contemporary art in the United States, the Phillips Memorial Gallery, is founded in Washington, D.C. Works: Schiele (Vienna), "The Family"; Rietveld (Holland), "Red and Blue Chair"; Man Ray (New York), "Aerographs."

Woodrow Wilson, president of United States, presents his "Fourteen Points" on self-determination and world peace to U.S. Congress. Civil war in Russia. Great War ends; Austria-Hungary in defeat. Spanish flu epidemic kills millions.
OCTOBER 29-31 Declaration of the independence of Czechoslovakia. Croatia secedes from Hungary and joins in formation of Serbo-Croatian-Slovene kingdom. Successful leftist revolution in Vienna. The "Chrysanthemum Revolution" in Hungary—a left-wing, democratic government takes power under leadership of Count Mihály Károlyi.
NOVEMBER-EARLY DECEMBER Emperor-King Charles IV abdicates as emperor of Austria (but not as king of Hungary), and Hungarian, Austrian, and Czech-Slovakian republics are declared in Budapest, Vienna, and Prague, respectively. Leftist and communist revolutions break out in Berlin, Munich, and other German cities. Journalists Béla Kun and Tibor Számuelly return from Russian captivity to Hungary and help found the Hungarian Communist party. Hungarian territory is occupied by Czechs in north, Serbians and French in south, and Romanians in east. Ethnic Romanians of Transylvania and eastern Hungary declare their union with Romania.

1919

Ernő Kállai goes on a scholarship to Germany, remaining there until 1934.
JANUARY An exhibition of graphic art is held at the Ma gallery; a trend toward abstraction is evident, especially in the works of Bortnyik and Uitz. Also exhibiting are Máttis Teutsch, Schadl, Ruttkay, Spangher, and Vera Biller.
FEBRUARY 20 Formation of the "Activists," (the renaming of the Ma group), is announced in a lecture by Kassák. The act of renaming the group, as well as the contents of the lecture, underline the assumption of a more politically active role by the artists around *Ma*. László Moholy-Nagy formally joins the group around this time. *Ma* publishes a translation of Guillaume Apollinaire's "The Cubist Painters" by journalist and critic Zsófia Dénes. The text is soon published in a *Ma* edition as a separate booklet.
SPRING Imre Szobotka returns to Budapest from internment in France and seeks contacts with the Activists. After 1919 he abandons cubism and turns to figurative landscape painting. He eventually becomes one of the major members of the Gresham Circle of painters, a group of late post-impressionist artists in Budapest between the world wars.
MARCH 20 *Ma* publishes Hevesy's study "Beyond Impressionism," dealing with futurism, expressionism, and cubism in detail, as well as with the new tendencies in Hungarian art.
MARCH 21 György Lukács is appointed people's deputy commissar

In Moscow, Malevich exhibits his white-on-white paintings at the Tenth State Exhibition: Non-Objective Creation and Suprematism, the high point of the suprematist movement; Rodchenko paints his first black-on-black and line paintings; and the first OBMOKhU exhibition takes place. Chagall resigns as director of the Vitebsk Practical Art Institute and is replaced by Malevich. Tatlin teaches at SVOMAS in Moscow and Petrograd; he begins work on his *Monument to the Third International*. Puni leaves Russia and goes to Berlin. Walter Gropius is elected chairman of the Arbeitsrat für Kunst, which unites with the Novembergruppe in Berlin; Gropius later founds the Bauhaus in Weimar. In Berlin, Hausmann founds *Der Dada*. Schwitters makes his first collages and initiates his "Merz" art; he shares an exhibition at Der Sturm gallery with Johannes Molzahn and Klee; and Willy Baumeister paints his first geometrical-abstract murals. Eggeling and Richter work on abstract films in Klein-Koelzig, Germany. Berlin Dada and Cologne Dada are in full flower. The first issue of Louis Aragon's *Littérature* appears in Paris. American painter Frank Duveneck dies. In New York, the de Zayas Gallery is established. Man Ray's "Aerographs" are displayed at the Daniel gallery, and he publishes the single issue of *T.N.T.* Late in the year, 153 works by Malevich are displayed at the Sixteenth State Exhibition in Moscow. After the exhibition, Malevich declares the end of suprematism. Works: El Lissitzky (Vitebsk), "Proun" pictures; Höch (Berlin), "Cut with the Kitchen Knife"; Ernst (Cologne), "Fruit of a Long Experience"; Brâncusi (Paris), "Bird in Space"; József Csáky (Paris), abstract

for culture and education of the new Hungarian Soviet Republic.
MARCH 25 The Activists issue a manifesto greeting the new communist-dominated republic.
MARCH-JULY Under the soviet republic, radical artists, including the Activists, assume important roles in artistic life: *Ma* becomes a widely distributed journal, with a sizable influence in the cultural sphere. In Budapest and provincial cities the Activists hold well-attended matinée propaganda performances in which Péri and Kassák's wife Jolán Simon play leading roles. Bertalan Pór and Róbert Berény teach at the reorganized Academy of Fine Arts. Béla Uitz founds and heads the Workshop for Proletarian Art where Nemes Lampérth also teaches. Uitz designs frescoes for the planned House of Work, and some former members of The Eight plan a summer camp for artists at Lake Balaton. Károly Kernstok establishes a free art school for young proletarian artists at Nyergesújfalu. Among his students is Gyula Derkovits. Mácza is appointed assistant director of the national theater. The soviet republic's directorate for art and museums is established and begins the reorganization of cultural life in the country. Among its members are Berény and Pál Pátzay. The directorate initiates a program of art acquisition for public collections, including works by The Eight and the Activists; works by Moholy-Nagy are acquired by a public institution for the first time. Berény, Uitz, Nemes Lampérth, and Kmetty design recruiting posters for the hastily organized Hungarian army. Pécs native Alfréd Forbát, under the influence of Theodor Fischer, his professor at the Technische Hochschule in Munich, takes part in planning the reform of architectural education at Budapest Technical University.
MAY On May Day there are organized mass demonstrations in Budapest. Béla Uitz participates in the decoration of city streets and squares. Sándor Bortnyik exhibits his Activist art at the Ma gallery.
JUNE *Ma* features Bortnyik's Activist art. This same issue reproduces Kassák's "Letter to Béla Kun in the Name of Art," in which Kassák addresses attacks by Kun (*de facto* leader of the Soviet republic) and others; Kun responds by labeling *Ma* "an excrescence of bourgeois decadence." Soon afterward, *Ma* is effectively proscribed. The painter Tivadar Csontváry Kosztka dies.
JULY The last Hungarian-based issue of *Ma* appears, dated July 1. Kassák's attempts to publish again on July 14 fail. He leaves Budapest for a vacation at Lake Balaton.
EARLY AUGUST With the collapse of the Hungarian Soviet Republic, Moholy-Nagy leaves Budapest and returns to Szeged.
AUGUST-DECEMBER The Republic of Councils (Soviets) is replaced by a succession of ever more conservative regimes. Several of the Activists and other avant-garde cultural figures are imprisoned. All are soon released, and most go to Vienna and Berlin. Hevesy, Márffy, Derkovits, and Pátzay, among others, elect to stay. Fred Forbát goes to Germany, where he soon joins Walter Gropius's architectural firm in Berlin. Pór and Mácza return to their homes in Upper Hungary, by then part of the newly created state of Czecho-Slovakia. After obtaining a Czechoslovak passport, Mácza goes to Vienna to join the Activists.
OCTOBER Moholy-Nagy and Sándor Gergely decide to leave the country, but hold an exhibition in Gergely's studio beforehand, including their own works and those of Gergely's fiancée Erzsébet Milkó. The poet Gyula Juhász opens the exhibition, and gives it rave reviews in local papers.
FALL The first forum of the Hungarian émigrés in Vienna, the *Bécsi Magyar Újság* [Viennese-Hungarian Journal], begins publication. It becomes a major source of support for the Activists in Vienna through the (paid) publication of articles by Kassák, and supportive reviews of their activities by writer Andor Németh. Margit Téry-Adler accompanies Johannes Itten from his school in Vienna to the Bauhaus, becoming the first Hungarian there. Gyula Pap leaves his studies at the Academy of Applied Arts in Budapest and moves to Vienna, where he meets Uitz and Berény. Later in the year he visits Berlin and becomes acquainted with the work of the artists of the Der Sturm circle.
NOVEMBER-DECEMBER Moholy-Nagy leaves Szeged for Vienna, where, by Kassák's account, he advises Moholy-Nagy to go to Berlin. After about six weeks in Vienna, Moholy-Nagy leaves for the German capital, as does Nemes Lampérth.

sculptures; Joseph Stella (New York), "Brooklyn Bridge."

Peace talks under way in Paris; signing of Treaty of Versailles with Germany. Hitler founds National Socialist German Workers' Party. Germany adopts Weimar Constitution. Mussolini founds Fascist party in Italy. Comintern founded in Moscow. Civil war continues in Russia; Allied intervention against Bolsheviks fails. "Red scare" in United States reflects anxiety about left-wing revolutions in Europe; persecution of American left begins, continuing until about 1927. Prohibition enacted in United States. United Artists founded by Chaplin, Pickford, and Fairbanks. John Reed: *Ten Days that Shook the World*.
JANUARY 15 Murder of Rosa Luxemburg and Karl Liebknecht in Berlin.
MARCH 21 Declaration of Hungarian Soviet Republic; government consists of left-wing social democrats, communists, and other radicals; its most influential member is Béla Kun.
APRIL 6 Proclamation of soviet republic in Munich; it lasts until end of month.
APRIL 16 Romanian army attacks Hungary; Hungarian army attempts to defend borders.
JUNE 24 Attempt is made in Budapest to overthrow soviet republic; as opposition grows, government response becomes more forceful; a red terror ensues as republic crumbles.
JULY 30 Victory of Romanian forces over those of Hungarian Soviet Republic.
AUGUST 1 Romanian army occupies and loots Budapest. Hungarian Soviet Republic collapses; Kun and members of government flee to Vienna; an interim government of trade unionists is formed.
AUGUST 9 Admiral Miklós Horthy takes command of Hungarian army.
NOVEMBER 16 As Romanian army withdraws, Miklós Horthy and his army enter Budapest; some of his officers initiate white terror against suspected participants in the soviet republic.

1920

In Berlin, László Péri proceeds with his architectural studies. Pécs-native Marcel Breuer goes to the Viennese academy on a scholarship, but soon leaves it and enrolls that fall at the Bauhaus on the advice of his friend Forbát. Gyula Pap has an exhibition at the Haus der Jungen Künstlerschaft in Vienna. Some of the Budapest avant-gardists withdraw to Pécs in southern Hungary, still under Serbian-French occupation. An avant-garde flyer titled *1920* is published there, followed by the more long-lived journal *Krónika*. Farkas Molnár returns to Pécs where he founds and leads the Pécs Artists' Circle. Max Hevesy publishes Uitz's album of figurative expressionist aquatints, *Versuche*, in Vienna. Béla Kádár and Hugó Scheiber move from Budapest to Vienna and eventually to Berlin.

JANUARY János Mácza considers enrolling at the Bauhaus, but joins the Communist party instead, and on the advice of György Lukács becomes cultural editor for the Hungarian daily *Kassai Munkás* [Kassa Worker] in Czechoslovakia.

FEBRUARY Sándor Gergely leaves for Berlin where he becomes an artistic advisor to the Fritz Gurlitt gallery.

MARCH Kassák arrives in Vienna. Lajos Tihanyi has an exhibition in Vienna at the Moderne Galerie. The critic Oskar Reichel calls Tihanyi's work "a worthy representative of modern expressionism." Tihanyi soon moves to Berlin.

MAY 1 The first issue of *Ma* in exile appears in Vienna. In "To the Artists of All Countries!" Kassák calls for the independence of art from political ideologies.

SUMMER Kassák begins work on dada collages, very much influenced by the works of Schwitters that were reproduced in German art journals. Dadaism first exerts a strong influence on the work of the Activists at this time.

OCTOBER Moholy-Nagy and Nemes Lampérth's first foreign exhibition, arranged with Gergely's help, takes place at the Fritz Gurlitt gallery in Berlin. Moholy-Nagy exhibits illustrations to Walter Hasenclaver's drama "Die Menschen." During a visit to Stockholm, Nemes Lampérth becomes mentally ill, returns to Hungary, and is hospitalized. In Vienna, Gyula Pap hears of Itten's teaching and decides to enroll at the Bauhaus. He distinguishes himself with his work in the metal workshop.

NOVEMBER Uitz's first exhibition in exile opens in Vienna, where he shows his new non-naturalistic works. Bortnyik completes work on his album of six abstract linocuts, the first examples of Hungarian geometrical abstract art. Konstantin Umansky, a *Tass* correspondent and author of *Neue Kunst in Russland* (a survey of contemporary Soviet art, published in 1920 in Germany), lectures in Vienna on new art, music, and poetry from Soviet Russia, in a "Russian Evening" organized by the Ma group. Included is a slide presentation of works by Altman, Goncharova, Kandinsky, Malevich, Rodchenko, and Tatlin, among others. This is one of the first public presentations of Soviet avant-garde art in Europe outside of Russia. The deepest impression seems to be made on Béla Uitz. Divisions begin to emerge among the Activists, as the majority turn to dada rather than the Russian direction. Nevertheless, Béla Uitz and Sándor Barta, the Activist most closely identified with the dada direction in the group, continue to coexist as assistant editors of *Ma*. At the Activists' First Viennese Matinée, held at the hall of the Freie Bewegung (a center for new culture), Activist poets read their own works and those of Kassák; Jolán Simon performs works by Huelsenbeck, Schwitters, and Apollinaire; and Barta reads his dada manifesto "The Green-Headed Man." Piano pieces by Bartók and Debussy are also performed.

Malevich founds the UNOVIS group in Vitebsk; El Lissitzky and the Polish Katarzyna Kobro join, among others. In May, INKhUK (Institute of Artistic Culture) is founded in Moscow under Kandinsky; affiliates later are established in Petrograd (under Tatlin and Punin) and at Vitebsk (under Malevich). By the end of the year Kandinsky leaves INKhUK. It is reorganized by Rodchenko, Stepanova, Babichev, and Briusova on theoretical, laboratory principles, and they set up the program for the VKhUTEMAS school. Naum Gabo designs kinetic constructions. In August, Gabo and Pevsner's *Realist Manifesto* is published in conjunction with their exhibition. In Berlin, Erwin Piscator's Proletarian Theater opens, the First International Dada Fair is held, Huelsenbeck's *Dada Almanach* is published, and Schwitters' first one-man show is displayed at the Der Sturm gallery. Ernst and Baargeld publish *Die Schammade* in Cologne. Hausmann, Huelsenbeck, and Baader go on a dada performance tour to Leipzig, Teplitz-Schönau, Prague, and Karlsbad. Mondrian's *Le Néo-plasticisme* appears. Tzara arrives in Paris, where dada is at its height. Also in Paris, Le Corbusier and Ozenfant found *L'Esprit nouveau*. In New York, Katherine Dreier, Man Ray, and Duchamp found the Société Anonyme; William Carlos Williams and Robert McAlmon publish *Contact*; Charles Demuth develops "precisionism" as a style of painting; and the Wildenstein Galleries hold an exhibition of the New Society of Artists. A major exhibition of modern art is presented at the Pennsylvania Academy of Fine Arts in Philadelphia. The Phillips Memorial Art Gallery opens in Washington, with an important collection of modernist art. Works: Mendelsohn (Berlin), Einstein Tower; Hausmann (Berlin), "Tatlin at Home"; Matisse (Paris), "Odalisque"; Léger (Paris), "The Mechanic"; Duchamp (New York), "L.H.H.O.Q."

League of Nations founded in Geneva. First radio stations established in Britain, United States, and Holland. Women's suffrage achieved in United States.

FEBRUARY 29-MARCH 1 Restoration of monarchy in Hungary. Admiral Horthy is elected to the regency.

JUNE 4 Hungarian government signs Versailles Treaty. Hungary loses 60% of population and two-thirds of territory, including bulk of natural resources; one of every three ethnic Hungarians remains outside new boundaries.

1921

The journal *Ma* and the performances of the Activists continue to be dominated by the dada spirit. Kassák begins to paint. Péri begins work on his non-objective concrete reliefs. Lajos Kudlák publishes an album of dada-constructive linocuts at Rimaszombat, Czechoslovakia (formerly Hungary). He exhibits his work in Kassa (Košice) with the Czech cubists. Máttis Teutsch has exhibitions in Vienna and Brassó (Braşov) in Romania (formerly Hungary). Later in the year, Bortnyik paints in the mode of the purists. In *Nyugat*, Hevesy writes on Imre Szobotka's cubist art, praising him as the only Hungarian cubist to reach a near-total abstraction from reality in his work. Aurél Bernáth moves to Vienna. Réth has a one-man show in Budapest. Ödön Palasovszky begins to revive avant-garde life in Budapest with his theatrical performances in workers'

In Moscow, Rodchenko, Medunetsky, Stepanova, Ioganson, Gan, and the Stenberg brothers form the first constructivist group at the INKhUKH. The term "constructivism" appears in print for the first time in an exhibition catalogue of works of Medunetsky and the Stenbergs; Osip Brik coins the term "productivism" at an INKhUK lecture; El Lissitzky is appointed head of the architectural faculty of VKhUTEMAS; the constructivists organize the show 5 × 5 = 25; Rodchenko develops his hanging constructions; and Alfréd Kemény lectures on new German art and on the OBMOKhU group at the INKhUK. Rodchenko, Popova, Vesnin, and others leave INKhUK to devote themselves entirely to applied design. Kandinsky emigrates to Berlin. The first exhibition of abstract art takes place in Warsaw, with works by Stażewski, Szczuka, Kobro, and others. In Zagreb Ljubomir Micić establishes the journal *Zenit*. Schwitters and Hausmann perform in Prague. Adolf Loos is appointed

85. KÁROLY KERNSTOK, Last Supper, 1921-23

centers. The sculptor Béni Ferenczy moves from Budapest to Vienna, where he lives during the 1920s. Articles on the new Hungarian art by Kudlák and Kállai appear in the German journal *Der Ararat*.

EARLY 1921 An exhibition of the Pécs Artists' Circle is held. Future Bauhäusler Farkas Molnár, Henrik Stefán, Andor Weininger, Lajos Cačinovič, and Hugó Johann, as well as Jenő Gábor, take part.

JANUARY Sándor Barta's dada-absurd play *Igen* [Yes], illustrated by a Bortnyik linocut, appears in an edition of *Ma*. Béla Uitz goes to Berlin where he meets fellow Activists Moholy-Nagy, Kemény and Kállai, as well as Herwarth Walden. He soon leaves for Moscow and the Third Comintern. *Ma*'s cover features a dadaist visual poem by Kassák, his first publication of visual art. The issue also presents Sándor Barta's dada manifesto, "The Green-headed Man," and Kurt Schwitters's "Merz" art.

FEBRUARY Lajos Kassák's book of dada poetry, *Új versek* [New Poems] (also referred to by its cover page inscription as "1-Ma Kassák"), appears in a *Ma* edition, illustrated by four of Kassák's own dada-constructivist woodcuts. This is the first of a series of illustrated volumes of his writing published in Vienna.

MARCH Bortnyik's album of six colored dada-constructivist linocuts appears in a *Ma* edition of 25, after five months of preparation. In the introduction Kassák first uses the term *képarchitektúra* [architecture of the picture] (*Bildarchitektur* in German) in describing Bortnyik's works. *Ma* features new art by Uitz, Bortnyik, Kassák, Máttis Teutsch (for the last time), and Moholy-Nagy (for the first time). Kassák designs *Ma*'s first geometrical-abstract cover.

APRIL *Magyar Írás* [Hungarian Writing] appears in Budapest, a journal edited by the critic Tivadar Raith and devoted to new art and literature. Molnár, Johann, and Stefán, on the advice of fellow Pécs-native Alfréd Forbát, decide to leave Pécs and go to Weimar to enroll at the Bauhaus. On their way, they travel through Italy and sketch the towns and the landscape in a loose, analytical cubist style. *Ma* features the art of Alexander Archipenko. Moholy-Nagy is listed for the first time as the German correspondent for *Ma*. An exhibition of Lajos Tihanyi's work is held at the Möller gallery in Berlin.

JUNE-JULY In Moscow, Uitz becomes acquainted firsthand with the work of the constructivists at the exhibition organized for the Third Comintern. According to Uitz, he sends material on the constructivists to Kassák, and Kassák does not publish it. Ernő Kállai publishes his first piece in *Ma* under the pseudonym Péter Mátyás.

JULY-AUGUST Máttis Teutsch exhibits at Der Sturm gallery along with Klee, Archipenko, Chagall, and others.

AUGUST A dada linocut by Moholy-Nagy appears in *Der Sturm*. *Ma* features the "Diagonal Symphonies" of Viking Eggeling and Hans

chief architect of the Siedlungsamt in Vienna. In Berlin, Piscator's Proletarian Theater closes, and Ivan Puni exhibits at Der Sturm. Moholy-Nagy, Hausmann, Arp, and Puni publish the "Elementarist Manifesto" in the October issue of *De Stijl*. Van Doesburg moves to Weimar. Not offered a position at the Bauhaus, he organizes his De Stijl Course outside it. The first Donauschingen Festival of new music takes place. Michel Seuphor and Jozef Peeters establish *Het Overzicht* [The Review] in Antwerp. Max Ernst and Man Ray have their first exhibitions in Paris. Also in Paris, the second purist exhibition is presented at the Galerie Druet; Mondrian develops the style of his "Compositions"—orthogonal patterns of heavy black lines enclosing rectangles of primary colors, greys and white; and the first and second sales of the Kahnweiler estate are held. Evola leads dada activities in Rome; *Bleu* appears in Mantua. In New York, Marsden Hartley's *Adventures in the Arts* is published; Man Ray and Duchamp publish *New York Dada*; a large exhibition of Paintings by Modern French Masters is on display at the Brooklyn Museum, the de Zayas gallery closes, and a major modernist show is held at the Metropolitan Museum. Much new American art is displayed in an Exhibition of Paintings and Drawings Showing the Later Tendencies in Art at the Pennsylvania Academy of the Fine Arts in Philadelphia. The Modern Artists of America society is founded, with Henry Fitch Taylor its first president. Man Ray and Duchamp leave New York for Paris, marking the end of New York dada. Margaret Anderson relocates to Paris with *The Little Review*. Works: Ernst (Cologne), "The Elephant Celebes"; Grosz (Berlin), "Grauer Tag"; Miró (Paris), "The Farm"; Picasso (Paris), "The Three Musicians" and "Grande baigneuse"; Léger (Paris): "Le grand déjeuner"; Man Ray (New York), "Gift"; Duchamp, "Why not sneeze Rrose Sélavy"; Stuart Davis, "Lucky Strike."

The NKVD (secret police) founded in Soviet Russia. Famine in Soviet Russia; introduction of New Economic Policy. Count István Bethlen becomes prime minister of Hungary, and a process of political consolidation begins. Two attempts to restore Habsburg monarchy in Hungary fail. National Origins Act in United States restricts immigration from southern and eastern Europe.

Richter. Pécs comes under the administration of the conservative regime in Budapest, and most of the avant-gardists leave. Some decide to attend the Weimar Bauhaus, while others go to nearby Újvidék (Novi Sad, Yugoslavia since 1920), where they regroup.
SEPTEMBER Farkas Molnár, Lajos Cačinovič, Hugó Johann, Henrik Stefán, and Andor Weininger enroll at the Weimar Bauhaus. *Ma* announces the publication of Kassák's manifesto *Képarchitektúra*, accompanied by seven of his own linocuts. The issue presents the "mechano-dada" art of Moholy-Nagy. The Activists' Second Viennese Matinée is held at the Konzerthaus. Dada continues to dominate.
FALL Uitz leaves Moscow for Berlin, where he meets Moholy-Nagy and Kállai. After his return to Vienna, Uitz begins work on his constructivist-inspired linocuts and paintings ("icon analyses").
OCTOBER A drawing by László Péri appears in *Der Sturm*, probably the first publication of his work.
NOVEMBER *Ma* features Kassák's *Képarchitektúra*, with an accompanying study by Ernő Kállai.

1922

In transition from dada to international constructivism, *Ma* is developing into one of the premier forums of the international avant-garde. Works by Hungarian avant-gardists are featured in many non-Hungarian journals such as *De Stijl*, *Der Sturm*, *Mécano*, *Veshch'/Gegenstand/Objêt*, *L'Esprit nouveau*, *Zenit*, *Secession*, and *Broom*. Kassák tries his hand at sculpture and architecture (advertising kiosks), while continuing to paint and make collages. Ödön Palasovszky steps up his efforts at reviving the Budapest avant-garde when he publishes his manifesto *Az új stáció* [The New Station] in Budapest. In it he calls for a "collective" art for the masses. In *The Agony and Reincarnation of Art*, Iván Hevesy attacks képarchitektúra, which he believes reintroduces a discredited "art for art's sake" attitude. At the Bauhaus, Molnár and Henrik Stefán publish an album of 12 lithographs of drawings made on their trip to Italy. Uitz completes work on 23 abstract linocuts, which he publishes in Vienna as an album entitled *Analízis*. He makes three-dimensional constructions in the manner of the Russian constructivists. In Berlin, Moholy-Nagy prepares a screenplay (film score) entitled "The Dynamics of the Metropolis" for a film that eschews linear narrative. It is later published in *Ma* and in his book *Painting, Photography, Film*. Important works of 1922 are his enamel "Telephone Pictures." Moholy-Nagy expounds on his ideas related to these works in his article "Production—Reproduction," which appears in *De Stijl* in July. Péri begins work on his *Raumkonstruktion* [Spatial construction] series.
JANUARY Béla Uitz breaks with the Activists.
FEBRUARY Moholy-Nagy and Lászlo Péri exhibit their new constructivist art at Der Sturm in Berlin, the first public exhibition of

Proletkult loses its government subsidy; Naum Gabo leaves Russia for Germany. In Moscow, Popova designs sets for Meyerhold's production of *The Magnanimous Cuckold*; Popova, Stepanova, and Rodchenko do design work for a textile factory, and Rodchenko becomes interested in photography. The Zenit International Gallery for New Art is established in Zagreb. Strzemínski and Kobro return to Poland from Moscow; Strzemínski publishes *Zwrotnica*. The Polish Blok group of nonobjective artists is founded at Łodz. In Berlin, the First Russian Exhibition takes place at the Galerie van Diemen, El Lissitzky and Ilya Ehrenburg publish the journal *Veshch'/Gegenstand/Objêt*, and Raoul Hausmann and Péri publish a proposal in *Der Sturm* for "Pré," a constructivist theater of abstract form, dance, and music. Kandinsky assumes a professorial position at the Weimar Bauhaus. The International Congress of Progressive Artists takes place in Düsseldorf in May, while the Weimar Congress of Constructivists and Dadaists is held in September. Van Doesburg, under the pseudonym I. K. Bonset, publishes a dada journal, *Mécano*. A Mondrian retrospective is held at the Stedelijk museum in Amsterdam. Gorham Munson establishes *Sezession* in Vienna, and Harold Loeb first publishes *Broom* in Rome. Max Ernst moves to Paris. A major exhibition of Picabia's works is held in Barcelona. James Joyce's *Ulysses* is published. Works: El Lissitzky, "The Story of Two Squares"; Schlemmer (Weimar), *Triadic Ballet*; Man Ray (Paris), "Rayograms"; Joseph Stella, "New York Interpreted" series; Alexander Gan (Moscow), *Constructivism*. Karl Kraus (Vienna), *Die letzten Tage der Menschheit* [The Last Days of Mankind]; Henrik Berlewi (Berlin), "Mechano-Faktur" painting.

Mussolini marches on Rome and becomes prime minister of Italy. Declaration of Union of Soviet Socialist Republics.

35. BÉLA CZÓBEL, Reclining Woman, 1922

119. DEZSŐ ORBÁN, Still Life with Cactus, Books, and Dishes, 1911

Péri's concrete reliefs and Moholy-Nagy's reliefs and metal constructions. Walter Gropius is especially impressed with Moholy-Nagy's works in metal. *Ma* presents the art of Ivan Puni. An album of hand-colored expressionist lithographs by Aurél Bernáth is published in Vienna.
MARCH *Ma* features the art of Hans Arp. On an Activist performance tour of Czechoslovakia, dada dominates the poetry and performance, and tensions become apparent between Kassák and Mácza.
APRIL The young Hungarian avant-garde artists who fled to Újvidék publish the first issue of their journal *Út* [Way].
MAY The critic Gyula Laziczius publishes a study on Hungarian Activism in *Magyar Írás*. The third issue of *Veshch'* presents a work by Kassák, as well as an appreciation of the Hungarian avant-garde by El Lissitzky. Kássak produces a sumptuous double issue of *Ma*, which includes works by international constructivists and dadaists. The journal *Egység* [Unity] is published in Vienna, edited by Uitz and other former Activists. Politically to the left of *Ma*, *Egység* attacks Kassák for his allegedly "bourgeois" constructivism. Published in Hungarian translation are Gabo and Pevsner's *Realist Manifesto* and Rodchenko and Stepanova's *Program of the Constructivist Group* (both of 1920), their first non-Russian publication. (This is the material which Uitz claimed Kassák did not publish in 1921.) At the Activists' Fourth Viennese Matinée, it is apparent that the influence of dada is on the wane.
JUNE *Der Sturm* features a design for one of Péri's concrete *Raumkonstruktionen* on its cover. The second issue of *Egység* includes an article by Uitz on new Russian art.
JULY A *De Stijl* special issue appears on the Activists; in turn, *Ma* publishes a special issue on the De Stijl group.
SUMMER Unable to attend the International Congress of Progressive Artists held in Düsseldorf in late May, the Activists formulate a position in July and publish it in the August issues of *Ma* and *De*

Stijl. In it, they call for an international organization of artists, suggesting the name "International Organization of Creators with a Revolutionary World View." This is the final unified stand taken by the Activists. Though *Ma* continues to identify itself as an "Activist" journal, "Activism" is for all intents and purposes a thing of the past when the remaining original members of the group break with Kassák over the summer. Moholy-Nagy and his wife Lucia begin work on photograms and on the kinetic "light-space modulator."

AUGUST Kassák publishes his "Notes on the New Art" in *Bécsi Magyar Újság*. *Ma* features a cover page with a sketch for El Lissitzky's "Proun 43." Kassák replies to the attacks made on him in *Egység*.

SEPTEMBER A linocut version of Moholy-Nagy's "The Great Wheel" appears on the cover of *Der Sturm*. The *Új művészek könyve/ Buch neuer Künstler* [Book of New Artists], edited by Kassák and Moholy-Nagy, appears in Hungarian and German. It becomes Kassák's most successful publishing effort and sets the standards for later compendia of new art. Bortnyik and Mácza plan a new journal, to be called *Kritika*, but Bortnyik leaves for Weimar, and the journal fails to materialize. "Uitz" by Zsófia Dénes appears in *Bécsi Magyar Újság*. *Egység* 3 presents extensive material on the Soviet constructivists, and an article on suprematism. In "The Squared World View," Iván Hevesy attacks Kassák's képarchitektúra. The Dada-Constructivist Congress opens in Weimar; Moholy-Nagy, Bortnyik, and Kemény attend. Bortnyik takes a studio in Weimar and remains there until late 1924.

FALL Bernáth moves to Berlin, where he becomes associated with the Der Sturm group; he remains there until 1926.

OCTOBER In Vienna, Kassák and Andor Németh publish the only issue of their avant-garde literary journal *2 × 2*. Among the works published is Kassák's major dada epic "The Horse Dies, the Birds Fly Away." *Ma* appears in a new, larger format. Included are an abridged version of Kassák's képarchitektúra manifesto in German translation, and Hungarian translations of El Lissitzky's "Proun" manifesto (1920) and Raoul Hausmann's "Optophonetics."

WINTER Moholy-Nagy and his wife Lucia share a studio in Weimar with Kurt Schwitters. Moholy-Nagy creates collages. Andor Weininger, Molnár and Bortnyik attend van Doesburg's studio seminars in Weimar.

NOVEMBER The first issue of Sándor Barta's left-wing dada journal *Akasztott Ember* [The Hanged Man] appears in Vienna. In it, he satirizes Kassák and *Ma*, especially for their uncritical glorification of machines. Kassák and his wife Jolán Simon travel to Berlin to see the Erste Russische Kunstausstellung [First Russian Art Exhibition]. Kassák, Simon, and Kállai hold an evening performance at the Der Sturm gallery. A Kassák képarchitektúra work appears on the cover of *Der Sturm*.

DECEMBER *Der Sturm*'s special issue on the Hungarians includes Alfréd Kemény and Moholy-Nagy's "Dynamic-Constructive System of Forces," and works by Péri, Kassák, and Bortnyik. Bortnyik has his only exhibition at Der Sturm gallery. Farkas Molnár drafts the Constructive-Utilitarian-Rational-International (KURI) manifesto at the Weimar Bauhaus, the first constructivist stand taken by students there. It is signed by many, including the Hungarians Molnár, Weininger, and Stefán, as well as Cačinovič. It later appears in *Út*. The second issue of *Akasztott Ember* introduces a "Debate on the Problem of New Content and New Form." Moholy-Nagy's contribution to this issue is a defense of nonobjectivity and experimentation in art. Ernő Kállai and George Grosz join the debate as well. *Ma* focuses on the First Russian Exhibition, with a review by Kassák and reproductions of works by members of the Russian avant-garde.

1923

Ma becomes the most important international constructivist journal in Central Europe once *Veshch'* is no longer published. Kassák publishes material on purism, De Stijl, Russian art, German international constructivism, the Bauhaus, and the Belgian moderns. Hungarian avant-garde works are featured in *L'Esprit nouveau*, *Der Sturm*, *Broom*, and *Het Overzicht* [The Review], among others. Articles in *Ma* reflect the formation of a new circle of Hungarian international constructivist artists and theorists around Kassák. Erno Kállai, Róbert Reiter, and László Grünhut contribute further to the development of the theory of Hungarian international constructivism, and képarchitektúra works by Kassák, the Prague-Hungarian poet

The Exhibition of All Tendencies takes place in Petrograd. Mayakovsky publishes the journal *LEF* in Moscow. The first constructivist exhibition in Poland is held at Vilna (now in Lithuania), and includes, among others, works of Strzemínski, Stażewski, Szczuka, and Kobro. Berlewi returns to Poland from Berlin. Szczuka exhibits at Der Sturm. Karel Teige, Kurt Seifert, and Krejčar publish *Disk* in Prague. Micić leaves Zagreb and continues to publish *Zenit* in Belgrade. Hans Richter, El Lissitzky, and Ilya Ehrenburg publish the journal *G* [Gestaltung] in Berlin. In *Broom*, Moholy-Nagy's "Light: a Medium of Plastic Expression" appears along with four of his photograms. Moholy-Nagy exhibits in Hannover at the Kestner Society, which publishes an album of six of his lithographs of 1922. In April he joins the Bauhaus as co-director of the metal work-

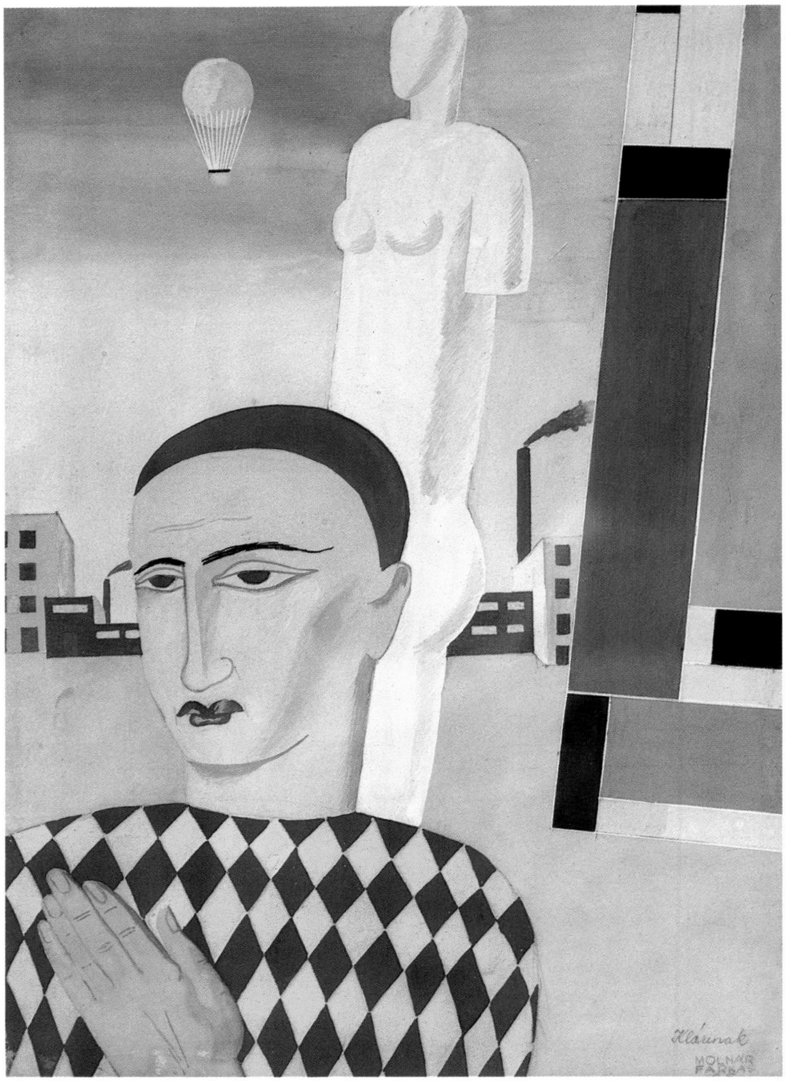

110. FARKAS MOLNÁR, Harlequinade, 1926

Henrik Glauber and the Viennese Hans Suschny are reproduced. Alfréd Forbát designs three international style buildings for clients in Hungary, the first such buildings in the country. Lajos Tihanyi moves from Berlin to settle in Paris. Béla Uitz breaks with constructivism, turning toward the development of an "ideology of form," for use in representational, ideologically infused art. Uitz has his second Viennese exhibition, at the Österreichisches Museum. Herwarth Walden publishes an album of lithographic *Raumkonstruktionen* by Péri, with an accompanying essay by Alfréd Kemény. Péri and Moholy-Nagy exhibit together at the Grosse Berliner Kunstaustellung. Aurél Bernáth and Béla Kádár have their first exhibitions at Der Sturm. At the Bauhaus, Farkas Molnár makes figurative drawings of athletic youths among international style buildings. In Budapest, Vilmos Aba-Novák and former Activist István Szőnyi (both heavily influenced by the art of Cézanne and Uitz), constitute an informal grouping together with photographer André Kertész.

JANUARY Editorial offices of *Egység* move to Berlin without Uitz. An attempt is made to unite the Hungarian international constructivists working in Germany around *Egység* at a meeting in Moholy-Nagy's Berlin apartment, attended by former Activists Aladár Komját, Moholy-Nagy, Péri, and Kállai, as well as Aurél Bernáth and a few others. Bortnyik has a show at the Nierendorf gallery in Berlin. Iván Hevesy writes on Máttis Teutsch and abstract expressionism in *Nyugat*. In *Akasztott Ember*, Bortnyik attacks van Doesburg and J.J.P. Oud, van Doesburg's former colleague in the De Stijl group, as representatives of "bourgeois" constructivism.

FEBRUARY *Der Sturm* features two works by Péri from his album (including one on the cover) and poetry by Kassák. Péri and Moholy-Nagy again exhibit together at Der Sturm. As a result of the January meeting, Kállai, Péri, Moholy-Nagy, and Kemény announce their joining *Egység* in a declaration published in that journal. The final issue of *Akasztott Ember* includes a declaration of the Vienna Union of Communist Hungarian Artists, with Sándor Barta, Béla Uitz, and János Mácza as signatories; Bortnyik's contribution to the debate on the "New Content and New Form;" and Kállai's review of the First Russian Exhibition in Berlin.

MARCH The *Ma-Buch*, a collection of Kassák's poems in German translation illustrated with the author's képarchitekturá woodcuts, appears in Berlin. Sándor Barta joins Béla Uitz in bringing out the journal *Ék* [Wedge] in Vienna. Barta leaves dada behind him, and Uitz abandons abstract art for a strictly proletkult line. Uitz publishes his "Experiment Toward an Ideology of Form." George Grosz and Lajos Tihanyi contribute to the "New Content and New Form" series begun in *Akasztott Ember*.

APRIL Gropius invites Moholy-Nagy to replace Johannes Itten as professor of the obligatory preparatory course at the Weimar Bauhaus, and to codirect the metal workshop.

APRIL-MAY Farkas Molnár writes on the "Constructive Conception" in new art and architecture for *Magyar Írás*. In the fifth issue of *Egység*, the editors announce their break with Kemény and Kállai. Though Moholy-Nagy and Péri are not named, the attack extends to them by implication. Ernő Kállai soon rejoins the Ma group through the publication of his essay "Constructivism."

JUNE The young painter Gyula Derkovits moves from Budapest to Vienna. He absorbs the art of expressionism.

JULY-OCTOBER A major exhibition of Bauhaus accomplishments is held in Weimar to which the Hungarian Bauhäusler Breuer, Molnár, Pap, Forbát, and Moholy-Nagy contribute. Having completed his Bauhaus studies, Pap leaves for Transylvania.

JULY Kassák produces a thoroughly international constructivist issue of *Ma* with contributions from Léger, Hans Richter, Kassák, Farkas Molnár, Kállai, and Willy Baumeister.

AUGUST Iván Hevesy writes on "Suprematism and Képarchitektúra" for *Kékmadár* [Bluebird], the Budapest journal of new art and letters.

SEPTEMBER The final issue of *Ék* appears in Vienna.

NOVEMBER Ernő Kállai's article on "Pictorial Problems of Today's Art" appears in the Budapest art journal *Ars Una*. In Budapest, the Mentor bookshop organizes a window display of new book design. In the back room, an exhibition of "Modern Graphic Art" is opened, with works by Béla Kádár, Máttis Teutsch, Uitz, Bortnyik, and others. This may have been the first display of avant-garde art in Budapest after 1919. In *Ma*, Kállai defends constructivism against the accusation that it is "art for art's sake." The first shops and of the preliminary courses. Schwitters founds *Merz* in Cologne. The *Institut für Sozialforschung* (Institute for Social Research) is founded in Frankfurt. Huszár breaks with the De Stijl group. Van Doesburg moves to Paris and collaborates with Cornelis van Eesteren on designs for buildings. Also in Paris, a De Stijl exhibition is held at the *Galerie de l'effort moderne*, and Berenice Abbott becomes Man Ray's assistant. In *Noi* the futurists declare their support for the fascist government. In New York, the Brooklyn Museum presents exhibitions of African Art and Contemporary Russian Paintings and Sculpture; and the first large exhibitions of Kandinsky and of German Expressionist art in North America are held at the Société Anonyme and the Valentiner gallery respectively. Archipenko moves to the United States. Demuth begins his series of "Poster Portraits." Works: El Lissitzky (Grosse Berliner Kunstausstellung), "Proun-Room"; Le Corbusier (Paris), *Vers une architecture*.

French army occupies Ruhr region of Germany. Height of monetary inflation in Germany. Failure of Hitler's Munich "Putsch." Hungary admitted to League of Nations. Calvin Coolidge becomes president of United States.

and only issue of Kassák's journal *Kortárs* [The Contemporary] appears in Vienna.
DECEMBER Moholy-Nagy writes Rodchenko a letter in which he outlines his plans for a series of books on new art. These plans later materialize as the *Bauhausbücher* of 1925-27.

1924 *Ma* continues to publish in the international constructivist spirit on a wide variety of topics and artists. Kassák's political-theoretical tract "Standpoint: Facts and Possibilities" and his poetic account of the events of 1919, "The Stakes Sing," are published in Vienna. He begins to design commercial advertising for various firms. Works by members of the Hungarian avant-garde continue to appear in the international avant-garde press, particularly in *L'Esprit nouveau*, *Der Sturm*, *Het Overzicht*, and the Romanian journal *Contimporanul*. Bortnyik begins to include figures in the architectonic space of his abstract painting. As he becomes more critical of "bourgeois" constructivism, these figural elements take on a satirical character. At the Bauhaus, Moholy-Nagy, Farkas Molnár, and Oskar Schlemmer prepare *Theater at the Bauhaus*; and Moholy-Nagy works on his book *Painting, Photography, Film*. Molnár, Bortnyik, Breuer, and Weininger publish their *Egység* declaration in *Magyar Írás*. In Holland, a young Dezső Korniss meets Vilmos Huszár and is exposed to the art of the De Stijl group. Iván Hevesy gives Péri's *Der Sturm Album* a positive review in *Nyugat*. Béla Kádár and Hugó Scheiber exhibit at Der Sturm. Scheiber's work is featured on the pages of *Der Sturm* regularly until 1930. Derkovits exhibits at the Hagenbund's spring show.
FEBRUARY Moholy-Nagy and Scheiber exhibit together at Der Sturm. Kassák has an exhibition with two Austrian artists at the Würthle gallery in Vienna.
MAY An exhibition of works by Kassák and the German-Hungarian painter and set-designer Nikolaus Braun is held at Der Sturm. Nemes Lampérth dies of tuberculosis in Hungary. The final issue of *Egység* appears in Berlin. The art critic Pál Bor writes about new art and architecture, and about Le Corbusier in particular, for *Magyar Írás*.
JUNE An exhibition of works by Bernáth and Béni Ferenczy opens at Der Sturm, and an appreciation of Bernáth's art by Ernő Kállai appears in *Der Sturm*.
JULY A Máttis Teutsch exhibition opens in Vienna.
JULY-AUGUST *Der Sturm*'s Zweites Vierteljahrheft [second quarterly issue] focuses on the Hungarians, including works by Kassák, Moholy-Nagy, Scheiber and Máttis Teutsch. The critic and theorist Endre Gáspár's *Kassák Lajos: Az ember és munkája* [Kassák: The Man and His Work] appears in Vienna. As part of a series on the documents of the international avant-garde, *Magyar Írás* republishes the "Realist Manifesto," the "Program of the Constructivists," and Malevich's "Suprematism." Marcel Breuer graduates from the Bauhaus and leaves Weimar for Paris.
SEPTEMBER Tivadar Raith asks the international modern art community about their opinions on what he terms "the crisis in art," and publishes the results in *Magyar Írás*. Included are replies from Robert Delaunay, Jean Metzinger, Fernand Léger, Kees van Dongen, Gino Severini, Marc Chagall, József Csáky, Sándor Bortnyik, Marcel Breuer, Farkas Molnár, and Andor Weininger. Subsequent issues publish the responses of János Kmetty, Pál

Punct is established in Bucharest, edited by Scarlat Calimanchi. The First Zenit International Exhibition of New Art takes place in Belgrade. *Blok* is founded in Poland, and the Blok group's first exhibition takes place at the Laurin-Clement car dealership in Warsaw. The first issue of *Pásmo*, edited by Karel Teige, appears in Brno. In September, Friedrich Kiesler's International Exhibition of Stagecraft opens in Vienna. Ernst May becomes the chief town planner of Frankfurt. In Berlin, Bruno Taut becomes the architect for the GEHAG housing authority, the artists' group "The Blue Four" (Feininger, Jawlensky, Klee, Kandinsky) is founded, Péri designs a monument to the memory of Lenin, and Alfréd Kemény (Durus) becomes the art critic for the communist journal *Rote Fahne*, a position he maintains until 1933. Schwitters begins work on his "Merzbau" in Hannover. In Holland van Doesburg develops his "elementarist" concept of painting using the diagonal. In Paris, *La Révolution surréaliste* is established by Breton and others. André Masson's first one-man show is held at the Galerie Simon; he and Miró join the surrealist group. American modernist painter Maurice B. Prendergast dies. In New York, the Metropolitan Museum of Art opens its American wing; *Sezession* and *Broom* cease publication. Works: Thomas Mann (Germany), *The Magic Mountain*; Oud, designs for public housing in Hoek van Holland; Rietveld (Utrecht), Schroeder House; André Breton (Paris), *First Surrealist Manifesto*; Ernst (Paris), "The Forest"; Léger (Paris) *Ballet mécanique*.

Death of Lenin; Petrograd renamed Leningrad.

Pátzay, and Béla Uitz, among others. Béla Kádár's portrait of Herwarth Walden appears on the cover of *Der Sturm*. Contained within is Endre Gáspár's "Die Bewegung der ungarischen Aktivisten," [The Hungarian Activist Movement], a history and account of the current state of Hungarian Activism. Kassák publishes a Special Music and Theater Issue of *Ma* in German, Hungarian, Italian, and French on the occasion of Friedrich Kiesler's International Exhibition of Stagecraft in Vienna. Among the material published is Moholy-Nagy's screenplay for "The Dynamics of the Metropolis." The new *Egység* [Unity], the union of the Viennese *Ék* and the Berlin *Egység*, appears, with Komját, Uitz, Barta, and Mácza (from Moscow) as contributors.
OCTOBER Uitz goes to Paris. Péri has an exhibition at Der Sturm with Nell Walden and Ludwig Hilberseimer.
LATE 1924 Bortnyik leaves Weimar, goes to Kassa (Košice) in Czechoslovakia to organize an exhibition of his works, and returns home to Budapest.
DECEMBER Kassák exhibits his képarchitektúra works at Ion Vinea's International Exhibition of New Art in Bucharest. The first issue of the avant-garde journal *Is* [Also] appears in Budapest with contributions by critic Árpád Mezei, the theorist and filmmaker György Gerő, and writer Imre Pán. The First Propaganda Evening of the Free Union of New Artists takes place in Budapest, with the participation of poets and critics Erwin Ember, Ágost Karly, Ödön Palasovszky, and Iván Hevesy, as well as the composer Pál Kadosa.

1925

Ernő Kállai's book *Neue Malerei in Ungarn* [New Painting in Hungary] appears in Hungarian and German editions, becoming the most widely consulted book on the Hungarian avant-garde until well into the 1960s. As *Ma*'s Hungarian audience in Czechoslovakia, Romania, and Yugoslavia shrinks, an unsuccessful attempt is made to reach a German-speaking audience in Vienna. Marinetti visits Vienna and meets with Kassák; the meeting is not friendly. The works of Hungarian avant-gardists appear more frequently in East-Central European avant-garde journals such as the Polish *Blok*, the Romanian *Integral* and *Contimporanul*, and the Czech *Pásmo*, as well as in *Der Sturm*. The Yugoslavian-Hungarian avant-garde journal *Út* ceases publication as does *Is* in Budapest. Sándor Barta emigrates to the USSR. Farkas Molnár returns from Weimar to Budapest permanently. Béla Uitz designs sets for a Paris production of Gorky's play *Mother*. Three of István Csók and János Vaszary's students at the Academy of Fine Arts in Budapest form an informal group concerned with new art. The group initially includes Dezső Korniss, György Kepes, and Sándor Trauner. A section on Hungarian art is included in Katherine Dreier's *Modern Art* (New York). In Budapest Iván Hevesy publishes a book and establishes a short-lived journal on film theory. Béla Kádár exhibits at Der Sturm. André Kertész moves from Budapest to Paris.
JANUARY *Ma*'s lavish tenth anniversary issue appears, a major document of international constructivism. The "flyer" *Fundamentum* appears in Szeged. Though no editor is given, *Fundamentum* contains poems by members of the current *Ma* group, as well as a full-page woodcut by Moholy-Nagy. The *Ma* group's Fifth Viennese Matinée is held, again at the Vienna Konzerthaus.
FEBRUARY Art historian István Genthon's article on Malevich's painting appears in *Magyar Írás*. Sándor Bortnyik has an exhibition at the Mentor bookshop in Budapest. He paints very little after this, becoming more interested in stage, advertising, and book design. Derkovits exhibits at the Weichburg gallery in Vienna.
MARCH Farkas Molnár exhibits his Bauhaus works at the Mentor bookshop in Budapest. He notes in the catalogue that the material was also exhibited in Hannover, Weimar, Berlin, and Stuttgart during 1923-24. The first issue of the Hungarian avant-garde journal *Periszkóp* [Periscope] appears in Arad, Romania (formerly Hungary), edited by György Szántó. Moholy-Nagy and Hugó Scheiber again exhibit together at Der Sturm. The Ma group organizes its First German Propaganda Evening, the group's last performance in Vienna. A special German-language issue of *Ma* appears in conjunction with the propaganda evening. The first performance of the dada "Green Donkey Theater" takes place in Budapest with the participation of Ödön Palasovszky, Iván Hevesy, Gyula Lazicziusz, Bortnyik, and Molnár, among others.

In Bucharest, H. M. Maxy founds *Integral*, and *Punct* merges with *Contimporanul*. In Warsaw, the Blok group disintegrates. In Prague, the Devětsil group issues the journal *Tvorba*, which lasts until the following year. The Bauhaus moves from Weimar to Dessau, occupying new buildings specially designed for the purpose by Gropius. At the Bauhaus, the industrial production and marketing of their designs begins; Herbert Bayer and Josef Albers are hired, Breuer takes over the carpentry workshop, and Moholy-Nagy launches the *Bauhausbücher* series. El Lissitzky and Hans Arp publish *Die Kunstismen*. The Neue Sachlichkeit exhibition opens in Dresden. *Die Form* is published by the Deutsche Werkbund and others. Mondrian breaks with van Doesburg and De Stijl. The last issue of *Het Overzicht* appears in Antwerp. El Lissitzky returns to Russia. In Paris, the birth of Art Deco is signaled at the *Exposition international des arts décoratifs et industriels modernes*. Melnikov designs the Soviet pavilion, where Rodchenko designs an interior for a Workers' Club; and Le Corbusier designs the Pavilion de l'esprit nouveau. Meanwhile, *L'esprit nouveau* ceases publication. Also in Paris, *L'art d'aujourdhui* [Art of Today] exhibition includes works by Moholy-Nagy, Baumeister, Dexel, Domela, Exter, Servanckx, and Vordemberge-Gildewart; the first exhibition of Miró's surrealist paintings is held at the Pierre gallery; Yves Tanguy joins the surrealist movement; the surrealists engage in *cadavre exquis* games; and their first group exhibition is organized at the Pierre gallery. De Chirico exhibits at L'Effort moderne, and Klee's first one-man show is held; American modernist painter John Singer Sargent dies. In New York, Martha Graham founds her dance company, Alfred Stieglitz organizes an exhibition of American moderns at the Anderson gallery (later he opens the Intimate Gallery), and an exhibition of new works by Léger is held at the Société Anonyme. Works: Karel Teige (Prague), "Poetism"; Kafka (Prague), *The Trial*; Klee (Dessau), "Fish Magic"; Breuer (Dessau), "Wassily" chair; Oud (Rotterdam), Café de Unie; Miró (Paris), "The Birth of the World"; Edward Hopper (United States), "House by the Railroad."

Trotsky dismissed from Russian revolutionary military council. Hitler publishes first volume of *Mein Kampf* [My Struggle].

46. LAJOS D'ÉBNETH, Composition, 1926

Prominent Hungarian artist Tibor Pólya visits Toronto and meets members of the Canadian nativist avant-garde Group of Seven painters. He declares the work of the theosophist painter Lawren Harris to be of international significance.
APRIL The first issue of *365*, an attempt to establish a Budapest edition of *Ma*, appears under the nominal editorship of Aladár Tamás. A small retrospective exhibition of Lajos Tihanyi's art is held at *Le Sacre du printemps* in Paris.
MAY *Periszkóp* 3 includes reproductions of works by Tihanyi, Léger, and Kudlák.
JUNE Bortnyik's pantomime "The Green Donkey" appears in *Periszkóp* 4 with the accompanying set and costume designs. Also included is van Doesburg's "The End of Art," Farkas Molnár's "Life at the Bauhaus," and reproductions of works by Moholy-Nagy, Brâncuşi, Natalia Goncharova, and Mikhail Larionov. The second performance of "Green Donkey Theater" takes place in Budapest. The expressionist graphic artist Tibor Gergely has an exhibition in Vienna. The final issue of *Ma* and the second issue of *365* appear simultaneously in Vienna and Budapest, respectively, with nearly identical contents. They feature the work of the Silesian group of artists and architects, *Das Junge Schlesien* (Young Silesia), as well as an article on surrealism. Both *Magyar Írás* and "Green Donkey Theater" receive disparaging comments in a review of current events.

1926

The *Új Föld* (New Ground) group is formed in Budapest, mainly from participants in the previous year's "Green Donkey Theater." Several books are published by the group, including Palasovszky's *Punalua*, with constructivist covers and graphic design by Bortnyik. Ernő Schubert joins the group of students at the Academy of Fine Arts in Budapest consisting of Korniss, Kepes, and Trauner. They exhibit together in the town of Vác, near Budapest. János Mácza publishes his *Iskusstvo sovremennoi Evropy* [Art of Contemporary Europe] in Moscow . The young Pécs artist Ferenc Martyn goes to Paris to study. As one avant-garde journal after another goes under, *Der Sturm* continues to publish material by Moholy-Nagy, Scheiber, Kádár, d'Ébneth, Péri, and Réth. Róbert Berény returns to Hungary after six years abroad. He continues his painting, while engaging in graphic design work. The traveling exhibit of the Société Anonyme collection tours North America during 1926-27. At the Toronto exhibition alone 16 works by five Hungarian artists (Huszár, Moholy-Nagy, Péri, Kádár, Scheiber) are shown.
JANUARY The last issue of *Periszkóp* appears in Arad. Derkovits returns to Hungary.
FEBRUARY The journal *Korunk* [Our Age] first appears in Kolozsvár (Cluj), Romania. The editor, László Dienes, concerns himself with new thinking and new art.
MARCH Kassák gives the last performance of his poetry in Vienna. The first performance of the Új Föld group is held in Budapest at the Academy of Music.
MAY The works of Uitz, Bortnyik, Kassák, Kudlák, and Máttis Teutsch are exhibited at the Exhibition of Western Revolutionary Art in the Academy of Arts and Sciences in Moscow. The Hungarian material is mainly drawn from János Mácza's Moscow collection. The second Új Föld performance of literature and theatrical skits takes place in Budapest.
JUNE Kassák makes a trip to Paris, where he and remaining members of the Ma group deliver a reading at the Société des savants before many of the major figures of the Paris avant-garde. Uitz organizes a demonstration to disrupt the performance. The confrontation is settled by giving Uitz time after the Ma program to air his opinions. In Paris, Kassák meets, among others, Éluard, Cocteau, Seuphor, Le Corbusier, Tzara, Goll, Aragon, and Chagall.
JULY *Korunk* publishes Kassák's "Let Us Live in Our Time." Kassák returns to Vienna and prepares to move back to Hungary to take advantage of the government's new policy of greater tolerance of left-wing political émigrés.
OCTOBER Béla Uitz emigrates to the Soviet Union. The third Új Föld performance is held in Budapest.
NOVEMBER Kassák returns to Hungary permanently. Although not harrassed by the authorities initially, his writings of the late 1920s would eventually land him in trouble, and briefly in jail by 1938. Other artists and writers with close links to Kassák such as

Béla Uitz's exhibition is held at the state art academy in Moscow. *Zenit* is banned in Belgrade, and ceases publication; Micić leaves for Paris. The last issue of *Blok* appears in conjunction with the First International Exhibition of Modern Architecture in Warsaw. The Praesens group develops out of the Blok group; a journal of the same name appears. The final issue of *Pásmo* is published in Brno. El Lissitzky designs a room for abstract art at the Internationale Kunstausstellung in Dresden. Gyula Pap is hired by Johannes Itten to teach drawing at the Itten Schule in Berlin, where he remains until 1933. Gropius asks Breuer to design furniture and interiors for the new buildings and masters' houses at Dessau. The "Wassily" chair is the centerpiece of Breuer's exhibition at the Dessau Kunsthalle. Mies van der Rohe is appointed vice-president of the Deutsche Werkbund. In November, *Der Sturm* features the work of Lajos d'Ébneth, and Der Sturm gallery presents works by d'Ébneth, Arnold Topp, and Schwitters. By year's end, the first issue of *Bauhaus* appears, with Moholy-Nagy as editor. Van Doesburg, Arp, and Sophie Tauber begin designs for the interior of the Café Aubette in Strasbourg. Christian Zervos founds *Cahiers d'art* in Paris. American impressionist Mary Cassatt dies. Katherine Dreier organizes the International Exhibition of Modern Art at the Brooklyn Museum; the show tours the United States and Canada in 1926-27. Friedrich Kiesler brings The International Stagecraft Exhibition to New York, and emigrates to the United States. Also in New York, the Little Review gallery opens, a retrospective exhibition of the works of Stuart Davis is held at the Downtown gallery, and the second one-man show of works by Arthur Dove is displayed. Works: János Mácza (Moscow), *Art of Contemporary Europe*; Kafka (Prague): *The Castle*; George Grosz (Berlin), "Pillars of Society"; Ernst, "The Great Forest"; Theodore Dreiser (United States), *An American Tragedy*.

Pilsudski takes power in Poland. Germany admitted to League of Nations. Germany signs treaty of friendship and neutrality with Soviet Union. Process of political consolidation in Hungary progresses to the point where left-wing émigrés begin to return. Communist party still banned in Hungary, but Social Democratic party is legal.

48. LAJOS D'ÉBNETH, Composition, 1926

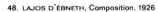

47. LAJOS D'ÉBNETH, Composition, 1926

Nádass, Tibor Déry, Gyula Illyés, and Endre Gáspár also return to Budapest. They plan a new journal.
DECEMBER The first issue of Kassák's new journal *Dokumentum* [Document] appears in Budapest. *Dokumentum* soon becomes an important organ of late international constructivism.

1927 With the launching of the journal *Új Föld* [New Ground] in February, there are now three avant-garde reviews being published in Budapest: *Új Föld, Dokumentum,* and *Magyar Írás*. By May, all three had ceased publication. *Korunk* and the new left-wing cultural journal *100%* fill the resulting gap. Books of poetry notable for their excellent typography and book design are brought out in *Dokumentum* and *Új Föld* editions, designed by Kassák and Bortnyik, respectively, both of whom begin to establish themselves as graphic designers. Extensive Hungarian material appears in *Der Sturm* 18. Two exhibitions of the art of Hugó Scheiber are held at Der Sturm. After living in Paris for several years, Dezső Czigány returns to Hungary. Károly Kernstok returns to Budapest from exile in Berlin.
JANUARY The second issue of *Dokumentum* appears. In *Korunk,* Lajos Gró praises Kassák for *Dokumentum,* while the writer Zoltán Fábry attacks him in "Reserve Activism."
FEBRUARY The first issue of *Új Föld* appears, edited by Tamás Aladár and Zsigmond Reményik. Included are contributions by Bortnyik, Molnár, Adolf Behne, Alfréd Forbát, and Marcel Breuer.

In Moscow, INKhUK is closed, and Béla Uitz works on plans for the Park of Rest and Culture. He is appointed, but does not accept, the position of director of the Revolutionary Poster Workshop at the VKhUTEIN (formerly VKhUTEMAS). Szczuka publishes the journal *Dzwignia*. *ReD* appears in Prague as an organ of the Devětsil group; it lasts until 1932. Hannes Meyer is appointed head of the architectural department of the Bauhaus. In June, the *Wohnung* exhibition at Stuttgart-Weissenhof is organized by Mies van der Rohe. Many major modernist French, Dutch, Swiss, and German architects build model houses there. Breuer exhibits his furniture and designs interiors for Mart Stam's and Gropius's houses. In Berlin, Gropius designs a "Total Theater" for Erwin Piscator, while Breuer designs Piscator's apartment, and a Malevich retrospective is held at the Grosse Berliner Kunstaustellung, with the artist in attendance. Van Doesburg publishes the ten-year jubilee issue of *De Stijl*. In Paris, the first exhibition of the photographs of André Kertész is displayed at Le Sacre du Printemps, the first one-man show of Yves Tanguy's art is held at Galerie Surréaliste, and the American avant-garde literary review *Transition* is founded. In New York, the Machine-Age Exposition is held, and the Museum of Living Art is founded at New York University. Works: Strzemínski, "Unism"; Malevich, *The Non-*

67. BÉLA KÁDÁR, Longing, c1925

MARCH Tivadar Raith greets the appearance of *Dokumentum*, *Új Föld*, and other new journals in his own *Magyar Írás*. *Dokumentum* 3 includes material by László Moholy-Nagy, El Lissitzky, Malevich, Tatlin, and Marcel Janco. *Új Föld* publishes contributions by Bortnyik, Molnár, and Oskar Schlemmer. *Korunk* publishes a positive review of *Új Föld*, and an article on Kassák's new poetry.
APRIL In *Dokumentum* 4, an account is given of the July-September 1927 Werkbund Exhibition at Stuttgart. *Új Föld* 3 publishes an important article by Kállai on Forbát's art and architecture, and other material by Molnár, Walter Dexel, and Henrik Stefán. The fourth and fifth (final) Új Föld performances are held in Budapest.
MAY *Dokumentum* 5 contains new material on the Young Silesia group and Walter Benjamin's "Russian Cinema." Both *Dokumentum* and *Új Föld* cease publication for lack of funds. Shortly afterward, the final issue of *Magyar Írás*, which had been published since 1921, appears.
AUGUST The first issue appears of *100%*, the legal journal of the illegal Hungarian Communist party, edited by Aladár Tamás. Farkas Molnár designs the constructivist cover.
NOVEMBER In the Viennese-Hungarian communist journal *Új Március* [New March], Uitz defends Soviet and European constructivism in "The Path of Revolutionary Art." The pioneer Hungarian modernist József Rippl-Rónai dies.

Objective World; Miró (Paris), "Landscape with Rooster"; Masson (Paris), sand paintings; Proust (Paris), *Le Temps retrouvé*.

Hungarian government signs treaty of friendship with Italy. Trotsky expelled from Communist party. Charles Lindbergh makes first nonstop solo trans-Atlantic flight. First "talkie" movie produced in United States.

135. HUGÓ SCHEIBER, The Charleston, c1928

1928 Róbert Berény collaborates with Bortnyik on his commercial poster designs. Bortnyik's painting embraces the style of the German "Neue Sachlichkeit" (New objectivity) of the mid-20s. Sztavropulosz, owner of the Modiano cigarette paper franchise in Budapest, commissions the major representatives of the new design to produce posters for the firm. Included in this advertising campaign (which lasts into the 30s) are designs by Bortnyik, Berény, and Kassák. Kállai regularly contributes to *Das neue Frankfurt* and *Korunk*. Lajos Vajda and Béla Hegedűs join the New Progressive group (Korniss, Kepes, Trauner, Schubert) at the Academy of Fine Arts in Budapest. They become interested in the avant-garde and study Bauhaus publications, including the writings of Moholy-Nagy. Dezső Korniss paints purely constructivist paintings. Trauner and Schubert exhibit together at the Mentor bookshop. Writings by Palasovszky appear in *Der Sturm* 19 (1928-29). There is a proliferation of avant-garde theatrical productions and performances, organized by members of the Új Föld group; the "battle of the journals" is replaced by a "battle of the performances" in Budapest, as the Új Föld and Kassák groups compete for audiences. Béni Ferenczy sculpts Egon Schiele's memorial in Vienna.

JANUARY Gábor Gaál takes over editorial work for *Korunk* in Kolozsvár.

The Oktyabr group of artists (concerned especially with design and photography) forms in Moscow; Klucis, the Vesnin brothers, Mácza, and Uitz join. In Bucharest, Victor Brauner, Maxy, and others found the journal *UNU*, which lasts until 1932. Gropius, Moholy-Nagy, Bayer, and Breuer leave the Bauhaus, and Hannes Meyer is named director. The emphasis at the Bauhaus now shifts to architecture, especially housing. Meyer hires Ernő Kállai as the editor of *Bauhaus*. In Berlin,

FEBRUARY The first "Cikk-Cakk" evening of avant-garde theatrical performance takes place in Budapest, with Palasovsky, Hevesy, Tamás, Tibor Boromissza, and Ágnes Kövesházy, among others, participating. The Új Művészek Egyesülete [Society of New Artists] holds an exhibition at the National Salon in Budapest. Included are works by the young avant-garde painter Gyula Hincz.
MARCH The second and third "Cikk-Cakk" evenings are given by the Új Föld group in Budapest. The first performance of the *"Független Új Művészek"* [Independent New Artists], an alias for the Dokumentum group, is held in Budapest, with Kassák, Jolán Simon, Tibor Déry, Gyula Illyés, and others participating.
APRIL Fourth and final "Cikk-Cakk" evenings are held. The Independent New Artists group hold their second performance.
MAY In *100%*, material by Le Corbusier and Saugnier, Farkas Molnár, and Moholy-Nagy is presented.
JUNE Marcel Breuer is listed as representing Hungary at the founding conference of *Les Congrès internationaux de l'architecture moderne* (CIAM) at Château de Sarraz in Switzerland.
AUGUST In Budapest, Virgil Birbauer begins publishing *Tér és Forma* [Space and Form] a journal devoted to modern architecture. In *100%*, Farkas Molnár reviews Kasimir Malevich's *The Non-Objective World*, one of the last Bauhaus books designed by Moholy-Nagy.
SEPTEMBER Kassák starts a new journal, *Munka* [Work], which emphasizes social, political, ideological, and pedagogical issues, and sport rather than the fine arts. Nevertheless, extensive material appears on new art, writing, film, architecture, dance, and theater in the 65 issues produced by 1938.
OCTOBER Kassák designs a new cover for *Korunk*. *Munka* publishes Moholy-Nagy's "The Renewal of Photography." The première performance of the "Rendkívüli Szinpad" [Stage Extraordinaire] takes place at the Zeneművészeti Főiskola [Academy of Music] under the direction of Andor Tiszay and Palasovszky. In Budapest, Bortnyik opens the "Műhely" (workshop) school of design (also known as the "Budapest Bauhaus"). The faculty includes Iván Hevesy (art history, film), Kálmán Kovács (stage design), Farkas Molnár ("elemental" architecture), Pál Ligeti ("construction," cultural history) and Bortnyik (painting, graphic design, advertising design). Among others, Győző Vásárhelyi (Victor Vasarely) and his future wife Klára enroll.
FALL Kassák has an exhibition of his képarchitektúra works at the Mentor bookshop. At the exhibition he meets the New Progressives, who soon join the Munka group. The influence of El Lissitzky's photomontages on the New Progressives is strong, though they absorb this influence in their drawing and painting, rather than by creating photomontages. By 1935 this combination of the "constructive" superposition of images and their "surreal" emotive effect leads to what Vajda termed the "constructive-surreal thematic," probably the most important home-grown avant-garde art movement in Hungary between the wars.
DECEMBER In *100%*, Sándor Vajda attacks Kassák's *Munka* as being "petit-bourgeois constructivist."

Breuer begins a private practice in architecture; Moholy-Nagy engages in free-lance design work, especially for the stage; and Alfréd Forbát accepts a position at the Itten Schule, remaining there until 1932. *Les Congrès internationaux d'architecture moderne* (CIAM) is founded at Château de la Sarraz in Switzerland. César Domela makes his first neoplastic reliefs in Paris. In New York, Brâncuşi successfully sues to recover a customs fee charged for his "Bird in Space," purchased by Edward Steichen. Works: Mácza (Moscow), *Art of the Epoch of Mature Capitalism in the West*; El Lissitzky (Cologne), design for the Soviet pavilion at the International Pressa Exhibition; Breton (Paris), *Le Surréalisme et la peinture*; Magritte, "The Lovers"; Ozenfant (Paris), *Foundations of Modern Art*; Charles Demuth, "The Figure 5 in Gold."

Stalin consolidates power in Soviet Union; First Five-Year Plan initiated; Trotsky deported to Central Asia; collectivization of agriculture begins, with great human costs. Left wins in French elections. Herbert Hoover becomes President of United States.

1929

Sándor Bortnyik delivers a lecture, "Art of the Machine Age," at the Mentor bookshop. The flowering of avant-garde performance in Budapest continues. The art of Gyula Hincz is displayed at Der Sturm in the gallery's last exhibition of the work of a Hungarian artist.
JANUARY *Munka* publishes a review of Jan Tschichold's *Die neue Typographie* [The New Typography] as well as a painting by Ozenfant.
FEBRUARY In *100%*, Farkas Molnár reviews Albert Gleizes's *Cubisme*. The Új Föld group holds the third Prizma performance at the Budapest Academy of Music. Bortnyik's "Green Donkey Pantomime" is performed, as well as works by Tristan Tzara ("The Gas-Burning Heart"), Herwarth Walden ("The Fourth"), Manci Wurm ("Movement Composition").
MARCH Kassák's designs a constructivist cover for *Korunk*. *Munka* publishes Endre Gergő's "The Culture of the Photograph."
SPRING The police raid János Vaszary and István Csók's classes at the Academy of Fine Arts in Budapest. They find what they consider "subversive" material (including "socio-photomontages") by students in the New Progressives group. The students are expelled from the academy.

In Moscow, a retrospective of Malevich's works is held at the Tretiakov Gallery, and the first exhibition of the Oktyabr group is held with Uitz, Rodchenko, El Lissitzky, and Klucis, among others, taking part. Lunacharsky is relieved of his position as Commissar of Instruction and replaced by a cultural conservative. Uitz is elected dean of VKhUTEIN in Moscow and attempts without success to reform the institution; subsequently, he becomes ill and resigns. In Poland, Strzemínski, Kobro, and Stażewski leave the Praesens group and found the journal *a.r.* [revolutionary artists]. The International Film and Photo Exhibition of the German Werkbund is presented in Stuttgart and Berlin. Moholy-Nagy designs stage sets in Berlin and, with Gropius and Herbert Bayer, the Berlin Werkbund Exhibition installation. A Russian exhibition is mounted at the Zurich Museum of Applied Art; El Lissitzky is involved in its organization. Giacometti and Dali join the surrealists. The last issues of *La Révolution surréaliste* and *The Little Review* appear in Paris. In New York, Stieglitz's Intimate Gallery closes, and the Museum of Modern Art opens, with an exhibition of works by Cézanne, Gauguin, Seurat, and van Gogh. Works: Dziga Vertov (Moscow) *Man with a Movie Camera*; Moholy-Nagy (Dessau), *From Material to Architecture*; Breton (Paris), *Second Manifesto of Surrealism*; Picasso (France), "bone" paintings; Dali and Buñuel (Paris) *Un Chien Andalou*; Mies van der Rohe, design

MAY An exhibition of works by Gyula Hincz, Máttis Teutsch, and László Mészáros takes place at the Tamás gallery.
OCTOBER An exhibition of Ferenc Martyn's abstract-surrealist Paris paintings opens at the Tamás gallery.
NOVEMBER *Munka* displays reproductions of works by the New Progressives.
DECEMBER 31 The New Progressives break with Kassák and the Munka group. Kassák nevertheless continues to reproduce their work in *Munka*.

of the German pavilion at the Barcelona World's Fair.

Royal dictatorship established in Yugoslavia. Trotsky sent into exile from Soviet Union. In October, the New York Stock Market crashes; ensuing Great Depression has particularly strong effect on fragile Hungarian economy.

1930

Győző Vásárhelyi leaves Bortnyik's Műhely and moves to Paris. The communist painters István Dési Huber and Andor Sugár create constructive still lifes that include copies of Bauhaus book covers, Kassák publications, and the journal *100%* as a form of silent protest. Vásárhelyi has an exhibition at the Ákos Kovács salon in Budapest. Kassák stops painting his képarchitektura works.
JANUARY AND FEBRUARY Bortnyik has a one-man exhibition of his paintings, photographs, and photomontages at the Tamás gallery. The critics are supportive. Though works painted from 1921 on are included, this is the first exhibition of his metaphysical-satirical painting done in Hungary in the late 1920s.
MARCH The final issue of *100%* is published, as the journal is banned by the authorities. The first and only exhibition of the New Progressives is held at the Tamás gallery. After the exhibition closes, most of the New Progressives leave the country: Kepes goes to work for Moholy-Nagy (with whom he had been in correspondence) in Berlin, while Vajda, Korniss, Trauner, and Hegedűs go to Paris. Vajda remains until 1935, doing photomontages for the most part. Korniss goes to Holland.

In Mosow, Malevich publishes his last essay while preparing for an unrealized exhibition of his works; Uitz founds the International Office of Revolutionary Artists and acts as secretary until its dissolution in 1935; *SA* [Soviet Architecture] ceases publication. Mayakovsky commits suicide. The *a.r.* group begins assembling works for the Łodz gallery's collection of abstract art, the second such collection after Hamburg's. Hannes Meyer leaves the directorship of the Bauhaus; Ludwig Mies van der Rohe is named as his successor. In Berlin, the Photomontage exhibition is held at the Staatliches Museum. Moholy-Nagy, Bayer, and Breuer help Gropius organize a German Werkbund exhibition at the Salon des artistes decorateurs in Paris; Moholy-Nagy exhibits his and István Sebők's "light-space modulator," while Breuer designs three room interiors. Kállai leaves the Dessau Bauhaus with Meyer, moves back to Berlin, and writes on art regularly for the weekly *Die Weltbühne* [The World Stage]. He organizes the exhibition Vision and Language of Form held at the Galerie Ferdinand Müller. Ernst May and his Frankfurt planning team leave for Moscow. In Paris, the journal *Surréalisme au service de la révolution* is published, the first Circle et Carré exhibition is held at the Galerie 23; three issues of *Circle et Carré* appear; van Doesburg publishes one issue of *Art Concret*. Together he, Carlslund, Hélion, Tutundjian, and Wantz publish *Manifesto of Constructive Art*, and he designs a studio house for Bertalan Pór, a former member of The Eight. Alfred Stieglitz opens his gallery, An American Place. Works: Magritte, "The Key of Dreams"; Picasso, "Bather on the Beach."

Nazis win 107 seats in Reichstag in Berlin.

116. HENRIK NEUGEBOREN, Composition, 1930

137. HUGÓ SCHEIBER, In the Park, c1930

Select Bibliography

This bibliography is designed to be of maximum use to the Western user without a reading knowledge of Hungarian. Thus, it is divided in two parts. The first lists works in English, French, German, Italian, and Dutch; when a particular work has appeared in more than one of these languages, priority is given to English publication. This omits only a few publications on the Hungarian avant-garde that have appeared in Finnish, Polish, Romanian, Russian, Serbo-Croatian, Slovak, and Swedish.

Part II lists publications in Hungarian. Not included are those works, or a close version thereof, that have appeared in English, French, German, Italian, or Dutch, and therefore are listed in Part I.

Each part is subdivided into sections on general literature, primary literature, and publications devoted to individual artists and critic-theorists. Many of the original documents appeared in journals and books which are now very difficult to obtain. The exhibition catalog *The Hungarian Avant-Garde: The Eight and the Activists* (see entry in Part I) provides a list of the important period journals and most essential articles and books. Accordingly, primary sources in this bibliography include only those that have appeared since World War II in one of the five languages of Part I, or have been recently republished in Hungarian (Part II). Original sources (for example *Ma*, 1919) are indicated where known.

Exhibition catalogues are listed in alphabetical order by title, unless the catalogue was evidently the work of an individual, in which case it is listed by the author's name. Selected dealer catalogues are listed by title. Multiple works by the same author appear in chronological order.

For artists connected with the Hungarian avant-garde only at some periods of their careers, such as Moholy-Nagy and Máttis Teutsch, the emphasis is on literature concerned with those periods of contact. Material on Hungarian avant-garde literature, architecture, and the applied arts is included where it also relates to the fine arts (painting, the graphic arts, and sculpture). When seen as useful or desirable, short annotations are appended to individual entries.

I. LITERATURE IN ENGLISH, FRENCH, GERMAN, ITALIAN, AND DUTCH

General

"Allegro Barbaro": Béla Bartók and the East European Avant-Garde Art. With articles by Tamás Štraus, Lajos Németh, and Árpád Mezei. New York: Matignon Gallery, n.d. Dealer catalogue.

Allegro Barbaro: Béla Bartók und die bildende Kunst. Duisburg: Wilhelm-Lehmbruck Museum, 1981. Exhibition catalogue.

Apollonio, Umbro. Recherches d'art visuel en Europe orientale. *Vingtième Siècle* 29, no. 28 (June 1967): 46-56.

Aradi, Nóra. Les enseignements de la vie culturelle sous la "dictature du proletariat." In Dautrey and Guerlain, eds., 67-78.

———. Berlin-Budapest in Klaus Kändler, Helga Karolewski, and Ilse Siebert, eds., *Berlin Bewegnungen: Ausländerische Künstler in Berlin 1918 bis 1933*, [East] Berlin: Dietz Verlag, 1987: 219-34.

L'art en Hongrie, 1905-1930: Art et révolution. Saint Etienne and Paris: Musée d'Art et d'Industrie, Saint Etienne; and Musée d'Art Moderne de la Ville de Paris, 1980. Exhibition catalogue prepared by Krisztina Passuth and Júlia Szabó. Versions also appeared in Hungarian, Swedish, Finnish, Italian and Serbo-Croation. For the English version, see entry *The Hungarian Avantgarde*.

L'art hongrois du XXe siècle. Publications Artistiques de la Musée Janus Pannonius 18. Pécs: Janus Pannonius Múzeum, 1974. Catalogue of an exhibition held at the Palais du Rhin, Strasbourg, 1974.

Art of the Twenties. New York: Matignon Gallery, n.d. [1979]. Dealer catalogue.

Artisti ungheresi dell' 1900. Introductory essay by Lajos Németh. Milan: Palazzo Reale, 1976. Exhibition catalogue.

The Arts Council of Great Britain; *The Hungarian Avant-Garde: The Eight and the Activists*. See listing under volume title.

Avant-Garde Art of Hungary, 1918-1935, From the Collection of Paul K. Kövesdy. Camden, N.J.: Stedman Art Gallery, Rutgers University, 1983. Exhibition catalogue.

L'avante-garde en Hongrie 1910-1930. Paris: Galerie Franka Berndt, 1984. Dealer catalogue, with an essay by Krisztina Passuth.

The Avant-Garde in Hungary, 1919-1939. New York: Matignon Gallery, 1980. Dealer catalogue.

Avant-Garde of Non-objective Art. Basel: Galerie Schreiner, 1978. A dealer catalogue including works by Kassák, Kádár, Moholy-Nagy, and Scheiber.

Avantgarde Osteuropa, 1910-1930. Berlin: Deutsche Gesellschaft für Bildende Kunst (Kunstverein Berlin) and the Akademie der Künste, 1967. Exhibition catalogue.

Avantgarde: Progressive ungarische Kunst des 20. Jh. Munich: Heseler, 1975. Exhibition catalogue.

Bajkay-Rosch, Éva. Tendenzen und Meinungsverschiedenheiten in der ungarischen Emigrationskunst im Zeitraum, 1920-1925. In *Kunst im Klassenkampf: Arbeitstagung zur proletarisch-revolutionären Kunst*. Berlin: Akademie der Künste der DDR, Humboldt University, 1979.

———. Les Activistes Hongrois en émigration. In *Bulletin analytique des périodiques d'Europe de l'Est*. Art, Architecture, Design 24. Paris: Centre Georges Pompidou (October 1981): 17-22.

———. Die ungarische Avantgard-Kunst im Wiener Exil, 1920-1925. *Alte und moderne Kunst 27*, no. 182 (May 1982): 34-37.

———. Die Bildarchitekturtheorie in Wien in Verbindung mit der Architektur: Ein ungarischer Beitrag zum Konstruktivismus. *XXV Internationaler Kongress für Kunstgeschichte* (Vienna) 1983: 109-96.

———. *Klassiker der Avantgarde, Die Ungarischen Konstruktivisten*. Innsbruck: Galerie im Taxis-Palais, 1983. Exhibition catalogue.

———. Künstler im Exil. In *Wechselwirkungen*, 37-46.

———. Die KURI-Gruppe. In *Wechselwirkungen*, 260-66.

Bakos, Sylvia. The Synthesis of the Arts and the Desire for Cosmic Unity: The Hungarian Literary Avant-Garde, 1915-1925. In Kish, ed., 73-89.

———. Nature and Intellect: The Ideas of the Emergent Hungarian Avant-Garde. *Hungarian Studies Review 7*, no. 1 (Spring © 1988).

———. *The Emergence of the Hungarian Avant-Garde, 1900-1919*. Unpublished Ph.D. dissertation, Rutgers University, 1989.

Bálint, Endre. The Szentendre School. *The New Hungarian Quarterly* 11, no. 38 (1970): 187-92.

Baudin, Antoine. Centralità e periferia: il contributo dell' Europa Centrale. *Rassegna* no. 12 (Architettura nelle riviste d'avanguardia/Architecture in the Avant-Garde Magazines): 12-21.

Béládi, Miklós. Le surréalisme hongrois. In Dautrey and Guerlain, eds., 253-60.

———. Le constructivisme hongrois. In Dautrey and Guerlain, eds., 254-59.

Belgique, Autriche, Hongrie: échanges dans le cadre du réseau international des années vingt. Brussels. In *Bruxelles-Vienne. Reflects croisés 1890-1938*. Brussels: Palais des Beaux-Arts, 1987. Exhibition catalogue.

Béothy et l'avant-garde Hongroise. Paris: Galerie Franka Berndt, 1985. Dealer catalogue.

Berend, Iván T. From the Millennium to the Republic of Councils. In Éri and Jobbágyi, eds., *A Golden Age: Art and Society in Hungary, 1896-1914*.

Bogner, Dieter. Wien 1920-1930: "Es war als würde Utopia Realität werden." *Alte und Moderne Kunst* no. 190-91 (1983).

Bojtár, Endre. The Avant-Garde in Central and Eastern European Literature. *Art Journal* 49, no. 1 (Spring 1990): 56-62.

Bori, Imre. L'activisme: forme de l'art d'une époque révolutionaire. In Dautrey and Guerlain, eds., 94-103.

Botar, Oliver A.I. Constructed Reliefs in the Art of the Hungarian Avant-Garde: Kassák, Bortnyik, Uitz, and Moholy-Nagy, 1921-1926. *The Structurist* no. 25-26 (1985-86): 87-95.

———. Constructivism, International Constructivism and the Hungarian Emigration. In Kish, ed., 90-98.

———. Connections Between the Hungarian and American Avant-Gardes during the Early Twenties. *Hungarian Studies Review* 15, no. 1 (Spring 1988).

———, ed. *Tibor Pólya and the Group of Seven. Hungarian Art in Toronto Collections, 1900-1949*. Toronto: Justina M. Barnicke Gallery, Hart House, 1989. An exhibition catalogue including material on members of The Eight and the Activists. In some cases, catalogue entries on individual artists by Botar, Sylvia Bakos, and Melanie Fisher are listed separately in this bibliography.

Brendel, János. Dada Ungarn. *Tendenzen der zwanziger Jahre*, 3: 102/105.
——. From Material to Architecture: On the Hungarian Avant-garde of the 1920s. *Polish Art Studies* no. 4 (1983): 47-60.
——. Der deutsche Einfluss von Scheerbart und Wilhelm Ostwald auf die ungarische Konstruktivismustheorie. In *Wechselwirkungen*, 173-79.
Breuer, János. Schoenberg's Paintings: Visions, Impressions, and Fantasies, a 1912 Exhibition in Budapest. *The New Hungarian Quarterly* 29, no. 111 (1988): 215-21.
Bromig, Christian. Aesthetik des Augenblicks: Ungarische Fotografen in der Bildpresse der Weimarer Republik. In *Wechselwirkungen*, 501-21.
Brühl, Georg. *Herwarth Walden und "Der Sturm."* Leipzig: Edition Leipzig, 1983.
Budapest, 1890-1919: L'anima e le forme. Milan: Gruppo Electa, 1981. This is the best-produced and best-presented picture of pre-World War I intellectual life in Hungary in any language, and it treats the rise of the avant-garde as well.
Chétrieux, Jacqueline. *Surréalisme français et avant-garde hongrois 1919-1940. Bulletin de Liaisons*, no. 6 (March 1977). Paris: Centre Nationale de la Rercherche Scientifique.
——. Hungarians at the Bauhaus. *Cahier ICSAC*, no. 6-7 (1987): 97-112.
——, ed. *Ungarische Grafik in Ausland: Deutschland 1919-1933*. Budapest: Magyar Nemzeti Galéria and Petőfi Irodalmi Múzeum, 1989.
Congdon, Lee. *The Young Lukács*. Chapel Hill: University of North Carolina, 1983.
Crevier, Richard. L'Activisme entre l'esthétique et l'éthique dans la politique révolutionnaire. In Dautrey and Guerlain, eds., ix-xvii.
Csorba, Géza, Edit Plesznivy, and Anna Szinyei-Merse. *Le rôle de l'Ecole de Paris dans la peinture hongroise*. Dijon: Hôtel de Ville, 1986. Exhibition catalogue.
Dabrowski, Magdalena. *Contrasts of Form: Geometric Abstract Art, 1910-1980*. Introduction by John Elderfield. New York: The Museum of Modern Art, 1985.
D'Alessandro M. Dal futurismo all'avanguardia ungherese. *Annali Sezione Slava* (Naples), no. 20-21: 273-94.
Dautrey, Charles, and Jean-Claude Guerlain, eds. *L'activisme hongrois*. Montrouge: Editions Goutal-Darly, 1979. The illustrative material is haphazardly arranged and poorly documented. Nevertheless, this is one of the most important anthologies on the Hungarian avant-garde. There are essays by many historians, as well as documentation in French translation; some are listed separately in this bibliography.
Deák, István. The Decline and Fall of Habsburg Hungary, 1914-1918. In Völgyes, ed.
Eckelt, Frank. The Internal Policies of the Hungarian Soviet Republic. In Völgyes, ed.
European and Hungarian Avant-garde, 1910-1930. With articles by Robert Rosenblum and Krisztina Passuth. New York: Modernage Gallery, n.d. [1985]. Dealer catalogue.
Fauchereau, Serge. Futurism: A Temptation, a Reticence. In Kish, ed., 99-106.
Fehér, D. Zsuzsa, and Gábor Ö. Pogány. *Twentieth Century Hungarian Painting*. Budapest: Corvina, 1971.
Finizio, Luigi Paolo. *L'arte contemporanea l'astrattismo costruttivo. Suprematismo e Costruttivismo*. Bari and Rome: Edition Laterza, 1990. Part 3 is on Constructivism in Poland and Hungary.
Forgács, Éva. The Rediscovery of Hungarian Art Deco. *The New Hungarian Quarterly* 27, no. 102 (1980): 178-80.
——. The Bauhaus in Budapest. *The New Hungarian Quarterly* 29, no. 111 (1988): 185-87.
Futurismo e Futurismi. Venice: Palazzo Grassi, 1986. An exhibition catalogue including a fair amount of material on Hungarian artists.
Gassner, Hubertus. "Ersehnte Einheit" oder "erpresste Versöhnung": Zur Kontinuität und Diskontinuität ungarischer Konstruktivismus-Konzeption. In *Wechselwirkungen*, 183-221. Part of this article appeared in English as: "Lukács and Popper: The Philosophical Foundations of The Eight." In Kish, ed., 107-10.
——, ed. *Wechselwirkungen: Ungarische Avantgarde in der Weimarer Republik*. See listing under volume title.
Gluck, Mary. *Georg Lukács and His Generation, 1900-1918*. Cambridge: Harvard University Press, 1985.
A Golden Age: Art and Society in Hungary, 1896-1914. With essays by Iván T. Berend, Lajos Németh, and Ilona Sármány-Parson. A joint publication of Corvina (Budapest), Barbican Art Gallery (London), and the Center for the Fine Arts (Miami), 1989.
Haulisch, Lenke. L'influence des photomontages d'El Lissitzky sur l'art hongrois. *Annales de la Galerie Nationale Hongroise* 2 (1974): 105-16.
Haus, Andreas. Die Präsenz des Materials: Ungarische Fotografen aus dem Bauhaus-Kreis. In *Wechselwirkungen*, 472-90.
Hegyi, Loránd. Konstruktivistische Tendenzen in der ungarischen Kunst. In *Ungarische konstruktivistische Kunst, 1920-1977*.
Herzogenrath, Wulf and Stefan Kraus. *Bauhaus Utopien: Arbeiten auf Papier*. Stuttgart: Editions Cantz, 1988. Catalogue of an exhibition held in Budapest, Madrid, and Cologne in 1988.
Horváth, Edit. Ungarn und das Bauhaus. *Wissentschaftliche Zeitschrift der Hochschule für Architektur und Bauwesen Weimar*, no. 5-6 (1976).
Humblet, Claudine. *Le Bauhaus*. Paris: Editions l'Age d'Homme, 1980. Contains a chapter on Moholy-Nagy and the Bauhaus, which includes two sections on Kassák as well.
Hungarian Art: 1920-1970. Boston: Northeastern University Art Gallery, 1981. Catalogue of an exhibition of works from the collection of Paul Kövesdy.
Hungarian Art: The Twentieth Century Avant-Garde. Thomas T. Solley, ed., with essays by Árpád Mezei and Leslie Singer. Bloomington, Ind.: Indiana University Art Museum, 1972. Exhibition catalogue.
The Hungarian Avant-Garde: The Eight and the Activists. Introduction by John Willet; essays and chronology by Krisztina Passuth and Júlia Szabó. London: The Arts Council of Great Britain, 1980. Catalogue of the exhibition held at the Hayward Gallery, London, 1980. Until now, this is the most important publication to appear on the Hungarian avant-garde in English. Articles are listed separately in this bibliography.
Internationaler Avantgarde 1927-1935. Die Abstrakten. Hannover: Sprengel Museum, 1987. An exhibition catalogue including works by Moholy-Nagy and others.
János, Andrew C.: *The Politics of Backwardness in Hungary, 1825-1945*. Princeton: Princeton University Press, 1982.
Kállai, Ernst. *Neue Malerei in Ungarn: Die Junge Kunst in Europa*. Prof. Dr. Georg Biermann, ed. Band II. Leipzig: Klinkhardt und Biermann Verlag, 1925.
Karádi, É. and E. Vezér, eds. *Georg Lukács, Karl Mannheim und der Sonntags-Kreis*. Frankfurt am Main, Sendler Verlag, 1985.
Karádi, Éva. Der "Sonntagskreis" und die Weimar Kultur. In *Wechselwirkungen*, 526-534.
Kassák, Lajos. Histoire de *A Tett* et *Ma*. In Dautrey and Guerlain, eds. 151-71.
Kish, John, ed. *The Hungarian Avant-Garde, 1914-1933*. Storrs, Conn.: The William Benton Museum of Art, 1987. Exhibition catalogue. Articles are listed separately in this bibliography.
Kohut, Leo. Bauhaus Ungarn-Tschechoslovakei. In *Bauhaus-Archiv Museum. Sammlungskatalog*. Berlin: Gebr. Mann Verlag, 1981, 283-86.
Körner, Éva. Künstler der Ungarischen Räterepublik, *Acta Historiae Artium* 6, no. 1-2 (1959): 169-91.
——. *Die ungarische Kunst zwischen den beiden Weltkriegen*. Dresden: VEB Verlag der Kunst, 1974. Originally published as *Magyar művészet a két világháború között*. Budapest, 1963.
——. L'art d'avant-garde en Hongrie, de 1920 á 1930-32. In *Bulletin analytique des périodiques d'Europe de l'Est*. Art, Architecture, Design 24. Paris: Centre Georges Pompidou (October 1981), 23-30.
——. Tatlin: Outlines of a Career in the Context of Contemporary Russian Avant-Garde Art as Related to Eastern and Western Tendencies. *Acta Historiae Artium* 31, no.1-7, (1985).
Die Kunst Osteuropas im 20. Jahrhundert. Bochum: Museum Bochum, 1980.
Kunst in Ungarn, 1900-1950. With reprints of essays by Lajos Németh, Júlia Szabó, and Éva Körner. Lucerne: Kunstmuseum Luzern, 1975. Exhibition catalogue.
Leclanhe-Boulé, Claude. Typographes Constructivistes des avant-gardes Russe et Hongroise. In *Bulletin analytique des périodiques d'Europe de l'Est*. Art, Architecture, Design 24. Paris: Centre Georges Pompidou (October 1981), 43-53.
Levinger, Esther. Hungarian Avant-Garde Typography and Posters. In Kish, ed., 112-22.
Linder, L. Lajos Kassák Retrospektive zum 100. Geburtstag. *Kunstwerk* 40 (September 1987), 130-31.
Lindner, Amalie Maria. Tendenzen der ungarischen Avantgarde im Spiegel der

Zeitschriften. In *Wechselwirkungen*, 68-72.

The "Ma" Circle: Budapest and Vienna, 1916-1925. Moraga, Calif.: Hearst Art Gallery, Saint Mary's College, 1985. An exhibition of works from the collection of Paul Kövesdy.

Mansbach, S.A. Gabo's Template for Utopia: Linear Construction in Space No. 1. *Bulletin of the Museum of Fine Arts* 8 (Houston), no. 3 (Winter 1984).

_____. Revolutionary Events, Revolutionary Artists: The Hungarian Avant-Garde until 1920. In Stephen C. Foster, ed., *"Event" Arts and Art Events*. Ann Arbor: UMI Research Press, 1988, 31-60.

_____. Confrontation and Accomodation in the Hungarian Avant-garde. *Art Journal* no. 49 (Spring 1990): 7-20.

_____, ed. From Leningrad to Ljubljana: The Suppressed Avant-gardes of East-Central Europe during the Early Twentieth Century. *Art Journal*, no. 49 (Spring 1990).

Master works of the Hungarian Avant-Garde, 1916 to 1933. With an essay by John E. Bowlt. New York: Kövesdy Gallery, 1987. Dealer catalogue.

Mezei, Ottó. Ecoles d'art libres en Hongrie entre 1896 et 1944. *Acta Historiae Artium 28* (1982): 175-209.

_____. Ungarische Architekten am Bauhaus. In Wechselwirkungen, 339-346.

Mezey, Katalin. The History of Kassák's *Ma*. *The New Hungarian Quarterly* 15, no. 54 (1974): 84-92.

Mihály, Ida F. Die Beziehungen der ungarischen Kunst zum Bauhaus. *Ars Kunsthistorischen Revue der Slowakischen Akademie der Wissenschaften*, no. 2 (1968).

Moderne-Postmoderne. Deux cas d'ecole: L'avant-garde russe et hongroise 1916-1925/Giorgio de Chirico 1928-1934. Geneva: Cabinet des Estampes/Tricone, 1987.

Nagy, Zoltán. Hungarian Activism. *The New Hungarian Quarterly* 15, no. 54 (1974): 180-82.

Nagy, Zsuzsa. The Secret Papers of István Bethlen, *The New Hungarian Quarterly* 14, no. 49.

Németh, Lajos. *Modern Hungarian Art*. Budapest: Corvina, 1968. This is the authoritative work on modern Hungarian art in both Hungarian and English. It does not deal extensively with the avant-garde, however.

_____. Symbolism and Surrealism in Modern Hungarian Art. *The New Hungarian Quarterly* 13, no. 45 (1972): 194-96.

_____, ed. *Artisti ungheresi del'900*. Milan: Palazzo Reale, 1976. Exhibition catalogue.

The 1920s in Eastern Europe. With essays by John E. Bowlt, Szymon Bojko, among others. Cologne: Galerie Gmurzynska, 1975. Bilingual German-English dealer catalogue.

The Non-Objective World, 1924-1939. London: Annely Juda Fine Art, 1971. Dealer catalogue with works by Bortnyik, Kassák, and Moholy-Nagy.

The Non-Objective World, 1914-1955. London: Annely Juda Fine Art, 1973. Dealer catalogue with works by Bortnyik, Kassák, and Moholy-Nagy.

The Non-Objective World: Twenty-Five Years, 1914-1939. London: Annely Juda Fine Art, 1978. Dealer catalogue with works by Bortnyik, Kassák, Moholy-Nagy, and Péri.

Novák, Zoltán. The Sunday Society. *Annales Universitatis Scientiarum Budapestiensis de Rolando Eötvös* 11 (1977): 103-28.

Osteuropäischer Konstruktivismus. Bottrop: Moderne Galerie Bottrop, 1976. Exhibition catalogue.

Osteuropäischer Avantgarde. Bochum: Museum Bochum, 1988. An exhibition catalogue containing much Hungarian material.

Overy, Paul. Hungarian Avant-Garde in London. *The New Hungarian Quarterly* 21, no. 80 (1980): 167-69.

Passuth, Krisztina. "Les Huit": le prèmier groupe hongrois de tendence constructive analyse par genres de leur peinture. *Acta Historiae Artium* 8 (1962): 299-318.

_____. Hungarian Art in the European Avantgarde. *Actes du XIIe Congrès International d'Histoire de l'Art* (Budapest), 1969.

_____. La genesi dell' avanguardia artistica ungherese. *Ungheria d'Oggi* (Rome, July-August 1971).

_____. Kurt Schwitters, Theo van Doesburg, et le "Bauhaus." *Bulletin du Musée des Beaux Arts* 40 (Budapest, 40 1973).

_____. Berlin, centre de l'avantgarde internationale. In *Paris-Berlin*. Paris: Centre Georges Pompidou, 1978, 98-104. Exhibition catalogue.

_____. L'utopie de l'avant-garde hongroise. In *L'art comme utopie*. Le Havre: Maison de la Culture du Havre en collaboration avec le Musée des Beaux Arts André Malraux et la Bibliothèque Municipale, 1979. Exhibition catalogue.

_____. Hongrie: Art et Pouvoir. *Canal* (Paris), no. 27 (1979).

_____. Les relations internationales de la revue *Ma* à Vienne. In Dautrey and Guerlain, eds., 266-69.

_____. The International Connections of the Eight and the Activists. In *The Hungarian Avant-Garde*. 19-27.

_____. Gli "Otto", gli "Attivisti" e *Ma*. In *Budapest, 1890-1919: L'anima e le forme*, 92-95.

_____. Les Huit on Hongrie et en Tchécoslovaquie. *Cahiers du Musée National d'Art Moderne*, no. 3 (1980).

_____. Contacts between the Hungarian and Russian Avant-Garde in the 1920s. In *The First Russian Show*. London: Annely Juda Fine Art, 1983.

_____. Autonomie der Kunst und sozialistische Ideologie in der ungarischen Avantgardekunst. In *Wechselwirkungen*, 12-26.

_____. "Der Sturm" der Ungarn. In *Wechselwirkungen*, 56-60.

_____. *Le rôle de l'avant-garde hongroise (Moholy-Nagy, Kassák, Péri) dans le développement des mouvements d'avante-garde est-ouest (1909-1926)*. Thesis for Doctorat d'Etat, Université de Paris I, Panthéon, Sorbonne, 1987.

_____. *Les avant-gardes de l'Europe Centrale*. Paris: Flammarion, 1988.

Peternák, Miklós. Licht und Klang aus Ungarn. Bemerkungen zur Geschichte des Intermedia in den zwanziger Jahren. In *Wechselwirkungen*, 456-60.

Richard, Lionel. Dans le sillage d'une révolution écrasée. In Dautrey and Guerlain, eds., 275-85.

Schröder-Kehler, Heidrun. Künstler erobern die Warenwelt: Neue Typographie der Werbegestaltung. In *Wechselwirkungen*, 388-412.

Solley, Thomas T., ed. See *Hungarian Art: The Twentieth Century Avant-Garde*.

Die Spracheder Geometrie. Bern: Kunstmuseum Bern and Benteli Verlag, 1984. An exhibition catalogue including material by Huszár, Kassák, and Moholy-Nagy.

Stecker, R. Wer hat Angst vor Moholy-Nagy? Ungarischer Künstler in Deutschland. *Kunstwerk* 40 (September 1987): 154.

Štraus, Tomáš. Der ost und mitteleuropäische Konstruktivismus im Lichte seiner programmatischen Theorien. *Ars Kunsthistorischer Revue der Slowakischen Akademie der Wissenschaften*, no. 2 (1969).

Szabadi, Judit. An Outline of the History of Hungarian Art Nouveau Ideas. *Acta Historiae Artium* 28 (1982): 117-30.

_____. *Jugendstil in Ungarn*. Vienna and Munich: Verlag Anton Schroll, 1982.

_____. Major Modern Hungarian Painters, Parts 1 and 2. *The New Hungarian Quarterly* 25, nos. 95 and 96 (1984).

Szabó, Júlia. Gedanken zu den Hauptströmungen der ungarischen Malerei 1896-1945 and L'histoire de l'Activisme Hongrois. In *Kunst in Ungarn, 1900-1950*, n.p.

_____. Some Influences of Italian Futurism on Hungarian Painters. *Acta Historiae Artium* 24, no. 1-4 (1978): 436-37.

_____. L'activisme hongrois et son époque. In Dautrey and Guerlain, eds., 56-84.

_____. Return of the Activists. *The New Hungarian Quarterly* 21, no. 80 (1980): 169-73.

_____. Ideas and Programmes: The Philosophical Background of the Hungarian Avant-Garde. In *The Hungarian Avant-Garde*, 9-18.

_____. Le rayonnement de l'avant garde Hongroise en Yougoslavie, en Transylvanie et en Slovaquie entre les deux guerres mondiales. In *Bulletin analytique des périodiques d'Europe de l'Est*. Art, Architecture, Design 24. Paris: Centre Georges Pompidou (October 1981), 31-42.

_____. The Exhibitions of the International Avant-garde in Budapest, Vienna, and Berlin and Their Influence on the History of the Hungarian Avant-Garde Movements. In *Der Zugang zum Kunstwerk: Schatzkammer, Salon, Ausstellung, Museum. Proceedings of the XXV International Congress for the History of Art* (CIHA) 4 (Vienna, 1983): 127-206.

_____. Twentieth Century Hungarian Art. *The New Hungarian Quarterly* 25, no. 95 (1984): 158-59.

_____. Der Expressionismus und die ungarische Kunst von 1915-1927. In *Wechselwirkungen*, 74-100.

_____. La Tour de Tatline et son influence sur l'avant-garde de l'Europe centrale et orientale, *Ligeia* (Paris), no. 5-6 (April-

September 1989): 65-69.
Tendenzen der Zwanziger Jahre. 15. Europäische Kunstausstellung. Berlin: Dietrich Reimer Verlag, 1977. This important source book contains a fair amount of Hungarian material.
Turowski, Andrzej. *Existe-t-il un art de l'Europe de l'est? Utopie & ideologie.* Paris: Editions de la Villette, 1986.
Ungarische Avantgarde. Berlin: Galerie Kunze, 1975. Exhibition catalogue.
Ungarische Avantgarde. Nuremberg: Galeria R. Johanna Ricard, (1976). Catalogue of an exhibition organized by Galerie von Bartha in Basel.
Ungarische Avantgarde, 1909-1930. With an introductory essay by Éva Körner. Munich: Galleria del Levante, 1971. Dealer catalogue.
Ungarische Avantgarde. Hamburg: Galerie Levy, 1989. Dealer catalogue.
Ungarische konstruktive Kunst. With articles by Ferenc Romváry and Tamás Aknai. Düsseldorf: Kunstmuseum Düsseldorf, 1979. Exhibition catalogue.
Ungarische konstruktivistische Kunst, 1920-1977. Munich: Kunstverein München, 1979. Exhibition catalogue.
Vanci, Marina. Les relations entre l'avant-garde hongroise et l'avant-garde roumaine. In *Bulletin analytique, des périodiques de l'Europe de l'Est.* Art, Architecture, Design 24. Paris: Centre Georges Pompidou (October 1981), 54-56.
Vann, Philip. The Hungarian Visual Arts, 1900-1945. *Contemporary Review* 250, no. 1454 (March 1987): 142-7.
Venezia, Italia e Ungheria tra decadentismo e avanguardia. Proceedings of a Conference held in Budapest, 1986. Budapest: Akadémiai, (in press).
Völgyes, Iván, ed.. *Hungary in Revolution, 1918-1919: Nine Essays.* Lincoln, Nebr.: 1971.
von Bartha, Miklós, and Carl László. *Die ungarische Künstler im Sturm. Berlin, 1913-1932.* Basel: Editions Galerie von Bartha and Editions Panderma, Carl László, 1983.
Wechselwirkungen: Ungarische Avantgarde in der Weimarer Republik. Edited by Hubertus Gassner. Marburg: Jonas Verlag, 1986. Catalogue of the 1986-87 exhibition held in Kassel and Bochum. This is the best anthology to date of original articles and documents on the Hungarian avant-garde in any language. Articles and translated primary literature are listed separately in this bibliography.
Wessely, Anna. Die Diskurs über die Kunst im Sonntagskreis. In *Wechselwirkungen*, 541-53.
Whelan, Richard. *Robert Capa, a Biography.* New York: Alfred A. Knopf, 1985. Includes material on Capa as a member of the *Munka* Circle in Budapest.
Wien und die ungarische Konstruktivisten. Vienna: Collegium Hungaricum, 1987. Exhibition catalogue.
Willet, John. *Art and Politics in the Weimar Period: The New Sobriety, 1917-1933.* New York: Pantheon Books, 1978. Willet gives the Hungarian émigrés in Weimar Germany serious consideration.

Primary Literature

Activists, the Hungarian. Questions du Bureau Provisoire international des Artistes Créateurs (Moscow) aux Artistes Activistes Hongrois (*Ma*, 1920). In Dautrey and Guerlain, eds. (trans. G. Kassai), 106-11.
Bortnyik, Sándor. Programm des ungarischen Bauhauses. Neue Weg des "Kunstgewerbe"-Unterrichts (1928). Reprinted as Dokument 99 in *Wechselwirkungen, 376-79.*
Forbát, Alfréd. Ungarische Künstler in Berlin und am Bauhaus. Reprinted as Dokument 92 in *Wechselwirkungen*, pp. 346-48.
Fülep, Lajos. Écrits sur Cézanne. *Acta Historiae Artium* 20 (1974): 107-24.
Gáspár, Endre. Die Bewegung der ungarischen Aktivisten (*Der Sturm*, 1924). Reprinted as Dokument 7 (excerpt) in *Wechselwirkungen*, 34-36.
Hevesy, Iván. Culture de masse, art de masse. (*Ma*, 1918). In Dautrey and Guerlain, eds. (trans. G. Kassai), 91-93.
_____. L'affiche nouvelle (*Ma*, 1919). In Dautrey and Guerlain, eds. (trans. G. Kassai), 104-05.
Hungarian Painters of Two Centuries: 1820-1970. Washington, D.C.: American University Press, 1991.
Kállai, Ernö. The Social and Intellectual Perspectives of Constructive Art. (*Ma*, 1922). In *The Hungarian Avant-Garde* (trans. George Cushing), 118-19.
_____. *Neue Malerei in Ungarn.* Leipzig: Klinkhardt and Biermann, 1925.
_____. Malerei und Photographie (*i 10*, 1927). Reprinted in Jürgen Klaus, ed., Kunst Heute, Hamburg: Rohwolt, 1965, 162-164. It is a debate with Moholy-Nagy.
_____. Konstruktivismus. Reprinted as Dokument 43 (excerpt) in *Wechselwirkungen*, 163-67.
_____. Pictorial Photography (1928). In Christopher Phillips, ed, *Photography in the Modern Era* (trans. Joel Agee). New York: The Metropolitan Museum of Art and Aperture, 1989.
Kállai, Ernő, Alfréd Kemény, László Moholy-Nagy and László Péri. Manifesto (*Egység*, 1923). In *The Hungarian Avant-Garde.* (trans. George Cushing), 120-21.
Kassák, Lajos. The Poster and New Painting (*Ma*, 1916). In *The Hungarian Avant-Garde* (trans. George Cushing), 112-113.
_____. En avant dans nôtre vie (*Ma*, 1918). In Dautrey and Guerlain, eds. (trans. László Csejdy), 39-41.
_____. Activism (*Ma*, 1919). *The Structurist*, no. 25-26 (1985-86) (trans. Esther Levinger), 85-86.
_____. Auf dem ersten Agitationsabend der *Ma* (*Vörös Lobogó*,1919). Reprinted as Dokument 4 (excerpt) in *Wechselwirkungen*, 30-31.
_____. Lettre à Béla Kun au nom de l'art (Budapest, 1919). In Dautrey and Guerlain, eds. (trans. L'Atelier Hongrois, Paris), 143-48.
_____. An die Künstler aller Länder! (*Ma*, Vienna, 1920). Reprinted as Dokument 10 in *Wechselwirkungen*, 49-51.
_____. Bilan et suite (*Ma*, 1920). In Dautrey and Guerlain, eds., 138-41.
_____. Lettre aux jeunes ouvriers (*Ma*, 1920). In Dautrey and Guerlain, eds. (trans. G. Kassai), 262-66.
_____. Képarchitektúra (Vienna, 1921). In *The Hungarian Avant-Garde* (trans. George Cushing), 114-17. Revised translation by Oliver Botar in *The Structurist*, no. 25-26 (1985-86), 96-98.
_____. Der Weg zur elementarischen Typographie (*Magyar Grafika*, 1928). Reprinted as Dokument 102 in *Wechselwirkungen*, 412-16.
_____. *Lasst uns leben in unserer Zeit: Gedichte Bilder und Schriften zur Kunst.* Selected and with an afterword by József Vadas. Budapest: Corvina, 1989 [copyright Kassák-Museum, Budapest]. Contains five of the writings cited individually above, as well as many others.
Kassák, Ludwig, and László Moholy-Nagy. *Buch neuer Künstler.* Postscript by Éva Körner. Budapest: Corvina Verlag/ Magyar Helikon, 1977. Facsimile edition of the original German edition, published by Kassák in Vienna, 1922.
Kemény, Alfréd. Vorträge und Diskussion am INChUK, (Moscow, 1921). Reprinted as Dokument 49 (excerpt) in *Wechselwirkungen*, 226-30.
_____. Bemerkungen zur Ausstellung der russichen Künstler in Berlin (*Egység*, February 4, 1923). Reprinted as Dokument 52 in *Wechselwirkungen*, 232-33.
_____. Die abstrakte Gestaltung vom Suprematismus bis heute (*Kunstblatt* [Berlin] 1924). Reprinted as Dokument 55 in *Wechselwirkungen*, 234-38.
_____. Photomontage, Photogram (1931). Photomontage as a Weapon in Class Struggle (1932). In Christopher Phillips, ed. *Photography in the Modern Era*, (trans. Joel Agee). New York: The Metropolitan Museum of Art and Aperture, 1989.
Lukács, György. The Ways Have Parted (*Nyugat*, 1910). In *The Hungarian Avant-Garde* (trans. George Cushing), 106-108.
Mácza, János. Le théâtre total (*Ma*, 1919). In Dautrey and Guerlain, eds. (trans. V. Charaire), 204-19.
Máttis Teutsch, Hans. *Kunstideologie: Stabilität und Aktivität im Kunstwerk.* Bucharest: Kritérion, 1977. A new edition of the original published by Müller & Kiepenheuer, Potsdam, 1931.
Moholy-Nagy, László. Various writings in English translation in Passuth, *Moholy-Nagy.*
_____. Various writings in English translation in Christopher Phillips, ed. *Photography in the Modern Era* (trans. Carolina Fawkes and Joel Agee). New York: The Metropolitan Museum of Art and Aperture, 1989.
_____. *The New Vision* (trans. Daniel M. Hoffman). New York: W. W. Norton & Co., Inc. 1938. Reprinted since 1938.
_____. *Vision in Motion.* Chicago: Paul Theobald and Company, 1947. Reprinted since 1947.
_____. *The New Vision* and *Abstract of an Artist.* The Documents of Modern Art, edited by Robert Motherwell. New York: Wittenborn, Schultz, Inc., 1949.
_____. *Painting, Photography, Film*, London: Lund Humphries, 1969. English translation

of *Malerei, Fotografie, Film*, Bauhausbücher 8, 2d ed. Munich: Albert Langen, 1927.

Moholy-Nagy, László, with Oskar Schlemmer, and Farkas Molnár. *The Theatre of the Bauhaus*. Middletown, Conn: Wesleyan University Press, 1961. English translation, with some pictorial modifications, of *Die Bühne im Bauhaus*, Bauhausbücher 4. Munich: Albert Langen, 1925.

Molnár, Farkas. KURI-Manifest (*Út*, Dec. 1922 and Weimar, 1923). Reprinted as Dokument 72 in *Wechselwirkungen*, 266-68.

______. Das Leben im Bauhaus (*Periszkóp*, 1925). Reprinted as Dokument 76 in *Wechselwirkungen*, 270-74.

______. Über die Fotomontage (Budapest, 1931). Reprinted as Dokument 103 in *Wechselwirkungen*, 416-19.

Nemes Lampérth, József. Letter from Berlin (1920). Reprinted as Dokument 37 in *Wechselwirkungen*, 138-39.

Scheiber, Hugó. Autobiographische Notizen (1923). Reprinted as Dokument 32 in *Wechselwirkungen*, 125-27.

Szélpál, Árpád. Art révolutionnaire ou art de parti (*Ma*, 1919). In Dautrey and Guerlain, eds. (trans. G. Kassai), 86-90.

______. A Béla Kun (*Ma*, 1919). In Dautrey and Guerlain, eds., 148-50.

Uitz, Béla. Hier mit der Diktatur! (*Vörös Újság*, 1919). Reprinted as Dokument 3 in *Wechselwirkungen*, 28-30.

Literature on Individuals

Róbert Berény

Szíj, Béla. La vie de Róbert Berény, de son enfance à son émigration à Berlin. *Bulletin de la Galerie Nationale Hongroise* 4 (1963): 5-30.

______. Róbert Berény. *Acta Historiae Artium* 12 (1966): 155-202.

Aurél Bernáth

Frank, János, ed. *Bernáth Aurél emlékkiállítás/Aurél Bernáth commemorative exhibition*. With an essay by Lajos Németh. Budapest: Ernst Museum, 1985. Bilingual Hungarian-English exhibition catalogue.

______. The Aurél Bernáth Exhibition. *The New Hungarian Quarterly* 26, no. 99 (1985): 227-30.

Genthon, István. Aurél Bernáth, the Painter. *The New Hungarian Quarterly* 3, no. 5 (1962): 121-28.

Illyés, Mária. Aurél Bernáth and Vilmos Perlrott Csaba's Paintings. *The New Hungarian Quarterly* 19, no. 69 (1978): 168-73.

Kállai, Ernő. Aurél Bernáth (1925). Reprinted as Dokument 20 in *Wechselwirkungen*, 112-17.

Meier-Graefe, Julius. Aurél Bernáth. In *Wechselwirkungen*, 115.

Németh, Lajos. The Oeuvre of Aurél Bernáth. *The New Hungarian Quarterly* 14, no. 50 (1973): 187-89.

Mihály Biró.

Haiman, György. A Dangerous Man. Mihály Biró designed roaring posters that inspired people to action. *Print*, (New York, March-April 1989): 102-11.

Dezső Bokros-Birman

Illyés, Mária. Dezső Bokros-Birman. In *Wechselwirkungen*, 150-51.

Sándor Bortnyik

Borbély, László. Sándor Bortnyik et la République des Conseils. *Annales de la Galerie Nationale Hongroise* no. 2 (1974): 127-35.

______, ed. *Bortnyik Sándor emlékkiállítás/Sándor Bortnyik Retrospective*. Budapest: Galerie Nationale Hongroise, 1977. Bilingual Hungarian-French exhibition catalogue.

Haulisch, Lenke. Die Ungarischen Bezüge der Kunst Oskar Schlemmers. *Acta Historiae Artium*, 23, no. 3-4 (1987-88): 345-56.

Hevesy, Iván. L'album de Sándor Bortnyik. In Dautrey and Guerlain, eds. (trans. G. Kassai), 169-70.

Kassák, Lajos. Sándor Bortnyik. In *Wechselwirkungen*, 221.

Kemény, Alfréd. Bilder und Grafiken Bortnyiks (*Ma*, 1919). Reprinted as Dokument 48 in *Wechselwirkungen*, 222-25.

Körner, Éva. *Bortnyik Sándor*. Budapest: Corvina Kiadó, 1975. A loose-leaf album with essay in Hungarian, English, German, and Russian.

Nagy, Zoltán. Two Activists in the Hungarian National Gallery (Sándor Bortnyik, Béla Uitz), *The New Hungarian Quarterly* 18, no. 68 (1977): 180-82.

Neumann, Eckhard, ed. *Bauhaus and Bauhaus People*. New York: Van Nostrand Rheinhold, 1970. Includes Bortnyik's "Something on the Bauhaus."

Pénzes, Éva and Gábor Ö. Pogány, eds. *Bortnyik Sándor kiállítása/Exposition de Sándor Bortnyik*. Budapest: Galerie Nationale Hongroise, 1969. Bilingual Hungarian-French exhibition catalogue.

Sándor Bortnyik: Ölbilder, Gouachen, Zeichnungen. With an introductory essay by Eckhard Neumann. Cologne: Galerie Gmurzynska and Bargera, 1972. Dealer catalogue.

Il vento dell'est degli anni 20. Milan: Galleria Breton, 1971. Dealer catalogue with material by Bortnyik and Kassák.

Marcel Breuer

Gassner, Hubertus. Zwischen den Stühlen sitzend sich im Kreise drehen. Marcel Breuer und Gyula Pap als Bauhaus-Gestalter. In *Wechselwirkungen*, 312-27.

Major, Máté. Marcel Breuer and Hungary. *The New Hungarian Quarterly* 23, no. 85 (1982): 179-83.

Dezső Czigány

Bakos, Sylvia. Entry on Czigány in Botar, ed., 23-25.

Béla Czóbel

Béla Czóbel. Foreword by Dunoyer de Segonzac. Paris: Galerie Zak, 1962. Dealer catalogue.

Frank, János, and Mimi Kratchowill. *Czóbel*. Budapest: Corvina, 1983. In a trilingual French, English, and German edition.

Frank, János. The Centenary of Béla Czóbel, the Painter. *The New Hungarian Quarterly* 25, no. 94 (1984): 173-76.

Gachot, François. Béla Czóbel. *Nouvelle Revue de Hongrie* (March 1941).

Homage to Béla Czóbel 1883-1976. With foreword by Stanley R. Johnson. Chicago, 1981. Exhibition catalogue.

Kállai, Ernő. Béla Czóbel (*Forum*, Bratislava, 1935). Reprinted as Dokument 25 in *Wechselwirkungen*, 119-20.

Németh, Lajos. The Art of Béla Czóbel. *The New Hungarian Quarterly* 12, no. 44 (1971): 178-79.

Pataky, Dénes. A Hungarian Painter in Paris. *The New Hungarian Quarterly* 4, no. 11 (1963): 103-08.

Philipp, Clarisse. Les oeuvres du jeune Béla Czóbel. *Bulletin de la Galerie Nationale Hongroise* 4 (1963): 31-44.

______. *Czóbel*. Budapest, 1970.

Weise, E. Béla Czóbel (*Das Kunstblatt*, 1920). Reprinted as Dokument 23 in *Wechselwirkungen*, 117-19.

Westheim, Paul. Béla Czóbel (1920). Reprinted as Dokument 24 in *Wechselwirkungen*, 119.

Valéria Dénes

Mezei, Ottó. Les Galimberti: Couple d'artistes Hongrois, des années 1910. *Acta Historiae Artium* 23 (1977): 329-55.

Gyula Derkovits

Borbély, László. *Retrospective de Gyula Derkovits (1894-1934)/Derkovits Gyula (1894-1934) emlékkiállítása*. Budapest: Galerie Nationale Hongroise, 1979. Bilingual French-Hungarian exhibition catalogue.

Németh, Lajos. Das Gemälde von Gyula Derkovits "Drei Generationen." *Acta Historiae Artium* 7 (1961): 103-14.

Pogány, Gábor Ö. The Life and Art of Gyula Derkovits. *New Hungarian Quarterly* 2, no. 1 (1961): 109-19.

Szabó, Júlia. Die Holzschnittfolge "1514" von Gyula Derkovits. *Acta Historiae Artium* 10. no. 1-2 (1964): 171-210.

______. The Paintings of Derkovits: A Memorial Exhibition. *New Hungarian Quarterly* 7, no. 21 (1966): 84-190.

Szabó, Júlia and Anna Oelmacher. *Derkovits Gyula emlékkiállítása/Gyula Derkovits Retrospective*. Budapest: Galerie Nationale Hongroise, 1965. Bilingual Hungarian-French exhibition catalogue.

Rudolf Diener-Dénes

Gachot, François. Rudolf Diener-Dénes. *The New Hungarian Quarterly* 17, no. 64 (1976): 160-63.

Lajos d'Ébneth

de Gruyter, Jos. *Lajos d'Ébneth: studie van een ontwikkelingsgang*. The Hague: A. A. M. Stols, 1946.

Schmalenbach, Werner. *Kurt Schwitters*. New York: Harry N. Abrams, 1967. Includes information on d'Ébneth's friendship with Schwitters.

Scholten d'Ébneth, Maria. *Lajos d'Ébneth Retrospectiva*. Lima, 1983.

József Egry

Éri, István, ed. *Egry József Emlékmúzeum, Badacsony/Musée Egry József*, Badacsony. Text by Béla Szíj. Badacsony: Veszprém Megyei Múzeumi Igazgatóság, n.d. Bilingual Hungarian-French museum catalogue.

Frank, János. Centenary of József Egry. *The New Hungarian Quarterly* 24, no. 91 (1983): 160.

Kállai, Ernő. József Egry (*Jahrbuch der Jungen Kunst*, Leipzig, 1924). Reprinted as Dokument 26 in *Wechselwirkungen*, 120-22.

Láncz, Sándor. József Egry. *The New Hungarian Quarterly* 2, no. 4 (1961): 103-15.

Németh, Lajos. La peinture de József Egry (1883-1951). *Acta Historiae Artium* 7 (1961): 303-35.

———. József Egry Retrospective. *The New Hungarian Quarterly* 13, no. 47 (1972): 105-7.

Szabó, Júlia. Les éléments picturaux et graphiques des oeuvres de József Egry. *Acta Historiae Artium* 20, no. 3-4 (1974): 317-26.

Béni Ferenczy

Genthon, István. Béni Ferenczy. *The New Hungarian Quarterly* 1, no. 1 (1960): 147-57.

Illyés, Mária. Béni Ferenczy. In *Wechselwirkungen*, 147-49.

Noémi Ferenczy

de Tolnay, Charles. Noémi Ferenczy (*Forum*, Bratislava, 1934). Reprinted as Dokument 39 in *Wechselwirkungen*, 144-46.

Jankovich, Júlia. Noémi Ferenczy (*Panoráma*, Pécs, 1937). Reprinted as Dokument 40 in *Wechselwirkungen*, 141-43.

Nagy, Zoltán. Retrospective of Noémi Ferenczy's Tapestries. *The New Hungarian Quarterly* 20, no. 75 (1979): 188.

Alfréd (Fréd) Forbát

Fréd Forbát: Architekt und Stadtplaner. Darmstadt: Bauhaus-Archiv, 1969. Exhibition catalogue.

Lajos Fülep

de Tolnay, Charles. Les écrits de Lajos Fülep sur Cézanne. *Acta Historiae Artium* 20 (1974): 103-05.

Tímár, Árpád. Lajos Fülep (1885-1970). *The New Hungarian Quarterly* 26, no. 98 (1985): 165-72.

Jenő Gábor

Thirteen Re-Discoveries. Basel: Editions Panderma, 1976. Dealer catalogue with material on Jenő Gábor and Lajos Kassák.

Sándor Galimberti

Bakos, Sylvia. Entry on Galimberti in Botar, ed., 30-31.

Aknai, Tamás. Sándor Galimberti's "Amsterdam": A Major Hungarian Painting of the 1910s. In *The Hungarian Avant-Garde*, 28-30.

Mezei, Ottó. Les Galimberti: Couple d'artistes Hongrois, des années 1910. *Acta Historiae Artium* 23 (1977): 329-55.

Lajos Gulácsy

Szabadi, Judit. The Life and Art of Lajos Gulácsy. *Acta Historiae Artium* 16, no. 3-4 (1970): 293-315.

———. Pencil-Drawings on Palm-Size Cards (Lajos Gulácsy). *The New Hungarian Quarterly* 24, no. 90 (1983): 156-58.

Vilmos Huszár

Bajkay-Rosch, Éva. A Hungarian Founder of the Dutch Constructivists. *Acta Historiae Artium* 30 (1984): 311-26. (Commemorates the 25th anniversary of Vilmos Huszár's death).

Ex, Sjarel. Vilmos Huszár en de toegepaste kunsten. *Bijvoorbeeld* 13, no. 4 (1981): 28-32.

———. Vilmos Huszár. In *De Stijl: The Formative Years*, 1917-1922. Cambridge: The MIT Press, 1986, 77-121.

Ex, Sjarel and Els Hoek. *De Mechanisch dansende Figuur van Vilmos Huszár.* Utrecht, 1984.

———, *Vilmos Huszár. Schilder en ontwerper 1884-1960*. Utrecht: Reflex, 1985. Exhibition catalogue; the definitive work on Huszár.

Gaugham, M. I. Vilmos Huszár: The Move Into Radical Abstraction, 1915-1923. Ph.D. dissertation, University of East Anglia, Norwich, 1975.

Szabó, Júlia. A Hungarian Artist in the Netherlands (Vilmos Huszár). *The New Hungarian Quarterly* 27, no. 102 (1980): 186-87.

Troy, Nancy. *The De Stijl Environment*. Cambridge: The MIT Press, 1983.

———. Figures of the Dance in De Stijl. *The Art Bulletin* 66, no. 4 (December 1984): 645-56.

Béla Kádár

Béla Kádár 1877-1956: A Leading Expressionist in the Twenties of "Der Sturm" in Berlin. New York: Kövesdy Gallery, 1985. Dealer catalogue.

Kállai, Ernő. Béla Kádár (from *Neue in Ungarn*, 1925). Reprinted as Dokument 28 in *Wechselwirkungen*, 122-23.

Fisher, Melanie. Entry on Kádár in Botar, ed., 33-35.

Ernő Kállai

Botar, Oliver A. I. Ernő Kállai and the Hidden Face of Nature. *The Structurist*, no. 23-24 (1984-85): 77-80.

Forgács, Éva. Ernő Kállai: Art Critic of a Changing Age. *The New Hungarian Quarterly* 17, no. 64 (1976): 174-81.

———. Der Konstruktivismus von Ernő Kállai. In *Wechselwirkungen*, 158-63.

———. Ernő Kállai. In Dautrey and Guerlain, eds.

Frank, T. Hannes Meyer und Ernst Kállai: eine freundliche Kontroverse am Bauhaus. *Bildende Kunst* 33, no. 10 (1985): 475-76.

———, ed. *Ernst Kállai: Vision und Formgesetz*. Leipzig and Weimar: Kiepenheuer, 1986.

Lajos Kassák

Ausstellung Lajos Kassák. Cologne: Galerie Gmurzynska, 1971. Dealer catalogue.

Brendel, János. The *Bildgedichte* of Lajos Kassák: Constructivism in Hungarian Avant-Garde Poetry. In *The Hungarian Avant-Garde*, 31-37.

Bortnyik, Sándor. Mes souvenirs de Kassák. In Dautrey and Guerlain, eds. (trans. V. Charaire), 172-73.

Bowlt, John E. Lajos Kassák: The Wolf Outside the Cage. In *Lajos Kassák, 1887-1967* (New York), 7-13.

Catalogue de l'exposition Lajos Kassák. Paris: Galerie Denise Renée, 1967. Dealer catalogue.

Csaplár, Ferenc. Kassák e Bartók. In *Budapest, 1890-1919. L'anima e le forme*, 198-200.

———. *Kassák és Párizs* [Kassák and Paris.] Budapest: Kassák Emlékmúzeum, 1990. Bilingual Hungarian-French exhibition catalogue.

———. *Kassák festmények, grafikák magángyűjteményekből* [Kassák paintings and graphic works from private collections]. Budapest: Kassák Emlékmúzeum, 1989. Bilingual Hungarian-German exhibition catalogue.

———. *Kassák reklámterv*, [Kassák advertising designs]. Budapest: Kassák Emlékmúzeum, 1977. Exhibition catalogue.

———. Lajos Kassák in Berlin. In *Lajos Kassák, 1887-1967* (East Berlin), 20-27.

———. Nach meinem eigenen Gesetz: Porträtskizze Lajos Kassák. In *Lajos Kassák, 1867-1957*. (East Berlin). Exhibition catalogue.

———, and Krisztina Horányi, eds. Kassák 1887-1967. *Arion*, no. 16 (Budapest: Corvina, 1988). A special issue devoted to the poetry and art of Kassák, with translation of his writings into several languages.

Erki, Edit. Interview with Lajos Kassák. *The New Hungarian Quarterly* 5, no. 16 (Winter 1964): 192-96.

Exhibition Lajos Kassák. With introductions by Michel Seuphor and Gábor Ö. Pogány. Paris: Galerie Denise Renée, 1960. Catalogue of the first exhibition of the Hungarian avant-garde in the West after the Stalinist period; also Kassák's first in Paris.

Ferenczi, László. Lajos Kassák. The Triumph of Will and Conviction. *The New Hungarian Quarterly* 28, no. 106 (1987): 73-86.

Forgács, Éva. Lajos Kassák Memorial Museum in Old Buda. *The New Hungarian Quarterly* 18, no. 67 (1977): 196-98.

Hajnal-Neukäter, Ildikó. Herwarth Walden und Lajos Kassák: ein Porträt. In *Wechselwirkungen*, 61-67.

Kassák. Basel: Editions Panderma Carl László, 1968.

Körner, Éva. Kassák the Painter in Theory and Practice. *The New Hungarian Quarterly* 7, no. 21 (1966).

———. In Memoriam Lajos Kassák. *The New Hungarian Quarterly* 8, no. 28 (1967): 107-12.

Konstruktive Kunst: Elemente und Prinzipien. Nürnberg: Institut für Moderne Kunst, 1969. Catalogue of the exhibition of the Nuremberg Biennale. The Hungarian section includes works by Kassák.

Lajos Kassák 1887-1967. Vienna: Galerie Nächst St. Stephan, 1971. Dealer catalogue.

Lajos Kassák 1887-1967. East Berlin: Akademie der Künste der Deutsche Demokratische Republik, 1987. Exhibition catalogue.

Lajos Kassák 1887-1967. With introduction by Wilfried Skriener. Graz: Neue Galerie am Landesmuseum Joanneum, 1971. Exhibition catalogue.

Lajos Kassák 1887-1967. With introduction by Paul Kövesdy and essays by John E. Bowlt and Éva Körner. New York: Matignon Gallery, 1984. Dealer catalogue.

Lajos Kassák 1887-1967. Düsseldorf: Heinrich-Heine-Institut, 1989. Exhibition catalogue.

Lengyel, Balázs. The Other Kassák. *The New Hungarian Quarterly,* 30, no. 115 (1989): 148-51.

Lengyel, József. Lajos Kassák, le maître. In Dautrey and Guerlain, eds. (trans. V. Charaire), 174.

Levinger, Esther. Lajos Kassák, *Ma* and the New Artist, 1916-1925. *The Structurist* no. 25-26 (1985-86): 78-86.

———. Kassák's Reading of Art History. *Hungarian Studies Review* 15, no. 1 (Spring 1988).

Matustik, Robert and Elena Sevcakova. Lajos Kassák: Tragödie und Heroismus des ungarischen Konstruktivismus. *Muzaika* (Bratislava) 10 (1970).

Nemes-Nagy, Ágnes. In Memoriam Lajos Kassák: From Odd Job Tramp to Avant-Garde Artist. *The New Hungarian Quarterly* 7, no. 28 (1967): 94-97.

Passuth, Krisztina. Lajos Kassák e l'avanguardia ungherese. *Proceedings of the Conférence au X. Convegno di Mitteleuropa.* Gorizia, 1975.

Rózsa, Gyula. Lajos Kassák's Collages in the Petőfi Museum. *Hungarian Review* (1971).

Sik, Csaba. Kassák in the Museum. *The New Hungarian Quarterly* 15, no. 54 (1974): 74-87.

Spielmann, Peter, ed. *Ausstellung Lajos Kassák 1887-1967.* Bochum: Museum Bochum, 1973.

Stein, Donna. The Rediscovery of Lajos Kassak (sic). *Artnews* (Summer 1984): 56-61.

Štraus, Tomáš. Kassák: *A Hungarian Contribution to Constructivism..* Cologne: Galerie Gmurzynska, 1975.

Szabó, Júlia. Kassák and the International Avant-Garde. *The New Hungarian Quarterly* 28, no. 106 (1987): 117-24.

Thirteen Re-Discoveries. Basel: Editions Panderma, 1976. Dealer catalogue including material on Kassák and Jenő Gábor.

Il vento dell'est degli anni 20. Milan: Galleria Breton, 1971. Dealer catalogue including material by Kassák and Bortnyik.

György Kepes

Major, Máté. One-man Show of György Kepes in Budapest. *The New Hungarian Quarterly* 17, no. 64 (1976): 164-66.

Károly Kernstok

Horváth, Béla. Károly Kernstok (1873-1940). *Acta Historiae Artium* 13 (1967): 353-87. In French.

János Kmetty

Nagy, Zoltán. János Kmetty (1889-1975). *The New Hungarian Quarterly* 17, no. 62 (1976): 185-86.

Dezső Korniss

Hegyi, Loránd. *Korniss Dezső kiállítása/ Exposition de Dezső Korniss.* Budapest: Galerie Nationale Hongroise, 1980. Bilingual Hungarian-French exhibition catalogue.

Körner, Éva. A Stubborn Abstract Painter (Dezső Korniss). *The New Hungarian Quarterly* 11, no. 39 (1970): 180-85.

János Mácza

Mácza, János. Souvenirs de ma jeunesse. In Dautrey and Guerlain, eds. (trans. V. Charaire), 214-16.

Szabó, Júlia. János Mácza, 1893-1974. In Dautrey and Guerlain, eds. (trans. V. Charaire), 198-204.

Ödön Márffy

Frank, János. Ödön Márffy's Rediscovery. *The New Hungarian Quarterly* 25, no. 96 (1984): 180-81.

János (Hans) Máttis Teutsch

Banner, Zoltán. *Hans Máttis Teutsch.* Bucharest: Kritérion, 1974. In German.

Csaplár, Ferenc. *Máttis Teutsch.* Budapest: Kassák Emlékmúzeum, 1983. Exhibition catalogue.

Deac, Mircea: *Máttis Teutsch, si realismul constructiv und der konstruktive Realismus.* Cluj-Napoca, 1985.

Hevesy, Iván. János Máttis Teutsch (*Ma,* 1918). In Dautrey and Guerlain, eds. (trans. V. Charaire), 147-49.

Passuth, Krisztina. Les oeuvres de Máttis Teutsch au Musée de Beaux Arts. *Bulletin de Musée Hongrois des Beaux Arts,* (Budapest) no. 45-46 (1977): 105-34.

———. The Abstract Vision of Máttis Teutsch. *The New Hungarian Quarterly* 25, no. 95 (1984): 149.

Szabó, Júlia. *Máttis Teutsch.* Budapest, 1983. Includes a German summary.

Vida, Gheorghe. Hans Máttis Teutsch and the European Dialogue of Forms. *Romanian Review,* no. 12 (1984): 94-101.

László Moholy-Nagy

Botar, Oliver, ed. Documents on László Moholy-Nagy. *Hungarian Studies Review* 15, no. 1 (Spring 1988): 77-87.

Caton, Joseph Harris. *The Utopian Vision of Moholy-Nagy: Technology, Society, and the Avant-Garde. An Analysis of the Writings of Moholy-Nagy on the Visual Arts.* Ann Arbor: UMI Research Press, 1984.

Fawkes, Caroline. Photography and Moholy-Nagy's Do-It-Yourself Aesthetic. *Studio International* (July-August 1975).

Haus, Andreas. *Moholy-Nagy: Photographs and Photograms.* Translated from the German by Frederic Samson. New York: Pantheon Books, 1980.

Hight, Eleanor M., with Andrea Kaliski Miller and Nancy Nugent. *Moholy-Nagy: Photography and Film in Weimar Germany.* Wellesley, Mass.: Wellesley College Museum, 1985.

In Memoriam László Moholy-Nagy. New York: Solomon R. Guggenheim Museum, 1947. Exhibition catalogue.

Jánosi, Ilona. László Moholy-Nagy: His Early Life in Hungary (1895-1919). Unpublished master's thesis. Indiana University, Bloomington, 1979.

Kepes, György. László Moholy-Nagy: The Bauhaus Tradition. *Print* (January-February 1969).

Keserű, Katalin. The Beginnings of László Moholy-Nagy. Early Portrait Sketches. *The New Hungarian Quarterly* 16, no. 57 (1975): 187-89.

Kostelanetz, Richard, ed. *Moholy-Nagy.* New York: Praeger Publishers, 1970.

Kovacs, Istvan. Totality through Light: The Work of László Moholy-Nagy. *Form* 6 (December 1967).

László Moholy-Nagy. Chicago: The Museum of Contemporary Art; New York: The Solomon R. Guggenheim Museum, 1969. Exhibition catalogue.

László Moholy-Nagy/László Péri. Zwei Künstler der ungarischen Avantgarde in Berlin 1920-1925. With essays by Krisztina Passuth and Wolfgang Werner. Bremen: Kunsthandel Wolfgang Werner, 1987.

László Moholy-Nagy. Constructivist Works 1920-1943. New York: Prakapas, 1987. Dealer catalogue.

László Moholy-Nagy. Berlin: Bauhaus-Archiv, 1972. Exhibition catalogue.

Lusk, Irene-Charlotte. *Montagen ins Blaue. László Moholy-Nagy: Fotomontagen und collagen, 1922-1943.* Berlin: Anabas, 1980. Published for the exhibition at the Werkbund-Archiv in West Berlin.

Mansbach, S. A. *Visions of Totality: László Moholy-Nagy, Theo van Doesburg, and El Lissitzky.* Ann Arbor: UMI Research Press, 1980.

———. Science as Artistic Paradigm: A 1920s Utopian Vision. *The Structurist* no. 21-22 (1981-1982): 33-39.

———. Attitudes Towards Nature Among Some Early Twentieth Century Artists. *The Structurist,* no. 23-24 (1983-84): 87-90.

Moholy, Lucia. *Moholy-Nagy. Marginal Notes. Documentary Absurdities.* Krefeld: Scherpe, 1972.

Moholy-Nagy. Eindhoven: Stedelijk van Abbemuseum, 1967. Exhibition catalogue.

Moholy-Nagy, Sibyl. *Moholy-Nagy: Experiment in Totality.* Cambridge: The MIT Press.

Neumann, Eckhard, ed. *Bauhaus and Bauhaus People.* New York: Van Nostrand Rheinhold, 1970. Includes information on Moholy-Nagy and Bortnyik.

Passuth, Krisztina. Debut of László Moholy-Nagy. *Acta Historiae Artium* 19, no. 1-2 (1973): 125-42.

———. Moholy-Nagy et Walter Benjamin. *Cahiers du Musée National d'Art Moderne* no. 5 (1980).

———. *Moholy-Nagy.* London: Thames and Hudson, 1985. This is the most extensive monograph on Moholy-Nagy published to date.

———. László Moholy-Nagy: la grande rue. *Art Press,* no. 131 (December 1988): 12-13.

Péter, László. The Young Years of Moholy-Nagy. *The New Hungarian Quarterly* 17, no. 21 (1972): 62-72.

Phillips, Sandra S. Man Ray and Moholy-Nagy: Rayographs and Photograms. *Arts in Virginia* 25, no. 2-3 (1985): 48-63.

Rave, H., and J. Heusinger von Waldegg. *László Moholy-Nagy: Z IX, 1924.*

Mannheim: Städtische Kunsthalle, 1982. Exhibition catalogue.
Reichardt, Jasia. Moholy-Nagy and Light Art as an Art of the Future. *Studio International* 174, no. 894 (November 1967): 184-85.
Rice, Leland D., and David W. Steadman, eds. *Photographs of Moholy-Nagy from the Collection of William Larson*. Claremont, Calif.: The Galleries of the Claremont Colleges, 1975. Exhibition catalogue.
Rondolino, Gianni. *László Moholy-Nagy: Pittura, fotografia, film*. Turin: Martano Editore, 1975.
Senter, Terence A., and Krisztina Passuth. *L. Moholy-Nagy*. London: Arts Council of Great Britain, 1980. Exhibition catalogue.
Sers, Philippe. Les recherches expérimentales de Moholy-Nagy pour inventer l'art du 20e siècle. *Connaissance des arts*, no. 2989 (December 1976): 82-89.
Sinkovits, Péter. Moholy-Nagy Exhibition in Buda Castle. *The New Hungarian Quarterly* 17, no. 62 (1976): 176-78.
Steckel, Hannah. László Moholy-Nagy, 1895-1946: Entwurf seiner Wahrnehmungslehre. Ph.D. dissertation, Freie Universität Berlin, 1974.
Szabó, Júlia. An Unknown Correspondence of László Moholy-Nagy. *The New Hungarian Quarterly* 16, no. 57 (1975): 189-93.
van der Marck, Jan "László Moholy-Nagy: Konstruktion in Emaille 1." *Art Press*, no. 106 (September 1986): 84-86.
Verre, P., and J. Saul. *Moholy-Nagy: Fotoplastiks, the Bauhaus Years*. New York: The Bronx Museum, 1983. Exhibition catalogue.
———. *Licht-Visionen: Ein Experiment von Moholy-Nagy*. Berlin: Bauhaus-Archiv, 1972.
Weitemeier, Hannah, Wulf Herzogenrath, and Tilman Osterwold. *László Moholy-Nagy*. Stuttgart: Gerd Hatje, 1974.

József Nemes Lampérth
Csaplár, Ferenc. *Nemes Lampérth*. Budapest: Kassák Emlékmúzeum, 1984. Exhibition catalogue.
Forgács, Éva. József Nemes Lampérth. In *Wechselwirkungen*, 134-38.
Mezei, Ottó. József Nemes Lampérths unbekannte Berliner Bilder und deren Platz in seinem Lebenswerk. *Acta Historiae Artium* no. 1-2 (1975): 151-65.
Szabó, Júlia. József Nemes Lampérth (1891-1924). *The New Hungarian Quarterly* 26, no. 98 (1985): 178-80.

Dezső Orbán
Dévényi, Iván. Desiderius Orbán, a Hungarian-Australian Painter. *The New Hungarian Quarterly* 17, no. 63 (1976): 173-75.
Halász, Zoltán. An Hour with Dezső (Desiderius) Orbán at the Threshold of 100. *The New Hungarian Quarterly* 24, no. 91 (1983): 167-70.
Waldmann, A. Desiderius Orbán: A Critical Assessment of an Australian Romantic. *Art and Australia* 22, pt. 2 (Summer 1984): 212-15.

Gyula Pap
Bajkay, Éva. Gyula Pap: the Last Hungarian Bauhaus Artist. *The New Hungarian Quarterly* 25, no. 94 (1984): 185-87.
Gassner, Hubertus. Zwischen den Stühlen sitzend sich im Kreise drehen: Marcel Breuer und Gyula Pap als Bauhaus-Gestalter. In *Wechselwirkungen*, 312-28.
Haulisch, Lenke. Der Maler Gyula Pap. In *Wechselwirkungen*, 284-88.
———. Die ungarische Bezüge der Kunst Oskar Schlemmers. *Acta Historiae Artium* 23, no. 3-4 (1987-88): 345-56.
Kállai, Ernő. Das neue Helldunkel: Zu den Bildern von Julius Pap (*Forum*, Bratislava, 1934). Reprinted in *Wechselwirkungen*, 289-91.

László (Peter) Péri
Herzogenrath, Wulf, ed. *László Péri: Werke 1920-1924 und das Problem des "Shaped Canvas."* Basel: Editions Panderma Carl László, 1973. Catalogue of the exhibition held at the Kölnischer Kunstverein, Cologne, 1973.
Kállai, Ernő. László Péri (from *Neue Malerei in Ungarn*, 1925). Reprinted as Dokument 66 in *Wechselwirkungen*, 248-49.
Kemény, Alfréd. Die konstruktive Kunst und Péris Raumkonstruktionen (1922, Berlin). Reprinted as Dokument 64 in *Wechselwirkungen*, 244-47.
László Moholy-Nagy/László Péri. Zwei Künstler der ungarischen Avantgarde in Berlin 1920-1925. With essays by Krisztina Passuth and Wolfgang Werner. Bremen: Kunsthandel Wolfgang Werner, 1987.
László Péri, 1899-1967, Arbeiten in Beton: Reliefs, Skulpturen, Graphik(sic). Berlin: Neue Gesellschaft für Bildende Kunst Berlin, Skulpturenmuseum, 1982. Exhibition catalogue.
Mosta-Heirt, C. László Péri. *Opus International* (Winter 1982): 24-25.
Passuth, Krisztina. L'utopie de László Péri. *Bulletin analytique des périodiques d'Europe de l'Est*, no. 23. Paris: Centres Georges Pompidou, 1981.
Stratmann, N. Der Verwandelte Avantgardist: Peter (László) Péri 1899-1967. *Bildende Kunst* (East Berlin), part 8 (1982): 410-63.

Vilmos Perlrott Csaba
Illyés, Mária. Aurél Bernáth's and Vilmos Perlrott Csaba's Paintings. *The New Hungarian Quarterly* 19, no. 69 (1987): 168-73.

Bertalan Pór
Bakos, Sylvia. Entry on Pór in Botar, ed., 56-60.
Oelmacher, Anna. *Pór Bertalan (1880-1964) emlékkiállítása/Bartholomé Pór (1880-1964) Retrospective*. Budapest: Galerie Nationale Hongroise, 1966. Bilingual Hungarian-French exhibition catalogue.

József Rippl-Rónai
Humbert, Agnès. *Les Nabis et leur époque*. Geneva, 1954.
Rippl-Rónai. Le Havre: Musée des Beaux-Arts André Malraux, 1983. Exhibition catalogue.
Rippl-Rónai 1861-1927. Pittore grafico, decoratore. Rome: Multigrafia Editrice, 1983. Exhibition catalogue.
Stump, Jean, et al. *Ritual and Reality: Prints of the Nabis*. Lawrence, Kansas: Spencer Museum of Art, 1979.
Szabadi, Judit. József Rippl-Rónai et l'art nouveau. *Acta Historiae Artium* 26, no 1-2 (1980): 285-316.

Hugó Scheiber
Botar, Oliver A. I. Entry on Scheiber in Botar, ed. 63-66.
Hugó Scheiber. Zurich: Galerie Dr. I. Schlegl, 1982. Dealer catalogue.
Kállai, Ernő. Hugó Scheiber (from *Neue Malerei in Ungarn*, 1925). Reprinted as Dokument 33 in *Wechselwirkungen*, 127-28.
Nagy, Zoltán. The Rediscovery of Hugó Scheiber (1873-1950). *The New Hungarian Quarterly* 28, no. 105 (1987): 200-3.
Schmidt, Ernst von, ed. *Hugó Scheiber: Leben und Werk*. Basel: Edition Inter Art Galerie, 1982.

Armand Schönberger
Szij, Béla. *Schönberger Armand kiállítása/Exposition de Armand Schönberger* (sic). Budapest: Galerie Nationale Hongroise, 1970. Bilingual Hungarian-French exhibition catalogue.

Imre Szobotka
Imre Szobotka: Oils, Watercolours, and Drawings. Milan: Galleria dell'incisione, 1973. Dealer catalogue.

Lajos Tihanyi
Desnos, Robert. *Tihanyi, peintures*. Paris, 1936.
Exhibition Lajos Tihanyi. Paris: Galerie Entremonde, 1970. Dealer catalogue.
Fülep, Lajos. Lajos Tihanyi. The Portrait on Its Painter. In *The Hungarian Avant-Garde* (trans. George Cushing), 109-11.
Kállai, Ernő. Lajos Tihanyi (*Jahrbuch der Jungen Kunst*, 1924). Reprinted as Dokument 34 in *Wechselwirkungen*, 128-31.
Passuth, Krisztina. La carrière de Lajos Tihanyi. *Acta Historiae Artium* 20, no. 1-2 (1974): 124-49.
———. *Tihangi*. Dresden: VEB Verlag der Kunst, 1977.
Tihanyi Lajos emlékkiállítása/Exposition de Lajos Tihanyi. Budapest: Galerie Nationale Hongroise, 1973. Bilingual Hungarian-French exhibition catalogue.

Sándor (Alexander) Trauner
Bajkay, Éva. Alexander Trauner's Film Sets in the Hungarian National Gallery. *The New Hungarian Quarterly* 22 (1981): 198-99.
———. A Hungarian Stage-Designer of the Bauhaus. *The New Hungarian Quarterly* 24, no. 92 (1983): 199-201.

Béla Uitz
Bajkay, Éva. Quatre cents oeuvres inconnus de Béla Uitz. *Annales de la Galerie Nationale Hongroise* no. 2 (1974): 117-26.
———. *Uitz Béla*. Budapest: Corvina Kiadó, 1977. A loose-leaf album with essay in Hungarian, English, German, and Russian.
———. Béla Uitz. In Dautrey and Guerlain, eds., 150-57.
Kontha, Sándor. L'Art de Béla Uitz. *Acta Historiae Artium* 29 (1973): 305-27.

Nagy, Zoltán. The Luddite Etchings of Béla Uitz. *The New Hungarian Quarterly* 13, no. 48 (1972): 182-85.

______. Two Activists in the Hungarian National Gallery (Sándor Bortnyik, Béla Uitz). *The New Hungarian Quarterly* 18, no. 68 (1977): 180-82.

Németh, Lajos. The Art of Béla Uitz. *The New Hungarian Quarterly* 9, no. 29 (1968): 176-80.

Victor Vasarely (Győző Vásárhelyi)

Hahn, Ottó. *Le musée imaginaire de Vasarely*. Paris: Duculot, 1978. This volume includes Vasarely's own remembrances of his early years in Hungary.

Mezei, Ottó. Vasarely Revisited. *The New Hungarian Quarterly* 13, no. 48 (1972): 192-97.

Sík, Csaba. Victor Vasarely. *The New Hungarian Quarterly* 8, no. 25 (1967): 188-94.

Spies, Werner. *Victor Vasarely*. Schaumberg: Verlag M. de Mont, 1971.

The Unknown Vasarely. Neuchâtel: Editions du Griffon, 1977.

Vadas, József. Vasarely at the Budapest Museum of Fine Arts. *The Hungarian Quarterly* 24, no. 90 (1983): 154-56.

Andor Weininger

Bajkay-Rosch, Éva. A Hungarian Stage-Designer of the Bauhaus. *The New Hungarian Quarterly* 24, no. 92 (1983): 199-201.

Michaelsen, Kathrin. Andor Weiningers Bühnenprojekte am Bauhaus. In *Wechselwirkungen*, 427-33.

Svestka, Jiri, ed., *Andor Weininger: Vom Bauhaus zur konzeptuellen Kunst*, Düsseldorf, 1990. Exhibition catalogue with several essays.

II. LITERATURE IN HUNGARIAN

General

Aradi, Nóra, Mária Cseh, György Theisler, and Sándor Győrffy. *A Magyar Tanácsköztársaság művészete* [Art of the Hungarian Soviet Republic]. Budapest: Képzőművészeti Alap, 1979.

Bajkay-Rosch, Éva. *A magyar grafika külföldön. Bécs, 1919-1933* [Hungarian Graphic Art Abroad. Vienna 1919-1933]. Budapest: Petőfi Irodalmi Múzeum, 1982.

______. Magyar kiállítás a kasseli Neue Galerie-ban [A Hungarian Exhibition in the Kassel Neue Galerie]. *Művészet* 28, no. 2 (February 1987): 48-51.

______. Ember vagy kocka!? A korai Bauhaus magyar rajzairól [Man or Cube!? Hungarian Drawings of the Early Bauhaus]. *Művészet* 27, no. 8 (1988): 6-7, 60-62.

Bajomi, Endre Lázár. *A szürrealizmus*. Budapest: Gondolat, 1968. Includes material on surrealism among the Hungarians.

______, ed. *A magyar Párizs* [The Hungarian Paris]. Budapest: Gondolat, 1978.

Bálint, Endre. Konstruktiv tendenciák a magyar művészetben [Constructive Tendencies in Hungarian Art], *Magyar Műhely* (Paris) 7, no. 28 (1 September 1968): 48-52.

Bakos, Katalin. A magyar és orosz művészet kapcsolatai, 1917-1925. [Connections Between Hungarian and Russian Art 1917-1925]. *Ars Hungarica* 5 (1977).

Bánszky, Pál. Képtár Kecskeméten [Gallery in Kecskemét]. *Művészet* 24, no. 11 (November 1983): 34-37.

Beke, László. Magyar nem-ábrázoló művészet I [Hungarian Non-Figurative Art I]. *Kritika* 9, no. 1 (1971).

______. Képzőművészet a *Ma* tiz évfolyamában [Fine Art in the Ten Volumes of *Ma*]. *Kritika* no. 3 (1971).

Béládi Miklós. Az avantgard mozgalom [The Avant-Garde Movement]. *Kortárs* 29, no. 1 (1985): 116-42.

Bojtár, Endre. *A kelet-európai avantgarde irodalom* [East European Avant-garde Literature]. Budapest: Akadémiai, 1977.

Bori, Imre. *A szecessziótól a dadáig* [From Secession to Dada]. Újvidék (Novi Sad, Yugoslavia): Fórum Könyvkiadó, 1969.

Csaplár, Ferenc. Kassák Lajos folyóirata: a Dokumentum [Lajos Kassák's Journal: *Dokumentum*]. *Tiszatáj* (March 1967).

______. A Munka-kör képzőművészeti tevékenysége [The Artistic Activity of the Munka Circle], *Művészettörténeti Értesítő* 21, no. 2 (1972).

______. Kisérlet a "Ma" hazai folytatására (*A Dokumentum*) [An Attempt to Continue *Ma* in Hungary (*Dokumentum*)]. *Literatura* no. 3-4 (1975): 102-27.

______. *Magyar avantgarde plakátművészet 1916-1930* [Hungarian avant-garde poster design 1916-1930]. Budapest: Kassák Emlékmúzeum, 1985. Exhibition catalogue.

______. *A kollázs a magyar művészetben, 1920-1954* [Collage in Hungarian Art, 1920-1965]. Budapest: Kassák Emlékmúzeum, 1982. Exhibition catalogue.

______. *Il Futurismo*. Budapest: Kassák Emlékmúzeum, 1981. Exhibition catalogue.

______. A Karavántól az Új művészek könyvéig [From *Karaván* to *The Book of New Artists*]. *Magyar Könyvszemle* 98 (1982): 379-82.

______. *Avantgarde Budapest 1920-1930*. Budapest: Kassák Emlékmúzeum, 1980. Exhibition catalogue.

______. Avantgárd és Proletkult: A Munka-kör 1928-1932 [Avant-garde and Proletkuit: The Munka Circle 1928-1932]. Budapest: Kassák Emlékmúzeum, 1988. Exhibition catalogue.

______. *Kassák Körei* [Kassák's Circles]. Budapest: Szépirodalmi, 1987.

______, ed. *Avant-garde folyóiratok 1920-1930* [Avant-garde Periodicals 1920-1930]. With introduction by Júlia Szabó. Budapest: Kassák Emlékmúzeum, 1978. Exhibition catalogue.

______, ed. Kassák Lajos levelesládájából [From the Letter Box of Lajos Kassák]. *Új Symposion* (Újvidék/Novi Sad) no. 165 (15 February 1979).

Czine, Mihály. Egy évtized (1915-1925) Pécs képzőművészeti életében [A Decade in the Artistic Life of Pécs]. In *Csuka Zoltán. Az idő mérlegén* [Zoltán Csuka. On the Scales of Time]. Budapest: Magvető, 1977.

Dávid, Katalin. A XX század magyar művészete. I. Konstruktiv törekvések [Hungarian Art of the Twentieth Century I. Constructive Tendencies]. *Művészettörténeti Tanulmányok* (1960): 73-79, 81-82.

Dénes, Zsófia. *Tegnapi új művészek* [Yesterday's New Artists]. Budapest: Kozmosz, 1974. Writings on art, including the avant-garde.

______. *Szivárvány Pesttől Párizsig* [Rainbow from Budapest to Paris]. Budapest: Magvető, 1979. Memoirs and journalistic writings, including material on Béla Uitz, Lajos Kassák, and László Moholy-Nagy.

Éri, Gyöngyi and Zsuzsa O. Jobbágyi, eds. *Lélek és forma. Magyar művészet 1896-1914*. See listing under volume title.

Forgács, Éva. *Kölcsönhatások* [On *Wechselwirkungen*] *Kritika* 3 (1987).

Galambos, Ferenc. Képzőművészeti élet a bécsi magyar emigrációban [Artistic Life in the Viennese-Hungarian Emigration]. *Művészettörténeti Értesítő* 20, no. 1 (1971): 1-10.

Gara, György, ed. *A kubizmus* [Cubism]. Budapest: Gondolat, 1975. A general work that includes material on cubism and the Hungarians.

Géger, Melinda. Új állandó kiállítás a kaposvári Rippl-Rónai Múzeumban [A New Permanent Exhibition in the Kaposvár Rippl-Rónai Museum]. *Művészet* 27, no. 11-12 (November-December 1986): 88-93.

Gellér, Katalin. Néhány új adat a Julian Akadémiáról és az ott tanuló magyar művészekről [Some New Information on the Académie Julian and its Hungarian Students]. *Ars Hungarica* 7, no. 1 (1979): 89-94.

______. Szecesszió és avantgarde [Art Nouveau and Avant-garde]. *Művészet* 26, no.2 (Feburary 1985): 24-27.

György, Péter. Magyar avantgarde, 1920-1930. *Kritika* 3 (March 1981), pp. 36-37.

______, and Gábor Pataki. *A Dada Magyarországon* [Dada in Hungary]. Budapest: ELTE Esztétika és Művészettörténeti Tanszéke, 1982.

Hamvas, Béla and Katalin Kemény. *Forradalom a művészetben. Absztrakció és szürrealizmus Magyarországon* [Revolution in Art. Abstraction and Surrealism in Hungary]. Budapest: Misztótfalusi, 1947. Reissued in 1989.

Hán, Anna and Éva Körner. Lovasok a vízparton: Fekete négyzet fehér alapon. Az orosz és magyar avantgardizmus társadalmi funkciójáról, forma és nyelvújító tevékenységéről [Horsemen on the Shore: Black Rectangle on a White Ground. On the Social Function and Language-renewal Activities of Hungarian and Russian Avant-gardism]. *Művészet* 25, no. 8 (August 1984): 4-7.

Hárs, Éva and Ferenc Romváry, eds. *Modern Magyar Képtár Pécs*. Budapest: Corvina Kiadó, 1981.

Halász, Zoltán. Jövő—múlt időben. Gondolatforgácsok a párizsi futurizmus-kiállításról [The Future—In the Past Tense. Thoughts on the Paris Futurist Exhibition]. *Művészet* 15, no. 12 (December 1974): 40-41. Includes material on Hungarian-Futurist connections.

Haulisch, Lenke. *A szentendrei festészet* [Szentendre Painting]. Budapest: Akadémiai Kiadó, 1977.

Hegyi, Loránd. A magyar konstruktivista művészet korszakai [The Periods of the

Hungarian Constructivist Art]. *Művészettörténeti Értesítő* 31, no. 1 (1982): 20-28.

———. A Munka-kör képzőművészeti tevékenysége [Artistic Activity of the Munka Circle]. *Ars Hungarica* 11, no. 2 (1983): 283-95.

Horváth, Béla. Márffy Ödön kortársairól és a korról [On Ödön Márffy's Contemporaries and his Age]. *Jelenkor* (1961): 715-19.

———. Bartók és a Nyolcak [Bartók and The Eight]. *Művészettörténeti Értesítő* 23, no. 4 (1974): 328-32. With a summary in German.

Illés, Ilona. A bécsi *Ma* [The Viennese *Ma*]. *A Petőfi Irodalmi Múzeum Évkönyve* 7 (1967-68): 171-84.

Kállai, Ernő. *Cézanne és a XX. század konstruktív művészete* [Cézanne and Twentieth Century Constructive Art]. Budapest, 1944.

Kampis, Antal, ed. *Művészettörténeti Dokumentációs Központ Közleményei* III, Bauhaus Szám [Bauhaus Issue]. Budapest: A Múzeumok Központi Propaganda Irodája, 1963. Includes interviews with Kassák, Bortnyik, and Gyula Pap. The interviews were republished in: *Rozgonyi Iván. Párbeszéd művekkel. Interjúk*, 1955-1981 [Iván Rozgonyi: A Dialogue with Works. Interviews, 1955-1981]. Budapest: MTA Művészettörténeti Kutató Csoport, 1988.

Kántor, Lajos. *Kép, világkép. A régi "Korunk" az új művészetért* [Image, World-image. The Old *Korunk* for the New Art]. Bucharest: Kriterion, 1977.

Karádi, Éva, and Erzsébet Vezér. *A Vasárnapi Kör* [The Sunday Circle]. Budapest: Gondolat, 1980.

Kardos, László. Magyar Futurizmus [Hungarian Futurism]. *Alkotás* 3-4 (February-March 1947): 40-42.

Kassák, Lajos. *Képzőművészetünk Nagybányától napjainkig* [Our Art from Nagybánya to the Present], Budapest: Magyar Műkiadó, 1947.

———. *Az izmusok története* [History of the Isms]. Budapest: Magvető Könyvkiadó, 1972.

———, and Imre Pán. A modern művészeti irányzatok története [The History of Modern Trends in Art]. *Nagyvilág* nos. 1-12 (1957).

Keserű, Katalin. Avantgardizmus és a primitiv/népi művészet tradíciója [Avantgardism and the Tradition of Primitive/Folk Art]. *Ars Hungarica* 16, no. 1 (1988): 43-53. Includes a summary in German.

Kis, Endre and Kristóf János Nyiri, eds. *A magyar filozófiai gondolkodás a századelőn* [Hungarian Philosphical Thought at the Beginning of the Century]. Budapest: Kossuth, 1979.

Kiss, Dezső and Lajos Németh. *A Magyar Tanácsköztársaság képzőművészeti élete* [Artistic Life of the Hungarian Soviet Republic]. Budapest: Művészettörténeti Dokumentációs Központ, 1960.

Kiss, Éva. Iparművészet és nagyipar kapcsolata Magyarországon a két világháború között. [The Connection Between Applied Design and Industry in Hungary Between the World Wars]. *Ars Hungarica* no. 1 (1977): 87-105. Includes a summary in English.

Kocsis, Rózsa. *Igen és Nem. A magyar avantgard színjáték története* [Yes and No. The History of Hungarian Avant-Garde Theatre]. Budapest: Magvető Könyvkiadó, 1973.

Koczogh, Ákos, ed. *Az expresszionizmus*. Budapest: Gondolat, 1967. Includes material on expressionist elements in the Hungarian avant-garde.

Kontha, Sándor. Művészetünk a két világháború között [Our Art Between the World Wars]. *Művészettörténeti Értesítő* 29, no. 1 (1980): 1-5

———, ed. *Magyar művészet 1919-1945* [Hungarian Art 1919-1945]. 2 vols. Budapest: Akadémiai, 1985. The definitive publication on Hungarian art between the two World Wars.

———, Júlia Szabó, and Márta Kovalovszky. XX. századi magyar festészet és szobrászat. A Magyar Nemzeti Galéria kiállítása [Twentieth Century Hungarian Painting and Sculpture, Permanent Exhibition of the Hungarian National Gallery]. *Művészet* 25, no. 3 (March 1984): 8-17.

Körner, Éva. Szentendre és a kelet-európai avantgarde [Szentendre and the East European Avant-garde]. *Valóság* 2 (1971): 78ff.

———. Adalékok a magyar képzőművészeti avantgarde történetéhez a két világháború között [Addenda to the History of the Hungarian Artistic Avant-Garde Between the Two World Wars], *Művészettörténeti Értesítő* 22 (1973): 131-136.

Lélek és forma. Magyar művészet 1896-1914 [Spirit and Form: Hungarian Art, 1896-1914]. Edited by Gyöngyi Éri and Zsuzsa O. Jobbágyi. Budapest: Magyar Nemzeti Galéria, 1986. Exhibition catalogue.

Litván, György. Irányzatok és viták a bécsi magyar emigrációban [Movements and Controversies in the Viennese Hungarian Emigration]. In *Vélemények - viták a két világháború közötti Magyarországon* [Opinions and controversies in Interwar Hungary]. Budapest, 1984.

Lóska, Lajos. Elfelejtett remekművek a Kiscelli Múzeumban [Forgotten Masterpieces in the Kiscelli Museum]. *Művészet* 25, no. 7 (July 1984): 35-39.

———. Magyar avantgard plakátművészet, 1916-1930 [Hungarian Avant-garde Poster Art. 1916-1930]. *Művészet* (April 1986): 16-19.

Markovits, Györgyi. Egy rövid életű folyóiratról. *Új Föld* 1927 [A Short-lived Journal: *Új Föld*, 1927]. *Magyar Könyvszemle* 91 (1975): 82-85.

———. A Bécsi Magyar Újság 1919. október - 1923. december [The *Bécsi Magyar Újság*, October 1919-December 1923]. *Magyar Könyvszemle*: 93 (1977): 257-62.

Mezei, Ottó. *A Bauhaus. Válogatás a mozgalom dokumentumaiból* [The Bauhaus. Selections from the Documents of the Movement]. Budapest: Gondolat, 1975.

———. Magyarok a bauhausban. [Hungarians at the Bauhaus]. In *Műhelymunkák a weimari bauhausból 1919-1925* [Workshop Works from the Weimar Bauhaus 1919-1925]. Budapest: Műcsarnok, 1977. Exhibition catalogue.

———. A hazai Bauhaus mozgalom kezdetei. Molnár Farkas a Bauhausban. [The Beginnings of the Bauhaus Movement at Home. Farkas Molnár at the Bauhaus.] *Művészet* 77. Budapest: Corvina Kiadó, 1978: 64-67.

———. *A Bauhaus magyar vonatkozásai: Előzmények, együttműködés, és kisugárzás* [Hungarian Connections with the Bauhaus: Precursors, Cooperation, and Influence]. Budapest: Népművelődési Intézet and Művelődéskutató Intézet, 1981.

Mihály, Ida F. A magyar bauhäuslerek [The Hungarian *Bauhäusler*.] *Művészet* 11, no. 9 (September 1970): 8-12.

Nagy, Ildikó, and Ilona Sármány. A budapesti Schiffer-villa [The Schiffer Villa of Budapest]. *Művészettörténeti Értesítő* 31, no. 2 (1982): 74-88. Includes a summary in German.

Nagy, Sándor E. Az Új Föld és a Bauhaus [*Új Föld* and the Bauhaus]. *Alföld*, no. 5 (1978): 58-61.

Nagy, Zoltán. Mihályfi Ernő hagyatéka [Ernő Mihályfi's Bequest]. *Művészet* 22, no. 12 (December 1981): 18-23.

———. Nyolcak és aktivisták [The Eight and the Activists]. *Művészet* 22, no. 7 (July 1981): 16-21.

Németh, Lajos, ed. *Magyar művészet 1890-1919* [Hungarian Art 1890-1919]. 2 vols. Budapest: Akadémiai Kiadó, 1981. This is the definitive history of the period's art.

Novák, Zoltán. *A Vasárnap társaság* [The Sunday Society]. Budapest: Kossuth, 1979.

Pamlényi, Ervin. A Magyar Tanácsköztársaság kultúrpolitikájáról [On the Cultural Policy of the Hungarian Soviet]. *Századok* 93, no. 1: 109-16.

Passuth, Krisztina. *A Nyolcak és Aktivisták köre*. [The Eight and the Activists]. Székesfehérvár: István Király Múzeum, 1965. Bilingual French-Hungarian exhibition catalogue.

———. A Nyolcak forradalmi Kisérlete [The Revolutioary Attempt of the Eight]. *Új Írás*, no. 10 (1968).

———. *A Nyolcak festészete* [The Painting of The Eight]. Budapest: Corvina Kiadó, 1967.

———. XX. századi magyar művészet kiállítása Amerikában [Twentieth Century Hungarian Art Exhibit in America]. *Művészet* 14,no. 7 (July 1973): 11-12. On the Bloomington, Indiana exhibition of 1973. See also *Hungarian Art: The Twentieth Century Avant-Garde*.

———. *Magyar művészek az európai avantgarde-ban 1919-1925* [Hungarian Artists in the European Avant-Garde 1919-1925]. Budapest: Corvina Kiadó, 1974. A pioneering study on the role of the Hungarians in the international avant-garde.

———. Modern művészet Amerikában az első világháború idején [Modern Art in America Around the First World War], Parts 1 and 2. *Művészet* 15, no. 8-9 (1974).

———. A magyar aktivizmus és kelet-európai rokonai. [Hungarian Activism and its Eastern European Relatives]. *Ars Hungarica* 2, no. 1 (1974).

———, ed. *Huszadik századi művészet kiállításának katalógusa* [Catalogue of

the Exhibition of Twentieth Century Art]. Budapest: Szépművészeti Muzeum, 1975.
Pataky, Dénes. *Nyolcak és Aktivisták rajzkiállítása* [Exhibition of Drawings of The Eight and the Activists]. Budapest: Magyar Nemzeti Galéria, 1961. Exhibition catalogue.
Perneczky, Géza. A Nyolcak és az aktivisták köre [The circle of The Eight and the Activists]. *Kritika*, no. 4 (April 1966). Reprinted in *Tanulmányút a Pávakertbe*. Budapest: Magvető, 1969.
______. A fekete négyzettől a pszeudo kockáig. Kisérlet a Kelet-európai avantgarde tipológiájának megalapozására [From the Black Square to the Pseudo-Cube: An Attempt to Establish a Typology of the Eastern-European Avant-Garde]. In Géza Porneczky, *A Korszak mint műalkotás*. Budapest: Corvina, 1988.
Petrák, Katalin, and György Milei, eds. *A magyar Tanácsköztársaság művelődéspolitikája. Válogatott rendeletek, dokumentumok, cikkek.* [Cultural Policy of the Hungarian Soviet Republic. Selected Decrees, Documents, Articles]. Budapest: Gondolat, 1959.
Pogány, Ö. Gábor. *A magyar festészet forradalmárai* [The Revolutionaries of Hungarian Art]. *Ars Mundi* X. Budapest: Officina, n.d.
Pór, Bertalan. A magyar Tanácsköztársaság plakátjai [Posters of the Hungarian Soviet Republic]. *Magyar Grafika* 3, no. 5 (1959): 324-31.
Ruttkay, György. Egy aktivista festő vallomásai [Testimony of an Activist Painter]. *Irodalmi Szemle* no. 1 (1972): 42.
Sarkadi, E. Gondolatok a "Nyolcak" művészcsoport tudománytörténeti értékeléséhez [Thoughts on the Intellectual Historical Assessment of "The Eight"]. *Janus Pannonius Múzeum Évkönyve* 25 (1980): 337-49.
Sőni, Pál. *Avantgard sugárzás* [Avant-garde radiation]. Bukarest: Kriterion, 1973.
Subotič, Irina. Zenitizmus és avantgarde [Zenitism and Avant-Garde]. *Művészet* 35, no. 5 (February 1984): 36-39. Includes material on Hungarian-Yugoslav avant-garde connections.
______. *Az avantgarde Jugosláviában. A Zenit Köre 1921-1926* [The Avant-Garde in Yugoslavia: The Zenit Circle 1921-1926]. Budapest: Hungarian National Gallery, 1986. Exhibition catalogue.
Szabó, György. *A futurizmus* [Futurism]. Budapest: Gondolat, 1962. Includes material on futurist elements in Hungarian art and literature.
______. Az "Egység" elméleti platformja [The Theoretical Platform of *Egység*]. In Miklós Szabolcsi and László Illés, eds., *Tanulmányok a magyar szocialista irodalom történetébol* [Studies on the History of Hungarian Socialist Literature]. Budapest: Akadémiai Kiadó, 1962.
Szabó, Júlia. *Magyar rajzművészet 1890-1919* [Hungarian Graphic Art]. Budapest: Corvina, 1969.
______. *A magyar aktivizmus története* [History of Hungarian Activism]. Budapest: Akadémiai, 1971. Includes a summary of the text in French, which is reprinted in *Kunst in Ungarn, 1900-1950*.
______. Az 1922-es berlini szovjet-orosz kiállítás és a magyar avantgarde [The 1922 Berlin Soviet Exhibition and the Hungarian Avant-Garde], *Ars Hungarica* 1 (1973). Includes a summary in German.
______. ed. *Magyar Aktivizmus/Hungarian Activism*. A Janus Pannonius Múzeum művészeti kiadványai 16. Pécs: Janus Pannonius Múzeum, 1973. Bilingual Hungarian-English exhibition catalogue.
______. Kaposvár és a XX. századi magyar képzőművészet, 1902-1927 [Kaposvár and Twentieth Century Hungarian Art, 1902-1927]. *Művészet* 16, no. 10 (1975): 24-25.
______. *A magyar aktivizmus művészete, 1915-1927* [The Art of Hungarian Activism 1915-1927]. Budapest: Corvina, 1981. The most important monograph to date on the Hungarian avant-garde.
______. Közép-kelet-európai avantgarde (1905-1930) [East-Central European Avant-garde (1905-1930)]. *Muvészet* 35, no. 6 (June 1984): 2-5.
Szabolcsi, Miklós. *Jel és kiáltás. az Avantgarde művészet kérdései*. [Sign and Cry. The Issues of Avant-Garde Art]. Budapest, 1971.
Szabolcsi, Miklós and László Illés, eds. *Tanulmányok a magyar szocialista irodalom történetéből* [Studies on the History of Hungarian Socialist Literature]. Budapest: Akadémiai, 1962. Includes an article by György Szabó on *Egység*.
Szélpál, Árpád. *Forró hamu* [Hot Ashes]. Budapest: Magvető, 1984. Memoirs.
Szinyei Merse, Anna and Margit Egry, eds. *20. századi magyar festészet és szobrászat* [20th century Hungarian Painting and Sculpture]. Budapest: Képzőművészeti, 1986. Catalogue of the permanent collection of the Hungarian National Gallery.
Tiszay, Andor. A Magyar Tanácsköztársaság plakátművészete [Poster Art of the Hungarian Soviet Republic]. *Magyar Könyvszemle* no. 2 (1959): 203-8.
Vágel, László. Baloldali viták az avantgarderól [Left-wing Debates about the Avant-Garde]. *Új Symposion* (Újvidék/Novi Sad) no. 11 (1975): 122-23.
Zádor, Anna, ed., *Magyar művészet 1800-1945*. Budapest, 1962.

Primary Literature

Ady, Endre. *Az élet szobra. Ady Endre képzőművészeti írásai* [The Statue of Life. Endre Ady's Writings on Art]. Edited by Lajos Varga. Budapest: Corvina, 1977.
Bajkay, Éva, ed. *A konstruktivizmus: Válogatás a mozgalom dokumentumaiból* [Constructivism: Selections From the Documents of the Movement.] Budapest: Gondolat, 1979. This anthology includes the basic texts of Hungarian Constructivism, all of them omitted from Stephen Bann's similar English-language anthology *The Tradition of Constructivism* (New York: Viking, 1974).
Béládi, Miklós, and Béla Pomogáts, eds. *Jelzés a világba. A magyar irodalmi avantgarde válogatott dokumentumai* [A Message to the World. Selected Documents of the Hungarian Literary Avant-Garde]. Budapest: Magvető, 1988.
Botka, Ferenc, ed. *Független Szemle (1921-1923), Kékmadár (1923) Repertórium* [Index to Független Szemle (1921-1923), Kékmadár (1923)]. Budapest: Petőfi Irodalmi Múzeum, 1979.
Dienes, László. *Sejtelme egy földindulásnak. Kritikai irások (1921-1931)* [Stirrings of an Earthquake. Critical Writings (1921-1931)]. Bucharest: Kritérion, 1977.
Forgács, Éva, ed. *Kállai Ernő. Művészet veszélyes csillagzat alatt. Válogatott cikkek, tanulmányok.* [Art Under Dangerous Constellations: Selected Articles and Studies.] With introduction by the editor. Budapest: Corvina, 1981.
Fülep, Lajos. *A művészet forradalmától a nagy forradalomig* [From the Revolution in Art to the Great Revolution]. Árpád Tímár, ed., 2 vols. Budapest: Magvető, 1974.
Galambos, Lajos. *A bécsi magyar-nyelvű sajtó repertóriuma* [Index of the Viennese Hungarian-language Press]. Budapest: Unpublished manuscript in the Széchényi Library, n.d.
Gulácsy, Lajos. A Virágünnep vége [End of the Holiday of Flowers]. In Judit Szabadi, ed., *Collected Writings*. Budapest: Szépirodalmi, 1989.
Hevesy, Iván. *Válogatott tanulmányok* [Selected Essays]. Budapest: Magvető, 1979.
Illés, Ilona. *"A Tett" 1915-1916, "Ma" 1916-1925, "2 × 2" 1922, Repertórium* [Index to "A Tett", "Ma" and "2 × 2"]. A Petőfi Irodalmi Múzeum Bibliográfiai Füzetei B. Sorozat 6. Budapest: Petőfi Irodalmi Múzeum, 1975.
Kálmán, Mrs. László. *"Dokumentum" 1926-1927, "Munka" 1928-1929 Repertórium* [Index to "Dokumentum" and "Munka"]. A Petőfi Irodalmi Múzeum Bibliográfiai Füzetei B. Sorozat 1. Budapest: Petőfi Irodalmi Múzeum, 1972.
Kassák, Lajos. *Egy ember élete* [One Man's Life]. 2 vols. Budapest: Magvető, 1983. Parts of this superb autobiography, dealing with Kassák's life up to 1919, have been published in English in *The New Hungarian Quarterly* 6, no. 19 (1965): 35-46 and 28, no. 106 (Summer 1987): 101-16.
______. Az én hivatásom az, hogy tényekre világitsak rá [My Calling Is to Shed Light on the Facts]. Text of an interview conducted by Áron Tóbiás. *A Petőfi Irodalmi Múzeum Évkönyve* 8 (1969-70): 65-77.
______. *Csavargók, alkotók. Válogatott irodalmi tanulmányok* [Hobos, Creators. Selected Literary Essays]. Budapest: Magvető, 1975.
______. *Éljünk a mi idônkben. Írások a képzőművészetről* [Let Us Live in Our Time. Writings on Art.] Budapest: Magvető Könyvkiadó, 1978.
Kovács, János. *Periszkóp, 1925-1926. Antológia* [*Periszkóp* 1925-1926. Anthology]. Bukarest: Kritérion, 1979.
Lakatos, Éva. *Magyar Írás (1921-1927) Repertórium* [Index to *Magyar Irás* (1921-1927)]. Budapest: Petőfi Irodalmi Múzeum, 1973.
Ma [Today]. Budapest and Vienna (1916-1925). Facsimile edition: Budapest: Akadémiai, 1969. One issue (vol. 10, no. 2, 1925) was omitted, it was reissued by the Pesti Műhely (Budapest), in 1983.

Mácza, János. *Legendák és tények. Tanulmányok a XX. század művészettörténetéhez* [Legends and Facts. Studies on Twentieth Century Art History.] Compiled, edited, and provided with a postscript by Júlia Szabó. Budapest: Corvina, 1972.

Moholy-Nagy, László. *A festéktől a fényig.* Edited and with notes by Erzsébet Sugár. Bucharest: Kritérion, 1979. This compendium of Moholy-Nagy's writings on art includes the material he published in the Cluj-Kolozsvár journal *Korunk*, edited by Gábor Gaál during the thirties, some of it not published elsewhere.

Németh, Andor. *A szélén lehajtva* [Folded at the Edge]. Budapest: Magvető, 1973. An anthology of the critical writings of this critic of the avant-garde.

Palasovszky, Ödön. *Az új stáció* [The New Station]. Budapest: Manifesztum Kiadás, 1922. Facsimile: Kecskemét: Katona József Múzeum, 1980. Edited by Pál Bánszky, with an introduction by Júlia Szabó and an English translation by Oliver A.I. Botar.

———. *A lényegretörő színház* [The Theatre That Gets to the Heart of the Matter]. Budapest: Szépirodalmi, 1980.

Perneczky, Géza, ed. *Kortársak szemével. Írások a magyar művészetről* [With the Eyes of Contemporaries. Writings on Hungarian Art]. Budapest: Corvina, 1967. An anthology of 20th century Hungarian writings on art, including the avant-garde.

———. A Nyolcak és aktivisták köre, avagy a magyar avantgard [The Circle of The Eight and the Activists, or the Hungarian Avant-garde]. In *Tanulmányút a Pávakertbe. Magvető 1969, 27-53.*

Rippl-Rónai József emlékezései [Memoirs of József Rippl-Rónai]. Edited by Zoltán Farkas. Budapest: Szépirodalmi, 1957.

Tamás, Aladár. *A 100%.* Budapest: Akadémiai, 1964.

Tüskés, Tibor. *A Krónika repertóriuma* [Index to *Krónika*]. Pécs, 1978.

Literature on Individuals

Aurél Bernáth

Frankó, A. Bernáth Aurél "Graphik"-mappája 1922-ből [Aurél Bernáth's "Graphik" Album of 1922]. *Művészettörténeti Értesítő* 32, no. 1-2 (1983): 77-84.

Genthon, István. Bernáth Aurél. *Ars Hungarica* 1. Budapest: Bisztrai Farkas Ferencz Kiadása, 1932.

Kállai, Ernő. Bernáth Aurél újabb munkái [New Works by Aurél Bernáth] *Magyar Művészet* (1929): 241-52. Reprinted in Forgács, ed., 224-28.

Pataky, Dénes. *Bernáth Aurél.* Budapest: Corvina, 1972. Includes summaries in French, English, and German.

Sándor Bortnyik

Aradi, Nóra. Bortnyik Sándorról [On Sándor Bortnyik]. *Művészet* 9, no. 11 (November 1968): 14-21.

Bajkay-Rosch, Éva. Bortnyik Sándor köszöntése [Salutation of Sándor Bortnyik]. *Művészet* 14, no. 4 (April 1973): 16-18.

Bán, András. Bortnyik - utószó egy életmuhöz [Bortnyik - Afterword to an Oeuvre]. *Művészet* 77. Budapest: Corvina, 1978: 78-79.

Borbély, László. Bortnyik Sándor korai művészete. [The Early Art of Sándor Bortnyik] *Művészettörténeti Értesítő* 18, no. 1 (1969): 46-73.

———. *Bortnyik.* Budapest: Corvina, 1971. This small book is the only monograph to have appeared on Bortnyik.

Kiss, Sándor. Bortnyik Sándor plakátművészete [Sándor Bortnyik's Art of the Poster]. *Művészet* 4, no. 12 (December 1969): 7-11.

József Csáky

Csáky, József. *Emlékek a modern művészet nagy évtizedéből, 1904-1914* [Memoirs of the Great Decade of Modern Art, 1904-1914]. Budapest: Corvina, 1972.

Béla Czóbel

Borghida, István. Czóbel és Ziffer [Czóbel and Ziffer]. *Ars Hungarica* 5, no. 2 (1977): 341-44.

Czóbel Béla. With an essay by Lajos Kassák. Budapest: Nemzeti Szalon, 1958.

Genthon, István. *Czóbel.* Budapest, 1961.

Kállai, Ernő. *Czóbel Béla.* Ars Hungarica Series. Budapest: Bisztray Farkas Ferencz Kiadása, 1934.

———. Czóbel Béla Művészete [The Art of Béla Czóbel] *Magyar Művészet* 2 (1933): 577-64. Reprinted in Forgács, ed., 251-55.

Phillip, Clarisse. Czóbel Béla köszöntése [Salutation of Béla Czóbel]. *Művészet* 14, no. 1 (Jaunary 1973): 27-31.

Perneczky, Géza: Czóbel. In *Tanulmányút a Pávakertbe*, Magvető, 1969, 255-58.

Szíj, Béla. Czóbel Béla Múzeum Szentendrén [Béla Czóbel Museum in Szentendre]. *Mvészet* 25, no.1 (January 1984): 33-41.

Valéria Dénes

Dénes, Zsófia. *Galimberti Sándor és Dénes Valéria.* Budapest: Corvina, 1979.

Zolnay, László. A Galimberti házaspár művészete [Art of the Galimberti Couple]. *Művészettörténeti Értesítő* 23, no. 4 (1974): 318-22.

Gyula Derkovits

Artinger Imre. Derkovits Gyula. *Ars Hungarica* 6, 1934.

Derkovits, Gyuláné. *Mi ketten. Emlékezés Derkovits Gyulára* [We Two. Remembering Gyula Derkovits]. Second edition. Budapest: Képzőművészeti Alap, 1977.

Kállai, Ernő. A Dózsa-sorozat fametszetei [The Dózsa woodcuts]. Budapest: Gondolat, 1936. Reprinted in Forgács, ed., 222-23.

Körner, Éva. *Derkovits Gyula.* Budapest: Corvina, 1968. The definitive monograph on the artist.

Perneczky, Géza: A szőlőevő. Egy Derkovits-kép kompozíciója ["The Grape Eater": The Composition of a Derkovits Painting]. In *Tanulmányút a Pávakertbe.* Magvető, 1969, 53-77.

Szabó, Júlia. Derkovits és a magyar műkritika a két világháború között [Derkovits and Hungarian Critical Opinion between the Two World Wars]. *Művészettörténeti Értesítő* 15, no. 1 (1966): 40-51.

———. Derkovits Gyula ifjúkora és a Magyar Tanácsköztársaság [The Youth of Gyula Derkovits and the Hungarian Soviet Republic]. *Művészet* 9, no. 11 (November 1968): 26-28.

József Egry

Farkas, Zoltán. *Egry.* Budapest: Corvina, 1969.

Fodor, András, and Júlia Szabó, eds. *Egry József arcképe. Egry József írásai. Írások Egry Józsefről* [Portrait of József Egry. His writings. Writings about Him]. Budapest: Magyar Helikon, 1980.

Kállai, Ernő. Egry József. In Forgács, ed., 284-86. Originally published in German under pseud. Pester Lloyd, May 11, 1941.

Láncz, Sándor. *Egry.* Budapest: Képzőművészeti Alap, 1980.

———. A sugárzó tér [Space Radiating]. *Művészet* 24, no. 12 (December 1983): 12-15.

———. A kezdettől a kiteljesedésig [From the Beginning to Completion]. *Művészet* 24, no. 12 (December 1983): 6-11.

Béni Ferenczy

Illyés, Mária. Ferenczy Béni: a keresés évei (1917-1925) [Béni Ferenczy: The Years of Searching (1917-1925)]. *Művészettörténeti Értesítő* 31, no. 1 (1982): 34-40.

Alfréd (Fréd) Forbát

Mezei, Zsuzsa. Forbát Alfréd. Unpublished manuscript. Stockholm, n.d.

Galambos, Ferenc. Forbát Alfréd halálára [On the Death of Fréd Forbát]. *Művészet* 13, no. 9 (September 1972): 11.

Passuth, Krisztina. Forbát Alfréd (1897-1972). *Magyar Építőművészet* no. 2 (1973): 50-51.

Lajos Fülep

Tímár, Árpád, ed. *Fülep Lajos emlékkönyv. Cikkek, tanulmányok Fülep Lajos életéről és munkásságáról* [Memorial Volume for Lajos Fülep. Articles and Studies on Lajos Fülep's Life and Work]. Budapest: Magvető, 1985.

Jenő Gábor

Gábor Jenő. Pécs: A Janus Panonnius Múzeum Kiadványai 4, 1971.

Sándor Galimberti

Dénes, Zsófia. Galimberti Sándor és Dénes Valéria. Budapest: Corvina, 1979.

Zolnay, László. A Galimberti házaspár művészete [Art of the Galimberti Couple]. *Művészettörténeti Értesítő* 23, no. 4 (1974): 318-22.

Lajos Gulácsy

Szabadi, Judit. *Gulácsy.* Budapest: Corvina, 1969. Includes summaries in English, French, and German.

———, and Márta Kovalovszky. *Gulácsy Lajos emlékkiállítás* [Lajos Gulácsy Retrospective]. Székesfehérvár: István Király Múzeum, 1966.

———. Művészet és ábránd a századfordulón [Art and Fantasy at the Turn of the Century]. *Művészet* 23, no. 12 (December 1982): 28-29.

Szij, Béla. *Gulácsy Lajos.* Budapest: Corvina, 1979.

———. Gulácsy Lajos műveinek kiállításai 1986-ban [Lajos Gulácsy's Exhibitions in 1986]. *Művészet* 8, no. 3 (March 1987): 16-22.

Béla Hegedüs

Bajomi Lázár, Endre. Kisérlet Hegedűs Béla pályájának rekontstruálására [An Attempt at Reconstructing the Career of Béla Hegedűs]. *Művészettörténeti Értesítő* 31, no. 3 (1982): 213-16.

Körner, Éva. Függelék Bajomi Lázár Endre "Kísérlet Hegedűs Béla pályájának rekontstruálására" c. cikkéhez [Appendix to Endre Lázár Bajomi's article "An Attempt at Reconstructing the Career of Béla Hegedűs"]. *Művészettörténeti Értesítő* 31, no. 3 (1982): 216-19.

Iván Hevesy

Kozocsa, Sándor. Hevesy Iván élete és irodalmi munkássága [Iván Hevesy's Life and Literary Activity]. *Fotóművészet* 9, no. 1-2 (1966).

Takács, József. Review of Iván Hevesy's *Az új művészetért* [For the New Art]. *Művészet* 20, no. 8 (August 1979): 44-45.

Vilmos Huszár

Bajkay-Rosch, Éva. *Huszár Vilmos*. Budapest: Corvina, 1983.

Dévényi, Iván. Huszár Vilmosról halálának 10. évfordulója alkalmával [On Vilmos Huszár on the Occasion of the Tenth Anniversary of this Death]. *Magyar Építőművészet*, no. 6 (1970).

Forgács, Éva. Huszár Vilmos esete a De Stijl mozgalommal [Vilmos Husszár's Affair with the De Stijl Group]. *Kritika*, no. 1 (1986).

Gergely, Mariann. *Huszár Vilmos (1884-1960) Festő, Tervező*. Budapest: Magyar Nemzeti Galéria, 1985. Bilingual Hungarian-English exhibition catalogue.

Béla Kádár

Bedő, Rudolf. Kádár Béla (1877-1958). *Művészet* 12, no. 9 (September 1971): 34.

Kádár Béla. Budapest: Magyar Nemzeti Galéria, 1971. Exhibition catalogue.

Sümegi, György. Kádár Béla önéletrajzi vallomása [Béla Kádár's Autobiographical Statement]. *Művészet* 18, no. 11-12 (November-December 1987): 56-61.

Ernő Kállai

Forgács, Éva. Kállai Ernő és a konstruktivizmus. [Ernő Kállai and Constructivism]. *Ars Hungarica* 3, no. 2 (1975): 277-94. Includes a summary in German.

———. Kállai Ernő és a vizualitás [Ernő Kállai and visuality]. *Filmvilág*, no. 7 (1985).

———. Kritikus és művészeti író [A Critic and a Writer on Art]. *Kritika*, no. 11 (1979).

———, ed. *Ernő Kállai. Művészet veszélyes csillagzat allatt.* See listing under primary literature.

Kállai Ernő emlékezete [Remembrance of Ernő Kállai]. Budapest: Óbuda Galéria, 1982. Exhibition catalogue.

Nagy, Zoltán. Konstruktivizmus és bioromantika [Constructivism and Bioromanticism]. *Művészet* 23, no. 5 (May 1982): 34-38.

Szabó, Júlia. Kállai Ernő szellemi hagyatéka [Ernő Kállai's Intellectual Bequest]. *Művészet* 16, no. 8 (August 1975).

———. Kállai Ernő idézése [Quoting Ernő Kállai]. *Művészet* 24, no. 9 (September 1983): 51-53.

Lajos Kassák

Ácsay, Judit. Szellemidézés. Állandó Kassák-kiállítás Érsekújváron [Conjuring up a Ghost: Permanent Exhibition of Kassák's Works in Érsekújvár (Nové Zamký, Czechoslovakia)]. *Művészet* 28 (August 1987): 53.

Bori, Imre and Éva Körner. *Kassák irodalma és festészete* [Kassák's Literature and Painting]. Budapest: Magvető, 1967.

Csaplár Ferenc. Kassák és a Korunk [Kassák and *Korunk*]. *Irodalomtörténet*, no. 2 (1977): 406-14.

———. *Kassák Emlékmúzeum* [Kassák Memorial Museum]. Budapest: Kassák Emlékmúzeum, 1976. Brochure of the institution.

———, ed. *Magam törvénye szerint. Tanulmányok és dokumentumok Kassák Lajosról* [According to my Own Laws. Studies and Documents on Lajos Kassák]. Budapest: Petőfi Irodalmi Múzeum and Múzsák Közművelődési Kiadó, 1987. Although this publication focuses on Kassák's literary output, it provides important material on his art and general activities as well, including documentation published for the first time.

———. *Kassák Körei*. Budapest: Szépirodalmi, 1987. *Filmkultúra* 23, no. 8 (August 1987). Kassák issue.

Gáspár, Endre. *Kassák Lajos: Az ember és munkája* [Lajos Kassák. The Man and his Work]. Vienna: Verlag Julius Fischer, 1924.

György, Péter. Egy szétszóródott életmű [A Dispersed Oeuvre]. *Művészet* 27 (April 1986): 12-15.

———. Kassák 1926 után [Kassák after 1926]. *Valóság* (August 1986).

Haulisch, Lenke. Kassák és a fotó [Kassák and Photography]. *Fotóművészet* no. 3 (1967).

Hegyi, Loránd. A tárgynélküliség értelmezése Kassák képarchitektúrájában [The Interpretation of Non-Objectivity in Kassák's *Képarchitektúra*]. *Művészettörténeti Értesítő* 30, no. 3 (1981): 194-199. A summary in English was published in the *New Hungarian Quarterly* 23, no. 88 (1982): 170-171.

Illés, Ilona, and Ernő Taxner, eds. *Kortársak Kassák Lajosról* [Contemporaries on Lajos Kassák]. Budapest: A Petőfi Irodalmi Múzeum és a Népművelési Propaganda Iroda közös kiadványa, 1975.

Kállai, Ernő. [pseud. Mátyás Péter]. Kassák Lajos. *Ma*, 1921. Reprinted in Forgács, ed.

Kassák emlékkiállítás. Debrecen: Kossuth Lajos Tudományegyetem, 1969. With an essay by Géza Perneczky in Hungarian, English, and German.

Kassák Lajos kiállítása [Lajos Kassák's Exhibition]. Budapest: Petőfi Irodalmi Múzeum, 1973.

Kassák és Párizs. Budapest: Kassák Múzeum, 1990. Exhibition catalogue.

Kassák Lajos 1887-1967. Budapest: Magyar Nemzeti Galéria and Petőfi Irodalmi Múzeum, 1987. This is the catalogue of the major retrospective exhibition of Kassák's works held on the centenary of his birth. The publication includes the most extensive catalogue of Kassák's works published to date (in Hungarian and English), as well as articles on Kassák's art by Éva Körner, Árpád Mezei, Tomáš Štraus, Géza Perneczky, Loránd Hegyi, Gábor Andrási, Oliver A.I. Botar, Éva Bajkay-Rosch, Júlia Szabó, Miklós Peternák, Ferenc Csaplár, and Péter György.

Lengyel, Lajos. Kassák a tipográfus [Kassák the Typographer]. *Új Irás*, no. 3 (1967).

———. Kassák Lajosról [On Lajos Kassák]. *Képzőművészeti Almanach*. Budapest, 1969.

Mucsi, András, ed. *Kassák Lajos emlékkiállítás* [Lajos Kassák Retrospective Exhibition]. Szentendre: Szentendrei Képtár, 1985. Exhibition catalogue.

Nádass, József, ed. *Kassák Lajos hatvanadik születésnapjára*. Budapest, 1947.

Pátkai, Ervin, ed. Kassák issue of *Magyar Műhely/Atelier Hongrois* (Paris) (1 December 1965).

Perneczky, Géza. *Kassák Lajos emlékkiállításának katalógusa* [Catalogue of Lajos Kassák's Memorial Exhibition]. Székesfehérvár: István Király Múzeum. Exhibition catalogue.

Rónay, György. *Kassák Lajos*. Budapest: Szépirodalmi, 1971.

Rózsa, Endre. Kassák Lajos az ismeretlen festő [Kassák the Unknown Painter], *Művészet* 77. Budapest: Corvina Kiadó, 1978: 72-77.

Sik, Csaba. *Kassák két évtizede*. Budapest: Helikon, 1987.

Sinkovits, Péter. Kassák a mi időnkben [Kassák in Our Time]. *Művészet* 27 (April 1986): 8-11.

———. Művek és kétségek [Works and Doubts]. *Művészet* 28 (August 1987): 26-29. A favorable review of the centenary Kassák retrospective exhibition at the Magyar Nemzeti Galéria in 1987.

Standeisky, É. Kassák Annája [Kassák's Anna]. *Irodalomtörténeti közlemények* no. 5-6 (February 1986).

Takács, József. Kassák és az olasz futurizmus [Kassák and Italian Futurism]. *Filológiai Közlöny* no. 2 (1980): 236-40.

Új Írás 27, no. 5 (May 1987). Kassák issue.

Vadas, József. *Kassák a konstruktőr* [Kassák the Constructor]. Budapest: Gondolat Könyvkiadó, 1979.

Alfréd Kemény

Szilágyi, Jolán. Emlékezés Kemény Alfrédre [Remembering Alfréd Kemény], *Művészet* 4, no. 7 (July 1963): 24-25.

György Kepes

Bodri, Ferenc. Magyar művészek a nagyvilágban: Kepes György - Cambridge (USA) [Hungarian Artists in the Wide World: György Kepes - Cambridge (USA)]. *Művészet* 11, no. 10 (October 1970): 9-11.

———. Kepes György új szintézise [György Kepes' New Synthesis]. *Művészet* 18, no. 2 (Feburary 1977): 38-39.

Körner, Éva. Beszélgetés Kepes Györggyel [Conversation with György Kepes]. *Kritika* 1 (January 1980): 18-19.

Károly Kernstok

Dévényi, Iván. Kernstok Károly életútja [Károly Kernstok's Career]. *Jelenkor,* no. 5 (1960): 110-17.

Goda, Gábor. Emlékezés Kernstok Károlyra [Remembrance of Károly Kernstok]. *Művészet* 9, no. 11 (November 1968): 4-9.

Horváth, Béla. Megjegyzések Dévényi Iván "Kernstok Károly életútja" című cikkéhez [Remarks on Iván Dévényi's Article "Károly Kernstok's Career"]. *Művészettörténeti Értesítő* 10, no. 1 (1961): 225-30.

_____. Kernstok Károly: 1919. *Művészettörténeti Értesítő* 19, no. 1 (1970): 55-61.

_____. Kernstok Károly Komárom megyében [Károly Kernstok in Komárom County]. *Művészet* 20, no. 5 (May 1979): 30-33.

Kállai, Ernő. Kernstok Károly. Reprinted in Forgács, ed., 278-79. Originally in German as "Karl Kernstok (1813-1940)," June 11, 1940.

Körmendy, András. *Kernstok Károly.* Ars Hungarica 16. Budapest: Bisztray Farkas Ferencz Kiadása, 1936.

Nagy, Zoltán. Kernstok-kiállítás Szombathelyen [Kernstok Exhibition in Szombathely]. *Művészet* 23, no. 10 (October 1982): 28-32.

János Kmetty

Kállai, Ernő: Kmetty János újabb képei [New Pictures by János Kmetty]. Introduction to his exhibition in Budapest, November 1937. Reprinted in Forgács, ed., 248-50.

Kmetty, János. *Festő voltam és vagyok* [I Was and Am a Painter]. Budapest: Corvina, 1976.

Kmetty János emlékkiállítás [János Kmetty Commemorative Exhibition]. Budapest: Műcsarnok, 1978.

Ráth, Zsolt. Nézzük meg együtt Kmetty János Önarckép almával című képét [Let Us Take a Look at János Kmetty's "Self Portrait with Apple"]. *Művészet* 17, no. 3 (March 1976): 40-41.

Ury, Ibolya. *Kmetty János.* Budapest: Képzőművészeti Alap, 1979.

Dezső Korniss

Hegyi, Loránd. Korniss Dezső első alkotói korszaka, 1923-1933 [Dezső Korniss' First Creative Period]. *Ars Hungarica* 4, no. 1 (1976): 89-122. Includes a summary in English.

_____. *Korniss Dezső.* Budapest: Képzőművészeti Kiadó, 1982. Includes a summary in English.

Körner, Éva. *Korniss Dezső.* Budapest: Képzőművészeti Alap Kiadóvállalata, 1971.

Művészet. Korniss issue. 15, no. 11 (November 1974).

Nagy, Zoltán. Teljességvágytól a transzcendenciáig [From a Desire for Wholeness to Transcendence]. *Művészet* 24, no. 8 (August 1983): 36-38.

Anna Lesznai

Gergely, Tibor, ed. *Lesznai képeskönyv.* Budapest: Corvina, 1978.

Szabadi, Judit. *Lesznai Anna.* Budapest: 1978.

Ödön Márffy

Kállai, Ernő. Márffy Ödön újabb munkái [New Works by Ödön Márffy]. *Ars Una* (April 1924): 265-71. Reprinted in Forgács, ed., 209-12.

Papp, Júlia. Márffy Ödön kiállíása a Vigadó Galériában [Ödön Márffy's Exhibition in the Vigadó Gallery]. *Művészet* 30, no. 6 (June 1984): 61-64.

Passuth, Krisztina. *Márffy Ödön.* Budapest: Corvina, 1978. Includes summaries in French, English, and German.

Zolnay, László. *Márffy.* Budapest, 1966.

János (Hans) Máttis Teutsch

Bodri, Ferenc. Máttis Teutsch János. *Művészet* 12 (October 1971): 21.

Csaplár, Ferenc. *Máttis Teutsch.* Budapest: Kassák Emlékmúzeum, 1983. Exhibition catalogue.

Máttis Teutsch János linoleum-albuma [The Linocut Album of János Máttis Teutsch]. Budapest: *Ma* Edition, 1917. (Facsimile, Budapest: Pesti Műhely-Forma 5, 1983)

Nagy, Zoltán. Lélekvirágok. Máttis Teutsch kiállítás és album [Flowers of the Spirit. Máttis Teutsch Exhibition and Album]. *Művészet* 24, no. 12 (December 1983): 26-31.

Szabó, Júlia. *Máttis Teutsch János.* Budapest: Corvina, 1983.

László Moholy-Nagy

Apró, Ferenc. Moholy-Nagy László és Gergely Sándor 1919-es szegedi kiállítása [László Moholy-Nagy's and Sándor Gergely's 1919 Exhibition in Szeged]. *Művészet* 16, no. 3 (1975).

Beke, László. *Moholy-Nagy László munkássága* [The Oeuvre of László Moholy-Nagy]. Budapest: Corvina, 1980.

Bodri, Ferenc. Moholy-Nagy László. *Nagyvilág* no. 1 (1971): 723-35.

Czigány, Magda. A visszatért űrhajós [The Returned Astronaut]. In *Néző a képben* [Viewer in the Picture]. London: Szepsi Csombor Kör, 1973.

Kállai, Ernő [Mátyás Péter, pseud.]. Moholy-Nagy. *Ma,* 1921. Reprinted in Forgács, ed., 46-47.

Kántor, Lajos. Moholy-Nagy László és a *Korunk* kapcsolata [László Moholy-Nagy's Relations with the Journal *Korunk*]. *Valóság* (December 1976).

Keserű, Katalin. Moholy-Nagy László első világháborús rajzainak kiállítása [The Exhibition of László Moholy-Nagy's First World War Drawings]. *Művészet* 15, no. 8 (August 1974): 45.

Kocsis, Botond, ed. *Moholy-Nagy László első világháborús rajzainak kiállítása* [Exhibition of László Moholy-Nagy's Drawings of the First World War]. Introduction by Júlia Szabó. Hatvan: Hatvan Városi Múzeum, 1974. Exhibition catalogue.

Mihály, Ida F. *Moholy-Nagy László kiállítás* [László Moholy-Nagy's Exhibition]. Budapest: Magyar Nemzeti Galéria, 1975. Exhibition catalogue.

Pap, Gyula. Moholy-Nagy László kiállítása ürügyén [On the Pretext of László Moholy-Nagy's Exhibition]. *Ars Hungarica* 5,no. 1 (1977): 147-50.

Passuth, Krisztina, Moholy-Nagy László. *Nagyvilág,* no. 2 (1976).

Perneczky, Géza. Moholy Nagy kerestetik. Megjegyzések a fehérvári Moholy Nagy kiállítás után [Wanted: Moholy-Nagy. Notes on the Moholy-Nagy Exhibition in Székesfehérvár]. *Kritika* 7, no. 12 (December 1969): 28-32.

Szabó, Júlia. Piros kolllázs Moholy-Nagy László kiállításán [Red Collage at László Moholy-Nagy's Exhibition]. *Művészet* 17, no. 4 (1976): 20-23.

Farkas (Wolfgang) Molnár

Mezei, Ottó. *Molnár Farkas* Budapest: Műszaki, 1987.

Molnár Farkas munkái, 1923-1933-ig [Farkas Molnár's Works, 1923-1933] Új Építés 1. A Magyar Műhely Szövetség Könyvei. With introduction by László Moholy-Nagy. Budapest: Egyetemi Nyomda, 1933.

József Nemes Lampérth

Csaplár, Ferenc. *Nemes Lampérth.* Budapest: Kassák Emlékmúzeum, 1984.

Forgács, Éva: Nemes Lampérth József. *Jelenkor,* (Pécs, October 1989): 960-65.

Mezei, Ottó. Nemes Lampérth József grafikai stílusa [József Nemes Lampérth's Graphic Style]. *Művészettörténeti Értesítő* 31, no. 3 (1982): 207-12.

_____. *Nemes Lampérth József.* Budapest: Corvina, 1984. Includes summaries in French, German, and English.

Molnár, Zsuzsa. *Nemes Lampérth.* Budapest: Corvina, 1967.

Nemes Lampérth József emlékkiállítása. Budapest: Magyar Nemzeti Galéria, 1963. Exhibition catalogue.

Dezső Orbán

Bellák, Gábor, and László Szabó. *Orbán Dezső festőművész* (Ausztrália) gyűjteményes kiállítása [The Painter Dezso Orbán's (Australia) Retrospective Exhibition]. Budapest: Magyar Nemzeti Galéria, 1984.

_____. Orbán Dezső: Asztalnál ülő munkások [Dezső Orbán: "Workers Sitting at a Table"]. *Művészet* 25, no. 10 (October 1984): 42-43.

Passuth, Krisztina. *Orbán Dezső.* Budapest: Corvina Kiadó, 1977. Includes an English summary.

Gyula Pap

Mihály, Ida F. *Pap Gyula.* Budapest: Magyar Nemzeti Galéria, 1979. Exhibition catalogue with a chronology in German.

Haulisch, Lenke. *Pap Gyula.* Budapest: Corvina, 1974.

Ödön Palasovszky

Szabó, Júlia. Az új stáció. Palasovszky Ödön művészete [The New Station. The Art of Ödön Palasovszky]. *Művészet* 22, no. 2 (February 1981): 42-45.

Vilmos Perlrott Csaba

Benedek, Katalin. Perlrott Csaba Vilmos négy grafikájáról [On Four Drawings by Vilmos Perlrott Csaba]. *Művészet* 27, no. 11-12 (November-December 1986): 53-55.

Bornemissza, Géza. *Perlrott Csaba Vilmos.* Budapest, 1929.

Dévényi, Iván. Perlrott Csaba Vilmos. *Művészet* 11, no. 8 (August 1970): 9.

László Péri

Czigány, Magda. Szocialista realizmus a számuzetésben [Socialist Realism in

Exile]. In *Néző a képben* [Viewer in the Picture]. London: Szepsi Csombor Kör, 1973.

Bertalan Pór

Oelmacher, Anna. *Pór Bertalan*. Budapest: Corvina, 1980. Includes summaries in French, English, and German.

Pogány, Ö. Gábor. Pór Bertalan (1880-1964). *Művészet* 11, no. 10 (October 1970): 4-7.

Z. P. A. "Ki látott engem?" Az utolsó fejezet Pór Bertalan életregényébol ["Who Has Seen Me?" The Last Chapter of Bertalan Pór's Life Story]. *Művészet* 13, no. 4 (April 1972): 7-8.

József Rippl-Rónai

Aknai, Tamás. *Rippl-Rónai*. Budapest, 1971.

Balogh, Sára. Rippl-Rónai iparművészeti elvei és tevékenysége kiadatlan levelei nyomán [Rippl-Rónai's Applied Art on the Basis of his Letters]. *Művészettörténeti Értesítő* 12, 13 (1963, 1964).

Bernáth, Mária. *Rippl-Rónai*. Budapest: Gondolat, 1976.

Bodnár, Éva. *Rippl-Rónai József kiállítása* [József Rippl-Rónai's Exhibition]. Tihany: Magyar Nemzeti Galéria and Veszprém Megyei Múzeumi Igazgatóság, 1968.

Gellér, Katalin. Rippl-Rónai József és a távolkeleti művészet [József Rippl-Rónai and Far Eastern Art]. *Művészet* 18, no. 11-12 (November-December 1987): 50-55.

Genthon, István. Rippl-Rónai kiadatlan levelei [Rippl-Rónai's Unpublished Letters]. *Képzőművészeti Almanach* 1 (1969): 139-49.

———, and Judit Szabadi. *Rippl-Rónai József*. Budapest: Corvina, 1977.

Keserű, Katalin. Táblakép és építészeti dekoráció Rippl-Rónai József művészetében [Easel Painting and Architectural Decoration in the Art of József Rippl-Rónai]. *Építés, Építészettudomány* no. 3-4 (1973): 579-84.

Petrovics, Elek. *Rippl-Rónai*. Budapest: Athenaeum, n.d. [1942].

Szabadi, Judit. *Rippl-Rónai*. Budapest, 1978.

György Ruttkay

Losonczi, Miklós. Egy elfelejtett életmű. Ruttkay György pályaképe [A Forgotten Oeuvre. György Ruttkay's Career]. *Művészettörténeti Értesítő* 26, no. 2 (1977): 169-76.

János Schadl

Szabó, Júlia. Schadl János. *Művészet* 7 (March 1966): 26.

Hugó Scheiber

Láncz, Sándor. Egy mappa története. Scheiber Hugóról [The History of a Portfolio. On Hugó Scheiber]. *Művészet* 26, no. 11-12 (November-December 1985): 28-33.

Scheiber Hugó emlékkiállítása. Budapest: Magyar Nemzeti Galéria, 1964. Exhibition catalogue.

Armand Schönberger

András, Edit. *Schönberger Armand*. Budapest: Corvina, 1984.

Baki, Miklós. Schönberger Armand. *Művészet* 6, no. 8 (1965).

Dévényi, Iván. Schönberger Armand. *Műgyűjtő*. (1972-73): 42-43.

Schönberger Armand festőművész kiállítása [Exhibition of the Painter Armand Schönberger]. Budapest: Műcsarnok, 1958. Exhibition catalogue.

Ferenc Spangher

Andrási, Gábor. Eleven robbanáscentrumok. Spangher Ferenc művészetéről [Live Centres of Explosion. On the Art of Ferenc Spangher]. *Művészet* 28, no. 10 (October 1987): 2-5.

Imre Szobotka

Bodnár, Éva, ed. *Szobotka Imre emlékkiállítása* [Imre Szobotka's Retrospective Exhibition]. Budapest: Magyar Nemzeti Galéria, 1971.

Lajos Tihanyi

Dévényi, Iván. *Tihanyi*. Budapest: Corvina, 1968.

Fehér, D. Zsuzsa. Gondolatok egy kiállítás rendezése közben. Gondolatok Tihanyi Lajosról [Thoughts During the Preparation of an Exhibition. Thoughts on Lajos Tihanyi] *Művészet* 14, no. 7 (July 1973): 41-42.

Mezei, Ottó. Megjegyzések Tihanyi Lajos ismeretlen portréjához [Comments on Lajos Tihanyi's Unknown Portrait]. *Művészet* 16, no. 9 (September 1975): 19-20.

Sándor Trauner

Bajkay, Éva. *Trauner*. Budapest: Magyar Nemzeti Galéria, 1981.

Bodri, Ferenc. Trauner Sándor tárlatának élménye és tanulságai [The Experience and Lessons of Sándor Trauner's Exhibition]. *Művészet* 23, no. 6 (June 1982): 46-47.

Béla Uitz

Bajkay, Éva. *Uitz Béla*. Budapest: Gondolat, 1974.

———. Uitz Béla kiállítása [Béla Uitz' Exhibition]. *Művészet* 77. Budapest: Corvina, 1978: 205-207.

———. Forradalmiság és formalizmus (Uitz Béla alkotói útja 1926-35). [Revolutionariness and Formalism (Béla Uitz's Creative Path 1926-35)] *Művészettörténeti Értesítő* 28, no. 4 (1979).

———. *Uitz Béla*. Budapest: Képzőművészeti, 1987. Oeuvre-catalogue.

Dénes, Zsófia. Uitz Béla. In *Szivárvány Pesttől Párizsig*. Budapest: Gondolat, 1979: 89-93.

Kontha, Sándor, ed. *Uitz Béla kiállítása* [Béla Uitz' Exhibition]. Budapest: Magyar Nemzeti Galéria and Kulturális Kapcsolatok Intézete, 1968. Exhibition catalogue, with some of its contents also in French.

———. Uitz Párizsban [Uitz in Paris]. *Művészet* 9, no. 11 (November 1968).

Körner, Éva, ed. *Uitz*. Budapest: Corvina, 1967.

Kővágó, S. Uitz Béla "Vörös katonák előre" című plakátjának előzményeiről [Antecedents of Béla Uitz' Poster "Red Soldiers Forward"]. *Művészettörténeti Értesítő* 31, no. 3 (1982): 231-32.

Művészet 12, no. 6 (June 1972). Uitz issue.

Nagy, Zoltán. Uitz Béla első moszkvai évei. [Béla Uitz' First Moscow Years]. *Ars Hungarica* 6, no. 2 (1978): 245-73. English summary.

Németh, Lajos. Uitz Béla művészete [The Art of Béla Uitz]. *Kritika* 5, no. 11 (November 1967): 54-56.

———. Uitz és az FMNI [Uitz and the International Bureau of Revolutionary Artists]. *Művészettörténeti Értesítő* 29, no. 3 (1980): 44-46.

Szabó, Júlia. Uitz Béla művészeti és mozgalmi pályájáról [On the Artistic and Political Career of Béla Uitz]. *Művészet* 3, no. 7 (July 1962).

Uitz, Béla. A Ludditákról [On the Luddites]. *Muvészet* 12, no. 5 (May 1971): 12-16.

Uitz Béla kiállítása a szovjet múzeumokban és a művész tulajdonában lévő művekből [Béla Uitz' Exhibition of Works in the Posession of the Artist and of Soviet Museums]. Budapest: Magyar Nemzeti Galéria, 1968.

Uitz Múzeum, Pécs. Az állandó kiállítás vezetője. [Uitz Museum, Pécs. A Guide to the Permanent Exhibition]. A Janus Pannonius Múzeum Művészeti Kiadványai 39. Pécs: Janus Pannonius Múzeum, 1978.

Victor Vasarely (Győző Vásárhelyi)

Körner, Éva. Vasarely és Magyarország [Vasarely and Hungary]. Afterword by Gaston Diehl. *Vasarely*. Budapest: Corvina, 1979.

Sik, Csaba. Program és ideológia. Vasarely esztétikája és eszmerendszere [Program and Ideology. Vasarely's Aesthetics and System of Thought]. *Művészet* 32, no. 8 (August 1981): 10-15.

Vasarely. Budapest: Műcsarnok, 1969. Exhibition catalogue.

Andor Weininger

Bajkay-Rosch, Éva. A Bauhaustól New Yorkig. Weininger Andor 85 éves [From the Bauhaus to New York. Andor Weininger is 85]. *Művészet* 30, no. 6 (June 1984): 46-48.

Height precedes width in all given dimensions of works. Dimensions are stated in centimeters (cm) and inches (in). To avoid confusion for the non-metric reader, dimensions of smaller graphic works, usually given in millimeters, have been also stated in centimeters. Approximate dates are indicated by a "c" (circa) before the given date. Artists' biographies were compiled by Gábor Bellák (GB) and András Zwickl (AZ) of the staff of the Hungarian National Gallery, whose initials appear after their respective entries, revised and supplemented by Richard V. West.

Róbert Berény (1887–1953) Born in Miskolc, Berény began his art studies in Budapest in 1904, leaving the following year to study with J. P. Laurens at the Académie Julian in Paris. While in Paris, he was influenced by the color usage of the Fauves and by the structuralism of Cézanne. In 1911, after his return to Hungary, he joined The Eight, and exhibited with them at the National Salon. In 1915, the artist was invited to exhibit at the Panama-Pacific International Exposition in San Francisco. Berény had a wide range of interests: he studied music and was in close touch with such composers as Leó Weiner and Béla Bartók, whose portraits he painted. In 1919, he participated in the administration of the arts during the Hungarian Soviet Republic; his works during this period include the famous poster *To Arms! To Arms!* (Fegyverbe! Fegyverbe!). After the collapse of the revolution, he emigrated to Berlin, where he temporarily gave up painting in favor of music composition. In 1926, he returned to Hungary. He designed commercial posters, including a series for Modiano cigarette papers, and continued to paint in a more lyric style. From 1948, he taught at the Academy of Fine Arts in Budapest and was later awarded the Kossuth and Munkácsy prizes. Ten years after his death, he was honored with a retrospective exhibition. AZ

1. **Self-portrait with Straw Hat** (Szalmakalapos önarckép), 1906
   oil on canvas, 60 x 45 cm (23⅝ x 17¾ in)
   inscribed lower left: B.R.
   Hungarian National Gallery, Budapest (Inv. 56.208 T)
   Illustrated page 48
2. **Woman in Red Dress** (Nő piros ruhában), 1908
   oil on paper, 92 x 58.5 cm (36¼ x 23 in)
   inscribed upper right: Berény, Paris 1908
   Janus Pannonius Museum, Pécs Inv. 75.215
   Illustrated page 114
3. **To Arms! To Arms!** (Fegyverbe! Fegyverbe!), 1919
   lithograph, 123.5 x 184.5 cm (48⅝ x 72⅝ in)
   inscribed lower left: Berény
   Museum of the Modern Age, Budapest (Inv. 6.1.1)
   Illustrated page 47
4. **Flóra Terpentine Soap** (Flóra Terpentinszappan), 1927
   lithograph, 125.5 x 94 cm (49⅜ x 37 in)
   inscribed lower left: Berény
   Hungarian Advertising Agency Archives, Budapest (Inv. MM 056)
   Illustrated page 81
5. **Modiano**, c1927
   lithograph on paper, 124.5 x 94 cm (49 x 37 in)
   inscribed upper left: Berény
   Hungarian Advertising Agency Archives, Budapest (Inv. 20/059)
   Illustrated page 83

Aurél Bernáth (1895–1982) Bernáth's early development as an artist was influenced by the precepts of the Nagybánya school, where he studied in 1915 with István Réti and János Thorma. During World War I, he was an enlisted soldier; after the war, he returned briefly to Budapest, later emigrating to Vienna in 1921. In 1923, at the invitation of Herwarth Walden, he moved to Berlin. His prints during this period reflect the influence of German Expressionism. Around 1924, his artistic direction changed and he gradually reverted to a more naturalistic style. Returning to Hungary in 1926, he joined the Gresham Café circle, the goal of which was to rekindle the traditions of the Nagybánya school. From 1945 to 1974, Bernáth taught at the Academy of Fine Arts in Budapest. During this period, he also executed monumental murals, such as those at the Brussels International Exposition of 1958. He was represented at the Venice Biennale in 1962, awarded the Kossuth and Munkácsy prizes, and was given a retrospective exhibition in London in 1963. In his later years, he authored several popular autobiographical works. AZ

6. **Villages** (Faluk), 1920
   ink and gold paint on paper, 28 x 37.8 cm (11 x 14⅞ in)
   inscribed lower left: A.B.
   Hungarian National Gallery, Budapest (Inv. F 85.4/2)
   Illustrated page 132
7. **Tumble and Cry** (Zuhanás és kiáltás), 1922
   ink and gold paint on paper, 28.3 x 34.1 cm (11⅛ x 13⅜ in)
   inscribed lower right: B.A.
   Hungarian National Gallery, Budapest (Inv. F 85.4/1)
   Illustrated page 133

Mihály Biró (1886-1948) Biró studied in Budapest at the School of Applied Arts. In 1908, he travelled to Berlin, Paris, and eventually to London, where he spent two years as a member of C.R. Ashbee's Handicraft Guild. In 1910, he was awarded a prize in a poster competition sponsored by the British art journal *The Studio*. He designed his first significant poster for the Hungarian Social Democratic newspaper *Népszava* [The People's Voice] in 1911; the "man with a hammer" quickly became a party emblem. (Appearing over the years in several variants, it was most recently seen on Budapest walls during the 1990 elections). During the brief Hungarian Soviet Republic, Biró became commissar of poster propaganda. After 1919, he emigrated to France, returning to Hungary only in 1947, shortly before his death. GB

8. **The People's Voice** (Népszava), 1913
   lithograph, 126 x 95.5 cm (49⅝ x 37⅝ in)
   inscribed lower right: Bíró
   Hungarian National Gallery, Budapest (Inv. XY 59.01)
   Illustrated page 116
9. **We Want a Republic!** (Köztársaságot!), 1918
   lithograph, 126 x 94 cm (49⅝ x 37 in)
   inscribed lower right: Bíró
   Hungarian National Gallery, Budapest (Inv. XY 67.1)
   Illustrated page 150
10. **Farewell Requiem for the Austro-Hungarian Monarchy**, (Búcsúztató halotti ének az Osztrák-Magyar Monarchia felett), 1919
    lithograph, 126 x 95 cm (49⅝ x 37⅜ in)
    inscribed lower right: Bíró
    Museum of the Modern Age, Budapest (Inv. 57.7)
    Illustrated page 57
11. **May 1, 1919** (1919 május 1.), 1919
    lithograph, 128 x 95 cm (50⅜ x 37⅜ in)
    inscribed upper left: Bíró
    Hungarian National Gallery, Budapest (Inv. XY 58.157)
    Illustrated page 57

Sándor Bortnyik (1893–1976) Born in Marosvásárhely (now Tîrgu Mureş, Romania), Bortnyik moved to Budapest in 1910, and started his artistic training in 1913 studying with Károly Kernstok and József Rippl-Rónai. An early advocate of Activism and associate of Lajos Kassák, Bortnyik's linoleum cuts were published in *Ma* from 1918 on. After the fall of the Hungarian Soviet Republic, Bortnyik emigrated to Vienna where he published his portfolio of *Bildarchitektur* prints in 1921. The following year, he had a successful exhibition at Der Sturm gallery in Berlin. Moving to Weimar, he maintained close contacts with the Bauhaus until his return to Hungary in 1924. In Budapest, he was one of the founders of the "Green Donkey" avant-garde theater. In 1928, he opened the *Műhely* workshop, modelled after the precepts of the Bauhaus; among its early students was Victor Vasarely. During this period, Bortnyik combined modernist aesthetics with commercial needs to execute a number of outstanding advertising posters. From 1949 to 1956, he was Dean of the Budapest Academy of Fine Arts. A winner of the Kossuth prize, in his last years he broke with earlier avant-garde artistic traditions and painted mostly satirical pieces. AZ

12. **Composition with Six Figures** (Hatalakos kompozíció), 1918
    oil on canvas, 75.5 x 9gw5 cm (29¾ x 37⅝ in)

inscribed lower left: Bortnyik 1919 [the artist's post facto signature in error]
Hungarian National Gallery, Budapest (Inv. 75.102 T)
Illustrated page 55

13. **Red Sun** (Vörös nap), 1918-19
oil on paper, 70.4 x 50.3 cm (27¾ x 19¾ in)
inscribed lower left: Bortnyik 19
Museum of the Modern Age, Budapest (Inv. 57.30)
Illustrated page 14
14. **Red Factory** (Vörös gyár), 1919
oil on cardboard, 60 x 51 cm (23⅝ x 20 in)
unsigned
Janus Pannonius Museum, Pécs (Inv. 73.81)
Illustrated page 135
15. **Bildarchitektur 31**, 1921
watercolor on paper, 26 x 21.6 cm (10¼ x 8½ in)
inscribed lower left: Bortnyik Wien 1921
Museum of Modern Art, New York, The Riklis Collection of McCrory Corporation (fractional gift) (Inv. 858.83)
Illustrated page 176

Selections from the **Ma Album,** 1921

16. **Bildarchitektur** [I]
color pochoir print on paper, 30.5 x 24 cm (12 x 9½ in)
unsigned
Illustrated page 136
17. **Bildarchitektur** [II]
color pochoir print on paper, 30.5 x 24 cm (12 x 9½ in)
unsigned
Illustrated page 136
18. **Bildarchitektur** [III]
color pochoir print on paper, 30.5 x 24 cm (12 x 9½ in)
unsigned
Janus Pannonius Museum, Pécs (Inv. 79.71.1, 2, and 3)
Illustrated page 136
19. **Geometric Form in Space**, 1923
gouache on paper, 19 x 29.2 cm (7½ x 11½ in)
inscribed lower right: BORTNYIK/1923
Mr. and Mrs. Thomas O. Hecht, Montreal
Illustrated page 43
20. **Geometric Forms in Space**, 1923
oil on canvas, 46.4 x 60 cm (18¼ x 23⅝ in)
inscribed lower left: Bortnyik/Weimar–1923
Museum of Modern Art, New York, The Riklis Collection of McCrory Corporation (fractional gift) 1983 (Inv. 996.83)
Illustrated page 71
21. **Still Life with Jug**, 1923
oil on cardboard, 35 x 45.5 cm (13¾ x 17½ in)
inscribed upper left and lower right: Bortnyik 1923
Staatliche Museen Preussischer Kulturbesitz, Nationalgalerie, Berlin
Illustrated page 124
22. **The First of May in Hungary** (Magyar Május), 1923
ink and white gouache on paper, 61 x 66 cm (24 x 26 in)
inscribed lower right: Bortnyik
Museum of the Modern Age, Budapest (Inv. LTM Gr.11)
Illustrated page 152
23. **The New Adam** (Az új Ádám), 1924
oil on canvas, 48 x 38 cm (18⅞ x 15 in)
inscribed lower right: Bortnyik 1924
Hungarian National Gallery, Budapest (Inv. 64.85 T)
Illustrated page 76
24. **Modiano**, 1928
lithograph, 125 x 95 cm (49¼ x 37⅜ in)
inscribed lower left: Bortnyik
Hungarian National Gallery, Budapest (Inv. XY 60.62)
Illustrated page 82

Tivadar Csontváry Kosztka (1853–1919) One of the truly independent artists of the nineteenth century, Csontváry was born in Kisszeben (now Sabinov, Czechoslovakia). A pharmacist by trade, his artistic career was initiated at the age of 27 with a vision in which a voice predicted that the young man would become a painter greater than Raphael. However, before Csontváry would entirely commit himself to the world of art, he continued to work as a pharmacist for 14 years to become financially independent. He began his formal training in 1894 in Munich under Simon Hollósy, then later continued at Karlsruhe, and finally in 1896 moved to Paris to study at the Académie Julian. He then embarked on extensive travels in search of the "ultimate theme." In 1904-1905, he managed to reach Palestine where he painted works on biblical motifs. In 1907, he exhibited his gigantic canvases in Paris. Towards the end of his life, he wrote theoretical tracts. His contribution as a painter was realized only long after his death; a museum devoted to his work was founded in the Hungarian city of Pécs, and he received a posthumous gold medal at the Brussels World Exposition in 1958 for his artistic contributions. AZ

25. **The Praying Saviour** (Fohászkodó üdvözítő), 1903
oil on canvas, 100 x 82 cm (39⅜ x 32¼ in)
unsigned
Janus Pannonius Museum, Pécs (Inv. 73.250)
Illustrated page 102: withdrawn from exhibition.

Dezső Czigány (1883–1937) After graduating from the Budapest School of Applied Arts, Czigány continued his studies in Munich. Returning to Hungary, he spent two years in Nagybánya where he was a student of Károly Ferenczy. He participated in exhibitions organized by MIÉNK, the association of Hungarian impressionists and naturalists, and later became a member of The Eight. In 1915, he was represented in the Panama-Pacific International Exposition in San Francisco. Like fellow artist Róbert Berény, Czigány was well acquainted with contemporaneous Hungarian composers such as Leó Weiner and Béla Bartók, and was a musician himself. In 1922, he spent time in Paris and in the south of France. By 1935, he was once more in Hungary, becoming a member of KÚT (The Association of Young Fine Artists). Czigány committed suicide in 1937; by the terms of his will, Berény was directed to destroy the artist's remaining works, but declined to do so. AZ

26. **Hay Stacks** (Boglyák), 1909
oil on canvas, 55 x 61 cm (21⅝ x 24 in)
inscribed lower right: Czigány
Herman Ottó Museum, Miskolc (Inv. P.77.54)
Illustrated page 50
27. **Funeral of a Child** (Gyermektemetés), 1910
oil on canvas, 60.5 x 77 cm (23⅞ x 30¼ in)
inscribed lower right: Czigány
Hungarian National Gallery, Budapest (Inv. 89.52 T)
Illustrated page 51
28. **Still Life with Apples and Dishes** (Csendélet almákkal, edényekkel), 1910
oil on canvas, 62 x 61.5 cm (24⅜ x 24¼ in)
inscribed lower right: Czigány D.
Hungarian National Gallery, Budapest (Inv. 60.137 T)
Illustrated page 111
29. **Self-Portrait** (Önarckép), c1912
oil on canvas, 58 x 40 cm (22⅞ x 15¾ in)
inscribed lower right: Czigány
Rippl-Rónai Museum, Kaposvár (Inv. 55.371)
Illustrated page 50

Béla Czóbel (1883–1976) The artist began his training in Nagybánya under Béla Iványi Grünwald, leaving in 1902 to spend two years at the Munich Academy. He then moved to Paris to attend the Académie Julian. While there, he was strongly influenced by the Fauves and subsequently exhibited with them at the Salon d'Automne. In 1906, he returned to Nagybánya where he became a leader of the so-called "Neos" (Neo-Impressionists), a group that split with the more traditional art colony there. Through his friendship with Károly Kernstok, Czóbel joined The Eight and exhibited with them. During World War I, he moved to the neutral Netherlands, then worked in Berlin between 1919 and 1925. After 1925, he lived in Paris, spending only summers in Hungary. Czóbel was primarily influenced by French painting; in fact, he is considered the prime Hungarian exponent of the School of Paris. AZ

30. **Painter in the Open Air**, 1906
oil on canvas, 79 x 79.5 cm (31⅛ x 31¼ in)
inscribed lower right: Béla Czóbel
Museé d'Art Moderne Centre Georges Pompidou, Paris
Illustrated page 109
31. **Garden at Nyergesújfalu** (Nyergesújfalui udvar), c1906
oil on canvas, 72 x 80 cm (28⅜ x 31½ in)
inscribed lower right: Czóbel

Janus Pannonius Museum, Pécs (Inv. 62.6)
Illustrated page 147

32. **Working Boy** (Munkásfiú), 1917
watercolor on paper, 110 x 73 cm (43¼ x 28¾ in)
inscribed upper right: Czóbel 1917
Károly Ferenczy Museum, Szentendre (Inv. 72.89.)
Illustrated page 171
33. **Berlin Street** (Berlini utca), c1920
oil on canvas, 84 x 71 cm (33 x 28 in)
inscribed lower right: Czóbel
Béla Czóbel Museum, Szentendre (Inv. 76.10.)
Illustrated page 65
34. **In the Studio** (Műteremben), 1922
oil on canvas, 93.5 x 74 cm (36¾ x 29¼ in)
unsigned
Hungarian National Gallery, Budapest (Inv. FK 8742)
Illustrated page 168
35. **Reclining Woman** (Fekvő nő), 1922
oil on canvas, 50 x 38.5 cm (19⅝ x 15¼ in)
inscribed upper right: Czóbel
Hungarian National Gallery, Budapest (Inv. FK 9206)
Illustrated page 199

Lajos Deák-Ébner (1850-1934) Deák-Ébner studied painting in Munich from 1868 to 1873. An early adherent of naturalism, he had his first exhibition in Vienna in 1873. Later in the same year he moved to Paris, with occasional trips to Barbizon. He continued to winter in Paris, but returned to Hungary in 1874 at the invitation of August von Pettenkoffen to teach during the summers at the Szolnok art colony. In 1887, he was appointed director of the Budapest Women's Painting Academy. He continued to paint, primarily genre and historical painting, and developed a highly decorative style which led to a number of important mural commissions. GB

36. **Hungaria** (Hungária), 1896
oil on canvas, 125 x 90 cm (49¼ x 35⅜ in)
inscribed lower right: Lajos Ébner
Private collection, Budapest
Illustrated page 41

Valéria Dénes (Galimberti) (1877-1915) One of the pioneers of cubism in Hungary, Dénes studied in Budapest and Nagybánya, later moving to Paris to study with Henri Matisse. While in Paris, she became acquainted with Sándor Galimberti whom she married in 1911. With her husband, she exhibited at the Salon d'Automne and the Salon des Indépendents. At the outbreak of World War I in 1914, the two artists returned to Hungary via The Netherlands, showing their latest works jointly at the 1914 National Salon in Budapest. With Galimberti, her works were also selected to be shown at the 1915 Panama-Pacific International Exposition in San Francisco. Because of Galimberti's military duties, they moved to Pécs, where Dénes succumbed to ill health brought on by the strain of her escape from France and poor living conditions. GB

37. **The Street** (Utca), 1913
oil on canvas, 55 x 46 cm (21⅝ x 18¼ in)
inscribed lower right: G D V
Janus Pannonius Museum, Pécs (Inv. 73.1)
Illustrated page 117

Gyula Derkovits (1894–1934) Born in Szombathely, Derkovits was first an apprentice in his father's carpentry workshop, enlisting in the Austro-Hungarian army at the outbreak of World War I. In 1916, he was discharged as a disabled veteran and worked in Budapest as a carpenter. He began to study art under Károly Kernstok in 1918, soon developing a highly personal expressionist style. In 1923, he emigrated to Vienna where he had several exhibitions. Returning to Hungary in 1927, he created a powerful woodcut series depicting the Hungarian hero Dózsa leading the peasant uprisings of 1514; an obvious commentary on Hungary's immediate past history. Despite a successful exhibition at the Tamás gallery in 1929, the artist's finances worsened. In failing health, Derkovits died shortly after his fortieth birthday. AZ

38. **Self-Portrait** (Önarckép), 1921
oil on canvas, 52.5 x 42 cm (20⅝ x 16½ in)
inscribed upper right: Derkovits 1921
Hungarian National Gallery, Budapest (Inv. 9771)
Illustrated page 126
39. **Old Cemetery in Buda** (Régi temető), 1922
oil on canvas, 75 x 68 cm (29½ x26¾ in)
inscribed lower right: Derkovits 1922
Hungarian National Gallery, Budapest (Inv. FK 7803)
Illustrated page 186
40. **Last Supper** (Utolsó vacsora), 1922
oil on canvas, 150 x 145 cm (59 x 57 in)
inscribed lower right: Derkovits Gy.
Hungarian National Gallery, Budapest (Inv. 54.326)
Illustrated page 129
41. **Fleeing the Storm** (Menekülés viharban), 1926
oil on canvas, 114 x 185 cm (44-7/8 x 72-7/8 in)
inscribed lower right: Derkovits Gy. 1926
Hungarian National Gallery, Budapest (Inv. 54.325)
Illustrated page 62
42. **Encounter–The Itinerant Fire-Eater** (Találkozás–Tüzevő vándorartista), 1927
oil on canvas, 100 x 80 cm (39⅜ x 31½ in)
inscribed lower right: Derkovits Gyula 1927
Hungarian National Gallery, Budapest (Inv. FK 10.112)
Illustrated page 129

Selections from the **1514 Portfolio**, 1928

43. **Dózsa on the Ramparts** [V] (Dózsa a várfokon)
woodcut on paper, 49.7 x 44 cm (19½ x 17¼ in)
Illustrated page 45
44. **Clash of Armies** [VI] (Összecsapás)
woodcut on paper, 44 x 50.4 cm (17¼ x 19⅞ in)
Illustrated page 128
45. **Verböczy! Verböczy!** [X]
woodcut on paper, 51.6 x 43.8 cm (20¼ x 17¼ in)
Hungarian National Gallery, Budapest (Inv. 1955-4608, 4609, and 4613)
Illustrated page 128

Lajos d'Ébneth (1902–1982) Born in Szilágysomlyó, Hungary, d'Ébneth was one of the few Hungarian modernists to come from an aristocratic background. He studied at the Academy of Fine Arts in Budapest as well as studying architecture at the Technical School there. He moved to Munich in 1921, enrolling in master classes at the Franz von Stuck academy, soon having his first exhibition at that city's Glass Palace. In 1923, he moved to The Hague, there to work with Mies van der Rohe, Hans Arp, and Piet Mondrian in the avant-garde group i 10. He also maintained close contacts with the artists of De Stijl and became friends with Vilmos Huszár and Kurt Schwitters. Invited by Gropius to the Dessau Bauhaus in 1926, d'Ébneth also exhibited at Der Sturm gallery in Berlin, working closely with Herwarth Walden. The artist returned to The Netherlands in 1928, becoming a Dutch citizen in 1947. He moved to Peru in 1949, living in Lima until his death. A posthumous retrospective of his work was mounted in Lima in 1983. RVW

46. **Composition**, 1926
collage, 50.5 x 32 cm (19⅞ x 12⅝ in)
inscribed lower right: ÉL[ligature].26
Berlinische Galerie, Berlin (Inv. BG-G 2319/80)
Illustrated page 206
47. **Composition**, 1926
oil on canvas, 58 x 51 cm (22⅞ x 20 in)
inscribed lower right: ÉL[ligature].26
Berlinische Galerie, Berlin (Inv. BG-M 2305/80)
Illustrated page 207
48. **Composition**, 1926
oil on canvas, 46.3 x 36.5 cm (18¼ x 14½ in)
inscribed lower right: ÉL[ligature].26
Museum of Modern Art, New York, The Riklis Collection of McCrory Corporation (fractional gift), 1983 (Inv. 1004.83)
Illustrated page 207
49. **Composition**, 1927
collage, 50.5 x 32 cm (19⅞ x 12⅝ in)
inscribed lower right: ÉL[ligature].27
Berlinische Galerie, Berlin (Inv. BG-G 2318/80)
Illustrated page 74

József Egry (1883–1951) Son of a day laborer, Egry was awarded a scholarship to attend the Academy of Fine Arts in Budapest in 1906 under Károly Ferenczy after two years previous study in Munich and at the Académie Julian in Paris. In 1909, he had his first one-man exhibition. On a trip to France and Belgium in 1911, he became familiar with the work of Théophile Steinlen; as a result, the works he created during this period reflect a certain social consciousness. In 1916, Egry was sent to a hospital in Badacsony, near Lake Balaton, to recover from illness contracted in military service. There, he discovered the beauty of Lake Balaton and settled permanently with his wife at the end of the war in 1918. During the 1920s, the artist subsumed his earlier expressionist style into a more transcendent, lyrical painting, concentrating on the effects of light and often using biblical themes set in the local landscape. In 1926, Ernő Kállai organized exhibitions for him in the Fritz Gurlitt gallery in Berlin and the Emil Richter gallery in Dresden. During this period, Egry was closely associated with the Gresham Cafe circle. The artist continued to paint into the 1930s and 40s. In 1948, he was awarded the Kossuth Prize by the Hungarian government. AZ

50. **Red Truth** (Vörös igazság), 1919
watercolor and pastel on paper, 68 x 85 cm (26¾ x 33½ in)
inscribed lower right: Egry József Keszthely
Museum of the Modern Age, Budapest (Inv. 58.537)
Illustrated page 126

Károly Ferenczy (1862–1917) Born in Vienna, Ferenczy made a decision to pursue a career in art in 1884 at his wife's urging, only after receiving a law degree and completing some graduate work in economics. From 1887, the artist studied at the Académie Julian in Paris, and in 1889, he moved to Szentendre, the artists' colony near Budapest. Once there, he painted realist works influenced by the French artist Jules Bastien-Lepage. Between 1893 and 1896, he lived in Munich with his family where he was part of the Simon Hollósy circle. In 1896, he moved to Nagybánya where he became one of the leading personalities of the art colony there. His 1903 exhibition at Budapest was a great success; in 1906, he received an appointment to the Academy of Fine Arts at which time he moved to Budapest and spent only his summers at Nagybánya. In 1915, three of his paintings were selected for exhibiton at the Panama-Pacific International Exposition in San Francisco. In his late period, his *plein air* style of painting changed to a more decorative style focusing on delicate nudes. AZ

51. **Ruthenian Peasant Boy** (Rutén parasztfiú), 1898
oil on canvas, 128 x 67.5 cm (50⅜ x 26⅝ in)
inscribed upper right: Ferenczy Károly
Janus Pannonius Museum, Pécs (Inv. 76.104)
Illustrated page 104
52. **Woman Painter** (Festőnő), 1903
oil on canvas, 136 x 129.6 cm (53½ x 51 in)
unsigned
Hungarian National Gallery, Budapest (Inv. 2472)
Illustrated page 95
53. **Beech Woods** (Bükkös–Őszi napsütés), 1908
oil on canvas, 90.5 x 104 cm (35⅝ x 40⅞ in)
inscribed lower right: Ferenczy K.
Hungarian National Gallery, Budapest (Inv. FK 5341)
Illustrated page 95

Alfréd (Fréd) Forbát (1897-1972) Forbát began his studies in Budapest, later moving to Munich for further education. From 1920 to 1922 he was a colleague of Walter Gropius at the Weimar Bauhaus. As a painter, he focused on meticulously thought out, small format compositions; as an architect, he was primarily interested in the city-scape, as well as architectural and planning solutions, designing entire habitats in several European cities. After a stay in Moscow during 1932-33, he returned to Hungary, working in Pécs from 1933 to 1938. He then moved to Sweden, where he worked in Lund and in Stockholm until his death. GB

54. **Abstract Composition** (Absztrakt kompozíció), 1921
colored chalk on paper, 20.5 x 20.5 cm (8⅛ x 8⅛ in)
inscribed lower right with monogram
Museum of Fine Arts Budapest, (Inv. 76.1 B)
Illustrated page 77
55. **Abstract Composition**, c1925
pastel and pencil on paper, 27 x 35 cm (10½ x 13½ in)
inscribed upper right with monogram
Paul Kövesdy Collection, New York
Illustrated page 75
56. **Composition**, 1923
colored pencil on paper, 22 x 32 cm (8⅝ x 12⅝ in)
inscribed lower left with monogram
Dr. Nicholas Éber, Unterengstringen, Switzerland
Illustrated page 73

Sándor Galimberti (1883-1915) Galimberti started his artistic training in Nagybánya, studying with István Réti. Following the example of many of his fellow artists, he continued his studies in Munich and Técsó with Simon Hollósy, only to move again, this time to the Académie Julian in Paris in 1907. He soon became involved with the more advanced artists there, and exhibited regularly at the Salon d'Automne and the Salon des Indépendents between 1908 and 1913. Although not a member of the Gleizes-Metzinger circle or of the short-lived Section d'Or group, both of which adopted various forms of cubist idiom around 1912, Galimberti began experimenting with cubism. At the outbreak of the war, he returned to Hungary through The Netherlands with his wife, Valéria Dénes. With her, he had works exhibited at the 1914 National Salon in Budapest and had three works selected for inclusion in the Fine Arts Section of the 1915 Panama-Pacific Exposition in San Francisco. Despondent over his wife's death in 1915, Galimberti committed suicide on the day of her funeral. With Dénes, Galimberti was one of the Hungarian pioneers of cubism; his work consists primarily of still lives and cityscapes. GB

57. **Nagybánya Motive** (Nagybányai motívum), c1900
oil on canvas, 90 x 130 cm (35½ x 51¼ in)
inscribed lower right: Galimberti
Janus Pannonius Museum, Pécs (Inv. 81.148)
58. **View of Tabán** (Tabán), c1910
oil on canvas, 111 x 76 cm (43¾ x 29⅞ in)
unsigned
Hungarian National Gallery, Budapest (Inv. 74.84 T)
Frontispiece
59. **Roofs** (Háztetők), c1910
oil on canvas, 65 x 75 cm (25⅝ x 29½ in)
inscribed lower left: G.S.
Rippl-Rónai Museum, Kaposvár (Inv. 65.15)
Illustrated page 189
60. **Amsterdam**, 1914
oil on canvas, 92 x 92.5 cm (36¼ x 36⅜ in)
unsigned
Janus Pannonius Museum, Pécs (Inv. 72.18)
Illustrated page 117

Béla Iványi Grünwald (1867-1940) Iványi Grünwald was one of the founders of the artist colony of Nagybánya (now Baia Mare, Romania). Between 1882 and 1884 he studied in Budapest, later moving to Munich where he joined Simon Hollósy's circle. In 1887, he attended the Académie Julian in Paris. From 1896, he worked in Nagybánya. His Munich period was characterized by genre and historical scenes but in Nagybánya he developed a notable *plein air* landscape style. Between 1907 and 1909, he broke with naturalism and initiated a more decorative style in his painting. In 1910, he became director of the art school in Kecskemét which counted among its students such talents as Kassák, Kmetty, and Uitz. Six of his paintings were included in the 1915 Panama-Pacific International Exposition in San Francisco. In the 1920s and 30s, his art was largely commercialized. GB

61. **Nagybánya Landscape** (Nagybányai táj), 1900
oil on canvas, 90.5 x 100.5 cm (35⅝ x 39½ in)
inscribed lower right: Grünwald Béla Nagybánya 1900
Janus Pannonius Museum, Pécs (Inv. 81.188)
Illustrated page 93
62. **In the Valley** (Bércek között), 1901
oil on canvas, 121 x 150 cm (47⅝ x 59 in)
inscribed lower left: Grünwald B. N.B.
Hungarian National Gallery, Budapest (Inv. 65.65 T)
Illustrated page 188
63. **Villa Schiffer Panel Design** (A Schiffer-villa pannója), c1911
oil on canvas, 131 x 360 cm (51⅝ x 141¾ in)

unsigned
Hungarian National Gallery, Budapest (Inv. 81.34 T)
Illustrated page 191

Béla Kádár (1877-1956) Originally trained as a machinist in Budapest, Kádár began his art studies in 1896, travelling to Paris and Munich. He attended the Academy of Fine Arts in Budapest, winning the Kohner prize in 1910. After an early period of naturalism, his painting changed under the influence of Rippl-Rónai and the Vienna Secessionists. He had his first exhibition in Budapest in 1918, adopting an appealing and personal amalgam of modernism which he refined over the years. In 1921, he had a joint exhibition with Hugó Scheiber, and in 1923, Herwarth Walden's Der Sturm gallery featured fifty-seven of his works in Berlin. One of Walden's favorite artists at this time, Kádár continued to have his works exhibited at Der Sturm throughout the decade. In 1928, he spent a year in the United States, and from 1929 on, he returned to Budapest to have his works exhibited there. GB

64. **Still Life with Chessboard and Pipe**, c1920
oil on canvas, 93 x 83.5 cm (36⅝ x 32⅞ in)
inscribed lower left: KÁDÁR/BÉLA
Berlinische Galerie, Berlin (Inv. BG-M 3819/86)
Illustrated page 69
65. **Portrait of Herwarth Walden**, 1924
lithograph, 32.4 x 23.8 cm (12¾ x 9⅜ in)
inscribed lower right: KÁDÁR/BÉLA
Yale University Art Gallery, New Haven
Sociéte Anonyme Collection (Inv. 1941.513)
Illustrated page 131
66. **Village Departure**, c1925
oil on canvas, 99 x 76 cm (39 x 30 in)
inscribed lower right: KÁDÁR/BÉLA
Paul Kövesdy Collecton, New York
Illustrated page 131
67. **Longing** (Vágyakozás), c1925
tempera on paper, 35 x 45 cm (13¾ x 17¾ in)
inscribed lower right: KÁDÁR/BÉLA
Hungarian National Gallery, Budapest (Inv. 27.1501)
Illustrated page 209
68. **Constructivist Composition (Theater Piece)**, c1928
gouache on paper, 50.8 x 38.1 cm (20 x 15 in)
inscribed lower left: KÁDÁR/BÉLA
Paul Kövesdy Collection, New York
Illustrated page 131

Lajos Kassák (1887–1967) The greatest supporter and entrepeneur of Hungarian avant-garde movements for over three decades and one of the most outstanding advocates of international modernism in the twentieth century, Kassák started his career as a locksmith's apprentice. Initially active in the field of literature, in 1915 he founded the periodical *A Tett* [The Deed]; when *A Tett* was banned, he began the publication of *Ma* [Today] first in Budapest and then in Vienna from 1920 to 1925, after the fall of the Hungarian Soviet Republic. In the early 1920's, Kassák turned to creating art, formulating his theory of *Bildarchitektur* together with Sándor Bortnyik, and completing a number of prints, watercolors and collages. With Lászlo Moholy-Nagy, Kassák produced the highly influential *Buch neuer Künstler* [Book of New Artists] in 1922. Returning to Hungary in 1926, he devoted his energies to publication and literary activities once again. In the 1950s, when his literary activity was once more banned in Hungary for political reasons, he reverted to creating art, recalling his earlier constructivist style. AZ

69. **Noise** (Bruits), 1920
collage and ink on paper, 14.8 x 10.7 cm (5⅞ x 4¼ in)
inscribed lower right: Kassák 920
Kunsthalle Nürnberg (Inv. 24a/71)
Illustrated page 134
70. **Bildarchitektur**, 1921-26
gouache on paper, 41.5 x 29.2 cm (16⅜ x 11½ in)
inscribed lower right: LK
Anonymous loan, Baltimore, Maryland
Illustrated page 68
71. **Bildarchitektur**, 1922
oil on cardboard, 36 x 30.5 cm (14¼ x 12 in)
inscribed lower left: LK
Galerie Dr. I. Schlégl, Zürich
Illustrated page 134
72. **Bildarchitektur**, 1923
gouache on paper, 19.9 x 27.5 cm (7⅞ x 10⅞ in)
inscribed lower right: L.K.
Kunsthalle Nürnberg (Inv. 24j/71)
Illustrated page 78
73. **Bildarchitektur**, 1923
graphite on paper, 25.5 x 18.1 cm (10 x 7⅛ in)
inscribed lower left: Kassák/Bilderarchitektur 23
inscribed lower right: K.L.
Kunsthalle Nürnberg (Inv. 24k/71)
Illustrated page 133
74. **Forward** (Elõre), 1923
ink on paper, 16 x 16 cm (6¼ x 6¼ in)
inscribed lower right: Kassák
Kunsthalle Nürnberg (Inv. 24m/71)
Illustrated page 1

DUR Portfolio (DUR-Mappe), 1921

75. **DUR Cover**
ink and collage on paper, 34.2 x 25.1 cm (13½ x 9⅞ in)
inscribed: KASSÁK and titled: DUR
Illustrated page 140
76. **Drawing I**
ink on paper, 33.1 x 24.5 cm (13 x 9⅝ in)
inscribed lower right: KASSÁK
77. **Drawing II**
ink on paper, 33.1 x 24.5 cm (13 x 9⅝ in)
inscribed lower center: KASSÁK
78. **Drawing III**
ink on paper, 33.1 x 24.5 cm (13 x 9⅝ in)
inscribed lower left: KASSÁK
79. **Drawing IV**
ink on paper, 33.1 x 24.5 cm (13 x 9⅝ in)
inscribed lower center: KASSÁK
80. **Drawing V** (Inner Back Cover)
ink on paper, 34.2 x 25.1 cm (13½ x 9⅞ in)
inscribed: KASSÁK
Graphics Collection: Staatsgalerie Stuttgart (Inv. C 71/2124a-f)

Károly Kernstok (1873–1940) Kernstok started his studies at the Budapest School of Applied Arts, continuing in Munich under Simon Hollósy in 1892. From 1894 to 1896, he attended the Académie Julian in Paris, then participated in Gyula Benczúr's master classes for three years. Early on, his art reflected a certain social consciousness, which later played a lesser role in favor of a style influenced by French Post-Impressionism, particularly Matisse's early Fauve works. Kernstok played an important role in the founding of The Eight, and he was acknowledged as their leading artist, partly due to his ability to express his views and philosophy in the intellectual circles which supported early modernism in Hungary. In 1915, four works, including the *Portrait of Béla Czóbel*, were shown at the Panama-Pacific International Exposition in San Francisco. During the brief Hungarian Soviet Republic, he was appointed to head the department responsible for the arts. Upon the collapse of the revolution, he emigrated to Berlin; there he was influenced to some degree by German Expressionism. In 1926, he returned to Hungary, and returned, also, to a more naturalistic mode of painting. Kernstok's creative levels varied from period to period; he is, however, one of the founders of Hungarian modernism and was very influential for a number of Hungarian artists through example and by teaching. AZ

81. **Portrait of Béla Czóbel** (Czóbel Béla képmása), 1907
oil on canvas, 101 x 70 cm (39¾ x 27½ in)
inscribed upper left: KK
Hungarian National Gallery, Budapest (Inv. 6826)
Illustrated page 109
82. **Rider at Dawn** (Hajnali lovas), 1911
oil on canvas, 141.2 x 135.4 cm (55⅝ x 53¼ in)
inscribed lower left: Kernstok Károly
Hungarian National Gallery, Budapest (Inv. 68.47 T)
Illustrated page 110
83. **Nude Boy Leaning Against a Tree** (Fához támaszkodó fiúakt), 1911
oil on paper, 66 x 44 cm (26 x 17-3/8 in)

inscribed lower left: Kernstok Károly
Hungarian National Gallery, Budapest (Inv. 9035)
Illustrated page 146

84. **Storm** (Zivatar), 1919
oil on canvas, 184 x 201.5 cm (72½ x 79⅜ in)
inscribed lower right: Kernstok Károly 1919
Hungarian National Gallery, Budapest (Inv. FK 10.612)
Illustrated page 110

85. **Last Supper**, 1921-23
gouache on paper, 20 x 38 cm (7⅞ x 15 in)
inscribed lower right: K.K. Kernstok Károly
Hungarian National Gallery, Budapest (Inv. 9113)
Illustrated page 197

János Kmetty (1889-1975) A native of Miskolc, Kmetty had his early art training in Kassa (now Košice, Czechoslovakia). In 1909, he initiated private studies with Ferenc Szablya Frischauf, moving to Paris in 1911 for a year where he admired the work of Cézanne and Braque while enrolled at the Académie Julian. From 1912 on, he spent his summers at Kecskemét, and joined the activist Ma group around Lajos Kassák in 1918. The following year, he completed a poster with József Nemes Lampérth for the Hungarian Soviet Republic. Unlike most of his colleagues, he he did not emigrate after 1919, but did travel to Vienna, Paris, and to Nagybánya (by then, part of Romania) on occasion. Although he adopted some cubist techniques in his paintings, the objects in his paintings retain strong contours and volumes influenced by Cézanne. Kmetty was represented in the Venice Biennale exhibitions of 1936 and 1962. GB

86. **View of Kecskemét** (Kecskemét), 1912
oil on canvas, 92 x 72 cm (36¼ x 28⅜ in)
inscribed lower right: Kmetty 1912
Hungarian National Gallery, Budapest (Inv. 70.33 T)
Illustrated page 118

87. **Self Portrait** (Önarckép), 1913
oil on canvas, 53 x 44 cm (20⅞ x 17⅜ in)
inscribed lower right: Kmetty
Hungarian National Gallery, Budapest (Inv. 70.32 T)
Illustrated page 119

88. **Woman with a Cup** (Nő csészével), 1916
oil on canvas, 66 x 53.3 cm (26 x 21 in)
inscribed lower right: Kmetty
Janus Pannonius Museum, Pécs (Inv. 72.322)
Illustrated page 112

89. **Concert** (Koncert), 1918
oil on canvas, 80 x 100 cm (31½ x 39⅜ in)
inscribed lower right: Kmetty
Hungarian National Gallery, Budapest (Inv. 56.18 T)
Illustrated page 126

Aladár Körösfői Kriesch (1863–1920) Körösfői Kriesch began his art studies in 1880, under the direction of the noted history painter Bertalan Székely. From 1891 to 1892, a scholarship enabled the artist to study in Rome. In 1896, he attended the Académie Julian in Paris. Between 1897 and 1902, he was one of several artists who worked on the murals designed for the newly completed Hungarian Parliament building in Budapest. In 1901, he moved to Gödöllő, near Budapest, with his family where he founded an art colony influenced by the philosphy of John Ruskin and the English Arts and Crafts movement of William Morris. Following Tolstoy's precepts to break down the barriers between the so-called fine arts and the applied arts, Körösfői Kriesch established a weaving workshop and began the design of decorative rugs and tapestries. In 1907, he was awarded the Great Gold Medal of State for his work in the field of applied arts. Sixteen paintings, tapestries and weaving designs were selected for display at the Panama-Pacific International Exposition of 1915 in San Francisco. His murals decorate several significant Hungarian buildings, including the Academy of Music (1907) in Budapest and the Palace of Culture (1912) in Marosvásárhely (now Tîrgu Mureş, Romania). AZ

90. **Ego sum via, veritas et vita** (I am the Way, the Truth and Life Itself), 1903
oil on canvas, main section: 159 x 286.5 cm (62⅝ x 112¾ in), frame panel: 38.2 x 26 cm (15 x 10¼ in)
inscribed lower left: KA 903
Hungarian National Gallery, Budapest (Inv. 2485)
Illustrated page 106

Ödön Márffy (1878-1959) Márffy studied in Paris between 1902 and 1906, first with J.P. Laurens at the Académie Julian, followed by Fernand Cormon at the École des Beaux Arts. He exhibited works at the Salon d'Automne in Paris and from 1906 on had several exhibitions in Budapest. In 1909, he joined The Eight. He was among several Hungarian artists invited to exhibit works in the international section of the 1915 Panama-Pacific Exposition in San Francisco. Upon the collapse of the Hungarian Soviet Republic in 1919, he chose not to emigrate and remained in Budapest until his death. In 1928, his works were exhibited in Washington, DC and New York. In his early works, one can detect the succeeding influences of fauvism, expressionism and cubism, while his later style grew to resemble that of the School of Paris. GB

91. **Constructivist Self Portrait** (Önarckép), 1914
oil on canvas, 92 x 69.5 cm (36¼ x 27⅜ in)
inscribed lower right: Ödön Márffy
Hungarian National Gallery, Budapest (Inv. 4659)
Illustrated page 54

János Máttis Teutsch (1884-1960) Born in Brassó, Transylvania (now Braşov, Romania) to a Saxon family, Máttis Teutsch attended the Budapest School of Applied Arts in 1901–1902, then studied sculpture in Munich until 1905. From 1906 to 1908, he lived in Paris. From 1913, he was included in several exhibitions organized in Berlin by Herwarth Walden's Der Sturm Gallery. In 1917, Máttis-Teutsch joined the Ma group; his first independent exhibition was the first of a series of one-man exhibitions organized under the auspices of the Ma group. After 1919, he returned to Brassó, but continued to participate in exhibitions arranged by Ma. In 1923, he worked at the Bauhaus in Weimar for a brief period. In 1924, he participated at the first international exhibition of the Romanian Contimporanul group, and subsequently had works exhibited in Rome, Berlin, and Chicago. After 1933, except for some brief periods, he totally withdrew from artistic engagements. GB

92. **Still Life**, c1914
watercolor on paper, 25.4 x 33 cm (10 x 13 in)
inscribed lower left: MT
Paul Kövesdy Collection, New York
Illustrated page 123

93. **Landscape** (Tájkép), 1915-1916
oil on cardboard, 50 x 60 cm (19⅝ x 23⅝ in)
inscribed lower left: MT
Museum of Fine Arts, Budapest (Inv. 75.2.B)
Illustrated page 181

94. **Landscape in Sunshine** (Világos táj), 1916
oil on cardboard, 40 x 49 cm (15¾ x 19⅜ in)
inscribed lower left: MT
Janus Pannonius Museum, Pécs (Inv. 73.151)
Illustrated page 181

95. **Dark Landscape with Trees** (Sötét táj), 1918
oil on cardboard, 40 x 49 cm (15¾ x 19⅜ in)
inscribed lower left: MT
Janus Pannonius Museum, Pécs (Inv. 73.82)
Illustrated page 122

96. **Spiritual Flower**, c1923
oil on cardboard, 35 x 29 cm (13¾ x 11⅜ in)
inscribed lower right: MT
Dr. Nicolas Éber, Unterengstringen, Switzerland
Illustrated page 122

97. **Composition**, 1925
oil on cardboard, 35 x 29 cm (13¾ x 11⅜ in)
inscribed lower right: MT
Dr. Nicolas Éber, Unterengstringen, Switzerland
Illustrated page 183

László Moholy-Nagy (1895–1946) Born in Bácsborsod, Moholy-Nagy first studied law in Budapest. During World War I, he was an enlisted soldier. Severely wounded and captured on the Russian front, he took up drawing during his internment and convalescence in Odessa. He returned to Budapest upon his release and became involved with the circle of artists formed around Lajos Kassák and his periodical *Ma*. In 1919, he moved briefly to Vienna, then to Berlin where in 1922 he had his first exhibition at Der Sturm gallery, met several of the Russian Constructivists, (especially El Lissitsky), and collaborated with

Kassák on the influential *Buch neuer Künstler* [Book of New Artists] which did much to further the cause of constructivism. Invited to teach at the Bauhaus in 1923, where he became director of the metal workshop, Moholy-Nagy's growing preoccupation with the effects of light and motion led him to experiments in photography, film making, and three-dimensional objects constructed of metal, glass and plastic—the so-called "space modulators" and "light modulators." In 1928, he moved back to Berlin where he was primarily involved with stage design, experimental film, and applied design. Between 1932 and 1936, he also participated in the exhibitions of the Abstraction-Création group in Paris. In 1934, he left the repressive atmosphere of Germany to work in Amsterdam, moving to London in 1935, and finally settling in the United States in 1937 as director of the New Bauhaus in Chicago. In 1939, he founded his own school, the Institute of Design. *Vision in Motion*, the magnum opus on which he was working at the time of his death, was published posthumously in 1947, the same year as a major retrospective exhibition mounted by the Solomon R. Guggenheim Foundation. AZ

98. **Wounded Soldier–Prisoner of War** (Sebesült katona–Hadifogoly), 1917
ink and watercolor on paper, 40 x 28 cm (15¾ x 11 in)
inscribed lower left: Odessa Moholy Nagy
Levente Nagy collection, Budapest
Illustrated page 193
99. **Landscape–Tabán** (Táj–Tabán), 1919
graphite on paper, 31.5 x 44.5 cm (12⅜ x 17½ in)
inscribed lower right: Moholy Nagy
Hungarian National Gallery, Budapest (Inv. 1919-588)
Illustrated page 137
100. **Untitled Construction**, 1922
tempera and collage on panel, 30.2 x 30.2 cm (11⅞ x 11⅞ in)
inscribed on reverse: Moholy-Nagy 22
Galerie Dr. I. Schlégl, Zürich
Illustrated page 137

Kestner Portfolio (Kestnermappe 6), 1923

101. **Construction** (1)
lithograph, 60.3 x 43.9 cm (23¾ x 17 5/16 in)
Illustrated page 156
102. **Construction** (2)
lithograph, 60.1 x 44.5 cm (23 11/16 x 17½ in)
103. **Construction** (3)
lithograph, 59.7 bx 43.9 cm (23½ x 17 5/16 in)
104. **Construction** (4)
lithograph, 59.7 x 43.9 cm (23½ x 17 5/16 in)
105. **Construction** (5)
lithograph, 60.1 x 43.9 cm (23 11/16 x 17 5/16 in)
106. **Construction** (6)
lithograph, 60 x 43.9 cm (23⅝ x 17 5/16 in)
San Francisco Museum of Modern Art, anonymous gift (Inv. 67.11-.1-6)

Farkas Molnár (1897-1945) Born in Pécs, Molnár began his art and architectural studies in Budapest around 1910. In 1921, he visited Italy, executing drawings and sketches of the landscapes and hill towns there. Invited to the Weimar Bauhaus in 1921 by Alfréd Forbát, Molnár stopped over in Vienna to initiate contact with Kassák and the artists of the Ma circle. As a result of this contact, several of his works were subsequently published in *Ma*. Molnár worked with Gropius until 1925. With Oskar Schlemmer and Lászlo Moholy-Nagy at the Bauhaus, he developed the concept of a "total theater," the *U-Theater*. Returning to Hungary after 1925, Molnár worked as an architect; between 1929 and 1930, he was one of the Hungarian leaders of CIRPAC. He also contributed stage designs for the Green Theater of Palasovszky and Hevesy. Molnár was killed in the closing months of World War II when a bomb hit his studio. GB

107. **Title Page–Italia Portfolio** (Itália mappa), 1921
serigraph, 66.4 x 52 cm (26⅛ x 20½ in)
unsigned
Hungarian National Gallery, Budapest (Inv. G 84.17/14)
Illustrated page 138
108. **Fiorentina** (Fiorentina), 1921
lithograph, 32 x 24 cm (12⅝ x 9½ in)
inscribed lower right: Molnár Farkas
Janus Pannonius Museum, Pécs (Inv. 65.14)
Illustrated page 158
109. **Gropius Memorial–Study** (Gropius-emlékmű terve), 1923
lithograph, 14.5 x 20 cm (5¾ x 7⅞ in)
inscribed lower left: Märzgefallen Denkmal v. Gropius
inscribed lower right: Wf Molnár
Janus Pannonius Museum, Pécs (Inv. 65.15)
Illustrated page 153
110. **Harlequinade** (Klárinak), 1926
gouache on paper, 37 x 26 cm (14½ x 10¼ in)
inscribed lower right: 26/Klárinak/MOLNÁR FARKAS
Dr. Nicolas Éber, Unterengstringen, Switzerland
Illustrated page 202

József Nemes Lampérth (1891–1924) Born in Budapest, Nemes Lampérth began at the School of Applied Arts in 1909. He enrolled as an advanced student at the Academy of Fine Arts in 1911, and it was there that he met Béla Uitz and János Kmetty with whom he joined the Activist movement. In 1912, he studied in Nagybánya, although by that time he was an accomplished artist. The stress and strain of World War I brought on a severe nerve-related illness from which he was to suffer the rest of his life. Nevertheless, he participated in the revolutionary movement, and, with Kmetty, produced a poster for the Hungarian Soviet Republic. After the fall of the Republic, he emigrated to Berlin, but soon returned to Hungary where he was treated at various mental institutions. In his final years, he created drawings representing dramatic moods. AZ

111. **Self-Portrait** (Önarckép), 1911
oil on canvas, 75 x 60 cm (29½ x 23⅝ in)
inscribed lower left: Nemes Lampérth József
Hungarian National Gallery, Budapest (Inv. 65.28 T)
Illustrated page 121
112. **Standing Nude (Front)** (Szemben álló női akt), 1916
oil on canvas, 130 x 79 cm (51¼ x 31⅛ in)
inscribed lower right: Nemes Lampérth J. 1916
Hungarian National Gallery, Budapest (Inv. 59.147 T)
Illustrated page 121
113. **Turning Nude (Back)** (Női akt), 1916
oil on canvas, 128 x 77 cm (50⅜ x 30¼ in)
inscribed lower left: Nemes Lampérth J. 1916
Hungarian National Gallery, Budapest (Inv. 5509)
Illustrated page 121
114. **Landscape at Tabán** (Tabáni részlet), 1916
oil on canvas, 76 x 101 cm (29⅞ x 39¾ in)
inscribed lower left: Nemes Lampérth J. 1916
Janus Pannonius Museum, Pécs (Inv. 82.52)
Illustrated page 192
115. **Still Life with Lamp** (Lámpás csendélet), 1916
oil on canvas, 65.5 x 90 cm (25¾ x 35⅜ in)
inscribed lower left: Nemes Lampérth J. 1916
Janus Pannonius Museum, Pécs (Inv. 64.9)
Illustrated page 173

Henrik Neugeboren (Henri Nouveau) (1901-1959) Born to Saxon parents in the Transylvanian town of Brassó (now Braşov, Romania), Neugeboren had an active career as a musician, painter, and a poet. From 1913, he studied in Budapest; in 1921 he moved to Berlin to study music with, among others, Federico Busoni. Between 1925 and 1927, he furthered his musical studies in Paris wih Nadia Boulanger. Meanwhile, from 1923 on, he began creating works of abstract art. Returning to Berlin in 1927, he was invited to visit the Dessau Bauhaus by Ernő Kallai. Although not an official member of the faculty, his abstract metal *Monument to Johann Sebastian Bach* was published in the Bauhaus journal. During his sojourn in Dessau, which lasted until 1929, Neugeboren became well acquainted with Paul Klee and Wassily Kandinsky and their theories of art and pedagogy. Thereafter, he moved permanently to Paris, adopting a French version of his name, Henri Nouveau. The recommendation of Theo van Doesburg led to his first one-man exhibition in Paris in 1930. After World War II, Neugeboren/Nouveau was associated with Francis Picabia and was a regular participant in the Salon des Réalités Nouvelles. He received another one-man exhibition in Paris in 1950 and was posthumously honored by the Bauhaus Archives in 1966 with an exhibition in Darmstadt. GB

116. **Composition** (Kompozíció), 1930
collage, 20.7 x 16.8 cm (8¼ x 6⅝ in)
inscribed lower right: H.N.
Museum of Fine Arts, Budapest (Inv. K 72.5.K)
Illustrated page 211

Dezső Orbán (1884–1986) A native of Győr, Orbán started painting while a university mathematics major. His talent was recognized: in 1905 and 1906, his works were exhibited at the Art Pavilion (*Műcsarnok*, the equivalent of *Kunsthalle*) and at the National Salon in Budapest. He travelled to Paris in 1906 to continue his art studies, where he met and befriended Róbert Berény. Upon his return to Budapest, he set up a studio which became a meeting place for younger artists. It was there that The Searchers, the group that evolved into The Eight, was established. During World War I, he was an enlisted soldier. In 1919 he served in the Art Department set up during the Hungarian Soviet Republic; unlike many of his colleagues, however, he chose not to emigrate after its dissolution. Between 1925 and 1926, Orbán was in Paris again. From the 1920s, his art-related writings were also published, and in 1931, he founded an art school. In 1939, he moved to Sydney, Australia where he remained until his death. AZ

117. **Church Yard** (Templomkert), c1908
oil on canvas, 56 x 69 cm (22 x 27¼ in)
inscribed lower right: Orbán D.
Janus Pannonius Museum, Pécs (Inv. 69.148)
Illustrated page 53

118. **Still Life** (Csendélet)
oil on canvas, 56 x 73.5 cm (22 x 29 in)
inscribed lower right: Orbán
Hungarian National Gallery, Budapest (Inv. FK 10.321)
Illustrated page 111

119. **Still Life with Cactus, Books, and Dishes** (Csendélet–Kaktusz, könyvek, edények), 1911
oil on canvas, 71 x 87 cm (28 x 34-1/4 in)
inscribed lower right: Orbán
Hungarian National Gallery, Budapest (Inv. 5484)
Illustrated page 200

Jenő Paizs Goebel (1896-1944) The son of Hungarian parents of German descent, Paizs Goebel first studied glass painting at the School of Applied Arts in 1915-16, and from 1916 to 1924 was a student of István Réti at the Academy of Fine Arts in Budapest. Like many of his colleagues, he produced posters during the short-lived Hungarian Soviet Republic founded at the end of World War I. He resumed painting after the fall of the Republic and his works were exhibited from 1920 on. In 1924-25, he worked in Paris and in Barbizon, and in 1925, his works were exhibited in Paris. In 1928, he was one of the founding members of the Painters' Association of Szentendre, the art colony near Budapest. His later art focussed on landscape painting and dreamlike symbolism with flashes of fantasy. GB

120. **Lajos Kossuth's Message: Long Live the Republic!** (Kossuth Lajos azt üzente: Éljen a köztársaság!), 1918
lithograph, 126 x 96 cm (49⅝ x 37¾ in)
inscribed upper left: Paizs J. 918
Museum of the Modern Age, Budapest (Inv. 59.19.1.)
Illustrated page 150

László Péri (1889-1967) One of the leading constructivist artists of his time, Péri began as a mason. From 1918 to 1920, he was in close touch with Kassák and the Activists and made a brief visit to the Soviet Union in 1920. Starting in 1921, he created abstract reliefs in concrete based on designs developed first as watercolors or collages. In 1922, he had a joint exhibition with Moholy-Nagy at Der Sturm gallery in Berlin, and between 1922 and 1928, his works were published frequently in *Der Sturm*, which also published his 12-part portfolio of linoleum cuts in 1922 and 1923, including the *Berlin Mural Design*. In 1924, he became interested in architecture and city planning which occupied his attention for some time, but returned to painting in 1930. He moved to London with his British wife in 1934, where he completed his memoirs after World War II. GB

121. **Berlin Mural Design** (Wandgestaltung), c1923
tempera on linoleum cut, 30.5 x 45.8 cm (12 x 18 in)
inscribed along bottom: Wandgestaltung. Original Wandgrösse 17.7 m/ Grosse Berliner Kunstausstellung/Péri/1924 (Mural Design. Original Size of Wall 58 ft/Great Berlin Art Exhibition/ Péri/1924) [artist inscribed later date in error]
Anonymous loan, Berlin
Illustrated page 154

Vilmos Perlrott Csaba (1880–1955) Born in Békéscsaba, Perlrott Csaba started as an art student of Béla Iványi Grünwald in 1904 at the Budapest Academy of Fine Arts. With the assistance of Károly Ferenczy, he was awarded a scholarship to the Académie Julian in Paris, where he studied briefly before leaving to study with Henri Matisse, between 1906 and 1910. He travelled to Madrid in 1911, remaining until 1912. After his return to Hungary and a brief stay at Nagybánya (now Baia Mare, Romania), he moved to the art colony of Kecskemét. There, under the leadership of Iványi Grünwald, he joined with other young talents representing new directions in the Neo-Impressionist group dubbed "Neos." Perlrott Csaba significantly influenced Lajos Kassák and Béla Uitz when they visited Kecskemét in 1916. In the 1920s, he lived in Germany and in Paris. He returned to Hungary in the late 1930s and settled in Szentendre. AZ

122. **Self-Portrait with Model** (Önarckép modellel), c1910-1912
oil on canvas, 110 x 90 cm (43¼ x 35⅜ in)
inscribed upper right: W Perlrott Csaba
Janus Pannonius Museum, Pécs (Inv. 73.118)
Illustrated page 146

123. **Bathing Youths** (Fürdőző fiúk), c1910
oil on canvas, 77.5 x 91 cm (30½ x 35⅞ in)
unsigned
Janus Pannonius Museum, Pécs (Inv. 76.259)
Illustrated page 96

124. **Deposition from the Cross** (Levétel a keresztről), 1912
oil on canvas, 92 x 72 cm (36¼ x 28⅜ in)
unsigned
Hungarian National Gallery, Budapest (Inv. 5492)
Illustrated page 96

Bertalan Pór (1880–1964) Born in Bábaszék, Pór initially studied art in Budapest, then continued his training in Munich and at the Académie Julian in Paris. In 1904, he returned to Hungary, gradually moving toward expressionism in his work. He soon joined the MIÉNK group of impressionist and expressionist artists, then its spinoff, The Searchers, which evolved into The Eight. In 1915, three of his paintings, including *The Family*, and fifty-nine drawings, mostly studies for *The Worship of Reason*, were exhibited at the Panama-Pacific Exposition in San Francisco. Pór participated in World War I as a war artist. During the Hungarian Soviet Republic, he designed posters and was acting head of the Department of Art's painting division. After the fall of the Republic, he first emigrated to Bratislava, then to Vienna via Prague and Warsaw. From the 1920s, he lived in Berlin and later in Paris, punctuated by a brief stay in the Soviet Union in 1935. In 1948, he moved back to Hungary where he became a professor at the Academy of Fine Arts in Budapest and twice was awarded the Kossuth prize. AZ

125. **The Family** (Család), 1909
oil on canvas, 176.5 x 206 cm (69½ x 81⅛ in)
inscribed lower right: Pór Bertalan 1909
Hungarian National Gallery, Budapest (Inv. 60.136 T)
Illustrated page 53

126. **Workers of the World, Unite!** (Világ proletárjai egyesüljetek!), 1919
lithograph, 244.5 x 185 cm (96-1/4 x 72-7/8 in)
inscribed lower right: Pór B. 1919
Museum of the Modern Age, Budapest (Inv. 86.35.1)
Illustrated page 58

József Rippl-Rónai (1861–1927) Born in Kaposvár, Rippl-Rónai first went to Munich in 1884 to study art with the history and genre painter Johann Casper Herterich; three years later, he moved to Paris to continue his studies under Mihály Munkácsy. In 1892, he moved to Neuilly in the outskirts of Paris where he went through his "black period," painting works in sombre tonalities and simplified outline. In 1894, he got acquainted with Aristide Maillol and the Nabis art circle. Concurrently with Vuillard and Bonnard, Rippl-Rónai developed a new decorative style, exhibiting at the art nouveau galleries of Bing in Paris in 1892 and 1897. In 1900, he returned to Hungary where he was active not only as a painter but as a designer of tapestries, book bindings, and glass decoration. After a successful exhibition in 1906, he settled in Kaposvár where he developed his personal style of pointillism, a mosaic-like patterning of intense color. He published his memoirs in 1911. In 1915, ten of his paintings were exhibited at the Panama-Pacific Exposition in San Francisco and he was awarded a silver medal for painting. After World War I, he gradually gave up painting in oils in favor of pastels. His mastery of this medium reached a peak in a series of portraits of notable Hungarian artists and authors. Rippl-Rónai's art served as a bridge interpreting the accomplishments of French art in the development of Hungarian art. Two major retrospectives of his work were held in Budapest in 1947 and 1952. AZ

127. **Lady in a White Robe (Study)** (Tanulmány), 1898
oil on canvas, 178 x 76.5 cm (70 x 30⅛ in)
unsigned
Hungarian National Gallery, Budapest (Inv. 4087)
Illustrated page 99

128. **Sorrow** (Szomoruság), 1903
oil on cardboard, 67.5 x 49.5 cm (26⅝ x 19½ in)
inscribed upper left: Rónai
Hungarian National Gallery, Budapest (Inv. 6099)
Illustrated page 99

129. **Sour Cherry Trees in Bloom** (Meggyfavirágzás), 1909
oil on paper, 68 x 90 cm (26¾ x 35⅜ in)
inscribed lower left: Rónai
Rippl Rónai Museum, Kaposvár (Inv. 55.622.)
Illustrated page 100

130. **Models** (Aktok), 1910
oil on paper, 67 x 97.5 cm (26⅜ x 38⅜ in)
inscribed lower right: Rónai
Hungarian National Gallery, Budapest (Inv. 5929)
Illustrated page 144

131. **Painter in the Park** (Parkrészlet), 1910
oil on cardboard, wood, 69.5 x 100.5 cm (27⅜ x 39½ in)
inscribed lower left: Rónai
inscribed: parkban festem Lazarine-t és Anellát; Hepiéknek melegük van (I am painting Lazarine and Anella in a park; the Hepis feel hot)
Hungarian National Gallery, Budapest (Inv. 87.1 T)
Illustrated page 101

János Schadl (1892-1944) Born in Keszthely, Schadl studied art in Budapest. Several of his drawings were published in *Ma* in 1918, and he also participated in exhibitions organized by Lajos Kassák's Activist group. In Schadl's early works, one can observe cubist and expressionist influences. In the 1920s, however, he withdrew to the countryside and developed a more naturalistic mode of painting. GB

132. **Youth Reading** (Olvasó férfi), 1917
oil on canvas, 70 x 50 cm (27½ x 19⅝ in)
inscribed lower left: Schadl 917
Hungarian National Gallery, Budapest (Inv. 85.18 T)
Illustrated page 113

133. **Houses and Aurél Bernáth** (Város és Bernáth Aurél), 1919
oil on canvas, 95 x 75 cm (37⅜ x 29½ in)
inscribed lower right: S.J. 919. II.
Janus Pannonius Museum, Pécs (Inv. 77.63)
Illustrated page 124

134. **Village** (Falu), undated
oil on cardboard, 60 x 49.5 cm (23⅝ x 19½ in)
unsigned
Hungarian National Gallery, Budapest (Inv. F 77.113)
Illustrated page 123

Hugó Scheiber (1873-1950) Essentially a self-taught painter, Scheiber received only two years of formal training between 1898 and 1900 at the Budapest School of Applied Arts. He started his career as a sign painter apprenticed to his father, and painted mostly landscapes and cityscapes in his early years. After moving to Berlin, however, he rapidly developed a modernist style; by 1921, he was given a joint exhibition with Béla Kádár. His friendship with Herwarth Walden led to several exhibitions at Der Sturm gallery from 1924 on. His works were also displayed in London in 1924, in New York and La Paz in 1926, and in Vienna in 1930. Scheiber was a member of the Hungarian New Artists group and showed works in their exhibitions in Budapest. In 1933, at the invitation of Marinetti, he exhibited with the Futurists at the *Mostra Nazionale d'Arte Futurista* in Rome. After the expressionism of the 1920s, Scheiber switched to an art-deco-like style of painting in the 1930s. His favorite topic was life in the modern city, but he painted numerous landscapes, portraits, and self-portraits as well. GB

135. **The Charleston**, c1928
gouache on paper, 50 x 55 cm (19½ x 21½ in)
inscribed lower center: Scheiber/H
Paul Kövesdy Collection, New York
Illustrated page 208

136. **Portrait of Lajos Kassák**, c1930
pastel on paper, 54.6 x 44.1 cm (21½ x 17⅜ in)[sight]
inscribed lower left: Scheiber H
Anonymous loan, Washington, DC
Illustrated page 130

137. **In the Park**
gouache on paper, 67 x 54 cm (26⅜ x 21¼ in)
inscribed lower right: Scheiber H
Dr. Nicolas Éber, Unterengstringen, Switzerland
Illustrated page 212

138. **Theatre Interior**
gouache on paper, 66 x 54 cm (26 x 21¼ in)
inscribed lower center: Scheiber H
Dr. Nicolas Éber, Unterengstringen, Switzerland
Illustrated page 130

Armand Schönberger (1885-1974) Born in Galgóc, Schönberger studied art in Budapest and in Munich. Between 1906 and 1912, he spent his summers working in Nagybánya (now Baia Mare, Romania). In 1909, he visited Paris. He began exhibiting his works in 1910, and was included in the 1917 Hungarian National Salon. His early works were influenced by German Expressionism, but he was also interested in the theories of the Italian Futurists. From the 1920s on, he painted in a style derived from cubism; in 1925, he was included in Ernő Kállai's book, *New Painting in Hungary*. Later exhibitions of his work took place in 1923, 1930, and in Malmö, Sweden in 1938. GB

139. **Cafe Scene** (Kávéházi jelenet), 1924
oil on canvas, 75 x 90 cm (29½ x 35½ in)
inscribed lower left: Schönberger A. 1924
Hungarian National Gallery, Budapest (Inv. 83.39 T)
Illustrated page 171

140. **At the Well**, c1928
oil on cardboard, 33 x 37 cm (13 x 14½ in)
inscribed lower left: Schönberger A.
Dr. Nicolas Éber, Unterengstringen, Switzerland
Illustrated page 162

Imre Szobotka (1890-1961) Born in Zalaegerszeg, Szobotka began his studies at the Budapest School of Applied Arts with Ignác Ujváry in 1905. After a brief trip to Italy, he moved to Paris in 1910. There he was greatly influenced by cubism. In 1913, he exhibited at the Salon des Indépendents. At the outbreak of World War I in 1914, he was interned by the French authorities in Brittany until his repatriation to Budapest in 1919. As a result, his connection with the Activists in Hungary was confined primarily to correspondence, and he was never part of the Kassák circle. Szobotka remained in Hungary and was one of the founders of the Hungarian New Artists group. He was awarded the grand prize of the Szinyei Society in 1941 and the Munkácsy prize in 1955, as well as serving for a time as president of the painting section of the Hungarian Union of Artists. He was one of the first Hungarian representatives of cubism, although later in his career he mostly painted landscapes in a more naturalistic style. GB

141. **Pipe Smoker** (Pipázó férfi), c1914
oil on canvas, mounted on plywood, 30 x 35 cm (11¾ x 13¾ in)
unsigned
Janus Pannonius Museum, Pécs (Inv. 77.2)
Illustrated page 118

142. **Reclining Nude** (Fekvó akt), 1921
oil on cardboard, 131 x 100 cm (51½ x 39⅜ in)
inscribed lower left: Szobotka I. 921
Hungarian National Gallery, Budapest (Inv. 59.27 T)
Illustrated page 12

János Tábor (Taupert) (1890-1956) Better known as a graphic artist than a painter, Tábor studied art in Budapest and exhibited from 1913 on. In 1919, during the Hungarian Soviet Republic, he designed posters. From 1924 on, he was associated with the journal *Magyar Grafika* [Hungarian Graphic Art], and became a member of the Spiritual Artists Association. GB

143. **Red Soldiers, Forward!** (Vörös katonák előre!), 1919
lithograph, 127 x 96 cm (50 x 37¾ in)
inscribed lower right: Tábor
Museum of the Modern Age, Budapest (Inv. 57.10.1.)
Illustrated page 125

144. **Meinl Tea** (Meinl Tea), 1930
lithograph, 94.5 x 61 cm (37¼ x 24 in)
inscribed lower left: Tábor
Hungarian Advertising Agency Archives, Budapest
Illustrated page 80

Lajos Tihanyi (1885–1938) Tihanyi first attended the School of Applied Arts in Budapest in 1904-1905 before moving to Nagybánya (now Baia Mare, Romania) for further studies, between 1907 to 1910. He visited Paris as early as 1907 and was greatly influenced by the the art of Cézanne and the Fauves, especially Matisse. Returning to Budapest, Tihanyi joined The Eight, and later the Activists. During this period, he attempted to synthesize elements of expressionism with Cézanne's formal methodology, as can be seen in the portraits of outstanding personalities of Hungarian intellectual life he created around 1915-1918. Four of his paintings, including a self-portrait, were exhibited at the 1915 Panama-Pacific Exposition in San Francisco. After the fall of the Hungarian Soviet Republic in 1919, Tihanyi moved to Vienna where he remained until 1920. He then moved to Berlin, living there until 1924. He then took up permanent residence in Paris where he painted cubist and nonfigurative works. From 1933, he was a member of the Abstraction-Création group. His estate was returned to Hungary in 1970. AZ

145. **Reclining Nude**, 1917
oil on canvas, 49 x 56 cm (19¼ x 22 in)
inscribed lower left: Tihanyi L. 917
Hungarian National Gallery, Budapest (Inv. 5502)
Illustrated page 193

146. **Portrait of Lajos Kassák** (Kassák Lajos arcképe), 1918
oil on canvas, 86.5 x 70 cm (34 x 27½ in)
inscribed lower left: Tihanyi L. 1918
Hungarian National Gallery, Budapest (Inv. 70.134 T)
Illustrated page 114

147. **Working Class Family** (Család), 1921
oil on canvas, 116.7 x 90 cm (46 x 35⅜ in)
inscribed lower right: L. Tihanyi Berlin 921
Hungarian National Gallery, Budapest (Inv. 70.179)
Illustrated page 52

148. **Man at a Window** (Ablaknál álló férfi), 1922
oil on canvas, 140 x 106.5 cm (55¼ x 42 in)
inscribed lower left: L.Tihanyi Berlin Schöneberg 1922
Hungarian National Gallery, Budapest (Inv. 70.180 T)
Illustrated page 172

149. **Portrait of Tristan Tzara** (Tristan Tzara arcképe), 1926
oil on canvas, 103 x 73 cm (40½ x 28¾ in)
inscribed lower left: L.Tihanyi
Hungarian National Gallery, Budapest (Inv. 70.169 T)
Illustrated page 139

Béla Uitz (1887-1972) Born in Mehala, and trained as a locksmith, Uitz became one of the most influential representatives of the Activist movement. From 1908 to 1913, he attended the Academy of Fine Arts in Budapest, majoring in painting and graphic arts. His first exhibition in Budapest was arranged without any outside assistance in 1914; later, the bulk of this exhibition, consisting of eighteen paintings, was shown in San Francisco at the 1915 Panama-Pacific Exposition, where Uitz was awarded a gold medal. From 1915 to 1922, he was closely associated with Lajos Kassák and his journals *A Tett* [The Deed], and later *Ma* [Today]. In 1919, Uitz was one of the directors of the Proletarian Artists Workshop. After the fall of the Hungarian Soviet Republic, he was briefly imprisoned; after his release he moved to Vienna to join the Hungarian émigrés there who had formed around Kassák. In 1922, he disassociated himself from the Ma circle and launched his own periodical in Vienna called *Egység* [Unity]. Between 1924 and 1926, Uitz lived in Paris; he then moved to the Soviet Union where he remained until his death. GB

150. **Portrait of Iván Hevesy** (Hevesy Iván arcképe), 1918
oil on canvas, 87 x 69 cm (34¼ x 27⅛ in)
unsigned
Janus Pannonius Museum, Pécs (Inv. 75.197)
Illustrated page 145

151. **Composition with Trees and Houses** (Kompozíció fákkal és házakkal), 1918-19
oil and tempera on cardboard, 65 x 82.5 cm (25-5/8 x 32-1/2 in)
unsigned
Janus Pannonius Museum, Pécs (Inv. 78.53)
Illustrated page 120

152. **Seated Woman** (Ülő nő), 1918
oil on cardboard, 87 x 69 cm (34¼ x 27⅛ in)
inscribed upper left: Uitz B. 918
Janus Pannonius Museum, Pécs (Inv. 64.7)
Illustrated page 119

153. **Sewing Woman** (Varró nő), 1918-19
oil on canvas, 85.5 x 72 cm (33⅝ x 28⅜ in)
unsigned
Hungarian National Gallery, Budapest (Inv. 8988)
Illustrated page 120

154. **Red Soldiers, Forward!** (Vörös katonák előre!), 1919
lithograph, 126 x 192 cm (49⅝ x 75⅝ in)
inscribed lower right: Uitz B. 919. IV. = .
Museum of the Modern Age, Budapest (Inv. 57.28.1.)
Illustrated page 60

155. **Iconanalysis with the Holy Trinity** (Ikonanalízis Szentháromsággal), 1922
oil on canvas, 152 x 142 cm (59-7/8 x 55-7/8 in)
unsigned
Hungarian National Gallery, Budapest (Inv. 72.35.T)
Illustrated page 142

Selections from the **Analysis series (Analízis)**, 1922

156. **Analysis** (XXVI), 1922
linoleumcut, 32.3 x 20.4 cm (12¾ x 8 in)
unsigned
Illustrated page 159

157. **Analysis** (XXVIII), 1922
linoleumcut, 20 x 32.6 cm (7⅞ x 12⅞ in)
unsigned
Hungarian National Gallery, Budapest (Inv. G 69.26 and 27)
Illustrated page 159

158. **Compositional Analysis for Nedd Ludd**, c1923
colored pencil on silk paper, 37.5 x 50.5 cm (14¾ x 19⅞ in)
unsigned
Hungarian National Gallery, Budapest (Inv. 69.417)
Illustrated page 148

Selections from the **General Ludd series** (I-XIV), 1923

159. **Nedd Ludd** (I)
etching, 33.1 x 42.8 cm (13 x 16⅞ in)
Illustrated page 148

160. **Captain Nottingham** (VII) (Nottingham kapitány)
etching, 33 x 42.4 cm (13 x 16¾ in)
Illustrated page 60

161. **General Ludd** (XII)
etching, 42.5 x 33.2 cm (16¾ x 13 in)
Illustrated page 60

162. **White Terror** (XIV) (Fehérterror)
etching, 33 x 42.5 cm (13 x 16¾ in)
Hungarian National Gallery, Budapest (Inv. G 69.2, 11, 13, and 16)
Illustrated page 63

163. **Prolétaires de tous les pays, unissez-vous!** (Workers of the World, Unite!) [Stage design for Vaillant-Couturier's play *Le Monstre*], 1925-26
ink, watercolor, and collage on paper, 52.5 x 14.7 cm (20⅝ x 5¾ in)
unsigned
Hungarian National Gallery, Budapest (Inv. F 69.310)
Illustrated page 161

János Vaszary (1867–1939) Vaszary was enrolled at the Budapest School of Drawing from 1885 to 1887, then continued his studies at the Academy in Munich with Bertalan Székely von

Ádámos until 1889. In 1890, he moved to Paris for study at the Académie Julian with Adolphe Bouguereau and Robert Fleury. In 1891, he was in Rome and in 1893-1894 was again in Paris. Vaszary's talent as a painter was never in doubt: in 1900, he was awarded a bronze medal at the Exposition Universelle and in 1915 he was awarded a gold medal for oil painting at the Panama-Pacific Exposition in San Francisco where five paintings were shown, including *Woman with a Cat*. Upon his return to Hungary, he not only continued to paint, but also created works of applied arts in a style influenced by Puvis de Chavannes. After the turn of the century, Vaszary's art was characterized by frequent stylistic changes. In the first two decades of the 20th century, he painted naturalistic and impressionistic works which were later influenced by The Eight. During his so-called "blue period" after World War I, during which time incidentally he was employed as a newscaster, he created paintings based on biblical themes. From the beginning of the 1920s, in his "black period," his works were dominated by circus and theater related scenes. During his last, "white period," Vaszary painted mostly garden and seashore scenes. In 1920, he was appointed to the Academy of Fine Arts where he taught for twelve years, establishing a reputation as one of the most liberal instructors at that institution. AZ

164. **Woman with a Cat** (Lilaruhás nő macskával), c1900
oil on canvas, 150 x 40 cm (59 x 15¾ in)
inscribed upper left: Vaszary
Private Collection, Budapest

Andor (Andrew) Weininger (1899-1986) Born in Karams, Weininger studied architecture and fine arts in Budapest. In 1921, he moved to Weimar to attend the Bauhaus where he remained until 1928. At the Bauhaus, he was particularly active in the areas of mural painting and theater. For the Bauhaus theater he created scenic work and choreography, as well as creating designs for the ultimate abstract theater. An avid jazz pianist, Weininger formed a Bauhaus jazz ensemble and also performed as a mime in Oskar Schlemmer's "figurative cabinet." In 1928, he moved to Berlin, then to Paris, and then to The Netherlands, where in 1945 he became a member of the Creatic group. He moved to Toronto, Canada in 1951, finally settling in New York in 1958. In New York, he was able to reproduce some of his works from the Bauhaus period that were destroyed during World War II. GB

165. **Composition** (Kompozíció), 1922-62
oil on cardboard, 101 x 26 cm (39¾ x 10¼ in)
inscribed lower right: A.W. 1922-1962
Hungarian National Gallery, Budapest (Inv. F 83.14)
Illustrated page 72

166. **De Stijl Composition** (De Stijl kompozíció), 1922
tempera on board, 100 x 22 cm (39⅜ x 8⅝ in)
inscribed lower right: Weininger A. 1922
Janus Pannonius Museum, Pécs (Inv. 70.450)
Illustrated page 72

Sándor (Alexandru) Ziffer (1880-1962) Born in the Hungarian town of Eger, Ziffer began his artistic education at the Budapest School of Applied Arts, later moving to Munich to study at the Academy, the Ažbe School, and eventually, between 1904 and 1906, with Simon Hollósy. He then returned to Hungary to paint at the art colony of Nagybánya (now Baia Mare, Romania). With Béla Czóbel, he travelled to Paris to paint and was given an exhibition, followed by exhibitions in Berlin, Munich, and Hamburg. He returned to Munich in 1914 where he opened a short-lived art school which closed upon the outbreak of World War I. In 1918, he moved permanently to Nagybánya/Baia Mare where he continued to paint strongly colored decorative landscapes, still lives, and portraits. In the 1920s, he taught at the Free School of Painting in Baia Mare; he was honored with a retrospective exhibition there in 1957. GB

167. **Nagybánya Winter**, 1910
oil on canvas, 78 x 68 cm (30¾ x 26¾ in)
inscribed lower right: Ziffer Sándor/1910
Dr. Nicolas Éber, Unterengstringen, Switzerland
Illustrated page 49

168. **Ships on the River Seine** (Hajók a Szajnán), 1911
oil on canvas, 46 x 61 cm (18¼ x 24 in)
inscribed lower right: Ziffer Sándor Paris 1911
Hungarian National Gallery, Budapest (Inv. 88.13 T)
Illustrated page 190

Index

Photo Credits

Jörg P. Anders: 124, 154
Zsuzsa Bokor: 99, 188
Center for the Fine Arts, Miami, Florida: 106
The Chrysler Museum, Norfolk, Virginia: 41
Prudence Cuming: 176
Dr. Nicholas Éber: 49, 73, 122, 130, 162, 183, 202, 212
Galerie Dr. I. Schlégl, Zürich: 134, 137
Graphische Sammlung, Staatsgalerie Stuttgart: 140
Hungarian National Gallery, Budapest: 48, 49, 59, 61, 71, 74, 79, 138
Janus Pannonius Museum, Pécs: 53, 124, 147, 192
H.E. Kiessling: 69, 74, 206, 207
Kurt Paulus Fotostudio: 133
Levente Nagy Collection: 193
György Makky: 179
Tibor Mester: 197, 209
Phillipe Migeat: 109
Museum of Fine Arts, Budapest: 77, 181, 211
Museum of Modern Art, New York: 71, 176, 207
Katalin Nádor: 98, 108, 110
Paul Kövesdy Collection: 43, 75, 123, 131, 208
Kunsthalle Nürnberg: 1, 78, 81, 134
István Petrás: 108
Donald Saban: cover, frontispiece, 12, 14, 45, 47, 48, 50, 51, 52, 53, 54, 55, 58, 60, 62, 63, 65, 72, 76, 80, 81, 82, 83, 93, 95, 96, 99, 100, 101, 102, 104, 109, 110, 111, 112, 113, 114, 116, 117, 118, 119, 120, 121, 123, 125, 126, 128, 129, 132, 133, 135, 136, 137, 139, 142, 145, 144, 146, 150, 152, 153, 158, 159, 161, 168, 171, 172, 173, 181, 186, 189, 190, 191, 193, 199, 200
San Francisco Museum of Modern Art: 156
Bertalan Vilmos: 182
Yale University Art Gallery, New Haven: 61, 131